【英汉对照全译本】

AN INQUIRY INTO THE NATURE AND CAUSES OF THE WEALTH OF NATIONS

国民财富的性质与原理

［英］亚当·斯密 著

赵东旭 丁 毅 译

（五）

中国社会科学出版社

CHAPTER VIII
Conclusion Of The Mercantile System [1]

The mercantile system discourages the exportation of materials of manufacture and instruments of trade. It encourages the importation of materials although not of instruments of trade.

Though the encouragement of exportation, and the discouragement of importation, are the two great engines by which the mercantile system proposes to enrich every country, yet with regard to some particular commodities, it seems to follow an opposite plan: to discourage exportation and to encourage importation. Its ultimate object, however, it pretends, is always the same, to enrich the country by an advantageous balance of trade. It discourages the exportation of the materials of manufacture, and of the instruments of trade, in order to give our own workmen an advantage, and to enable them to undersell those of other nations in all foreign markets: and by restraining, in this manner, the exportation of a few commodities, of no great price, it proposes to occasion a much greater and more valuable exportation of others. It encourages the importation of the materials of manufacture, in order that our own people may be enabled to work them up more cheaply, and thereby prevent a greater and more valuable importation of the manufactured commodities. I do not observe, at least in our Statute Book, any encouragement given to the importation of the instruments of trade. When manufactures have advanced to a certain pitch of greatness, the fabrication of the instruments of trade becomes itself the object of a great number of very important manufactures. To give any particular encouragement to the importation of such instruments, would interfere too much with the interest of those manufactures. Such importation, therefore, instead of being encouraged, has frequently been prohibited. Thus the importation of

---

[1] [This chapter appears first in Additions and Corrections and ed. 3.]

第八章 关于重商主义的结论①

奖励出口和抑制进口是重商主义提出的两大富国手段；但对于某些特定商品而言，重商主义奉行的政策似乎又相反，即奖励进口和抑制出口。尽管自相矛盾，但重商主义宣称其最终目标是相同的，即通过贸易顺差，来使国家致富。它抑制工业原料和各行业生产工具的出口，以使我国手工业者处于有利地位，并使他们得以在外国市场上以低于其他国家的价格出售自己的货物。以同样的方式，它提出通过限制几种价值不大商品的出口，来使其他商品在数量和价值上都有大得多的出口。它又提出奖励工业原料的进口，从而使我国人民能以较低的成本来加工制成工业品，从而防止工业品在数量和价值上较大的进口。至少，在我国的《法律全编》中，我没看到过关于奖励生产性用具进口的法令。当制造业发展到一定程度时，生产性工具的制造，就成为许多极重要制造业的目标。所以，对这种工具的进口给予奖励，当然会大大妨碍国内制造业者的利益。因此，此类进口，不但不被奖励，而且往往被禁止。例如，羊毛梳具，除了从爱尔兰进口，或作为沉

重商主义抑制原料和生产工业、但它原料进口、鼓励工业材料行业的出口。鼓励材料不生产具的口。励工产进

---

① 本章最初出现在《补充》、《修订》以及第三版中。

wool cards, except from Ireland, or when brought in as wreck or prize goods, was prohibited by the 3d of Edward IV. ;① which prohibition was renewed by the 39th of Elizabeth, ② and has been continued and rendered perpetual by subsequent laws.

The importation of the materials of manufacture has sometimes been encouraged by an exemption from the duties to which other goods are subject, and sometimes by bounties.

<small>Various materials are exempt from customs duties.</small>
The importation of sheep's wool from several different countries,③of cotton wool from all countries, ④ of undressed flax, of the greater part of dying drugs, ⑤ of the greater part of undressed hides from Ireland or the British colonies, of seal skins from the British Greenland fishery, of pig and bar iron from the British colonies, as well as of several other materials of manufacture, has been encouraged by an exemption from all duties, if properly entered at the customhouse. The private interest of our merchants and manufacturers may, perhaps, have extorted from the legislature these exemptions, as well as the greater part of our other commercial regulations. They are, however, perfectly just and reasonable, and if, consistently with the necessities of the state, they could be extended to all the other materials of manufacture, the public would certainly be a gainer.

The avidity of our great manufacturers, however, has in some cases extended these exemptions a good deal beyond what can justly be considered as the rude materials of their work. By the 24 Geo. Ⅱ. chap. 46. a small duty of only one penny the pound was imposed upon the importation of foreign brown linen yarn, instead of much higher duties to which it had been subjected before, viz. of sixpence the pound upon sail yarn, of one shilling the pound upon all French and Dutch yarn, and of two pounds thirteen shillings and fourpence upon

---

① [C. 4.]

② [C. 14.]

③ [From Ireland, 12 Geo. Ⅱ., c. 21; 26 Geo. Ⅱ., c. 8. Spanish wool for clothing and Spanish felt wool. Saxby, *British Customs*, p. 263.]

④ [6 Geo. Ⅲ., c. 52, § 20.]

⑤ [8 Geo. I., c. 15, § 10]

船货物或捕获货物进口,根据爱德华四世三年的法令就被禁止了①;伊丽莎白女王三十九年,重新起用了这项禁令②;后世的君主继续实行,从而使这一禁止法令永久沿用。

国家有时采用豁免关税的方法对工业原料的进口进行奖励,有时采用津贴的办法。

从几个不同国家进口的羊毛③,从各国进口的棉花,从爱尔兰或英属殖民地进口的生麻④、大部分染料⑤和大部分生皮,从英属格林兰渔场进口的海豹皮,从英属殖民地进口的生铁和铁条,以及进口的其他几种工业原料,若按正当手续呈报海关,都可得到免除一切关税的奖励。这种免税特权,以及许多其他商业条例,也许都是我国商人和制造业者,出于私人利益考虑,硬要立法机构制定的。但这些要求是完全正当且合理的;要是符合国家需要,可把这些要求推广到一切其他工业原料,那一定是有利于人民大众的。

<small>多种原材料可以免征关税。</small>

可是有的时候,由于大制造业者的贪欲,免税对象竟大大超过可正当地看作加工原料的范围。乔治二世二十四年第46号法令规定,外国黄麻织纱每进口1磅,仅纳税1便士;而先前,帆布麻织纱进口1磅须纳税6便士,从法国和荷兰进口麻织纱1磅须纳税一先令,一切普鲁士产的麻织纱进口1百磅须纳2镑13

---

① 见第四号法令。
② 见第十四号法令。
③ 引自爱尔兰,乔治二世十二年第21号法令;乔治二世二十六年,第8号法令。西班牙羊毛用作织布,西班牙人喜爱羊毛。见萨克斯贝《英国关税税则》,第263页。
④ 乔治三世六年第52号法令第20节。
⑤ 乔治一世八年第15号法令第10节。

Yarn, though a manufactured article is free from duty, because the spinners are poor, unprotected people, and the master weavers are rich and powerful.

the hundred weight of all spruce or Muscovia yarn. ① But our manufacturers were not long satisfied with this reduction. By the 29th of the same king, chap. 15. the same law which gave a bounty upon the exportation of British and Irish linen of which the price did not exceed eighteen pence the yard, even this small duty upon the importation of brown linen yarn was taken away. In the different operations, however, which are necessary for the preparation of linen yarn, a good deal more industry is employed, than in the subsequent operation of preparing linen cloth from linen yarn. To say nothing of the industry of the flax-growers and flax-dressers, three or four spinners, at least, are necessary, in order to keep one weaver in constant employment; and more than four-fifths of the whole quantity of labour, necessary for the preparation of linen cloth, is employed in that of linen yarn; but our spinners are poor people, women commonly, scattered about in all different parts of the country, without support or protection. It is not by the sale of their work, but by that of the complete work of the weavers, that our great master manufacturers make their profits. As it is their interest to sell the complete manufacture as dear, so is it to buy the materials as cheap as possible. By extorting from the legislature bounties upon the exportation of their own linen, high duties upon the importation of all foreign linen, and a total prohibition of the home consumption of some sorts of French linen, they endeavour to sell their own goods as dear as possible. By encouraging the importation of foreign linen yarn, and thereby bringing it into competition with that which is made by our own people, they endeavour to buy the work of the poor spinners as cheap as possible. They are as intent to keep down the wages of their own weavers, as the earnings of the poor spinners, and it is by no means for the benefit of the workman, that they endeavour either to raise the price of the complete work, or to lower that of the rude materials. It is the industry which is carried on for the benefit of the rich and the powerful, that is principally encouraged by our mercantile system. That which is carried on for the benefit of the poor and the indigent, is too often, either neglected, or oppressed.

---

① [Smith has here inadvertently given the rates at which the articles were valued in the ' Book of Rates, ' 12 Car. Ⅱ. , c. 4, linstead of the duties, which would be 20 per cent. on the rates.]

先令 4 便士①。但我国制造业者,仍不能长久满足于这样的减税。于是,乔治二世二十九年第 15 号法令,即对输出价格为每码不超过 18 便士的不列颠和爱尔兰麻布给予津贴的法令,把对黄麻织纱进口所课的如此轻微的一点税也免除了。然而实际上,把亚麻纺成麻织纱的各种操作,比把麻织纱制成麻布的操作,需要使用多得多的劳动量。且不说要使一名织工有不断的工作,需要亚麻栽种者和亚麻梳理者的劳动,以及至少须有三名或四名纺工的劳动;单说制造麻布全过程所需要的全部劳动,有 4/5 以上,是用在麻织纱纺织上的。而我国的纺纱工人,都是穷苦人民(通常是妇女,散居国内各地,无依无靠且无保障)。但是售卖纺纱工的制品并不是我国大制造业者获取利润的途径,售卖织工的完全制品才是他们的生财之道。他们的利益,在于以尽可能高的价格售卖制成品,所以他们的利益,就在于以尽可能低的价格购买原材料。他们硬要立法机构对他们自己的麻布出口给予津贴,对一切外国麻布的进口,课以征收高关税,对法国输入的供国内消费的某几种麻布,一律禁止,从而来使自己的货物能以尽可能高的价格出售。通过奖励外国麻织纱输入,并使之与本国产品竞争,他们以尽可能低的价格购入贫穷纺工的制品。同时,他们还千方百计要压低自己所雇织工的工资,正如他们要压低贫穷纺工的收入一样。所以,他们企图提高完全制造品价格或减低原料价格,都不是为了工人的利益。重商主义所要奖励的产业,都是那些维护权贵利益的产业。至于为贫苦人民的利益而经营的产业,却往

虽然纱线是制成品,却免征税,为贫穷纺工没有保障,而雇主既富有又有势力。

①　这里,斯密根据《地方税则》(查理二世十二年第 4 号法令)的条款,错误地给出了 20% 的税率。

<small>This exemption and also the bounty on the exportation of linen are given by a temporary law.</small>

Both the bounty upon the exportation of linen, and the exemption from duty upon the importation of foreign yarn, which were granted only for fifteen years, but continued by two different prolongations, expire with the end of the session of parliament which shall immediately follow the 24th of June 1786.

The encouragement given to the importation of the materials of manufacture by bounties, has been principally confined to such as were imported from our American plantations.

<small>Bounties on imported materials have been chiefly given to American produce, such as naval stores.</small>

The first bounties of this kind were those granted, about the beginning of the present century, upon the importation of naval stores from America. ① Under this denomination were comprehended timber fit for masts, yards, and bowsprits; hemp; tar, pitch, and turpentine. The bounty, however, of one pound the ton upon masting-timber, and that of six pounds the ton upon hemp, were extended to such as should be imported into England from Scotland. ② Both these bounties continued without any variation, at the same rate, till they were severally allowed to expire; that upon hemp on the 1st of January 1741, and that upon masting-timber at the end of the session of parliament immediately following the 24th June 1781.

The bounties upon the importation of tar, pitch, and turpentine underwent, during their continuance, several alterations. Originally that upon tar was four pounds the ton; that upon pitch the same; and that upon turpentine, three pounds the ton. The bounty of four pounds the ton upon tar was afterwards confined to such as had been prepared in a particular manner; that upon other good, clean, and merchantable tar was reduced to two pounds four shillings the ton. The bounty upon pitch was likewise reduced to one pound; and that upon turpentine to one pound ten shillings the ton.

The second bounty upon the importation of any of the materials of

---

① [3 and 4 Ann, c. 10. Anderson. *Commerce*, A. D. 1703.]

② [Masting-timber (and also tar, pitch and rosin), under 12 Ann, st. 1, c. 9, and mastingtimber only under 2 Geo. Ⅱ., c. 35, § 12. The encouragement of the growth of hemp in Scotland is mentioned in the preamble of 8 Geo. I., c. 12, and is presumably to be read into the enacting portion.]

往被忽视、被压抑。

麻布出口津贴制度及外国麻织纱进口免税条例,颁布时原以15年为期,但以后经过两次延期,延续到今日,将于1786年6月24日国会议期终结时到期。

> 麻布出口津贴制度及免税条例是在一个暂行法令中给出的。

享受津贴的进口工业原料,主要是从美洲殖民地进口的原料。

这类津贴的第一批,是在本世纪初,给予从美洲进口的造船用品①。所谓造船用品,包括适于建造船桅、帆桁、牙樯的木材、大麻、柏油、松脂和松香油。但船桅木材进口每吨20先令的津贴、大麻进口每吨6磅的津贴,也推及到从苏格兰进口英格兰的船桅木材②。这两种津贴,按原先比例无变更地继续施行,一直到满期之时为止。即大麻进口津贴,于1741年1月1日国会议期终结时结束,船桅木材进口津贴,于1781年6月24日国会议期终结时结束。

> 进口给予奖金限于从美洲进口原料,主要如造船用品,对之主要产品。

柏油、松脂、松香油进口津贴额,在津贴制度的有效期间内,几经变更。原来,柏油和松脂进口每1吨得津贴4磅;松香油进口每1吨得津贴3磅。后来,每1吨得津贴4磅的奖励,仅限于按特殊方法制造的柏油,其他品质纯良的商用柏油,减为每吨44先令。松脂津贴减为每吨20先令;松香油津贴减为每吨1磅10先令。

按照时间先后,第二次发出的工业原料进口津贴,是根据乔

---

① 安妮女王三年、四年第10号法令,见安德森,《商业》,1703年。
② 仅限于安妮女王十二年,第1次会议,第9号法令和乔治二世二年第35号法令第12条所规定的船桅用的木材。鼓励大麻在苏格兰的种植,也在乔治一世八年第12号法令的序言中提到,并且相信已写进执行部分。

— 1363 —

<small>colonial indigo,</small> manufacture, according to the order of time, was that granted by the 21 Geo. II. chap. 30. upon the importation of indigo from the British plantations. When the plantation indigo was worth three-fourths of the price of the best French indigo, it was by this act entitled to a bounty of sixpence the pound. This bounty, which, like most others, was granted only for a limited time, was continued by several prolongations, but was reduced to four pence the pound. It was allowed to expire with the end of the session of parliament which followed the 25th March 1781.

<small>colonial hemp or undressed flax,</small> The third bounty of this kind was that granted (much about the time that we were beginning sometimes to court and sometimes to quarrel with our American colonies) by the 4 Geo. III. chap. 26. upon the importation of hemp, or undressed flax, from the British plantations. This bounty was granted for twenty-one years, from the 24th June 1764, to the 24th June 1785. For the first seven years it was to be at the rate of eight pounds the ton, for the second at six pounds, and for the third at four pounds. It was not extended to Scotland, of which the climate (although hemp is sometimes raised there, in small quantities and of an inferior quality) is not very fit for that produce. Such a bounty upon the importation of Scotch flax into England would have been too great a discouragement to the native produce of the southern part of the united kingdom.

<small>American wood,</small> The fourth bounty of this kind, was that granted by the 5 Geo. III. chap. 45. upon the importation of wood from America. It was granted for nine years, from the 1st January 1766, to the 1st January 1775. During the first three years, it was to be for every hundred and twenty good deals, at the rate of one pound; and for every load containing fifty cubic feet of other squared timber at the rate of twelve shillings. For the second three years, it was for deals to be at the rate of fifteen shillings, and for other squared timber, at the rate of eight shillings; and for the third three years, it was for deals, to be at the rate of ten shillings, and for other squared timber, at the rate of five shillings.

<small>colonial raw silk,</small> The fifth bounty of this kind, was that granted by the 9 Geo. III. chap. 38. upon the importation of raw silk from the British plantations. It was granted for twenty-one years, from the 1st January 1770, to the 1st January 1791. For the first seven years it was to be at the

治二世二十一年第 30 号法令发给从英国殖民地进口的蓝靛的津贴。当殖民地产的蓝靛在价值上等于法国蓝靛价格的 3/4 时,按这法令,便可享有每磅 6 便士的津贴。这个津贴的发给,亦是有限期的,但历经数次延期,减至每磅 4 便士,并于 1781 年 3 月 25 日国会议期终结时结束。

殖民地蓝靛,

第三次发出的工业原料进口津贴,是乔治三世四年第 26 号法令对进口英国殖民地大麻或生亚麻时所给予的津贴(在这期间,我国有时与北美殖民地交好,有时和它们冲突)。这个津贴以 21 年为期,有效期从 1764 年 6 月 24 日至 1785 年 6 月 24 日,每七年为一期。第一期每吨津贴 8 镑;第二期 6 镑;第三期 4 镑。苏格兰气候不宜于种麻,虽也种麻,但产量不多,且品质较劣,所以无资格享有此种津贴。因为,如果从苏格兰输入英格兰的亚麻,也能享有津贴,那对联合王国南部本地的生产,不能不说是极大的妨碍。

殖民地大麻或者生亚麻,

第四次给予的工业原料进口津贴,乃是乔治三世五年第 45 号法令对进口美洲木材所给予的津贴。这个津贴期限为九年,即从 1766 年 1 月 1 日至 1775 年 1 月 1 日。每三年为一期。第一期,每进口好松板 120 条,得补贴 20 先令;其他方板每进口 50 立方呎,得补贴 12 先令。第二期,每进口好松板 120 条,得补贴 15 先令;其他方板每进口 50 立方呎,得补贴 8 先令。第三期,每进口好松板 120 条,得补贴 10 先令;其他方板每 50 立方呎,得补贴 5 先令。

美洲木材,

第五次发出的工业原料进口津贴,是乔治三世九年第 38 号法令,对进口英国殖民地生丝所给予的津贴。有效期 21 年,即从 1770 年 1 月 1 日至 1791 年 1 月 1 日。每七年分为一期。第一

殖民地生丝,

rate of twenty-five pounds for every hundred pounds value; for the second, at twenty pounds; and for the third at fifteen pounds. The management of the silk-worm, and the preparation of silk, requires so much hand labour; and labour is so very dear in America, that even this great bounty, I have been informed, was not likely to produce any considerable effect.

<small>colonial barrel staves,</small> The sixth bounty of this kind, was that granted by 11 Geo. III. chap. 50. for the importation of pipe, hogshead, and barrel staves and heading from the British plantations. It was granted for nine years, from 1st January 1772, to the 1st January 1781. For the first three years, it was for a certain quantity of each, to be at the rate of six pounds; for the second three years, at four pounds; and for the third three years, at two pounds.

<small>Irish hemp.</small> The seventh and last bounty of this kind, was that granted by the 19 Geo. III. chap. 37. upon the importation of hemp from Ireland. It was granted in the same manner as that for the importation of hemp and undressed flax from America, for twenty-one years, from the 24th June 1779, to the 24th June 1800. This term is divided, likewise, into three periods of seven years each; and in each of those periods, the rate of the Irish bounty is the same with that of the American. It does not, however, like the American bounty, extend to the importation of undressed flax. It would have been too great a discouragement to the cultivation of that plant in Great Britain. When this last bounty was granted, the British and Irish legislatures were not in much better humour with one another, than the British and American had been before. But this boon to Ireland, it is to be hoped, has been granted under more fortunate auspices, than all those to America.

<small>These commodities were subject to duties when coming from foreign countries. It was alleged that the interest of the colonies and of the mother country was the same.</small> The same commodities upon which we thus gave bounties, when imported from America, were subjected to considerable duties when imported from any other country. The interest of our American colonies was regarded as the same with that of the mother country. Their wealth was considered as our wealth. Whatever money was sent out to them, it was said, came all back to us by the balance of trade, and we could never become a farthing the poorer, by any expence which we could lay out upon them. They were our own in every respect, and it was an expence laid out upon the improvement of our own property, and for the profitable employment of our own people.

期，每进口生丝价值100镑，给予津贴25镑；第二期，给予津贴20镑；第三期，给予津贴15镑。但养蚕造丝，需要如此多的手工，而在北美，劳动力又是如此昂贵，所以连这样大的津贴，也不能产生丝毫效果。

第六次发出的工业原料进口津贴，是乔治三世十一年第50号法令，给予从英国殖民地进口的酒桶、大桶、桶板、桶头板的津贴。有效期九年，从1772年1月1日至1781年1月1日。三年一期；第一期，进口货物一定量，得补贴6镑；第二期，得补贴4镑；第三期，得2补贴镑。殖民地酒桶。

第七次即最后一次发出的这一类津贴，乃是乔治三世十九年第37号法令，给予进口的爱尔兰大麻的津贴。有效期为21年，即从1779年6月24日至1800年6月24日，每七年为一期。每一期的津贴标准与给予从美洲进口的大麻及生亚麻的津贴一样，差别只在于，对美洲的津贴不推及到生亚麻。给予进口爱尔兰生亚麻的津贴，对不列颠的亚麻栽种，是太大的妨害了。在对爱尔兰大麻进口发给津贴时，不列颠议会和爱尔兰议会之间的交情，并不比以前不列颠和美洲的交情好，但我们总希望，前者是在比后者更有利的情况下发给的。爱尔兰大麻。

这几种商品，从美洲进口，我们会给予津贴，但若从任何其他国家进口，我们就会课以高的关税。我国美洲殖民地的利益，与母邦的利益，被认为是一致的。他们的财富，被认为是我们的财富。据说流到那里去的货币，会由于贸易顺差，全部回到我们这里来，无论怎样在他们身上花钱，都不会使我们的财富减少一分一毫。无论就哪一点来说，他们所拥有的就是我们所拥有的，钱用在他们身上，就等于用钱来增加我们自己的财富，是对我国人尚有些商品从外国进口时，要交税。据说殖民地和母邦的利益是一致的。

It is unnecessary, I apprehend, at present to say any thing further, in order to expose the folly of a system, which fatal experience has now sufficiently exposed. Had our American colonies really been a part of Great Britain, those bounties might have been considered as bounties upon production, and would still have been liable to all the objections to which such bounties are liable, but to no other.

The exportation of the materials of manufacture is sometimes discouraged by absolute prohibitions, and sometimes by high duties.

<small>The exportation of wool and live sheep is forbidden under heavy penalties,</small>

Our woollen manufacturers have been more successful than any other class of workmen, in persuading the legislature that the prosperity of the nation depended upon the success and extension of their particular business. They have not only obtained a monopoly against the consumers by an absolute prohibition of importing woollen cloths from any foreign country; but they have likewise obtained another monopoly against the sheep farmers and growers of wool, by a similar prohibition of the exportation of live sheep and wool. The severity of many of the laws which have been enacted for the security of the revenue is very justly complained of, as imposing heavy penalties upon actions which, antecedent to the statutes that declared them to be crimes, had always been understood to be innocent. But the cruellest of our revenue laws, I will venture to affirm, are mild and gentle, in comparison of some of those which the clamour of our merchants and manufacturers has extorted from the legislature, for the support of their own absurd and oppressive monopolies. Like the laws of Draco, these laws may be said to be all written in blood.

<small>at one time mutilation and death,</small>

By the 8th of Elizabeth, chap. 3. the exporter of sheep, lambs or rams, was for the first offence to forfeit all his goods for ever, to suffer a year's imprisonment, and then to have his left hand cut off in a market town upon a market day, to be there nailed up; and for the second offence to be adjudged a felon, and to suffer death accordingly. To prevent the breed of our sheep from being propagated in foreign countries, seems to have been the object of this law. By the 13th and 14th of Charles II. chap. 18. the exportation of wool was made felony, and the exporter subjected to the same penalties and forfeitures as a felon.

民有利的。这一理论的错误,已被现实所充分揭露(我们无须多费唇舌)。因为,我国的美洲殖民地,假如真是大不列颠的一部分,那么此种津贴便可认为是对生产的津贴,依然要受这类津贴所要受的一切非难,而不受其他的非难。

制造品原材料的出口,有时受到绝对禁止的打击,有时受到高额关税的抑制。

我国的呢绒制造者,就说服国会相信"国家的繁荣,依赖于呢绒制造这种业务的成功与推广"这一点来说,比任何其他种类的制造业者都更成功。他们不仅通过绝对禁止从外国进口呢绒,取得了妨害消费者的独占特权,而且从禁止活羊及羊毛出口,取得了一种妨害牧羊者及羊毛生产者的独占特权。我国保证财政收入的法律,有许多被人们义正词严地抨击为:对那些在法律未颁布前被认为无罪的行为加以严惩,实在过于苛酷。但我敢说,在与我国商人和制造业者强逼国会颁布的几部支持他们那种荒谬的、不正当的独占权的法律比较时,即便最苛酷的岁入法律,都会使人觉得温和宽大。以德拉科[1]法律为例,支持那种独占权的法律,可以说是用血写成的。

<small>重罚来禁止羊毛和活羊的出口。</small>

伊丽莎白第八年第3号法令规定,擅自出口绵羊、小羊、公羊者,初犯永久没收其全部货物,监禁一年,并在某一集市日,断其左手,钉在市镇上示众;再犯,即判为重罪犯人,处以死刑。这项法律的目的,就在于防止我国的羊种向外国扩散。查理二世十三年及十四年第18号法令,又宣布出口羊毛也犯重罪,擅自出口者

<small>曾一度采用残酷处罚和死刑来惩罚羊毛和活羊的出口。</small>

---

[1] 德拉古(Draco),雅典政治家,制定了雅典的法典(前621),该法典因其公平受到赞扬,但因其严酷而不受欢迎。

> but now twenty shillings for every sheep with forfeiture of the sheep and the owner's share in the ship,

For the honour of the national humanity, it is to be hoped that neither of these statutes were ever executed. The first of them, however, so far as I know, has never been directly repealed, and Serjeant Hawkins seems to consider it as still in force. It may however, perhaps, be considered as virtually repealed by the 12th of Charles II. chap. 32. sect. 3. which, without expressly taking away the penalties imposed by former statutes, imposes a new penalty, viz. That of twenty shillings for every sheep exported, or attempted to be exported, together with the forfeiture of the sheep and of the owner's share of the ship. The second of them was expressly repealed by the 7th and 8th of William III. chap. 28. sect. 4. By which it is declared that, "Whereas the statute of the 13th and 14th of King Charles II. made "against the exportation of wool, among other things in the said act "mentioned, doth enact the same to be deemed felony; by the sever"ity of which penalty the prosecution of offenders hath not been so " effectually put in execution: Be it, therefore, enacted by the authority " foresaid, that so much of the said act, which relates to the making "the said offence felony, be repealed and made void. "

> and three shillings for every pound of wool, with other pains and penalties.

The penalties, however, which are either imposed by this milder statute, or which, though imposed by former statutes, are not repealed by this one, are still sufficiently severe. Besides the forfeiture of the goods, the exporter incurs the penalty of three shillings for every pound weight of wool either exported or attempted to be exported, that is about four or five times the value. Any merchant or other person convicted of this offence is disabled from requiring any debt or account belonging to him from any factor or other person. Let his fortune be what it will, whether he is, or is not able to pay those heavy penalties, the law means to ruin him completely. But as the morals of the great body of the people are not yet so corrupt as those of the contrivers of this statute, I have not heard that any advantage has ever been taken of this clause. If the person convicted of this offence is not able to pay the penalties within three months after judgment, he is to be transported for seven years, and if he returns before the expiration of that term, he is liable to the pains of felony, without benefit of clergy. ①The owner of the ship knowing this offence forfeits all his interest in the ship and furniture. The master and mariners knowing this offence forfeit all their goods and chattels, and suffer three months imprisonment. By

---

① [4 Geo. I., c. II, § 6.]

须受重犯罪人同样的刑罚,货物也被没收。

出于国家的人道主义考虑,我们希望这两项法律都不实施。第一项,据我所知,虽至今尚未直接撤除,而且法学家霍金斯也认为至今仍然有效,但该法律,实际上根据查理二世十二年第32号法令第三节的规定,已形同取消了。因为查理二世的法令规定:凡出口或企图出口羊者,每一头罚金20先令,并没收全部羊及其所有者对船只的部分所有权。第二项法律,则被威廉三世七年、八年第28号法令第四节明令废除了。该法令宣称:"查理二世十三年及十四年颁布的禁止羊毛出口的法令,把羊毛出口视为重罪。因为刑罚过于苛重,及犯罪者的控诉,未能按法执行。因此,该法令关于视该犯罪行为为重罪一节,明令撤除,宣告为无效。"

但是,这个查理二世十二年的第32号法令虽较和缓,以及先前法令所规定而未经这项法令撤除的刑罚,都还是很严酷的:除了没收货物,出口者每出口或企图出口羊毛一磅,须缴罚金3先令。这个罚金是原价的四倍乃至五倍。而且,犯此罪的任何商人或其他人,都不得将罚金转嫁给其债务人。不管犯罪者财产状况如何,也不管其是否有能力交付这样重的罚款,该法律的目的就是想令他完全破产——但人民大众的道德还没败坏到同该法律的制定者那样,所以我也未曾听到过有任何人通过这项条款获利——倘若犯此罪的人,不能在判决后的三个月内交付罚款,即被处以七年的流放刑法;刑期未满逃归者,作为重犯处罚,并不得享受牧师的特典①。船主有知罪不报者,没收其船只及设备;船长水手知罪不告者,没收其所有动产和货物,并处以三个月的监禁,后又

---

① 乔治一世四年第2号法令第六节。

a subsequent statute the master suffers six months imprisonment. ①

<small>To prevent clandestine exportation the inland commerce of wool is much hampered by restrictions,</small>

In order to prevent exportation, the whole inland commerce of wool is laid under very burdensome and oppressive restrictions. It cannot be packed in any box, barrel, cask, case, chest, or any other package, but only in packs of leather or pack-cloth, on which must be marked on the outside the words *wool* or *yarn*, in large letters not less than three inches long, on pain of forfeiting the same and the package, and three shillings for every pound weight, to be paid by the owner or packer. ② It cannot be loaden on any horse or cart, or carried by land within five miles of the coast, but between sun-rising and sun-setting, on pain of forfeiting the same, the horses and carriages. ③ The hundred next adjoining to the sea coast, out of or through which the wool is carried or exported, forfeits twenty pounds, if the wool is under the value of ten pounds; and if of greater value, then treble that value, together with treble costs, to be sued for within the year. The execution to be against any two of the inhabitants, whom the sessions must reimburse, by an assessment on the other inhabitants, as in the cases of robbery. And if any person compounds with the hundred for less than this penalty, he is to be imprisoned for five years; and any other person may prosecute. These regulations take place through the whole kingdom. ④

<small>especially in Kent and Sussex,</small>

But in the particular counties of Kent and Sussex the restrictions are still more troublesome. Every owner of wool within ten miles of the sea-coast must give an account in writing, three days after shearing, to the next officer of the customs, of the number of his fleeces, and of the places where they are lodged. And before he removes any part of them he must give the like notice of the

---

① [Presumably the reference is to 10 and 11 W. Ⅲ., c. 10, § 18, but this applies to the commander of a king's ship conniving at the offence, not to the master of the offending vessel.]

② [12 Geo. Ⅱ., c. 21, § 10.]

③ [13 and 14 Car. Ⅱ., c. 18, § 9, forbade removal of wool in any part of the country between 8 P. M. and 4 A. M. from March to September, and 5 P. M. and 7 A. M. from October to February. 7 and 8 W. Ⅲ., c. 28, § 8, taking no notice of this, enacted the provision quoted in the text. The provision of 13 and 14 Car. Ⅱ., c. 18, was repealed by 20 Geo. Ⅲ., c. 55, which takes no notice of 7 and 8 W. Ⅲ., c. 28.]

④ [All these provisions are from 7 and 8 W. Ⅲ., c. 28.]

改为六个月的监禁。①

为防止羊毛出口,全国的羊毛贸易,都受到极繁琐的重重限制。例如,规定羊毛不得装在箱内、桶内、匣内,而只能用布或皮革包装,且外面要用至少三时长的大字"羊毛"或"毛线"注明;否则没收货物及盛器,且每磅罚金三先令,由所有者或包装者交纳②。又规定,一天中除了在日出及日落之间的时间,羊毛不可由马或马车搬运,也不可通过离海岸五哩以内的陆路搬运,否则没收货物及车马③;若通过海岸或邻近海岸运出或出口羊毛者,羊毛价值不足10磅时将在一年内处以罚金20镑,如羊毛价值在10镑以上时,则处以三倍于原价及三倍诉讼费的罚金。对居民中任何二人执行判决,判决金额根据其他居民的评判标准决定,就像盗窃案的判决一样。若有人私通官吏,以求减免罚金,则处以监禁五年;且任何人都可告发。这一法令,全国通行④。

肯特及萨塞克斯二郡,限制尤其繁琐。距海岸10哩以内的羊毛所有者,必须在剪下羊毛的三天内,以书面形式向最近的海关报告所剪羊毛的数量及储藏所。在移动其中任何部分以前,又

---

① 大概此处参考的是威廉三世十年、十一年第10号法令第18款,但这里只适用于纵容、勾结皇家舰船的船长,而不适用于一般犯罪舰船的主人。

② 乔治二世十二年第21号法令第10款。

③ 查理二世十三年和十四年第18号法令第9款规定,三月份到九月份的晚上8点到早上4点,和十月份到次年二月份的下午5点到早上7点,禁止在国家的任何地区搬运羊毛。威廉三世七年和八年第28号法令第8款,略过了此处,执行的是文中的条款。查理二世十三年和十四年第18号法令的规定,被乔治三世二十年第55号法令撤销,但后来被威廉三世七年和八年第28号法令放弃。

④ 所有的条款取自威廉三世七年和八年第28号法令。

number and weight of the fleeces, and of the name and abode of the person to whom they are sold, and of the place to which it is intended they should be carried. No person within fifteen miles of the sea, in the said counties, can buy any wool, before he enters into bond to the king, that no part of the wool which he shall so buy shall be sold by him to any other person within fifteen miles of the sea. If any wool is found carrying towards the sea-side in the said counties, unless it has been entered and security given as aforesaid, it is forfeited, and the offender also forfeits three shillings for every pound weight. If any person lays any wool, not entered as aforesaid, within fifteen miles of the sea, it must be seized and forfeited; and if, after such seizure, any person shall claim the same, he must give security to the Exchequer, that if he is cast upon trial he shall pay treble costs, besides all other penalties. ①

and so also is the coasting trade.
When such restrictions are imposed upon the inland trade, the coasting trade, we may believe, cannot be left very free. Every owner of wool who carrieth or causeth to be carried any wool to any port or place on the sea-coast, in order to be from thence transported by sea to any other place or port on the coast, must first cause an entry thereof to be made at the port from whence it is intended to be conveyed, containing the weight, marks, and number of the packages before he brings the same within five miles of that port; on pain of forfeiting the same, and also the horses, carts, and other carriages ; and also of suffering and forfeiting, as by the other laws in force against the exportation of wool. This law, however, (1 Will. Ⅲ. chap. 32.) is so very indulgent as to declare, that "this shall not hinder any "person from carrying his wool home from the place of shearing, "though it be within five miles of the sea, provided that in ten days "after shearing, and before he remove the wool, he do under his hand "certify to the next officer of the customs, the true number of fleeces, "and where it is housed; and do not remove the same, without certifying "to such officer, under his hand, his intention so to do, three days "before. " ② Bond must be given that the wool to be carried coast ways is to be landed at the particular port for which it is entered outwards; and if any part of it is landed without the presence of an officer, not only the forfeiture of the wool is incurred as in other goods, but the usual additional penalty of three shillings for every pound weight is likewise incurred.

---

① [9 and 10 W. Ⅲ. , c. 40.]

② [The quotation is not *verbatim*.]

必须以同样的形式报告所移动羊毛的捆数、重量、买者姓名住址，及移运地址。在这二郡内，凡居住在距海 15 哩内的人，在未向国王保证，不把如此购得的羊毛的任何部分再售给距海 15 哩内任何其他人以前，不得购买任何羊毛。若未作这样的报告和保证，就向这二郡的海边输运羊毛，一经查获，就没收其羊毛，且处以当事者罚金每磅三先令；倘若未作这样的报告，就把羊毛存放于距海 15 哩者，查封并没收其羊毛；倘在查封后，有人要求领还，则必须对国库作出保证；在败诉时，除了上述处罚外，还须交纳三倍的诉讼费①

当境内贸易如此受限时，我们有理由相信，沿海贸易也绝不会很自由。羊毛所有者，若要运送或意图运送羊毛到海岸任何港埠，再从那里沿海路运至沿海其他港埠，那么在将羊毛输运至距离出口港五哩以内的地方以前，须先到出口港报告所运羊毛的包数、重量及记号，否则没收羊毛，并没收马和马车或其他车辆；并且还要按照其他各种禁止羊毛出口迄今还有效的法律加以处罚。但威廉三世一年第 21 号法令，却又是如此宽大，它宣称："若在羊毛剪下 10 日内，将羊毛的真实捆数及储存地，亲自向最近的海关出示证明，并在羊毛搬运前的三日内②，亲自向最近的海关说明其意图，就可把羊毛从剪毛地点运回家中，尽管剪毛地点，是在距海五哩以内的地方。"向沿海输送的羊毛，必须保证在登记的某港口起运上陆；倘若没有负责官吏在场，自行起运，则没收其羊毛，并处以每磅 3 先令的罚金。

沿海贸易的状况也是如此。

---

① 威廉三世九年和十年第 40 号法令。
② 此处引文并不是逐字引用的。

国民财富的性质与原理

<small>The manufacturers alleged that English wool was superior to all others, which is entirely false.</small>

Our woollen manufacturers, in order to justify their demand of such extraordinary restrictions and regulations, confidently asserted, that English wool was of a peculiar quality, superior to that of any other country; that the wool of other countries could not, without some mixture of it, be wrought up into any tolerable manufacture; that fine cloth could not be made without it; that England, therefore, if the exportation of it could be totally prevented, could monopolize to herself almost the whole woollen trade of the world; and thus, having no rivals, could sell at what price she pleased, and in a short time acquire the most incredible degree of wealth by the most advantageous balance of trade. This doctrine, like most other doctrines which are confidently asserted by any considerable number of people, was, and still continues to be, most implicitly believed by a much greater number; by almost all those who are either unacquainted with the woollen trade, or who have not made particular enquiries. It is, however, so perfectly false, that English wool is in any respect necessary for the making of fine cloth, that it is altogether unfit for it. Fine cloth is made altogether of Spanish wool. English wool cannot be even so mixed with Spanish wool as to enter into the composition without spoiling and degrading, in some degree, the fabric of the cloth.

<small>These regulations have depressed the price of wool, as was desired.</small>

It has been shown in the foregoing part of this work, that the effect of these regulations has been to depress the price of English wool, not only below what it naturally would be in the present times, but very much below what it actually was in the time of Edward Ⅲ. The price of Scots wool, when in consequence of the union it became subject to the same regulations, is said to have fallen about one half. It is observed by the very accurate and intelligent author of the Memoirs of Wool, the Reverend Mr. John Smith, that the price of the best English wool in England is generally below what wool of a very inferior quality commonly sells for in the market of Amsterdam. To depress the price of this commodity below what may be called its natural and proper price, was the avowed purpose of those regulations; and there seems to be no doubt of their having produced the effect that was expected from them.

<small>but this has not much reduced the quantity of wool grown.</small>

This reduction of price, it may perhaps be thought, by discouraging the growing of wool, must have reduced very much the annual produce of that commodity, though not below what it formerly was, yet below what, in the present state of things, it probably would have been, had it, in consequence of an open and free market, been allowed to rise to the natural and proper price. I

第四篇 第八章

我国的呢绒制造者,为他们对国会要求施行这样异常的限制进行辩护,强词夺理说英国羊毛具有特殊品质,比任何其他国家的羊毛都好;并说他国的羊毛,若不掺入英国羊毛,就无法造出有质量合格的产品;精良呢绒,若非加以英国羊毛,根本不能织成;说英国若能完全防止本国羊毛出口,就能垄断几乎全世界的呢绒业,没有谁能成为竞争对手,它也就可以随意抬高呢绒售卖价格,并在短期间内,按照最有利的贸易顺差,取得非常大的财富。这一论调,如同大多数其他为人们所确信的说法一样,曾为多数人们所盲从,而且至今仍为他们所信从。至于一般不了解呢绒业或未曾研究过呢绒业的人,几乎是全部相信。实际上,英国羊毛,不但不是制造精良呢绒的必须原料,而且根本就不适合于制造精良呢绒。精良呢绒,全由西班牙羊毛织成;如果把英国羊毛掺到西班牙羊毛中去织造,还会在一定程度上,减低呢绒的质量。

> 商制造宣称英国羊毛质量超过任何其他国家出产的羊毛,而这完全是错误的。

本书曾经提过,这些法令法规,不仅把羊毛价格压低到现时应有价格以下,而且将其大大压低于爱德华三世时代的实际价格。英格兰苏格兰合并,这些法令法规即通行于苏格兰;据说,苏格兰羊毛价格因此暴跌一半。据约翰·斯密这位《羊毛研究报告》的精明作者的考察结果,最上等的英国羊毛在英国国内市场的价格,一般比阿姆斯特丹市场上极低劣羊毛的通常售卖价格还要低。这些法规公然提出的目的,是把该商品的价格,降至自然价格之下;毫无疑问,它们似乎确实产生了预期的效果。

> 这些规定像所预期的那样,压低了羊毛的价格。

也许有人认为,由于价格如此大幅度的降低,妨害了羊毛生产,因而必然大大减低这商品的年产额;虽不至于比从前低,但肯定会比当前状况下,任由市场公开自由运作所形成的价格调节时的年产额低。可是我却认为,其年产额虽多少会受这些法规的影

> 但并没有大大减少羊毛生产的数量。

am, however, disposed to believe, that the quantity of the annual produce cannot have been much, though it may perhaps have been a little, affected by these regulations. The growing of wool is not the chief purpose for which the sheep farmer employs his industry and stock. He expects his profit, not so much from the price of the fleece, as from that of the carcase; and the average or ordinary price of the latter, must even, in many cases, make up to him whatever deficiency there may be in the average or ordinary price of the former. It has been observed in the foregoing part of this work, that "Whatever regulations tend to sink the price, either of wool or "of raw hides, below what it naturally would be, must, in an improved "and cultivated country, have some tendency to raise the price of "butchers meat. The price both of the great and small cattle which "are fed on improved and cultivated land, must be sufficient to pay the "rent which the landlord, and the profit which the farmer has reason "to expect from improved and cultivated land. If it is not, they will "soon cease to feed them. Whatever part of this price, therefore, is "not paid by the wool and the hide, must be paid by the carcase. The "less there is paid for the one, the more must be paid for the other. "In what manner this price is to be divided upon the different parts of "the beast, is indifferent to the landlords and farmers, provided it is "all paid to them. In an improved and cultivated country, therefore, "their interest as landlords and farmers cannot be much affected by " such regulations, though their interest as consumers may, by the rise "in the price of provisions. " According to this reasoning, therefore, this degradation in the price of wool is not likely, in an improved and cultivated country, to occasion any diminution in the annual produce of that commodity; except so far as, by raising the price of mutton, it may somewhat diminish the demand for, and consequently the production of, that particular species of butchers meat. Its effect, however, even in this way, it is probable, is not very considerable.

<small>nor its quality,</small>   But though its effect upon the quantity of the annual produce may not have been very considerable, its effect upon the quality, it may perhaps be thought, must necessarily have been very great. The degradation in the quality of English wool, if not below what it was in former times, yet below what it naturally would have been in the present state of improvement and cultivation, must have been, it may perhaps be supposed, very nearly in proportion to the degradation of price. As the quality depends upon the breed, upon the pasture, and upon the management and cleanliness of the sheep, during the whole progress of the growth of the fleece, the attention to these circumstances, it

响,但不会大受影响。因为,牧羊者使用其劳动及资本的主要目标不是羊毛的生产;他更希望从售卖羊肉中获得利润。在大多数情况下,羊肉的平均或普通价格,能够补偿羊毛平均或普通价格的不足。本书的第一篇第十一章曾经说过:"在进步和耕种发达的国家,不论何种规定,如果能降低羊毛及羊皮价格,使之低于自然应有的程度,那么就必然能提高羊肉的价格。在改良的耕地上饲养的牲畜,无论大小,其价格必须能够足够支付地主的地租和农场主的利润。如果不够支付,其饲养不久就会停止。羊毛羊皮如不够支付这种租金和利润,那就必须由羊肉来支付。前者的贡献愈少,后者所做出的贡献必然就愈多。这种贡献,究竟是怎样由羊的各部分分担,地主与农场主是不关心的。他们所关心的,只是它们各自的租金和利润得到支付没有。这样看来,在进步及耕种先进的国家,地主与农场主的利益,不大容易受这些规定的影响,尽管作为消费者,他们可能会因这种规定导致食品价格提高,而不免受到影响。"所以,按照这种推理,在进步及耕种发达的国家,皮毛价格的极人降低,不致引起这种商品年产额的减少。只不过,由于它使羊肉价格上涨,所以可能会稍稍降低这种畜肉的需求,从而稍稍抑制此种家畜肉的生产。但尽管如此,其影响似乎并不是很大。

  不过,虽然对年产量的影响不是很大,但有人认为对于品质的影响却是非常大的。英国羊毛的质量,虽不比从前低,但比起如今农耕状态下所应有的程度来说却是要低的;也许有人认为,品质的低与价格的低成比例。因为羊毛的品质,既取决于羊种、牧草,又取决于羊毛生产全过程中对羊的管理与清洁,而牧羊者对于这些因素的关注,却取决于羊毛价格在何种程度上能弥补所

（也没有降低羊毛的质量，）

may naturally enough be imagined, can never be greater than in proportion to the recompence which the price of the fleece is likely to make for the labour and expence which that attention requires. It happens, however, that the goodness of the fleece depends, in a great measure, upon the health, growth, and bulk of the animal; the same attention which is necessary for the improvement of the carcase, is, in some respects, sufficient for that of the fleece. Notwithstanding the degradation of price, English wool is said to have been improved considerably during the course even of the present century. The improvement might perhaps have been greater if the price had been better; but the lowness of price, though it may have obstructed, yet certainly it has not altogether prevented that improvement.

<small>so that the growers of wool have been less hurt than might have been expected.</small>

The violence of these regulations, therefore, seems to have affected neither the quantity nor the quality of the annual produce of wool so much as it might have been expected to do (though I think it probable that it may have affected the latter a good deal more than the former); and the interest of the growers of wool, though it must have been hurt in some degree, seems, upon the whole, to have been much less hurt than could well have been imagined.

These considerations, however, will not justify the absolute prohibition of the exportation of wool. But they will fully justify the imposition of a considerable tax upon that exportation. To hurt in any degree the interest of any one order of citizens, for no other purpose but to promote that of some other, is evidently contrary to that justice and equality of treatment which the sovereign owes to all the different orders of his subjects. But the prohibition certainly hurts, in some degree, the interest of the growers of wool, for no other purpose but to promote that of the manufacturers.

<small>Though prohibition of exportation cannot be justified, a duty on the exportation of wool might furnish revenue with little inconvenience.</small>

Every different order of citizens is bound to contribute to the support of the sovereign or commonwealth. A tax of five, or even of ten shillings upon the exportation of every tod of wool, would produce a very considerable revenue to the sovereign. It would hurt the interest of the growers somewhat less than the prohibition, because it would not probably lower the price of wool quite so much. It would afford a sufficient advantage to the manufacturer, because, though he might not buy his wool altogether so cheap as under the prohibition, he would still buy it, at least, five or ten shillings cheaper than any foreign manufacturer could buy it, besides saving the freight and insurance, which the other would be obliged to pay. It is scarce possible to devise a tax which could produce any considerable revenue to the sovereign, and at the same time occasion so little inconveniency to any body.

第四篇 第八章

需要的劳动和成本——这是人们可以想象得到的。但羊毛质地的优劣，在很大程度上，又取决于羊的健康与发育状况；所以就改良羊肉所必要的某几点来说，亦就很够改良羊毛了。所以，英国羊毛价格虽低，但其品质，据说在本世纪中，也有相当的改良——价格要是好些，改良也许会大些；但价格的低贱，虽然阻碍了这种改良，但却并没有完全阻止这种改良。

所以，这些规定的粗暴，对羊毛年产量及其品质的影响，似乎并没有人们所预料的那么大（但我认为它们对质量的影响可能远大于对数量的影响）；羊毛生产者的利益，虽受到一定伤害，但总的来说，其伤害并不像一般所想象的那么大。

> 羊毛生产者受到的伤害不像预期的那样大。

但尽管如此，这些结论，绝不能证明绝对禁止羊毛出口是正当的；它们只不过充分证明，对羊毛出口课以重税，可能会是正当的。一国之君主，应公正对待其所属的各阶级人民；如果仅仅为了促进一个阶级的利益，而损害另一阶级的利益，显然是违反这一原则的。这种禁令，正是仅仅为了促进制造业者的利益而损害了羊毛生产者的利益。

> 虽然不认为禁止出口是正当的，但对羊毛出口征税却可以非常容易地得到收入。

各阶级人民本来都有纳税以支持君主或国家的义务。每出口羊毛一托德即38磅，收税5先令或甚至于10先令，将给君主带来很大收入。这种赋税，也许不像禁止出口那样对减低羊毛价格有那么大的作用，所以对羊毛生产者利益的损害程度，也许就会少一些。对于制造业者，它也会提供足够大的利益，因为他虽然不得不以高于禁止出口时的价格购买羊毛，但与外国制造业者比较，他至少能够少付5先令或10先令的价格，而且还可节省外国制造业者所必须支付的运费及保险费。要设计出既能为君主提供很大收入，同时又不会给任何人都引起困扰的赋税，那几乎是

The prohibition, notwithstanding all the penalties which guard it, does not prevent the exportation of wool. It is exported, it is well known, in great quantities. The great difference between the price in the home and that in the foreign market, presents such a temptation to smuggling, that all the rigour of the law cannot prevent it. This illegal exportation is advantageous to nobody but the smuggler. A legal exportation subject to a tax, by affording a revenue to the sovereign, and thereby saving the imposition of some other, perhaps, more burdensome and inconvenient taxes, might prove advantageous to all the different subjects of the state.

The exportation of fuller's earth, or fuller's clay, supposed to be necessary for preparing and cleansing the woollen manufactures, has been subjected to nearly the same penalties as the exportation of wool. ① Even tobacco-pipe clay, though acknowledged to be different from fuller's clay, yet, on account of their resemblance, and because fuller's clay might sometimes be exported as tobacco-pipe clay, has been laid under the same prohibitions and penalties. ②

By the 13th and 14th of Charles Ⅱ. chap. 7. the exportation, not only of raw hides, but of tanned leather, except in the shape of boots, shoes, or slippers, was prohibited;③ and the law gave a monopoly to our boot-makers and shoe-makers, not only against our graziers, but against our tanners. By subsequent statutes, our tanners have got themselves exempted from this monopoly, upon paying a small tax of only one shilling on the hundred weight of tanned leather, weighing one hundred and twelve pounds. ④ They have obtained likewise the drawback of two-thirds of the excise duties imposed upon their commodity, even when exported without further manufacture.

---

① [12 Car. Ⅱ., c. 32; 13 and 14 Car. Ⅱ., c. 18.]

② [13 and 14 Car. Ⅱ., c. 18, § 8. The preamble to the clause alleges that 'great quantities of fuller's earth or fulling clay are daily carried and exported under the colour of tobaccopipe clay'.]

③ [The preamble says that notwithstanding the many good laws before this time made and still in force, prohibiting the exportation of leather . . . by the cunning and subtlety of some persons and the neglect of others who ought to take care thereof; there are such quantities of leather daily exported to foreign parts that the price of leather is grown to those excessive rates that many artificers working leather cannot furnish themselves with sufficient store thereof for the carrying on of their trades, and the poor sort of people are not able to buy those things made of leather which of necessity they must make use of.]

④ [20 Car. Ⅱ., c. 5; 9 Ann., c. 6, § 4.]

不可能的。

禁止羊毛出口的这些禁令虽附有防止出口的各种罚则,却并没有有效防止羊毛的出口。人们都知道,每年的出口额仍是很大的。因为外国市场与本国市场上羊毛价格的巨大差额,对于走私的诱惑是那么大,以至于严酷的法律也不能加以阻止——可以说这种不合法的秘密出口,除了对走私者外,对任何其他人都无利。而相比而言,征收重税的合法出口,既给君主提供收入,又可免除其他更苛重、更难堪的赋税,可以说,对国内各阶级人民都有利。

漂白土,由于被用作呢绒制造及漂白的必需品,所以其私自出口所受的处罚,几乎和羊毛的私自出口相同①。而烟土,虽被公认为和漂白土不相同,但由于两者很相似,而且因为漂白土有时可作为烟土出口,也受到同样的禁止与处罚②。

<small>漂白土的私自出口也受到同样的处罚。</small>

查理二世十三年和十四年第 7 号法令规定,除皮靴、皮鞋和皮拖鞋外,一切生皮鞣皮都禁止出口③;这样,该法律就在妨害牧畜业和鞣皮业的前提下,给予了我国制靴者和制鞋者以独占权。随后,又有法律出台规定,鞣皮业对每 112 磅重的鞣皮纳轻税 1 先令,就可摆脱这种受垄断的状况④。这样,制皮者即使以为加工的鞣皮出口,也可在出口时,收回所纳国产税的 2/3。若是皮革

<small>禁止出口生牛皮、牛角。</small>

---

① 查理二世十二年第 32 号法令;查理二世十四年第 18 号法令。
② 查理二世十三年和十四年第 18 号法令,第八款。本条款的序言宣称,每天都有大量的漂白土以烟土的颜色被运输和出口。
③ 序言说到,尽管先前制定的那些仍在发挥效力的法律禁止皮革出口……因为某些人的狡猾和狡诈,以及本该有责任监管那些人的疏忽;每天都有皮革私私运出口,以至于价格剧涨,许多皮革加工工人没法糊口,而那些工作进行离不开皮革的人又买不起皮革。
④ 查理二世二十年第 5 号法令;安妮女王九年第 6 号法令第 4 款。

All manufactures of leather may be exported duty free; and the exporter is besides entitled to the drawback of the whole duties of excise. Our graziers still continue subject to the old monopoly. Graziers separated from one another, and dispersed through all the different corners of the country, cannot, without great difficulty, combine together for the purpose either of imposing monopolies upon their fellow-citizens, or of exempting themselves from such as may have been imposed upon them by other people. Manufacturers of all kinds, collected together in numerous bodies in all great cities, easily can. Even the horns of cattle are prohibited to be exported ; and the two insignificant trades of the horner and comb-maker enjoy, in this respect, a monopoly against the graziers.

woollen yarn and worsted, white cloths, watch cases, etc., also.

Restraints, either by prohibitions or by taxes, upon the exportation of goods which are partially, but not completely manufactured, are not peculiar to the manufacture of leather. As long as any thing remains to be done, in order to fit any commodity for immediate use and consumption, our manufacturers think that they themselves ought to have the doing of it. Woollen yarn and worsted are prohibited to be exported under the same penalties as wool. Even white cloths are subject to a duty upon exportation, and our dyers have so far obtained a monopoly against our clothiers. Our clothiers would probably have been able to defend themselves against it, but it happens that the greater part of our principal clothiers are themselves likewise dyers. Watch-cases, clock-cases, and dial-plates for clocks and watches, have been prohibited to be exported. Our clock-makers and watch-makers are, it seems, unwilling that the price of this sort of workmanship should be raised upon them by the competition of foreigners.

some metals.

By some old statutes of Edward Ⅲ. , Henry Ⅷ. , and Edward Ⅵ. , the exportation of all metals was prohibited. Lead and tin were alone excepted; probably on account of the great abundance of those metals; in the exportation of which, a considerable part of the trade of the kingdom in those days consisted. For the encouragement of the mining trade, the 5th of William and Mary, chap. 17. exempted from this prohibition, iron, copper, and mundic metal made from British ore. The exportation of all sorts of copper bars, foreign as well as British, was afterwards permitted by the 9th and 10th of William Ⅲ. chap. 26. The exportation of unmanufactured brass,

制成品，还可免税出口，这样，出口者还可收回所纳国产税的全部。但我国的牲畜饲养者，却要继续受先前垄断的损害。牲畜饲养者散居国内各地，彼此分离；要让他们团结起来，以威压他们的同胞接受他们的独占，或摆脱他人可能强加在他们身上的独占，在他们而言都是极其困难的。而各种制造业者，却都住在大都市，所以他们能够很容易团结起来。针对牲畜饲养者的垄断，由于捎带着连牛角也禁止出口，所以在这点上，制角器和制梳这两种细小的行业，也受到极大损害。

以禁止或征税方法限制半制成品的出口，并不是皮革制造业所独有的特权。当一件物品还需要加工才适于直接使用或消费时，我国该物品的制造业者便以为那应当由他们来完成——羊毛线与绒线和羊毛一样，禁止出口，私自出口受同样的处罚，甚至连白呢绒出口，也必须纳税；在这点上，我国的染业也取得了一种损害呢绒业的垄断权。我国的呢绒制造者，虽因此有能力保护他们自己，但大部分的大呢绒制造者，兼营染业。所以，也就用不着保护了。表壳、钟壳，表针盘、钟针盘，也都禁止出口。我国制表者和制钟者，似乎都不愿这一类半制成品的价格因外国人的竞争而抬高。_{羊毛线与绒线、白呢绒、表壳的出口都受到限制，}

爱德华三世、亨利八世和爱德华六世的一些法令，曾经明文规定禁止私自出口一切金属。但铅锡列为例外，可能因为这两种金属蕴藏量极为丰饶。而金属出口，却又是当时国家贸易相当大的组成部分。因此，为奖励开矿，威廉和玛利第5年第17号法令规定，由不列颠矿产制造的铁、铜和黄铜的出口，不受禁止。后来威廉三世九年和十年第26号法令都规定，铜块无论产自本国或产自外国，都获准出口。未经加工的黄铜，即所谓枪炮金属、钟_{某些金属。}

国民财富的性质与原理

of what is called gunmetal, bell-metal, and shroff-metal, still continues to be prohibited. Brass manufactures of all sorts may be exported duty free.

<small>On various other materials of manufacture considerable export duties are imposed.</small>

The exportation of the materials of manufacture, where it is not altogether prohibited, is in many cases subjected to considerable duties.

By the 8th George I. chap. 15. , the exportation of all goods, the produce or manufacture of Great Britain, upon which any duties had been imposed by former statutes, was rendered duty free. The following goods, however, were excepted: Alum, lead, lead ore, tin, tanned leather, copperas, coals, wool cards, white woollen cloths, lapis calaminaris, skins of all sorts, glue, coney hair or wool, hares wool, hair of all sorts, horses, and litharge of lead. If you except horses, all these are either materials of manufacture, or incomplete manufactures (which may be considered as materials for still further manufacture), or instruments of trade. This statute leaves them subject to all the old duties which had ever been imposed upon them, the old subsidy and one per cent. outwards.

By the same statute a great number of foreign drugs for dyers' use, are exempted from all duties upon importation. Each of them, however, is afterwards subjected to a certain duty, not indeed a very heavy one, upon exportation. Our dyers, it seems, while they thought it for their interest to encourage the importation of those drugs, by an exemption from all duties, thought it likewise for their interest to throw some small discouragement upon their exportation. The avidity, however, which suggested this notable piece of mercantile ingenuity, most probably disappointed itself of its object. It necessarily taught the importers to be more careful than they might otherwise have been, that their importation should not exceed what was necessary for the supply of the home market. The home market was at all times likely to be more scantily supplied; the commodities were at all times likely to be somewhat dearer there than they would have been, had the exportation been rendered as free as the importation.

<small>Gum senega has a peculiar history and is subject to a large export duty.</small>

By the above-mentioned statute, gum senega, or gum arabic, being among the enumerated dying drugs, might be imported duty free. They were subjected, indeed, to a small poundage duty, amounting only to three pence in the hundredweight upon their re-exportation. France enjoyed, at that time, an exclusive trade to the country most productive of those drugs, that which lies in the neighbourhood of the Senegal; and the British market could not be easily supplied by the immediate importation of them from the place of growth. By the 25th Geo. II. therefore, gum

铃金属或货币鉴定人金属(shroff-metal),却仍继续禁止出口。而各种黄铜制造品都可以免税出口。

不完全禁止出口的,却往往在出口时对之征收重税。

乔治一世八年第 15 号法令规定:英国的一切货物,无论是英国的农产品或制造品,若按以前法令规定,在出口时须纳税的,现在都可以免税出口。但下述各货物除外,即明矾、铅、铅矿、锡、鞣皮、绿矾、煤炭、梳毛机、白呢绒、菱锌矿、各种兽皮、胶、兔毛、野兔毛、各种毛、马匹、黄色氧化铅矿。这些物品,除了马匹外,其他都是工业原料,半制成品(即需要进一步加工的材料),或行业生产工具。这项法令,依然是要这些货物交纳以前须缴纳的税,即以前的补助税和 1% 的出口税。

_{多种制造原料出口征重税,对其他制造业原料出口,收税。}

该法令又规定,有许多用作染色的外国染料,在进口时可免纳一切税;但在后来出口时,须纳一定的税,但注意不能算重。这么做,我国染业者,似乎一面认为,免除进口税奖励这些染料进口,对自己有利,另一面又认为,稍稍阻碍其出口,对自己照样有利。但是,商人为逞自己贪欲而筹划出的这种高明的巧妙手法,却似乎在这里大失其所望。因为它必然使进口者注意,进口量不能超过国内市场需要。结果,国内市场上,这类商品的供给,总是不足;因而这类商品的价格,也总是比在自由进出口的情形下高些。

按照上述法令规定,美远志根胶或阿拉伯胶,因在染料之列,也得以能够在进口时免税。在再次转运出口时,要纳轻微的税——112 磅不过 3 便士的税。当时,法国垄断了与西尼加附近生产这种染料的国家之间的贸易,所以英国市场不容易从生产地直接进口来供应。于是,乔治二世二十五年规定,美远志根胶,允许从欧

_{美远志根胶有的特殊的历史,需要缴纳很重的赋税。}

senega was allowed to be imported (con trary to the general dispositions of the act of navigation), from any part of Europe. As the law, however, did not mean to encourage this species of trade, so contrary to the general principles of the mercantile policy of England, it imposed a duty of ten shillings the hundred weight upon such importation, and no part of this duty was to be afterwards drawn back upon its exportation. The successful war which began in 1755 gave Great Britain the same exclusive trade to those countries which France had enjoyed before. Our manufacturers, as soon as the peace was made, endeavoured to avail themselves of this advantage, and to establish a monopoly in their own favour, both against the growers, and against the importers of this commodity. By the 5th Geo. III. therefore, chap. 37. the exportation of gum senega from his majesty's dominions in Africa was confined to Great Britain, and was subjected to all the same restrictions, regulations, forfeitures and penalties, as that of the enumerated commodities of the British colonies in America and the West Indies. Its importation, indeed, was subjected to a small duty of six-pence the hundred weight, but its re-exportation was subjected to the enormous duty of one pound ten shillings the hundred weight. It was the intention of our manufacturers that the whole produce of those countries should be imported into Great Britain, and in order that they themselves might be enabled to buy it at their own price, that no part of it should be exported again, but at such an expence as would sufficiently discourage that exportation. Their avidity, however, upon this, as well as upon many other occasions, disappointed itself of its object. This enormous duty presented such a temptation to smuggling, that great quantities of this commodity were clandestinely exported, probably to all the manufacturing countries of Europe, but particularly to Holland, not only from Great Britain but from Africa. Upon this account, by the 14 Geo. III. chap. 10. this duty upon exportation was reduced to five shillings the hundred weight.

<small>beaver skins exported are charged seven pence,</small> In the book of rates, according to which the old subsidy was levied, beaver skins were estimated at six shillings and eight-pence a-piece, and the different subsidies and imposts, which before the year 1722 had been laid upon their importation, amounted to one-fifth part of the rate, or to sixteen-pence upon each skin; all of which, except half the old subsidy, amounting only to two-pence, was drawn back upon exportation. This duty upon the importation of so important a material of manufacture had been thought too high, and, in the year

洲各地进口(那与航海条例的本意是大相违背的)。但由于该法令的目的,不在于奖励这种贸易,所以是违反英国重商政策的普遍原理的;它规定在其进口时,每112磅须征税10先令,而在出口时,又不许退还任何部分。1755年开始的那场战争的胜利,使英国也获得同从前的法国一样,对那些生产染料各国享受专营贸易的特权;和议一经达成,我们的制造者即乘此良机,意欲建立一种有利于他们自己但有害于该商品生产者及进口者的垄断。所以,乔治三世五年第37号法令规定,从英王陛下非洲领土出口的美远志根胶,只允许输往不列颠;如同对所列举过的英属美洲殖民地和西印度殖民地的各商品一样,加上了同样的限制、规则、没收及处罚条例。虽然,在进口时,每112磅只须交纳轻税6便士,但当其再出口时,每112磅却须纳重税30先令。我国制造业者的意图,是要把该产品的全部产量运到英国来,而且,为使自己能够以自定的价格购买该商品,又规定其中无论何种数量的商品,除非负担高额费用,否则不能再出口。事实上,如此高的费用,已足够妨碍它的出口了。制造业者们在这里,如同在其他许多类似情形中一样,都是受着贪欲的驱使,但结果同样大失所望。可以说,这种重税实际上是走私该商品的引诱。大量该种商品,是经由英国和非洲,秘密输往欧洲各制造国的,尤其是荷兰。因此,乔治三世十四年第10号法令,把原先的出口税减为每112磅纳税5先令。

根据旧补助税条例的规定,海狸皮1件估定税为6先令8便士;1722年以前,海狸皮每件进口所纳的各种补助税和关税,约等于其地方税的1/5,即1先令4便士。在出口时,除了旧补助税的一半即仅仅2便士外,都可退还。如此重要的一种工业原料,在进口时,竟征收如此高的关税,未免有些过高;于是,在1722年,

海狸的出口征收7便士的赋税,

1722, the rate was reduced to two shillings and six-pence, which reduced the duty upon importation to six-pence, and of this only one half was to be drawn back upon exportation. The same successful war put the country most productive of beaver under the dominion of Great Britain, and beaver skins being among the enumerated commodities, their exportation from America was consequently confined to the market of Great Britain. Our manufacturers soon bethought themselves of the advantage which they might make of this circumstance, and in the year 1764, the duty upon the importation of beaverskin was reduced to one penny, but the duty upon exportation was raised to seven-pence each skin, without any drawback of the duty upon importation. By the same law, a duty of eighteen pence the pound was imposed upon the exportation of beaver-wool or wombs, without making any alteration in the duty upon the importation of that commodity, which when imported by British and in British shipping, amounted at that time to between four-pence and five-pence the piece.

<small>and coals five shillings a ton.</small>

Coals may be considered both as a material of manufacture and as an instrument of trade. Heavy duties, accordingly, have been imposed upon their exportation, amounting at present (1783) to more than five shillings the ton, or to more than fifteen shillings the chaldron, Newcastle measure; which is in most cases more than the original value of the commodity at the coal pit, or even at the shipping port for exportation.

<small>The exportation of the instruments of trade is commonly prohibited.</small>

The exportation, however, of the instruments of trade, properly so called, is commonly restrained, not by high duties, but by absolute prohibitions. Thus by the 7th and 8th of William III. chap. 20. sect. 8. the exportation of frames or engines for knitting gloves or stockings is prohibited under the penalty, not only of the forfeiture of such frames or engines, so exported, or attempted to be exported, but of forty pounds, one half to the king, the other to the person who shall inform or sue for the same. In the same manner by the 14th Geo. III. chap. 71. the exportation to foreign parts, of any utensils made use of in the cotton, linen, woollen and silk manufactures, is prohibited under the penalty, not only of the forfeiture of such utensils, but of two hundred pounds, to be paid by the person who shall offend in this manner, and likewise of two hundred pounds to be paid by the master of the ship who shall knowingly suffer such utensils to be loaded on board his ship.

<small>Similarly it is a grave offence to entice an artificer abroad.</small>

When such heavy penalties were imposed upon the exportation of the dead instruments of trade, it could not well be expected that the living instrument, the artificer, should be allowed to go free. Accordingly, by the 5 Geo. 1. chap. 27. the person who shall be convicted of enticing any artificer of, or in any of the manufactures of Great Britain, to go into any foreign parts, in order to

地方税减为 2 先令 6 便士，进口税也减为 6 便士。但在出口时，也只能退还此数额的一半。1755 年战争的胜利，使英国得以控制了产海狸最多的地方，而海狸皮又为所列举受限制商品之一，所以，其出口，就仅限于从美洲运至英国市场了。我国制造业者不久就想到利用这一良机。于是 1764 年，1 件海狸皮的进口税降为 1 便士，出口税则提高至每件 7 便士，并不得退还任何进口税。同法令又规定，海狸毛或海狸腹部出口，每磅须纳税 1 先令 6 便士；但对海狸皮的进口税却没有任何更改——由英国人用英国船进口的，所纳的税仍在 4 先令与 5 先令之间。

煤炭，即可当作工业原料，又可视为行业生产工具，所以对其出口，也征以重税；现在（1783 年）是每吨纳税 5 先令以上，或每纽卡斯尔度量单位的煤纳税 15 先令以上。这在多种情形下，简直比煤矿所在地的商品原价还要高，甚至高于出口港的商品原价。煤炭每吨征收 5 先令的赋税。

但对实际生产工具的出口，一般不是通过高关税，而是通过绝对禁止来限制的。所以，威廉三世七年和八年第 20 号法令第八条规定，织手套和长袜的织机或机械禁止私自出口；违者不仅把出口乃至企图出口的织机或机械没收，而且须交罚金 40 镑——一半上交给国王，一半赏给告发人。同样，乔治三世十四年第 71 号法令规定，棉制造业、麻制造业、羊毛制造业和丝制造业所用的一切用具禁止出口，违犯者则没收其货物，且须交罚金 200 镑，知情不报租出船只供其运输的船长，亦须交罚金 200 镑。普遍禁止生产工具的出口。

对物化工具的擅自出口，可以处以重罚；活的职业用具即技工自不能任其自如来去。所以，乔治一世五年法令第 27 号规定，凡引诱英国技工或制造业工人到国外去从业或传授技能者，初犯引诱工匠到国外去是严重的罪行。

practise or teach his trade, is liable for the first offence to be fined in any sum not exceeding one hundred pounds, and to three months imprisonment, and until the fine shall be paid; and for the second offence, to be fined in any sum at the discretion of the court, and to imprisonment for twelve months, and until the fine shall be paid. By the 23 Geo. Ⅱ. chap. 13. this penalty is increased for the first offence to five hundred pounds for every artificer so enticed, and to twelve months imprisonment, and until the fine shall be paid; and for the second offence, to one thousand pounds, and to two years imprisonment, and until the fine shall be paid.

By the former of those two statutes, upon proof that any person has been enticing any artificer, or that any artificer has promised or contracted to go into foreign parts for the purposes aforesaid, such artificer may be obliged to give security at the discretion of the court, that he shall not go beyond the seas, and may be committed to prison until he give such security.

<small>and the artificer who exercises or teaches his trade abroad may be ordered to return.</small> If any artificer has gone beyond the seas, and is exercising or teaching his trade in any foreign country, upon warning being given to him by any of his majesty's ministers or consuls abroad, or by one of his majesty's secretaries of state for the time being, if he does not, within six months after such warning, return into this realm, and from thenceforth abide and inhabit continually within the same, he is from thenceforth declared incapable of taking any legacy devised to him within this kingdom, or of being executor or administrator to any person, or of taking any lands within this kingdom by descent, devise, or purchase. He likewise forfeits to the king, all his lands, goods and chattels, is declared an alien in every respect, and is put out of the king's protection.

It is unnecessary, I imagine, to observe, how contrary such regulations are to the boasted liberty of the subject, of which we affect to be so very jealous; but which, in this case, is so plainly sacrificed to the futile interests of our merchants and manufacturers.

<small>The object is to depress the manufactures of our neighbours.</small> The laudable motive of all these regulations, is to extend our own manufactures, not by their own improvement, but by the depression of those of all our neighbours, and by putting an end, as much as possible, to the troublesome competition of such odious and disagreeable rivals. Our master manufacturers think it reasonable, that they themselves should have the monopoly of the ingenuity of all their countrymen. Though by restraining, in some trades, the number of apprentices which can be employed at one time, and by imposing the necessity of a long

处以100镑以下的罚金、三个月徒刑,并继续拘禁,直到罚金付清之时为止;再犯者则听凭法庭判决,处以罚金、12个月徒刑,并继续拘禁,到罚金付清之时为止。乔治二世二十三年第13号法令,加重了这种处罚,该初犯罚金为500镑,处12个月徒刑,并继续拘禁,到罚金付清之时为止;再犯者罚金1000镑,处二年徒刑,并继续拘禁,直到罚金付清之时为止。

按照上述二法令中第一个的规定,某一个人若被证明曾引诱某一技工,或某一技工如被证明受人引诱,答应或签订合同为上述目的前往国外,那么这样的技工,必须向法庭出具不出国的充分保证,而在未向法庭出具此种保证以前,须由法庭拘押。

<small>在国外从业或者传授技艺的技工会被勒令回国。</small>

若某一技工,确实擅自出国了,并在外国从业或传授技能,则在受到英王陛下的驻外公使或领事的警告,或受到当时阁员的警告后,必须在接到警告后的六个月内回国,并继续居住在本国,否则从那时候起,将被剥夺一切国内财产的继承权,也不得作国内任何人的遗嘱执行人或财产管理人,更不得继承、承受或购买国内任何土地。他本人所有的动产及不动产,也将被国王没收,并被作为外国人看待,不受国王保护。

我国一向自诩为爱护自由。但现在无须再费唇舌,这些规定与这夸大的自由精神是多么矛盾。很显然,这种自由精神,在这一情形下,为了商人和制造业者的徒劳利益而被牺牲掉了。

这一系列规定背后的堂皇动机,是发展我国的制造业。但发展的方法,不是改进自己的制造业,而是抑制我们邻邦的制造业,并尽可能消灭一切竞争者的叫恶竞争。我国制造业者理所当然地认为,他们应当独有本国同胞的技能和才干。通过限定某些职业在一段时间内可以雇佣的人数,并规定一切职业须有较长的学

<small>目的是抑制我们邻邦的制造业发展。</small>

国民财富的性质与原理

<small>The mercantile system absurdly considers production and not consumption to be the end of industry and commerce.</small> apprenticeship in all trades, they endeavour, all of them, to confine the knowledge of their respective employments to as small a number as possible; they are unwilling, however, that any part of this small number should go abroad to instruct foreigners.

Consumption is the sole end and purpose of all production; and the interest of the producer ought to be attended to, only so far as it may be necessary for promoting that of the consumer. The maxim is so perfectly self-evident, that it would be absurd to attempt to prove it. But in the mercantile system, the interest of the consumer is almost constantly sacrificed to that of the producer; and it seems to consider production, and not consumption, as the ultimate end and object of all industry and commerce.

<small>Restraints on importation of competing commodities sacrifice the interest of the consumer to the producer,</small> In the restraints upon the importation of all foreign commodities which can come into competition with those of our own growth, or manufacture, the interest of the home-consumer is evidently sacrificed to that of the producer. It is altogether for the benefit of the latter, that the former is obliged to pay that enhancement of price which this monopoly almost always occasions.

<small>and so do bounties on exportation.</small> It is altogether for the benefit of the producer that bounties are granted upon the exportation of some of his productions. The home-consumer is obliged to pay, first, the tax which is necessary for paying the bounty, and secondly, the still greater tax which necessarily arises from the enhancement of the price of the commodity in the home market.

<small>and the provisions of the Methuen treaty,</small> By the famous treaty of commerce with Portugal, the consumer is prevented by high duties from purchasing of a neighbouring country, a commodity which our own climate does not produce, but is obliged to purchase it of a distant country, though it is acknowledged, that the commodity of the distant country is of a worse quality than that of the near one. The home-consumer is obliged to submit to this inconveniency, in order that the producer may import into the distant country some of his productions upon more advantageous terms than he would otherwise have been allowed to do. The consumer, too, is obliged to pay, whatever enhancement in the price of those very productions, this forced exportation may occasion in the home market.

But in the system of laws which has been established for the

徒时期,他们企图以此来限制各行业的知识,使其仅为少数人所掌握,而且掌握的人愈少愈好;他们更不愿这少数人中的一些人到外国去传授技能给外国人。

消费才是一切生产的唯一目的,而生产者的利益,只有在消费者的利益能得到促进时,才应当顾及到。这原则是不言而喻的,根本用不着证明。但在重商主义下,消费者的利益,几乎都是为了保全生产者的利益而被牺牲了;这种主义似乎不把消费看作一切工商业的终极目的和目标,而是把生产看作工商业的终极目的和目标。

> 重商主义荒谬地把生产而不是消费看作一切工商业的目的。

对于那些凡是能与本国农产品和制造品进行竞争的一切外国商品,在进口时加以限制,显然意图是为了顾及国内生产者的利益而牺牲消费者的利益。为了前者的利益,后者不得不支付这种独占所造成的价格上升。

> 限制竞争性商品的进口,是为了生产者的利益而牺牲消费者的利益,

对于本国的某些产品,给予出口津贴,那也全是为了生产者的利益考虑。因为,国内消费者,第一不得不缴纳为支付津贴所要征收的赋税;第二不得不缴纳商品在国内市场上价格抬高所必然产生的更大赋税。

> 出口津贴也如此。

与葡萄牙签订的那个著名的通商条约,通过规定高关税,使我国消费者不能够从邻近的国家购买我国本国气候所不宜生产的商品,而必须从更遥远的国家购买这种商品,虽然明知该国这种商品的品质较差。为了保证本国生产者能在比较有利的条件下从这一个遥远国家输送某几种产物到国内,国内消费者,不得不忍受这种不便。这几种产物的强行进口在国内市场所引起的价格增高,也只得由消费者支付。

> 因梅休条约的规定,

但为管理我国美洲殖民地和西印度殖民地而制订的众多法

but the most extravagant case of all is that of the management of the American and West Indian colonies.

management of our American and West Indian colonies, the interest of the home-consumer has been sacrificed to that of the producer with a more extravagant profusion than in all our other commercial regulations. A great empire has been established for the sole purpose of raising up a nation of customers who should be obliged to buy from the shops of our different producers, all the goods with which these could supply them. For the sake of that little enhancement of price which this monopoly might afford our producers, the home-consumers have been burdened with the whole expence of maintaining and defending that empire. For this purpose, and for this purpose only, in the two last wars, more than two hundred millions have been spent, and a new debt of more than a hundred and seventy millions has been contracted over and above all that had been expended for the same purpose in former wars. The interest of this debt alone is not only greater than the whole extraordinary profit, which, it ever could be pretended, was made by the monopoly of the colony trade, but than the whole value of that trade, or than the whole value of the goods, which at an average have been annually exported to the colonies.

The contrivers of the whole mercantile system are the producers and especially the merchants and manufacturers.

It cannot be very difficult to determine who have been the contrivers of this whole mercantile system; not the consumers, we may believe, whose interest has been entirely neglected; but the producers, whose interest has been so carefully attended to; and among this latter class our merchants and manufacturers have been by far the principal architects. In the mercantile regulations, which have been taken notice of in this chapter, the interest of our manufacturers has been most peculiarly attended to; and the interest, not so much of the consumers, as that of some other sets of producers, has been sacrificed to it. ①

---

① [This chapter appears first in Additions and Corrections and ed. 3, and is doubtless largely due to Smith's appointment in 1778 to the Commissionership of Customs (Rae, *Life of Adam Smith*, p. 320). He had in his library W. Sims and R. Frewin, *The Rates of Merchandise*, 1782 (see Bonar, *Catalogue*, p. 27), and probably had access to earlier works, such as Saxby's *British Customs*, 1757, which give the duties, etc. , at earlier periods as well as references to the Acts of Parliament regulating them.]

律,与我国所有其他通商条例相比,都在更严重地牺牲国内消费者的利益,以保全生产者的利益。一个大的帝国已经建立起来,但其建立的唯一目的,却是为打造出一个顾客之国,即让我国国内的人民只能作为消费者,来从我国各生产者的店铺购买我国所能供给的各种物品。我国生产者通过这种垄断所造成的仅是价格的稍微提高,而我国消费者却要负担全部成本,以维持这个消费者帝国,捍卫这个消费者帝国。就是为了这一目的,仅仅就是为了这一目的,我国在最近的两次战争中,耗资二亿镑以上,借债一亿七千万镑以上;至于前此各次战争的花费,还不算在里面。单单借款这一项所需支付的利息,不仅大于殖民地贸易垄断所能得到的超额利润的全部,而且大于该项贸易的价值的全部;换言之,大于平均每年出口到殖民地的货物价值的全部。

到底谁是这重商主义理论体系的设计者,并不难确定。但我们可以相信,那绝不会是消费者,因为消费者的利益全被忽视了;真正的设计者一定是生产者,因为生产者的利益受到如此周到的关注。但在生产者中,我国的商人与制造业者,才是始作俑者。在本章所讨论的商业条例中,我国制造者的利益,得到了最特别的关注;而消费者,或更恰当地说是其他生产者的利益,就为了制造业者的利益而被牺牲掉了①。

---

① 本章最初出现在《修补目录》以及第三版中,而且毫无疑问在很大程度上是因为斯密在1778年被任命为关税委员(雷:《亚当·斯密的生平》,第27页)。他在自己写的关于 W. Sims 和 R. Frewin 的传记中写下了《商品税率》(1757年),并且涉及了早期的一些著作,例如萨克斯贝写的《不列颠关税税则》,这样既介绍了关税额,又介绍了国会管理关税的法案。

CHAPTER IX

Of The Agricultural Systems, Or Of Those Systems Of Political Economy, Which Represent The Produce Of Land As Either The Sole Or The Principal Source Of The Revenue And Wealth Of Every Country

The agricultural systems will require less lengthy explanation than the mercantile system.

The agricultural systems of political œconomy will not require so long an explanation as that which I have thought it necessary to bestow upon the mercantile or commercial system.

That system which represents the produce of land as the sole source of the revenue and wealth of every country has, so far as I know, never been adopted by any nation, and it at present exists only in the speculations of a few men of great learning and ingenuity in France. It would not, surely, be worth while to examine at great length the errors of a system which never has done, and probably never will do any harm in any part of the world. I shall endeavour to explain, however, as distinctly as I can, the great outlines of this very ingenious system.

Colbert adopted the mercantile system and favoured town industry,

Mr. Colbert, the famous minister of Lewis XIV. was a man of probity, of great industry and knowledge of detail; of great experience and acuteness in the examination of public accounts, and of abilities, in short, every way fitted for introducing method and good order into the collection and expenditure of the public revenue. That minister had unfortunately embraced all the prejudices of the mercantile system, in its nature and essence a system of restraint and regulation, and such as could scarce fail to be agreeable to a laborious and plodding man of business, who had been accustomed to regulate the different departments of public offices, and to establish the necessary checks and controuls for confining each to its proper sphere. The industry and commerce of a great country he endeavoured to regulate upon the same model as the departments of a public office; and instead of allowing every man to pursue his own interest his own way, upon the liberal plan of equality, liberty and justice, he bestowed up-

第九章 论重农主义即政治经济学中把土地的生产物视为各国赋税及财富的唯一来源或主要来源的学派

对于政治经济学中的重农主义,我觉得不需要进行长篇的解释;而关于重商主义,倒有详细说明的必要。据我所知,这种把土地生产物看作各国赋税及财富的唯一来源或主要来源的学说,从来没有被任何国家所采纳;现在它只存在于法国寥寥可数的博学多才学者的臆想之中。当然,对于一种过去从未、也许将来也永远不会危害世界上任何地方的学说的谬误,是不值得长篇大论去研究的。然而,我将尽我所能,明确说出这个具有巧妙构思体系的轮廓。

<small>与重商主义相比,重农主义不需要长篇的说明。</small>

科尔伯特,这个路易十四时代有名的权臣,为人正直,工作兢兢业业,知识渊博,对于公共账目的核查,既精通其中奥妙,又分毫不差。总之,在各方面,他的能力能将公共收入的征收与支出,搞得井井有条。然而不幸的是,这位大臣接受了重商主义的一切偏见。这种学说,就其性质与实质来说,就是一套限制与管制的学说,所以,对于一个习惯于管理国家各部,并设置必要的管制与控制,使各部各谋其政,而又辛苦工作的勤勉之士,是会欣然接受这套学说的。他用管理各部公务的方式来管制一个大国的工业及商业;他不允许个人在平等自由与正义的公平安排下,按照各自的方式来追求各自的利益,反而给予某些产业部门异常的特权,

<small>科尔伯特采纳了重商主义,重视城市产业发展,忽视了主要产业的发展。</small>

on certain branches of industry extraordinary privileges, while he laid others under as extraordinary restraints. He was not only disposed, like other European ministers, to encourage more the industry of the towns than that of the country; but, in order to support the industry of the towns, he was willing even to depress and keep down that of the country. In order to render provisions cheap to the inhabitants of the towns, and thereby to encourage manufactures and foreign commerce, he prohibited altogether the exportation of corn, and thus excluded the inhabitants of the country from every foreign market for by far the most important part of the produce of their industry. This prohibition, joined to the restraints imposed by the ancient provincial laws of France upon the transportation of corn from one province to another, and to the arbitrary and degrading taxes which are levied upon the cultivators in almost all the provinces, discouraged and kept down the agriculture of that country very much below the state to which it would naturally have risen in so very fertile a soil and so very happy a climate. This state of discouragement and depression was felt more or less in every different part of the country, and many different inquiries were set on foot concerning the causes of it. One of those causes appeared to be the preference given, by the institutions of Mr. Colbert, to the industry of the towns above that of the country.

with the result that the French philosophers who support the agricultural system undervalue town industry.

If the rod be bent too much one way, says the proverb, in order to make it straight you must bend it as much the other. The French philosophers, who have proposed the system which represents agriculture as the sole source of the revenue and wealth of every country, seem to have adopted this proverbial maxim; and as in the plan of Mr. Colbert the industry of the towns was certainly over-valued in comparison with that of the country; so in their system it seems to be as certainly under-valued.

There are three classes in their system: (1) proprietors, (2) cultivators, and (3) artificers, manufacturers and merchants.

The different orders of people who have ever been supposed to contribute in any respect towards the annual produce of the land and labour of the country, they divide into three classes. The first is the class of the proprietors of land. The second is the class of the cultivators, of farmers and country labourers, whom they honour with the peculiar appellation of the productive class. The third is the class of artificers, manufacturers and merchants, whom they endeavour to degrade by the humiliating appellation ① of the barren or unproductive class.

---

① [where the usefulness of the class is said to be admitted. In his exposition of physiocratic doctrine, Smith does not appear to follow any particular book closely. His library contained Du Pont's *Physiocratie*, but he probably relied largely on his recollection of conversations in Paris; see Rae, *Life of Adam Smith*.]

而给其他产业部门施以异常的限制。他不仅像欧洲其他大臣一样,更多地鼓励城市产业的发展,而很少鼓励农村产业;而且,为了支持城市产业,他还愿意压抑农村产业的发展。为了向城市居民供应廉价的食物,从而鼓励制造业与国外贸易,他彻底禁止谷物的出口;这样就把农村居民和他们产业产品的最重要部分与外国市场隔离开了。这种禁令,加上以往限制各省间谷物运输的各省法规,再加上各省对耕种者的横征暴敛,压得该国的农业不能依照其肥沃土壤和适宜的气候所应有的发展程度而发展了。这种令人失望和压制的状态,在全国各地都能多多少少感觉到;对于发生这种状态的原因,已经做出了许多不同的探讨。科尔伯特麾下各项鼓励城市产业超过鼓励农村产业的制度安排,似乎是其中原因之一。

<small>重农主义的哲学家们低估了城市产业,结果拥护一个国家体系法学低城市业。</small>

谚语说得好,矫枉必须过正。那些主张把农业看作各国赋税与财富唯一来源的法国学者们,似乎采纳了这个格言。在科尔伯特的制度中,与农村产业相比较,城市产业确是过于受到重视了;所以在重农主义的学说中,城市产业就必然受到轻视。

他们把一般认为在任何方式对一国土地和劳动力年产出物有所贡献的各阶层人民,分为三种。第一种,土地所有者阶级;第二种,耕种者、农业家和农村劳动者阶级,对于这一阶级,他们给予生产阶级这一特殊称号;第三种,工匠、制造者和商人阶级,对于这一阶级,他们给予不生产阶级这一带有侮辱性的称号①。

<small>在他们的体系中有三种阶级:(1)土地所有者;(2)耕种者;(3)工匠、制造者和商人。</small>

---

① 这种阶级的有用性应该得到承认。在他关于重农主义的论文中,斯密好像并没有遵循特定的某本书。他的图书馆中有杜蓬的著作。但他可能主要依靠他在巴黎和别人谈话的回忆(参见雷:《亚当·斯密的生平》)。

| 国民财富的性质与原理

Proprietors contribute to production by expenses on improvement of land.

    The class of proprietors contributes to the annual produce by the expence which they may occasionally lay out upon the improvement of the land, upon the buildings, drains, enclosures and other ameliorations, which they may either make or maintain upon it, and by means of which the cultivators are enabled, with the same capital, to raise a greater produce, and consequently to pay a greater rent. This advanced rent may be considered as the interest or profit due to the proprietor upon the expence or capital which he thus employs in the improvement of his land. Such expences are in this system called ground expences (depenses foncieres).

cultivators, by original and annual expenses of cultivation.

    The cultivators or farmers contribute to the annual produce by what are in this system called the original and annual expences (depenses primitives et depenses annuelles) which they lay out upon the cultivation of the land. The original expenses consist in the instruments of husbandry, in the stock of cattle, in the seed, and in the maintenance of the farmer's family, servants and cattle, during at least a great part of the first year of his occupancy, or till he can receive some return from the land. The annual expences consist in the seed, in the wear and tear of the instruments of husbandry, and in the annual maintenance of the farmer's servants and cattle, and of his family too, so far as any part of them can be considered as servants employed in cultivation. That part of the produce of the land which remains to him after paying the rent, ought to be sufficient, first, to replace to him within a reasonable time, at least during the term of his occupancy, the whole of his original expences, together with the ordinary profits of stock; and, secondly, to replace to him annually the whole of his annual expences, together likewise with the ordinary profits of stock. Those two sorts of expences are two capitals which the farmer employs in cultivation; and unless they are regularly restored to him, together with a reasonable profit, he cannot carry on his employment upon a level with other employments; but, from a regard to his own interest, must desert it as soon as possible, and seek some other. That part of the produce of the land which is thus necessary for enabling the farmer to continue his business, ought to be considered as a fund sacred to cultivation, which if the landlord violates, he necessarily reduces the produce of his own land, and in a few years not only disables the farmer from paying this racked rent, but from paying the reasonable rent which he might otherwise have got for his land. The rent which properly belongs to the landlord, is no more than the neat produce which remains after paying in the completest manner all the necessary expences which must be previously laid out in order to raise

所有者阶级,通过把钱花在土地改良上,花在建筑物、排水沟、围墙及其他改良或保养上,而对年产出物有所贡献。正是有了这些投入,耕种者就能以同样的资本,生产更多的产出,因而能支付更高的地租。这种增加的地租,可以看作是地主花费或投资改良其土地所应得的利息或利润。在这个学说中,这种费用被称为土地费用。

耕种者或农业家所以对年产出有贡献,是因为他们支出用于耕种土地。在重农主义体系中,这种费用称为原始费用和年度费用。原始费用固化在农具、耕牛、种子以及农业家的家属、雇工和牲畜的维持费。这种维持费用至少在第一年度耕种期间(至少在其大部分期间)或在土地有若干收获以前存在着。年度费用包括种子费用、农业用具的磨损以及农业家的雇工、耕畜和家属(只要家属中某些成员可以被看作农业雇工)每年的维持费。支付地租后剩下的那一部分土地产出物,首先应该足以在一个合适的时间内,至少在他耕种期间内,补偿他的全部原始费用和资本的平均利润;其次应该足以补偿他全部的年度费用,并提供资本的平均利润。这两种费用,是农业家在耕种时使用的两种资本;除非这两种资本能够经常地回流到他手中,并给他提供合理的利润,他才能与其他职业者处于同样的位置上;倘若不如此,为了自身的利益,他必然会尽快地放弃这种职业,而谋求其他职业。这部分确保农业家能继续工作所必需的那一部分土地产出物,应视为耕种农业神圣不可侵犯的基金。倘若地主加以侵犯,他就必然会减少他自己土地的产出;要不了多少时日,就会使农业家不但不能支付此种较高的地租,而且不能支付他原本可以支付的合理地租。地主应得的地租,就是先前用于生产总产出或全部产出所必

the gross, or the whole produce. It is because the labour of the cultivators, over and above paying completely all those necessary expences, affords a neat produce of this kind, that this class of people are in this system peculiarly distinguished by the honourable appellation of the productive class. Their original and annual expences are for the same reason called, in this system, productive expences, because, over and above replacing their own value, they occasion the annual reproduction of this neat produce.

_{These expenses should be free from all taxation.}

The ground expences, as they are called, or what the landlord lays out upon the improvement of his land, are in this system too honoured with the appellation of productive expences. Till the whole of those expences, together with the ordinary profits of stock, have been completely repaid to him by the advanced rent which he gets from his land, that advanced rent ought to be regarded as sacred and inviolable, both by the church and by the king; ought to be subject neither to tithe nor to taxation. If it is otherwise, by discouraging the improvement of land, the church discourages the future increase of her own tithes, and the king the future increase of his own taxes. As in a well-ordered state of things, therefore, those ground expences, over and above reproducing in the completest manner their own value, occasion likewise after a certain time a reproduction of a neat produce, they are in this system considered as productive expences.

_{All other expenses and orders of people are unproductive,}

The ground expences of the landlord, however, together with the original and the annual expences of the farmer, are the only three sorts of expences which in this system are considered as productive. All other expences and all other orders of people, even those who in the common apprehensions of men are regarded as the most productive, are in this account of things represented as altogether barren and unproductive.

Artificers and manufacturers, in particular, whose industry, in the common apprehensions of men, increases so much the value of the rude produce of land, are in this system represented as a class of people altogether barren and unproductive. Their labour, it is said, replaces only the stock which employs them, together with its ordinary profits. That stock consists in the materials, tools, and wages, advanced to them by their employer; and is the fund destined for their employment and maintenance. Its profits are the fund destined for the

须的一切费用完全付清之后留下来的净产出。正是因为耕种者的劳动,在支付完一切必要费用的之后,还能提供这种净产出,这个阶级才在这种学说中被尊称为生产阶级。而且由于同样的原因,在这个学说中,他们的原始费用和每年费用也被称为生产性费用。因为这种费用,除了补偿自身的价值外,还能使这个净产出每年再生产出来。

顾名思义,所谓土地费用,就是地主用来改良土地的费用,在这种学说中,亦被授予生产性费用的光荣称号。这些全部的费用及资本的平均利润,在还没有通过提高的地租完全补偿地主以前,这提高的地租,应视为神圣不可侵犯的。教会不应征收什一税,国王亦不应征收赋税。如果不是这样,由于阻碍土地的改良,就会损害教会自身未来什一税的增加,也损害国王自身的未来赋税的增加。因此,在管理良好的情形下,这些土地费用,除了再生产出它自身全部价值以外,还能在若干时间以后,把净产出再生产出来。所以在这种学说中,它也被称为生产性费用。

<small>这些费用应该免税。</small>

在这种学说中,只有三种费用,即地主的土地费用,再加上农业家的原始费用及年度费用,才被称为生产性费用。也由于这个原因,其他所有的费用和其他一切阶级的人民,即使一般常理认为最具生产性的那些人,被看作是完全不具备不生产性的。

<small>所有其他费用和其他一切阶级人民都是非生产性的。</small>

按人们的常识来看,工匠与制造者的劳动,能够极大地增加土地原始产出的价值。但在这种学说中,工匠和制造者却被视为完全不具备生产性的阶级。据说,他们的劳动,只能补偿雇佣他们的资本并提供其平均利润。这种资本存在于雇主提前垫付给他们的原材料、器具与工资中,是被指定用来雇佣他们、维持他们生活的基金。他们创造的利润是被指定用来维持他们雇主生活

artificers and manufacturers in particular, and the expense of employing them;

maintenance of their employer. Their employer, as he advances to them the stock of materials, tools and wages necessary for their employment, so he advances to himself what is necessary for his own maintenance, and this maintenance he generally proportions to the profit which he expects to make by the price of their work. Unless its price repays to him the maintenance which he advances to himself, as well as the materials, tools and wages which he advances to his workmen, it evidently does not repay to him the whole expence which he lays out upon it. The profits of manufacturing stock, therefore, are not, like the rent of land, a neat produce which remains after completely repaying the whole expence which must be laid out in order to obtain them. The stock of the farmer yields him a profit as well as that of the master manufacturer; and it yields a rent likewise to another person, which that of the master manufacturer does not. The expence, therefore, laid out in employing and maintaining artificers and manufacturers, does no more than continue, if one may say so, the existence of its own value, and does not produce any new value. It is therefore altogether a barren and unproductive expence. The expence, on the contrary, laid out in employing farmers and country labourers, over and above continuing the existence of its own value, produces a new value, the rent of the landlord. It is therefore a productive expence.

mercantile stock also.

Mercantile stock is equally barren and unproductive with manufacturing stock. It only continues the existence of its own value, without producing any new value. Its profits are only the repayment of the maintenance which its employer advances to himself during the time that he employs it, or till he receives the returns of it. They are only the repayment of a part of the expence which must be laid out in employing it.

The labour of artificers and manufacturers adds nothing to the value of the annual produce.

The labour of artificers and manufacturers never adds any thing to the value of the whole annual amount of the rude produce of the land. It adds indeed greatly to the value of some particular parts of it. But the consumption which in the mean time it occasions of other parts, is precisely equal to the value which it adds to those parts; so that the value of the whole amount is not, at any one moment of time, in the least augmented by it. The person who works the lace of a pair of fine ruffles, for example, will sometimes raise the value of perhaps a pennyworth of flax to thirty pounds sterling. But though at first sight he appears thereby to multiply the value of a part of the rude produce

的基金。他们的雇主,提前垫付他们工作所需的原材料、工具及工资,也同样垫付以维持他自己所需的费用。他所垫付的这种维持费,通常和他在产品价格上所预期得到的利润成比例。除非产品价格能够补偿他为自己而垫付的维持费,以及为劳动者而垫付的原材料、器具与工资,那他才能补偿他所投入的全部开支。所以,制造业资本的利润,和土地的地租不一样。地租是还清全部费用以后留下的净产出。农业家的资本,不仅能给自己创造利润,也能给资本所有者提供利润,但农业家能给他人提供地租,制造者却不能够。所以,用来雇佣并维持工匠、制造业工人生计的费用,只能简单维持——如果可以这样说——它自身价值的存在,并不能创造任何新的价值。这样,它是全无生产性或不生产的费用。反之,用来雇佣农场主或农村劳动者的费用,除了维持它本身价值的存在,还能生产一个新的价值,即地主的地租。因此,它是生产性费用。

<small>特别是工匠、制造者和雇佣他们的费用;</small>

和制造业资本一样,商业资本同样是不生产的。它只能延续它自身价值的存在,不能生产任何新价值。其利润,不过是雇主在投资期间内或取得报酬前为自身而垫付的维持费的补偿而已。它们只不过是它早先支出的所需费用的一部分的偿还而已。

<small>商业资本也是一样。</small>

工匠和制造业工人的劳动,对于土地原产出的全年产额价值,不会增加任何东西。确实,他们的劳动,对于土地原产出某特定部分的价值,确有极大的增加。但他们在劳动时要消费原产出的其他部分。他们对这部分的消费,恰好等于他们对那部分的增加。所以,无论什么时候,他们的劳动,对全部的价值,没有一丁点的增加。举例而言,制造一对花边的人,有时可以把1便士亚麻的价值提高到30镑。初看起来,他似乎把一部分原产出的价

<small>工匠和制造业工人的劳动,不会增加年产物的价值。</small>

about seven thousand and two hundred times, he in reality adds nothing to the value of the whole annual amount of the rude produce. The working of that lace costs him perhaps two years labour. The thirty pounds which he gets for it when it is finished, is no more than the repayment of the subsistence which he advances to himself during the two years that he is employed about it. The value which, by every day's, month's, or year's labour, he adds to the flax, does no more than replace the value of his own consumption during that day, month, or year. At no moment of time, therefore, does he add any thing to the value of the whole annual amount of the rude produce of the land: the portion of that produce which he is continually consuming, being always equal to the value which he is continually producing. The extreme poverty of the greater part of the persons employed in this expensive, though trifling manufacture, may satisfy us that the price of their work does not in ordinary cases exceed the value of their subsistence. It is otherwise with the work of farmers and country labourers. The rent of the landlord is a value, which, in ordinary cases, it is continually producing, over and above replacing, in the most complete manner, the whole consumption, the whole expence laid out upon the employment and maintenance both of the workmen and of their employer.

<small>Artificers, manufacturers and merchants can augment revenue only by privation.</small>   Artificers, manufacturers and merchants, can augment the revenue and wealth of their society, by parsimony only; or, as it is expressed in this system, by privation, that is, by depriving themselves of a part of the funds destined for their own subsistence. They annually reproduce nothing but those funds. Unless, therefore, they annually save some part of them, unless they annually deprive themselves of the enjoyment of some part of them, the revenue and wealth of their society can never be in the smallest degree augmented by means of their industry. Farmers and country labourers, on the contrary, may enjoy completely the whole funds destined for their own subsistence, and yet augment at the same time the revenue and wealth of their society. Over and above what is destined for their own subsistence, their industry annually affords a neat produce, of which the augmentation necessarily augments the revenue and wealth of their society. Nations, therefore, which, like France or England, consist in a great measure of proprietors and cultivators, can be enriched by industry and enjoyment. Nations, on the contrary, which, like

值,增加了约7200倍。但实际上,他对原产出全年的价值,毫无增益。花边的制造也许要费他两年的劳动时间。当花边制成后,他所得的那30镑,只不过补偿他这两年当工人时给自己垫付的生活资料而已。他每日、每月或每年的劳动,对于亚麻所增加的价值,恰好补偿这一日、一月或一年他自身消费掉的价值。因此,无论何时,他对土地原产出全年的价值,没有一点的增加。他继续消费的那部分原生产出的价值,总是等于他继续生产的价值。被雇在这种费力而又不重要的制造业上的人,绝大部分是处于赤贫状态的。这种现象,让我们感到欣慰的是,在通常的情形中,他们制造品的价格,并没有超过他们生活资料的价值。但就农业家及农村劳动者的工作来说,情况就大不相同了。在一般情况下,他们的劳动,除了完全补偿他们的全部消费以及雇佣并维持工人及其雇主的全部支出以外,还继续生产一个价值,这就是地主的地租。

工匠、制造业工人和商人们,只能靠节俭来增加社会的赋税与财富;或按这种学说的说法,只能靠克己,即剥夺用于维持自己生活资料基金的一部分,来增加社会的赋税或财富。他们每年所再生产的,没有别的,只是这种基金。因此,他们每年只有节省若干部分,只有每年自行剥夺若干部分的享受,社会的赋税与财富才会因他们的劳动而有所增加。相反,农业家及农村劳动者一方面可以享受其自己生活资料基金的全部,另一方面可以增加社会的赋税与财富。农业家及农村劳动者的劳动,除了给自己提供生活资料以外,还能每年提供一种净产出;增加这种净产出就等于增加社会的赋税与财富。所以,像法国、英国这样的国家里,地主和耕种者占人口相当大的比重,就能靠勤劳和享乐而发家致富。

> 工匠、制造业工人和商人们只能靠克己才能增加收入。

Holland and Hamburgh, are composed chiefly of merchants, artificers and manufacturers, can grow rich only through parsimony and privation. As the interest of nations so differently circumstanced, is very different, so is likewise the common character of the people. In those of the former kind, liberality, frankness, and good fellowship, naturally make a part of that common character. In the latter, narrowness, meanness, and a selfish disposition, averse to all social pleasure and enjoyment.

<small>The unproductive class is maintained at the expence of the other two,</small> The unproductive class, that of merchants, artificers and manufacturers, is maintained and employed altogether at the expence of the two other classes, of that of proprietors, and of that of cultivators. They furnish it both with the materials of its work and with the fund of its subsistence, with the corn and cattle which it consumes while it is employed about that work. The proprietors and cultivators finally pay both the wages of all the workmen of the unproductive class, and the profits of all their employers. Those workmen and their employers are properly the servants of the proprietors and cultivators. They are only servants who work without doors, as menial servants work within. Both the one and the other, however, are equally maintained at the expence of the same masters. The labour of both is equally unproductive. It adds nothing to the value of the sum total of the rude produce of the land. Instead of increasing the value of that sum total, it is a charge and expence which must be paid out of it.

<small>but is useful to them,</small> The unproductive class, however, is not only useful, but greatly useful to the other two classes. By means of the industry of merchants, artificers and manufacturers, the proprietors and cultivators can purchase both the foreign goods and the manufactured produce of their own country which they have occasion for, with the produce of a much smaller quantity of their own labour, than what they would be obliged to employ, if they were to attempt, in an aukward and unskilful manner, either to import the one, or to make the other for their own use. By means of the unproductive class, the cultivators are delivered from many cares which would otherwise distract their attention from the cultivation of land. The superiority of produce, which, in

反之，像在荷兰、汉堡那样的国家里，商人、工匠和制造业工人占人口中相当大的比例，却只能靠节俭与克己而致富。实际情况差异如此之大，利害关系也天差地别，所以国民的性格也迥异不同。在前一类国家中，宽大、坦诚和友爱，自然成为国民性格中共同的一部分。在后一类国家中，却极易养成狭隘、卑鄙和自私心，对一切社会性娱乐与享受厌恶之极。

不具备生产性的阶级，即商人、工匠、制造业工人的阶级，是靠其他两阶级——土地所有者阶级及耕种者阶级——维持与雇佣的。他们不仅供给这一阶级工作的材料，还供给这一阶级的生活资料基金。这一阶级在雇佣期间所耗费的谷物和牲畜，也是由他们来供给的。不具备生产性阶级的一切工人的工资以及他们一切雇主的利润，最终都由土地所有者阶级及耕种者阶级支付。这些工人和这些雇主，确切地说，是地主和耕种者的仆人。他们是在户外工作的仆人，而家仆在户内工作。两种人都依靠同一个主人来养活自己。他们的劳动，同样都不是生产性的，都不能增加土地原产出总额的价值。它非但不能增加这总额的价值，而且还是一种必须从这总额中支付的支出和花销。

<small>非生产性阶级是靠其他两个阶级来维持的，</small>

不过，对于其他两个阶级，这个不具有生产性的阶级，不仅有用，而且是大大的有用。有了商人、工匠和制造业工人的勤勉劳作，地主与耕种者才能够以少得多的自己劳动的产物，购得他们所需的外国货物及本国制造品。倘若他们企图笨拙地、不灵巧地亲自来进口或亲手来制造这些东西，那就要花大得多的劳动量，得不偿失了。借着不具有生产性阶级的帮助，耕种者省去了很多不必要的顾虑，能专心致志于耕种土地，不至于被其他事务而分心。这种专心的成果就是耕种者能生产的产品更多了。这种更

<small>但对它们有用。</small>

consequence of this undivided attention, they are enabled to raise, is fully sufficient to pay the whole expence which the maintenance and employment of the unproductive class costs either the proprietors, or themselves. The industry of merchants, artificers and manufacturers, though in its own nature altogether unproductive, yet contributes in this manner indirectly to increase the produce of the land. It increases the productive powers of productive labour, by leaving it at liberty to confine itself to its proper employment, the cultivation of land; and the plough goes frequently the easier and the better by means of the labour of the man whose business is most remote from the plough.

and it is not their interest to discourage its industry.

It can never be the interest of the proprietors and cultivators to restrain or to discourage in any respect the industry of merchants, artificers and manufacturers. The greater the liberty which this unproductive class enjoys, the greater will be the competition in all the different trades which compose it, and the cheaper will the other two classes be supplied, both with foreign goods and with the manufactured produce of their own country.

nor is it ever the interest of the unproductive class to oppress the others.

It can never be the interest of the unproductive class to oppress the other two classes. It is the surplus produce of the land, or what remains after deducting the maintenance, first, of the cultivators, and afterwards, of the proprietors, that maintains and employs the unproductive class. The greater this surplus, the greater must likewise be the maintenance and employment of that class. The establishment of perfect justice, of perfect liberty, and of perfect equality, is the very simple secret which most effectually secures the highest degree of prosperity to all the three classes.

Mercantile states similarly are maintained at the expense of landed states,

The merchants, artificers and manufacturers of those mercantile states which, like Holland and Hamburgh, consist chiefly of this unproductive class, are in the same manner maintained and employed altogether at the expence of the proprietors and cultivators of land. The only difference is, that those proprietors and cultivators are, the greater part of them, placed at a most inconvenient distance from the merchants, artificers and manufacturers whom they supply with the materials of their work and the fund of their subsistence, are the inhabitants of other countries, and the subjects of other governments.

but are greatly useful to them,

Such mercantile states, however, are not only useful, but greatly useful to the inhabitants of those other countries. They fill up, in some measure, a very important void, and supply the place of the merchants, artificers and manufacturers, whom the inhabitants of those countries ought to find at home, but whom, from some defect in their policy, they do not find at home.

It can never be the interest of those landed nations, if I may call

多的产品,足以充分补偿他们自己和地主的雇佣,并维持这一不具有生产性阶级所消耗的全部开支。商人、工匠和制造业工人的劳动,就其本身而言,虽是完全不具有生产性的,但却以这种方式间接有助于土地产出的增加。通过保障生产性劳动者专心于原来的职业,即耕种土地,他们的劳动,因而提高了生产性劳动者的生产力。往往由于与耕种业务毫不相关人的劳动,耕种这一业务,变得更加简易,也变得更好。

无论从哪一点出发,限制或压制商人、工匠及制造业工人的产业的发展,都不符合地主及耕种者的自身利益。这一不具备生产性阶级享受的自由越多,这一行业中各种职业之间的竞争越激烈,外国商品及本国制造品,就越能以低廉的价格供应给其他两个阶级。

<small>压制非生产性阶级的发展不符合其他两个阶级的自身利益。</small>

同样,压迫其他两个阶级,也不可能符合不具有生产性阶级的自身利益。维持并雇佣不具有生产性阶级的开支,乃是先补偿耕种者再维持地主以后剩下来的土地产出。这个剩余额越大,这一阶级的生计与就业规模,必将能够得到进一步地改进。因此,建立完全正义、完全自由和完全平等,就是这三个阶级达到最高层次繁华的最简易却又最有效的秘诀。

<small>压迫其他两个阶级,也不符合非生产性阶级的自身利益。</small>

在荷兰和汉堡这样主要由商人、工匠和制造业工人这一不具有生产性阶级构成的商业国家中,这一类的人,同样是由地主和土地耕种者来维持和雇佣的。唯一的区别在于,这些地主与耕种者,大部分都和这些商人、工匠和制造业工人隔得很远,来往不是很便利。换言之,提供给后者工作材料和生活资料资金的,是其他国家的居民,其他政府管理的人民。

<small>同样,商业国也是靠农业国来维持的,</small>

然而,这样的商业国,对其他各国居民而言,不仅有用,而且

<small>商业国对农业国非常有用,</small>

and it is not the interest of landed nations to discourage their industry by high duties; them so, to discourage or distress the industry of such mercantile states, by imposing high duties upon their trade, or upon the commodities which they furnish. Such duties, by rendering those commodities dearer, could serve only to sink the real value of the surplus produce of their own land, with which, or, what comes to the same thing, with the price of which, those commodities are purchased. Such duties could serve only to discourage the increase of that surplus produce, and consequently the improvement and cultivation of their own land. The most effectual expedient, on the contrary, for raising the value of that surplus produce, for encouraging its increase, and consequently the improvement and cultivation of their own land, would be to allow the most perfect freedom to the trade of all such mercantile nations.

Freedom of trade would in due time supply artificers, etc., at home. This perfect freedom of trade would even be the most effectual expedient for supplying them, in due time, with all the artificers, manufacturers and merchants, whom they wanted at home, and for filling up in the properest and most advantageous manner that very important void which they felt there.

in consequence of the increase of their capital, which would first employ manufacturers, The continual increase of the surplus produce of their land, would, in due time, create a greater capital than what could be employed with the ordinary rate of profit in the improvement and cultivation of land; and the surplus part of it would naturally turn itself to the employment of artificers and manufacturers at home. But those artificers and manufacturers, finding at home both the materials of their work and the fund of their subsistence, might immediately, even with much less art and skill, be able to work as cheap as the like artificers and manufacturers of such mercantile states, who had both to bring from a great distance. Even though, from want of art and skill, they might not for some time be able to work as cheap,

是大大地有用,它们使商人、工匠和制造业找到了他们合适的位置。这些人本来应该可以在国内找到的,但由于国家政策的某种缺点,不能在国内找到他们的位置。

> 商家动制国的不农业的益利抑业的符益;

对这些商业国的贸易或他们提供的商品征收高关税,而来损害或压制这些商业国产业的发展,绝不是有田地国家——如果我可以这样称呼地话——的利益。这种关税,会使这些商品的价格变得更加昂贵,就会降低用以购买商业国商品的它们自己土地的剩余产出或其价格的真实价值。这种关税只会妨碍这些剩余产出的增加,结果妨碍它们自己土地的改良与耕种。相反,提高这种剩余产出的价值,鼓励这种剩余产出的增加,从而鼓励国内土地改良及耕种的最有效策略,就是准许所有的商业国享有贸易上最完全的自由。

这种完全的贸易自由,在适当期间,能够以最有效的方法提供他们国内所缺少的工匠、制造业工人及商人,并且在最适当、最有利的情况下,使得他们在国内感到的那种最重要缺陷得到填补。

> 自由贸易在适当的时候会在国内提供工匠等。

土地剩余产出的持续增加,到了适当的时候,能够创造出更多的资本,其中必有一部分能按平均利润率投入到改良土地或耕种土地上。剩余中的一部分,自动会改用于在国内雇佣工匠与制造业工人。但是,能在国内找得工作材料和生活资料基金的国内工匠与制造业工人,即使技术与熟练程度不及他人,也能立即与商业国同类工匠及制造业工人,以同样低廉的价格,出售他们的产品。因为这些商业国同类工匠与制造业工人,必须从很远的地方获得所需的材料与生活资料。即使由于技术与熟练程度的匮乏,在一定时间内,他们不能和这些商业国同类工匠及制造业工

> 自本资量本加出己些首制业会雇佣造者,增了,资先来制用这本数增加,会用本

yet, finding a market at home, they might be able to sell their work there as cheap as that of the artificers and manufacturers of such mercantile states, which could not be brought to that market but from so great a distance; and as their art and skill improved, they would soon be able to sell it cheaper. The artificers and manufacturers of such mercantile states, therefore, would immediately be rivalled in the market of those landed nations, and soon after undersold and justled out of it altogether. The cheapness of the manufactures of those landed nations, in consequence of the gradual improvements of art and skill, would, in due time, extend their sale beyond the home market, and carry them to many foreign markets, from which they would in the same manner gradually justle out many of the manufactures of such mercantile nations.

<small>and afterwards overflow into foreign trade.</small> This continual increase both of the rude and manufactured produce of those landed nations would in due time create a greater capital than could, with the ordinary rate of profit, be employed either in agriculture or in manufactures. The surplus of this capital would naturally turn itself to foreign trade, and be employed in exporting, to foreign countries, such parts of the rude and manufactured produce of its own country, as exceeded the demand of the home market. In the exportation of the produce of their own country, the merchants of a landed nation would have an advantage of the same kind over those of mercantile nations, which its artificers and manufacturers had over the artificers and manufacturers of such nations; the advantage of finding at home that cargo, and those stores and provisions, which the others were obliged to seek for at a distance. With inferior art and skill in navigation, therefore, they would be able to sell that cargo as cheap in foreign markets as the merchants of such mercantile nations; and with equal art and skill they would be able to sell it cheaper. They would soon, therefore, rival those mercantile nations in this branch of foreign trade, and in due time would justle them out of it altogether.

According to this liberal and generous system, therefore, the

人,以同样低廉的价格,出售他们的产品,但也许可以在国内市场上,以同样低廉的价格出售他们的产品。原因在于这些商业国同类工匠及制造业工人制造的货物,必须由遥远的地方运来。而且,当他们的技术与熟练程度得到提高的时候,他们很快就能以更低的价格出售他们的产品。因此,这些商业国的工匠与制造业工人,将在那些农业国的市场上遇到强劲的竞争对手;不久以后,就不得不贱卖他们的产品,最后被赶出该国市场。随着技术与熟练程度的逐渐改善,这些农业国制成品价格低廉,在适当时期,将会使其制造品推广到国内之外的市场中去,即推销于许多国外市场,并在那里,按同样的做法,逐渐把这些商业国的许多制造商排挤出市场。

农业国原产出及制造品的不断增加,到了相当时期,会创造出更大的资本,其中必有一部分能够按平均利润率,投在农业或制造业上。这增加的资本,自然会投入到国外贸易上,用于出口上,把超过国内市场上需求的过剩的原产出及制造品,运到外国去。在出口本国产出时,农业国商人,将比来自商业国商人处于更加有利地位,这和农业国工匠及制造业工人,比商业国的工匠及制造业工人,处于更加有利地位一样。后者必须在远地找到货物、原料与食品,前者能在国内找得这些东西。所以,即使他们航海技术水平比较低,他们也能和商业国商人,以同样低廉的价格,在外国市场上出售他们的货物。如果有旗鼓相当的航海技术,就能以更低的价格出售货物了。因此,在对外贸易这一部门,不久他们就能和商业国的商人相竞争,并在相当期间,把这些商人全部排挤出去。

所以,根据这个宽宏制度,农业国要培育本国自己的工匠、制

<small>就对外贸易部分。随后溢出会到</small>

国民财富的性质与原理

<small>Freedom of trade therefore is best for introducing manufactures and foreign trade.</small> most advantageous method in which a landed nation can raise up artificers, manufacturers and merchants of its own, is to grant the most perfect freedom of trade to the artificers, manufacturers and merchants of all other nations. It thereby raises the value of the surplus produce of its own land, of which the continual increase gradually establishes a fund, which in due time necessarily raises up all the artificers, manufacturers and merchants whom it has occasion for.

<small>High duties and prohibitions sink the value of agricultural produce, raise mercantile and manufacturing profit,</small> When a landed nation, on the contrary, oppresses either by high duties or by prohibitions the trade of foreign nations, it necessarily hurts its own interest in two different ways. First, by raising the price of all foreign goods and of all sorts of manufactures, it necessarily sinks the real value of the surplus produce of its own land, with which, or, what comes to the same thing, with the price of which, it purchases those foreign goods and manufactures. Secondly, by giving a sort of monopoly of the home market to its own merchants, artificers and manufacturers, it raises the rate of mercantile and manufacturing profit in proportion to that of agricultural profit, and consequently either draws from agriculture a part of the capital which had before been employed in it, or hinders from going to it a part of what would otherwise have gone to it. This policy, therefore, discourages agriculture in two different ways; first, by sinking the real value of its produce, and thereby lowering the rate of its profit; and, secondly, by raising the rate of profit in all other employments. Agriculture is rendered less advantageous, and trade and manufactures more advantageous than they otherwise would be; and every man is tempted by his own interest to turn, as much as he can, both his capital and his industry from the former to the latter employments.

<small>and could only raise up manufacturers and merchants prematurely.</small> Though, by this oppressive policy, a landed nation should be able to raise up artificers, manufacturers and merchants of its own, somewhat sooner than it could do by the freedom of trade; a matter, however, which is not a little doubtful; yet it would raise them up, if one may say so, prematurely, and before it was perfectly ripe for them. By raising up too hastily one species of industry, it would depress another more valuable species of industry. By raising up too hastily a species of industry which only replaces the stock which employs it, together with the ordinary profit, it would depress a species of industry which, over and above replacing that stock with its profit, affords likewise a neat produce, a free rent to the landlord. It would depress productive labour, by encouraging too hastily that labour which is altogether barren and unproductive.

造业工人与商人,最有利的方法就是对一切其他国家的工匠、制造业工人与商人给予最完全的贸易自由。这样就能提高国内剩余土地产出的价值,而这种价值的不断增加就将逐渐建立起来一笔资金,而一笔资金在相当时期内,必然把所需的各种工匠、制造业工人及商人培育起来。

所以,自由贸易最有利于引入制造业对外贸易。

相反,如果农业国通过用高关税或禁令压抑外国人民的贸易,就会必然在两个方面阻碍它本身的利益。(一)会提高所有国外商品及各种制造品的价格,必然降低用以购买国外商品及各种制造品的本国剩余土地产出的真实价值;(二)给予本国商人、工匠与制造业工人以国内市场的垄断权力,就会相应提高工商业利润率,并使之高于农业利润率。这样就会把原来投在农业上的资本的一部分吸引到工商业去,或阻碍原要投在农业上的那一部分资本却不投入到农业。所以,这个政策在两个方面危害农业。(一)首先,降低农产物的真实价值,因而降低农业利润率;(二)其次,提高其他一切资本用途的利润率。农业因此而成为处于劣势的行业,而商业与制造业却因此变得更有利可图。个人出于自身的利益,都企图尽可能把资本及劳动从前一类用途改投到后一类用途之上。

高关税出口禁令降低了农产品的价值,提高了商业和制造业的利润,

农业国通过这种压制政策,虽能以比在贸易自由情况下稍大的速度(这大有疑问)培育本国的工匠、制造业工人及商人,但这是在其尚未十分成熟以前,过早地把他们培育起来(如果可以这样说)。过速地培育一种产业,结果就会压抑另一种更有价值的产业。对于仅能补偿所投资本并提供其普通利润的产业,如以过于急速的方法加以培育,结果就会压抑另一种产业,即除了补偿资本并提供其利润以外,还能提供一种纯产物作为地主地租的产

不能出地只能成熟培养制造业者和商人。

The distribution of the produce of land is represented in the Economical Table.

In what manner, according to this system, the sum total of the annual produce of the land is distributed among the three classes above mentioned, and in what manner the labour of the unproductive class does no more than replace the value of its own consumption, without increasing in any respect the value of that sum total, is represented by Mr. Quesnai, the very ingenious and profound author of this system, in some arithmetical formularies. The first of these formularies, which by way of eminence he peculiarly distinguishes by the name of the Œconomical Table, represents the manner in which he supposes this distribution takes place, in a state of the most perfect liberty, and therefore of the highest prosperity; in a state where the annual produce is such as to afford the greatest possible neat produce, and where each class enjoys its proper share of the whole annual produce. Some subsequent formularies represent the manner, in which, he supposes, this distribution is made in different states of restraint and regulation; in which, either the class of proprietors, or the barren and unproductive class, is more favoured than the class of cultivators, and in which, either the one or the other encroaches more or less upon the share which ought properly to belong to this productive class. Every such encroachment, every violation of that natural distribution, which the most perfect liberty would establish, must, according to this system, necessarily degrade more or less, from one year to another, the value and sum total of the annual produce, and must necessarily occasion a gradual declension in the real wealth and revenue of the society; a declension of which the progress must be quicker or slower, according to the degree of this encroachment, according as that natural distribution, which the most perfect liberty would establish, is more or less violated. Those subsequent formularies represent the different degrees of declension, which, according to this system, correspond to the different degrees in which this natural distribution of things is violated.

Nations can prosper in spite of hurtful regulations.

Some speculative physicians seem to have imagined that the health of the human body could be preserved only by a certain precise regimen of diet and exercise, of which every, the smallest, violation necessarily occasioned some degree of disease or disorder proportioned to the degree of the violation. Experience, however, would seem to show, that the human body frequently preserves, to all appearance at least, the most perfect state of health under a vast variety of different regimens; even under some which are generally believed to be very far from being perfectly wholesome. But the healthful state of the human body, it would seem, contains in itself some unknown principle of preservation, capable either of preventing or of correcting, in many respects, the bad effects even of a very faulty regimen. Mr. Quesnai,

业。过于急速地鼓励全不生产的劳动,必然压抑生产性劳动。

至于按照这个学说,土地年产物全部是怎样在上述那三个阶级之间进行分配,不生产阶级的劳动为什么只能补还它所消费的价值,而不增加那全额的价值,则由这一学说的最聪明、最渊博的创始者奎斯纳用一些数学公式表示出来了。在这些公式中,他对第一个公式特别重视,标名为《经济表》。他想象在最完全的自由状态下,因而是在最繁荣的状态下,在年产物能提供最大量纯产物,而各阶级能在全部年产物中享有其应得部分的情况下,他用第一个公式把想象的这种分配的进行方式表述出来。接着,有几个公式,又把在有各种限制及规章条例的状态下,在地主阶级和不生产阶级受惠多于耕种者阶级的状态下,在这两个阶级侵蚀生产阶级应得部分的状态下,把他所想象的这种分配的进行方式,表述出来。按照这个学说,最完全自由状态所确立的自然分配,每一次受侵蚀,每一次受侵害,都必然会或多或少不断地减少年产物的价值与总和,因而使社会收入与财富逐渐减少。减少的程度,必然会按照侵蚀程度,按照自然分配所受的侵害程度,而以较速或较缓的程度,日益加剧。这些公式,把这学说认为必和这自然分配所受不同侵害程度相适应的不同减少程度,表述出来。

<small>土地产物的分配在《经济表》中得到了表述。</small>

有些有思想的医生,以为人体的健康只能靠食物及运动的正确养生方法来保持,稍有违犯,即将按违犯程度的比例而引起相等程度的疾病。但经验似乎告诉我们,在各种不同的养生方法下,人类身体常能保持最良好的状态,至少从表面上看是这样,甚至在一般认为很不卫生的情况下,也能保持健康。其实,人体的健康状态,本身就含有一种未被发觉的保卫力量,能在许多方面预防并纠正极不良卫生方法的不良结果。奎斯纳自己就是一个

<small>有伤国家规章造成的损害,国家仍然可以繁荣富强。</small>

who was himself a physician, and a very speculative physician, seems to have entertained a notion of the same kind concerning the political body, and to have imagined that it would thrive and prosper only under a certain precise regimen, the exact regimen of perfect liberty and perfect justice. He seems not to have considered that in the political body, the natural effort which every man is continually making to better his own condition, is a principle of preservation capable of preventing and correcting, in many respects, the bad effects of a political œconomy, in some degree both partial and oppressive. Such a political œconomy, though it no doubt retards more or less, is not always capable of stopping altogether the natural progress of a nation towards wealth and prosperity, and still less of making it go backwards. If a nation could not prosper without the enjoyment of perfect liberty and perfect justice, there is not in the world a nation which could ever have prospered. In the political body, however, the wisdom of nature has fortunately made ample provision for remedying many of the bad effects of the folly and injustice of man; in the same manner as it has done in the natural body, for remedying those of his sloth and intemperance.

The system is wrong in representing artificers, etc., as unproductive, since: (1) they reproduce at least their annual consumption and continue the capital which employs them;

The capital error of this system, however, seems to lie in its representing the class of artificers, manufacturers and merchants, as altogether barren and unproductive. The following observations may serve to show the impropriety of this representation.

First, this class, it is acknowledged, reproduces annually the value of its own annual consumption, and continues, at least, the existence of the stock or capital which maintains and employs it. But upon this account alone the denomination of barren or unproductive should seem to be very improperly applied to it. We should not call a marriage barren or unproductive, though it produced only a son and a daughter, to replace the father and mother, and though it did not increase the number of the human species, but only continued it as it was before. Farmers and country labourers, indeed, over and above the stock which maintains and employs them, reproduce annually a neat produce, a free rent to the landlord. As a marriage which affords three children is certainly more productive than one which affords only two; so the labour of farmers and country labourers is certainly more productive than that of merchants, artificers and manufacturers. The superior produce of the one class, however, does not render the other barren or unproductive.

医生并且是个极有思想的医生,他似乎对于国家亦抱有同样的概念,以为只有在完全自由与完全公平的正确制度下,国家才能繁荣发达起来。他似乎没有考虑到,在国家内,各个人为改善自身境遇自然而然地、不断地所作的努力,就是一种保卫力量,能在许多方面预防并纠正在一定程度上是不公平和压抑的政治经济的不良结果。这种政治经济,虽无疑会多少阻碍一国趋于富裕繁荣的发展,但不能使其完全停止,更不能使一国后退。如果一国没有享受完全自由及完全正义,即无繁荣的可能,那世界上就没有一国能够繁荣了。幸运的是,在国家内,自然的智慧,对于人类的愚蠢及不公正的许多恶的影响,有了充分的准备来做纠正,正如在人体内,自然的智慧,有充分准备,来纠正人类的懒惰及无节制的不良结果一样。

但是,这种学说最大的谬误,似乎在于把工匠、制造业工人和商人看作全无生产或全不生产的阶级。这种看法的不适当,可由下面的话来说明。

第一,这种学说也承认这一阶级每年再生产他们自身每年消费的价值,至少是延续了雇佣他们和维持他们的那种资财或资本的存在。单就这一点来说,把无生产或不生产的名称加在他们头上,似乎很不妥当。只生一男一女来代替父母、延续人类而不能增加人类数目的婚姻,不能称为不生儿育女的婚姻。诚然,农业家与农村劳动者,除补偿维持他们和雇佣他们的资财以外,每年还再生产一种纯产物,作为地主的地租。生育三个儿女的婚姻,确比仅生育两个儿女的婚姻更有生产力,而农场主与农村劳动者的劳动,确比商人、制造业工人与工匠的劳动更有生产力。但是,一个阶级的更多的生产,绝不能使其他阶级成为无生产或不生产的。

这种学说将工匠等非生产性的,是错误的,原因在于:(1)他们每年再生产出至少他们的消费,使他们的资本得到了延续;

国民财富的性质与原理

(2) they are not like menial servants;
　　Secondly, it seems, upon this account, altogether improper to consider artificers, manufacturers and merchants, in the same light as menial servants. The labour of menial servants does not continue the existence of the fund which maintains and employs them. Their maintenance and employment is altogether at the expence of their masters, and the work which they perform is not of a nature to repay that expence. That work consists in services which perish generally in the very instant of their performance, and does not fix or realize itself in any vendible commodity which can replace the value of their wages and maintenance. The labour, on the contrary, of artificers, manufacturers and merchants, naturally does fix and realize itself in some such vendible commodity. It is upon this account that, in the chapter in which I treat of productive and unproductive labour, I have classed artificers, manufacturers and merchants, among the productive labourers, and menial servants among the barren or unproductive.

(3) their labour increases the real revenue of the society;
　　Thirdly, it seems, upon every supposition, improper to say, that the labour of artificers, manufacturers and merchants, does not increase the real revenue of the society. Though we should suppose, for example, as it seems to be supposed in this system, that the value of the daily, monthly, and yearly consumption of this class was exactly equal to that of its daily, monthly, and yearly production; yet it would not from thence follow that its labour added nothing to the real revenue, to the real value of the annual produce of the land and labour of the society. An artificer, for example, who, in the first six months after harvest, executes ten pounds worth of work, though he should in the same time consume ten pounds worth of corn and other necessaries, yet really adds the value of ten pounds to the annual produce of the land and labour of the society. While he has been consuming a half yearly revenue of ten pounds worth of corn and other necessaries, he has produced an equal value of work capable of purchasing, either to himself or to some other person, an equal half yearly revenue. The value, therefore, of what has been consumed and produced during these six months is equal, not to ten, but to twenty pounds. It is possible, indeed. that no more than ten pounds worth of this value, may ever have existed at any one moment of time. But if the ten pounds worth of corn and other necessaries, which were consumed by the artificer, had been consumed by a soldier or by a menial servant, the value of that part of the annual produce which existed at the end of the six months, would have been ten pounds less than

第二，无论怎样说，把工匠、制造业工人与商人，和家仆一样看待，似乎是完全不适当的。家仆的劳动，不能延续雇佣他们和维持他们的基金的存在。他们的维持与雇佣，全由主人出费用；他们所搞的工作，在性质上并没有偿还这种费用的可能。他们的工作，大都是随生随灭的事务，不固定在亦不实现在任何可卖商品上，以补偿他们工资及维持费的价值。反之，工匠、制造业工人与商人的劳动，却自然而然地固定在并实现在可卖商品上。因此，在讨论生产性和非生产性劳动那一章中，我把工匠、制造业工人及商人，归到生产性劳动者内，而把家仆归到无生产或不生产的劳动者内。（2）他们与家仆不同；

第三，无论根据何种假设，说工匠、制造业工人和商人的劳动，不增加社会的真实收入，都似乎是不妥当的。例如，即使我们假定（像这种学说所假定的一样），这一阶级每日、每月或每年所消费的价值，恰好等于他们每日、每月或每年所生产的价值，亦不能因此便断言，他们的劳动，对社会的真实收入，对社会上土地和劳动的年产物的真实价值，无所增加。例如，某一工匠，在收获后6个月时间，做了价值10镑的工作，那么即使他同时消费了值10镑的谷物及其他必需品，他实际上亦对社会的土地和劳动的年产物，增加了10镑的价值。在他消费半年收入即价值10镑的谷物及其他必需品时，他又生产了一个等价值的产品，使他自己或别人能购买相等的半年收入。所以，这6个月时间所消费及所生产的价值，不等于10镑，而等于20镑。诚然，无论在什么时候，只存在着这10镑的价值，但若这价值10镑的谷物及其他必需品，不为这工匠所消费，而为一兵士或一家仆所消费，那么在6个月终，还存在的那一部分年产物的价值，就比这工匠劳动的场合要少10镑（3）他们的劳动增加了社会的实际收入；

it actually is in consequence of the labour of the artificer. Though the value of what the artificer produces, therefore, should not at any one moment of time be supposed greater than the value he consumes, yet at every moment of time the actually existing value of goods in the market is, in consequence of what he produces, greater than it otherwise would be.

When the patrons of this system assert, that the consumption of artificers, manufacturers and merchants, is equal to the value of what they produce, they probably mean no more than that their revenue, or the fund destined for their consumption, is equal to it. But if they had expressed themselves more accurately, and only asserted, that the revenue of this class was equal to the value of what they produced, it might readily have occurred to the reader, that what would naturally be saved out of this revenue, must necessarily increase more or less the real wealth of the society. In order, therefore, to make out something like an argument, it was necessary that they should express themselves as they have done; and this argument, even supposing things actually were as it seems to presume them to be, turns out to be a very inconclusive one.

(4) for augmenting. annual produce parsimony is just as much required from farmers as from them;

Fourthly, farmers and country labourers can no more augment, without parsimony, the real revenue, the annual produce of the land and labour of their society, than artificers, manufacturers and merchants. The annual produce of the land and labour of any society can be augmented only in two ways; either, first, by some improvement in the productive powers of the useful labour actually maintained within it; or, secondly, by some increase in the quantity of that labour. The improvement in the productive powers of useful labour depend, first, upon the improvement in the ability of the workman; and, secondly, upon that of the machinery with which he works. But the labour of artificers and manufacturers, as it is capable of being more subdivided, and the labour of each workman reduced to a greater simplicity of operation, than that of farmers and country labourers, so it is likewise capable of both these sorts of improvement in a much higher degree. In this respect, therefore, the class of cultivators can have no sort of advantage over that of artificers and manufacturers.

The increase in the quantity of useful labour actually employed within any society, must depend altogether upon the increase of the capital which employs it; and the increase of that capital again must be exactly equal to the amount of the savings from the revenue, either

的价值了。所以，即使他所生产的价值，无论在什么时候，都没有超过他所消费的价值，但无论在什么时候，市场上货物实际存在的价值，都因为他的生产，大于没有他生产的东西时的价值。

此种学说的拥护者往往说，工匠、制造业工人与商人的消费，等于他们所生产的价值。在他们这样说时，其意思也许只是，他们的收入，或指定供他们消费的基金，等于他们所生产的价值。如果他们的话表达得确切些，如果他们只说，这一阶级的收入等于这一阶级所生产的价值，读者们也许更容易想到，这一阶级从这个收入节省下来的东西，必会多少增加社会的真实财富。但为了要说出一种像样的论据，他们不得不照他们本来的说法来说了。然而，即使假定事情真如他们所假设一样，那种议论亦是非常不得要领的。

第四，农业家及农村劳动者，如果不节俭，即不能增加社会的真实收入即其土地和劳动的年产物，这和工匠、制造业工人及商人是一样的。任何社会的土地和劳动的年产物，都只能由两种方法来增加。其一，改进社会上实际雇佣的有用劳动的生产力；其二，增加社会上实际雇佣的有用劳动量。有用劳动的生产力的改进，取决于：（一）劳动者能力的改进；（二）他工作所用的机械的改进。因为工匠及制造业工人的劳动，能比农业家和农村劳动者的劳动，实行更细密的分工，使每个工人的操作更为单纯，所以就工匠及制造业工人说，这两种改进都能达到高得多的程度。因此，在这方面，耕种者阶级并不比工匠及制造者阶级处于优越地位。

任何社会实际雇佣的有用劳动量的增加，必完全取决于雇佣有用劳动的资本的增加；这种资本的增加，又必恰好等于收入（资

of the particular persons who manage and direct the employment of that capital, or of some other persons who lend it to them. If merchants, artificers and manufacturers are, as this system seems to suppose, naturally more inclined to parsimony and saving than proprietors and cultivators, they are, so far, more likely to augment the quantity of useful labour employed within their society, and consequently to increase its real revenue, the annual produce of its land and labour.

_{and (5) trade and manufactures can procure that subsistence which the system regards as the only revenue.} Fifthly and lastly, though the revenue of the inhabitants of every country was supposed to consist altogether, as this system seems to suppose, in the quantity of subsistence which their industry could procure to them; yet, even upon this supposition, the revenue of a trading and manufacturing country must, other things being equal, always be much greater than that of one without trade or manufactures. By means of trade and manufactures, a greater quantity of subsistence can be annually imported into a particular country than what its own lands, in the actual state of their cultivation, could afford. The inhabitants of a town, though they frequently possess no lands of their own, yet draw to themselves by their industry such a quantity of the rude produce of the lands of other people as supplies them, not only with the materials of their work, but with the fund of their subsistence. What a town always is with regard to the country in its neighbourhood, one independent state or country may frequently be with regard to other independent states or countries. It is thus that Holland draws a great part of its subsistence from other countries; live cattle from Holstein and Jutland, and corn from almost all the different countries of Europe. A small quantity of manufactured produce purchases a great quantity of rude produce. A trading and manufacturing country, therefore, naturally purchases with a small part of its manufactured produce a great part of the rude produce of other countries; while, on the contrary, a country without trade and manufactures is generally obliged to purchase, at the expence of a great part of its rude produce, a very small part of the manufactured produce of other countries. The one exports what can subsist and accommodate but a very few, and imports the subsistence and accommodation of a great number. The other exports the accommodation and subsistence of a great number, and imports that of a very few only. The inhabitants of the one must always enjoy a much greater quantity of subsistence than what their own lands, in the actual state of their cultivation, could afford. The inhabitants of the other must always enjoy a much smaller quantity.

This system, however, with all its imperfections, is, perhaps,

本管理人的收入或资本出借人的收入）的节省额。如果商人、工匠和制造业工人，真如这一学说所设想的那样，自然而然地比地主及耕种者更有节俭储蓄的倾向，那么他们也就更能够增加本社会所雇佣的有用劳动量，因而更能够增加本社会的真实收入即土地和劳动的年产物。

第五，即使一国居民的收入，真如这一学说所设想的那样，全由其居民劳动所能获得的生活资料构成，在其他一切条件都相等的场合，工商业国的收入，亦必比无工业或无商业的国家的收入大得多。一国通过商业及工业每年能从外国进口的生活资料量，就比其土地在现有耕种状态下所能提供的多。城市居民，虽往往没有田地，亦能靠自身的劳动得到大量的他人土地原生产物，不仅获得工作的原料，而且获得生活资料基金。城市与其邻近农村的关系，往往即是一个独立国家与其他独立国家的关系。荷兰就是这样从其他国家得到他们生活资料的大部分。活牲畜来自霍耳斯廷及日兰德；谷物来自几乎欧洲各个国家。小量的制造品，能购买大量的原生产物。所以，工商业国自然以小部分本国制造品来交换大部分外国原生产物；反之，无工商业的国家，就大都不得不费去大部分本国原生产物，来购买极小部分的外国制造品。前者出口的话，仅能维持极少数人，供应极少数人使用，但所进口的，却是大多数人的生活资料及供应品。后者所出口的，是大多数人的供应品及生活资料，但所进口的却只是极少数人的供应品及生活资料。前一类国家的居民，总能享用比其土地在现有耕种状态下所能提供的多得多的生活资料。后一类国家的居民，却只能享用少得多的生活资料。

（5）商业和制造业能获得这个体系所认为的唯一收入。

这一学说虽有许多缺点，但在政治经济学这个题目下发表的

国民财富的性质与原理

<small>In spite of its errors the system has been valuable.</small> the nearest approximation to the truth that has yet been published upon the subject of political œconomy, and is upon that account well worth the consideration of every man who wishes to examine with attention the principles of that very important science. Though in representing the labour which is employed upon land as the only productive labour, the notions which it inculcates are perhaps too narrow and confined; yet in representing the wealth of nations as consisting, not in the unconsumable riches of money, but in the consumable goods annually reproduced by the labour of the society; and in representing perfect liberty as the only effectual expedient for rendering this annual reproduction the greatest possible, its doctrine seems to be in every respect as just as it is generous and liberal. Its followers are very numerous; and as men are fond of paradoxes, and of appearing to understand what surpasses the comprehension of ordinary people, the paradox which it maintains, concerning the unproductive nature of manufacturing labour, has not perhaps contributed a little to increase the number of its admirers. They have for some years past made a pretty considerable sect, distinguished in the French republic of letters by the name of, The Œconomists. Their works have certainly been of some service to their country; not only by bringing into general discussion, many subjects which had never been well examined before, but by influencing in some measure the public administration in favour of agriculture. It has been in consequence of their representations, accordingly, that the agriculture of France has been delivered from several of the oppressions which it before laboured under. The term during which such a lease can be granted, as will be valid against every future purchaser or proprietor of the land, has been prolonged from nine to twenty-seven years. The ancient provincial restraints upon the transportation of corn from one province of the kingdom to another, have been entirely taken away, and the liberty of exporting it to all foreign countries, has been established as the common law of the kingdom in all ordinary cases. This sect, in their works, which are very numerous, and which treat not only of what is properly called Political Œconomy, or of the nature and causes of the wealth of nations, but of every other branch of the system of civil government, all follow implicitly, and without any sensible variation, the doctrine of Mr. Quesnai. There is upon this account little variety in the greater part of their works. The most distinct and best connected account of this doctrine is to be found in a little book written by Mr. Mercier de la Riviere, sometime Intendant of Martinico, intitled, The natural and essential Order of Political Societies. The admiration of this whole sect for their master, who was himself a man of the greatest modesty

许多学说中,要以这一学说最接近于真理。因此,凡愿细心研讨这个极重要科学的原理的人,都得对它十分留意。这一学说把投在土地上的劳动,看作唯一的生产性劳动,这方面的见解,未免失之褊狭;但这一学说认为,国民财富非由不可消费的货币财富构成,而由社会劳动每年所再生产的可消费的货物构成,并认为,完全自由是使这种每年再生产能以最大程度增进的唯一有效方策,这种说法无论从哪一点说,都是公正而又毫无偏见的。它的信徒很多。人们大都爱好怪论,总想装作自己能理解平常人所不能理解的东西;这一学说与众不同,倡言制造业劳动是不生产的劳动,也许是它博得许多人赞赏的一个不小的原因。在过去数年间,他们居然组成了一个很重要的学派,在法国学术界中,取得了经济学家的名称。他们的作品,把许多向来不曾有人好好研究过的题目,提到大众面前讨论,并使国家行政机关在一定程度上赞助农业,所以对于他们的国家,他们确有贡献。就因为他们这种说法,法国农业一向所受的各种压迫,就有好几种得到了解脱。任何未来的土地购买者或所有者都不得侵犯的租期,已由九年延长到27年了。往昔国内各省间谷物运输所受各省的限制,完全废除了;出口谷物到外国的自由,在一切普通场合,亦由王国的习惯法所确认了。这个学派有许多著作,不仅讨论真正的政治经济学,即讨论国民财富的性质与原因,而且讨论国家行政组织其他各部门。这些著作,都绝对遵循奎斯纳的学说,不加任何修改。因此,他们的著作大部分都和他的学说相同。对于这学说,曾作最明白、最连贯的阐述的,乃是曾任马提尼科州长的里维埃所著《政治社会的自然与基本制度》那一小册子。这整个学派,对于他们的大师的赞扬,不下于古代任何哲学学派对其创立者的赞扬。不

and simplicity, is not inferior to that of any of the ancient philosophers for the founders of their respective systems. "There have been, since the world began, " says a very diligent and respectable author, the Marquis de Mirabeau, "three great inventions which have principally given stability to political societies, independent of many other inventions which have enriched and adorned them. The first, is the invention of writing, which alone gives human nature the power of transmitting, without alteration, its laws, its contracts, its annals, and its discoveries. The second, is the invention of money, which binds together all the relations between civilized societies. The third, is the Œconomical Table, the result of the other two, which completes them both by perfecting their object; the great discovery of our age, but of which our posterity will reap the benefit. "

<small>Some nations have favoured agriculture.</small>
As the political economy of the nations of modern Europe, has been more favourable to manufactures and foreign trade, the industry of the towns, than to agriculture, the industry of the country; so that of other nations has followed a different plan, and has been more favourable to agriculture than to manufactures and foreign trade.

<small>China, for example.</small>
The policy of China favours agriculture more than all other employments. In China, the condition of a labourer is said to be as much superior to that of an artificer; as in most parts of Europe, that of an artificer is to that of a labourer. In China, the great ambition of every man is to get possession of some little bit of land, either in property or in lease; and leases are there said to be granted upon very moderate terms, and to be sufficiently secured to the lessees. The Chinese have little respect for foreign trade. Your beggarly commerce! was the language in which the Mandarins of Pekin used to talk to Mr. de Lange, the Russian envoy, concerning it. Except with Japan, the Chinese carry on, themselves, and in their own bottoms, little or no foreign trade; and it is only into one or two ports of their kingdom that they even admit the ships of foreign nations. Foreign trade, therefore, is, in China, every way confined within a much narrower circle than that to which it would naturally extend itself, if more freedom was allowed to it, either in their own ships, or in those of foreign nations.

Manufactures, as in a small bulk they frequently contain a great value, and can upon that account be transported at less expence from one country to another than most parts of rude produce, are, in almost all countries, the principal support of foreign trade. In countries, besides, less extensive and less favourably circumstanced for interior

过,这学派的大师自己倒是非常谦虚、非常朴质的。有一位勤勉而可尊敬的作者米拉波说:"从有世界以来,有三个大发明在极大程度上给政治社会带来安定,这些发明,与其他丰富和装饰政治社会的许多发明无关。第一,是文字的发明,只有它使人类能把其法律、契约、历史和发明照原样传达下去。第二,是货币的发明,它使各文明社会联结起来。第三,是《经济表》,它是其他两种发明的结果,把这两者的目标弄得齐全,使它们完善了;这是我们这个时代的大发现,而我们的子孙将从此获得利益。"

近代欧洲各国的政治经济学,比较有利于制造业及国外贸易,即城市产业,比较不利于农业,即农村产业;其他各国的政治经济学,则采用不同的计划,比较有利于农业,比较不利于制造业及国外贸易。_{有些国家重视农业。}

中国的政策,就特别爱护农业。在欧洲,大部分地方的工匠的境遇优于农业劳动者,而在中国,据说农业劳动者的境遇却优于技工。在中国,每个人都很想占有若干土地,或是拥有所有权,或是租地。租借条件据说很适度,对于租借人又有充分保证。中国人不重视国外贸易。当俄国公使兰杰来北京请求通商时,北京的官吏以惯常的口吻对他说,"你们乞食般的贸易!"除了对日本,中国人很少或完全没有由自己或用自己船只经营国外贸易。允许外国船只出入的海港,亦不过一两个。所以,在中国,国外贸易就被局限在狭窄的范围,要是本国船只或外国船只能比较自由地经营国外贸易,这种范围当然就会大得多。_{例如,中国。}

制造品常常是体积小价值大,能以比大部分原生产物更小的费用由一国运至他国,所以在所有国家,它们都是国外贸易的主要支柱。而且在幅员不像中国那么广大而国内贸易不像中国那

国民财富的性质与原理

<small>China is itself of very great extent, but more foreign trade would be advantageous to it.</small> commerce than China, they generally requite the support of foreign trade. Without an extensive foreign market, they could not well flourish, either in countries so moderately extensive as to afford but a narrow home market; or in countries where the communication between one province and another was so difficult, as to render it impossible for the goods of any particular place to enjoy the whole of that home market which the country could afford. The perfection of manufacturing industry, it must be remembered, depends altogether upon the division of labour; and the degree to which the division of labour can be introduced into any manufacture, is necessarily regulated, it has already been shown, by the extent of the market. But the great extent of the empire of China, the vast multitude of its inhabitants, the variety of climate, and consequently of productions in its different provinces, and the easy communication by means of water carriage between the greater part of them, render the home market of that country of so great extent, as to be alone sufficient to support very great manufactures, and to admit of very considerable subdivisions of labour. The home market of China is, perhaps, in extent, not much inferior to the market of all the different countries of Europe put together. A more extensive foreign trade, however, which to this great home market added the foreign market of all the rest of the world; especially if any considerable part of this trade was carried on in Chinese ships; could scarce fail to increase very much the manufactures of China, and to improve very much the productive powers of its manufacturing industry. By a more extensive navigation, the Chinese would naturally learn the art of using and constructing themselves all the different machines made use of in other countries, as well as the other improvements of art and industry which are practised in all the different parts of the world. Upon their present plan they have little opportunity of improving themselves by the example of any other nation; except that of the Japanese.

<small>Egypt and the Gentoo government of Indostan favoured agriculture.</small>

The policy of ancient Egypt too, and that of the Gentoo government of Indostan, seem to have favoured agriculture more than all other employments.

<small>The people were divided into castes in these countries.</small> Both in ancient Egypt and Indostan, the whole body of the people was divided into different casts or tribes, each of which was confined, from father to son, to a particular employment or class of employments. The son of a priest was necessarily a priest; the son of a soldier, a soldier; the son of a labourer, a labourer; the son of a weaver, a weaver; the son of a taylor, a taylor; &c. In both countries, the cast of the priests held the highest rank, and that of the soldiers the next; and in both countries, the cast of the farmers and labourers was superior to the casts of merchants and manufacturers.

么有利的国家,制造业亦常需要国外贸易来支持。如果没有广阔的国外市场,那在幅员不大仅能提供狭小国内市场的国家,或在国内各省间交通不方便而国内某地生产物不能畅销国内各地的国家,制造业就没有好好发展的可能。必须记住,制造业的完善,全然依赖分工,而制造业所能实行的分工程度,又必然受市场范围的支配,这是我们曾经说过的。中国幅员是那么广大,居民是那么多,气候是各种各样,因此各地方有各种各样的产物,各省间的水运交通,大部分又是极其便利,所以单单这个广大国内市场,就够支持很大的制造业,并且容许很可观的分工程度。就面积而言,中国的国内市场,也许并不小于全欧洲各国的市场。假设能在国内市场之外,再加上世界其余各地的国外市场,那么更广大的国外贸易,必能大大增加中国制造品,大大改进其制造业的生产力。如果这种国外贸易,有大部分由中国经营,则尤有这种结果。通过更广泛的航行,中国人自会学得外国所用各种机械的使用术与建造术,以及世界其他各国技术上、产业上的各种改良。但在今日中国的情况下,他们除了模仿他们的邻国日本以外,却几乎没有机会模仿其他外国的先例,来改良他们自己。

_{本国幅员辽阔,如果进行更多由自身将会更加有利的贸易,中国身更加有利。}

古埃及和印度政府的政策,似亦比较有利于农业,比较不利于其他一切职业。

_{埃及和印度政府重视农业。}

古埃及和印度,都把全体人民分成若干阶级或部族,由父至子,世袭某一特定职业或某一种类职业。僧侣的儿子,必然是僧侣;士兵的儿子,必然是士兵;农业劳动者的儿子,必然是农业劳动者;织工的儿子,必然是织工;缝工的儿子,必然是缝工;依次类推。在这两国,僧侣阶级占最高地位,其次是士兵;而农业家及农业劳动者阶级,在地位上都高于商人及制造者阶级。

_{这些国家的人民按照世袭阶级来划分。}

国民财富的性质与原理

Irrigation was attended to there.

    The government of both countries was particularly attentive to the interest of agriculture. The works constructed by the ancient sovereigns of Egypt for the proper distribution of the waters of the Nile were famous in antiquity; and the ruined remains of some of them are still the admiration of travellers. Those of the same kind which were constructed by the ancient sovereigns of Indostan, for the proper distribution of the waters of the Ganges as well as of many other rivers, though they have been less celebrated, seem to have been equally great. Both countries, accordingly, though subject occasionally to dearths, have been famous for their great fertility. Though both were extremely populous, yet, in years of moderate plenty, they were both able to export great quantities of grain to their neighbours.

Egypt and India were dependent on other nations for foreign trade.

    The ancient Egyptians had a superstitious aversion to the sea; and as the Gentoo religion does not permit its followers to light a fire, nor cousequently to dress any victuals upon the water, it in effect prohibits them from all distant sea voyages. Both the Egyptians and Indians must have depended almost altogether upon the navigation of other nations for the exportation of their surplus produce; and this dependency, as it must have confined the market, so it must have discouraged the increase of this surplus produce. It must have discouraged too the increase of the manufactured produce more than that of the rude produce. Manufactures require a much more extensive market than the most important parts of the rude produce of the land. A single shoemaker will make more than three hundred pairs of shoes in the year; and his own family will not perhaps wear out six pairs. Unless therefore he has the custom of at least fifty such families as his own, he cannot dispose of the whole produce of his own labour. The most numerous class of artificers will seldom, in a large country, make more than one in fifty or one in a hundred of the whole number of families contained in it. But in such large countries as France and England, the number of people employed in agriculture has by some authors been computed at a half, by others at a third, and by no author that I know of, at less than a fifth of the whole inhabitants of the country. But as the produce of the agriculture of both France and England is, the far greater part of it, consumed at home, each person employed in it must, according to these computations, require little more than the custom of one, two, or, at most, of four such families as his own, in order to dispose of the whole produce of his own labour. Agriculture, therefore, can support itself under the discouragement of a confined market, much better than manufactures. In both ancient Egypt and Indostan, indeed, the confinement of the foreign market was in some measure compensated by the

这两国的政府都特别注意农业的利益。古埃及国王为使尼罗河灌溉各地而兴建的水利工程,在古代是很有名的;其遗迹至今还为旅行者所赞赏。印度古代各王公为使恒河及许多河流灌溉各地而兴建的同种工程,虽不如前者有名,但是一样伟大。所以,这两国虽亦偶有粮食不足情况,但都以粮食丰饶而闻名于世。那里虽都是人烟极其稠密,但在一般丰年,他们都能出口大量谷物到邻国去。

_{注意灌溉。那里意灌溉。}

古埃及有畏惧大海的迷信思想;印度教不许教徒在水上点火,因而不许教徒在水上烹调任何食物,所以实际上就等于禁止教徒作远海的航行。埃及和印度人都几乎完全依赖外国航运业,来出口他们的剩余生产物。这样的依赖,必然限制市场,所以必然阻碍剩余生产物的增加。而且,它对制造品增加的阻碍,在程度上必然大于对原生产物增加的阻碍。与最重要部分的土地原生产物比较,制造品需要大得多的市场。一个鞋匠一年可制造三百多双鞋,但其家属一年也许不会穿坏六双。所以,至少要有50家像他那样的家属来光顾他,不然,他自身劳动的全部产物即无法售脱。在任何一个大国,即使人数最多的那一类工匠,在国内居民中所占比例,很少在1/50或1/100以上。但在英国和法国那样的大国,据一些作家计算,以农业为职业的人数占全国居民1/2,据另一些作家计算,则为1/3,但据我所知,没有一个作家计算为1/5以下。英法两国的农产物,大部分在国内消费,那么照此等计算,每一家农场主,只需一家、两家至多四家像他那样的家属来光顾,就可售脱他的全部劳动生产物。所以,农业和制造业比较,更能在市场有限这个不利情况下来维持自己。诚然,在古埃及和印度,外国市场的狭窄,在一定程度上由内地航运的便利得

国民财富的性质与原理

conveniency of many inland navigations, which opened, in the most advantageous manner, the whole extent of the home market to every part of the produce of every different district of those countries. The great extent of Indostan too rendered the home market of that country very great, and sufficient to support a great variety of manufactures. But the small extent of ancient Egypt, which was never equal to England, must at all times have rendered the home market of that country too narrow for supporting any great variety of manufactures. Bengal, accordingly, the province of Indostan which commonly exports the greatest quantity of rice, has always been more remarkable for the exportation of a great variety of manufactures, than for that of its grain. Ancient Egypt, on the contrary, though it exported some manufactures, fine linen in particular, as well as some other goods, was always most distinguished for its great exportation of grain. It was long the granary of the Roman empire.

<small>The land tax gave eastern sovereigns a particular interest in agriculture.</small>

The sovereigns of China, of ancient Egypt, and of the different kingdoms into which Indostan has at different times been divided, have always derived the whole, or by far the most considerable part, of their revenue from some sort of land-tax or land-rent. This land-tax or land-rent, like the tithe in Europe, consisted in a certain proportion, a fifth, it is said, of the produce of the land, which was either delivered in kind, or paid in money, according to a certain valuation, and which therefore varied from year to year according to all the variations of the produce. It was natural therefore, that the sovereigns of those countries should be particularly attentive to the interests of agriculture, upon the prosperity or declension of which immediately depended the yearly increase or diminution of their own revenue.

<small>Ancient Greece and Rome discouraged manufactures and foreign trade, and carried on manufactures only by slave labour, which is expensive.</small>

The policy of the ancient republics of Greece, and that of Rome, though it honoured agriculture more than manufactures or foreign trade, yet seems rather to have discouraged the latter employments, than to have given any direct or intentional encouragement to the former. In several of the ancient states of Greece, foreign trade was prohibited altogether; and in several others the employments of artificers and manufacturers were considered as hurtful to the strength and agility of the human body, as rendering it incapable of those habits which their military and gymnastic exercises endeavoured to form in it, and as thereby disqualifying it more or less for undergoing the fatigues and encountering the dangers of war. Such occupations were considered as fit only for slaves, and the free citizens of the state were prohibited from exercising them. Even in those states where no such prohibition took place, as in Rome and Athens, the great body of the people were in effect excluded from all the trades which are now commonly exercised by the lower sort of the inhabitants of towns. Such trades were, at Athens and Rome, all occupied by the slaves of the rich, who exercised them for the benefit of their masters, whose wealth, power,

到补偿,内地航运十分有力地给本国各地各种生产物开拓了全国性的市场。而且,印度幅员很大,所提供的国内市场亦很大,足够支持许多种类制造业。但在古埃及,则幅员很小,不及英国,所以国内市场总是很小,不能维持许多种类制造业。以此之故,孟加拉,即通常出口谷物最多的印度一个省,所以引人注意,与其说因为它出口了许多谷物,不如说因为它出口了许多种类制造品。反之,古埃及虽亦出口若干制造品,尤其是精麻布及其他某几种货物,但终以出口大量谷物而闻名于世。有一个长时期,它是罗马帝国的谷仓。

中国和古埃及的各君主,以及印度各时代割据各王国的君主,其收入全部或绝大部分都是得自某种地税或地租。这种地税或地租,像欧洲的什一税一样,包含一定比例的土地生产物(据说是1/5),或由实物交付,或估价由货币交付;随各年收获丰歉的不同,租税也一年不同于一年。这样,此等国家的君主,当然特别注意农业的利益,因为他们年收入的增减,直接取决于农业的盛衰。

<small>地税使东方各国君主们在农业中有特殊的利益。</small>

古希腊各共和国和古罗马的政策,重视农业,而不重视制造业和国外贸易;但是,与其说他们直接地、有意识地奖励前一种职业,不如说他们妨害后一类职业。希腊古代各国,有些完全禁止国外贸易,有些把工匠及制造业工人的职业,看作有害于人类的体力与精神,使人们不能养成他们在军事训练和体育训练中所要养成的习惯,使人们不能忍受战争的劳苦和战争的危险。这种职业被认为只适宜于奴隶,不许国家自由市民从事经营。即使像罗马、雅典那样的国家,虽然没有这种禁令,但事实上,人民大众还是不许经营今日通常为下层城市居民所经营的各种职业。这一类职业,在雅典和罗马,全由富人的奴隶经营。此等奴隶,为其主

<small>古希腊和古罗马抑制造业和对外贸易的发展,制造业只由奴隶来进行,这是要耗费钱的。</small>

and protection, made it almost impossible for a poor freeman to find a market for his work, when it came into competition with that of the slaves of the rich. Slaves, however, are very seldom inventive; and all the most important improvements, either in machinery, or in the arrangement and distribution of work, which facilitate and abridge labour, have been the discoveries of freemen. Should a slave propose any improvement of this kind, his master would be very apt to consider the proposal as the suggestion of laziness, and of a desire to save his own labour at the master's expence. The poor slave, instead of reward, would probably meet with much abuse, perhaps with some punishment. In the manufactures carried on by slaves, therefore, more labour must generally have been employed to execute the same quantity of work, than in those carried on by freemen. The work of the former must, upon that account, generally have been dearer than that of the latter. The Hungarian mines, it is remarked by Mr. Montesquieu, though not richer, have always been wrought with less expence, and therefore with more profit, than the Turkish mines in their neighbourhood. The Turkish mines are wrought by slaves; and the arms of those slaves are the only machines which the Turks have ever thought of employing. The Hungarian mines are wrought by freemen, who employ a great deal of machinery, by which they facilitate and abridge their own labour. From the very little that is known about the price of manufactures in the times of the Greeks and Romans, it would appear that those of the finer sort were excessively dear. Silk sold for its weight in gold. It was not, indeed, in those times a European manufacture; and as it was all brought from the East Indies, the distance of the carriage may in some measure account for the greatness of the price. The price, however, which a lady, it is said, would sometimes pay for a piece of very fine linen, seems to have been equally extravagant; and as linen was always either a European, or, at farthest, an Egyptian manufacture, this high price can be accounted for only by the great expence of the labour which must have been employed about it, and the expence of this labour again could arise from nothing but the awkwardness of the machinery which it made use of. The price of fine woollens too, though not quite so extravagant, seems however to have been much above that of the present times. Some cloths, we are told by Pliny, dyed in a particular manner, cost a hundred denarii, or three pounds six shillings and eight pence the pound

人的利益,经营此等职业。这些富人既有财富和权力,又得到保护,所以贫穷的自由市民,要想在市场上以其产品与此等富人的奴隶的产品竞争,那几乎是办不到的。可是,奴隶很少能别出心裁,一切最重要的节省劳动、便利于劳动的改良办法,无论是机械方面或是工作安排与分配方面,都是自由人发现的。如果有一个奴隶提出这一类的改良办法,其主人往往认为此等提议是懒惰的表示,是奴隶想以主人为牺牲而节省自己的劳动。这样,可怜的奴隶不但不能因此得到报酬,也许还要因此受责骂,甚至受惩罚。所以,与自由人经营的制造业比较,奴隶经营的制造业,同量作业通常需要更大的劳动量。以此之故,后者的产品,通常必比前者的产品昂贵。孟德斯鸠曾说,与邻近的土耳其矿山比较,匈牙利的矿山虽不更为丰饶,但总能以较小的费用开采,因而能获取较大的利润。土耳其的矿山由奴隶开采,土耳其人所知道使用的机械只是奴隶的手臂。匈牙利矿山由自由人开采,并使用许多节省劳动、便易劳动的机械。关于古希腊和古罗马时代制造品的价格,我们知道得很少,但我们从这很少的一点知识中可以知道,精制造品似乎是非常昂贵的。丝与金以等重量相交换。当时,丝并非欧洲的制造品,全是从东印度运来的;长途运输,或可在一定程度上说明其价格的昂贵。但据说,当时贵妇人亦往往以同样高的价格,购买极精致的麻布,而麻布则大都是欧洲的制造品,至远亦不过是埃及的制造品。所以,此种高价的原因,就只是生产麻布的劳动所费很大,而此种劳动所费很大的原因,又只是所用机械过于粗笨。此外,精制呢绒的价格虽不这么昂贵,但比现今的价格高得多。普林尼告诉我们,按一种方式染的呢绒,1磅值100迪纳里,即3镑6先令8便士,而按另一种方式染的呢绒,1磅值

weight. Others dyed in another manner cost a thousand denarii the pound weight, or thirty-three pounds six shillings and eight pence. The Roman pound, it must be remembered, contained only twelve of our avoirdupois ounces. This high price, indeed, seems to have been principally owing to the dye. But had not the cloths themselves been much dearer than any which are made in the present times, so very expensive a dye would not probably have been bestowed upon them. The disproportion would have been too great between the value of the accessory and that of the principal. The price mentioned by the same author of some Triclinaria, a sort of woollen pillows or cushions made use of to lean upon as they reclined upon their couches at table, passes all credibility; some of them being said to have cost more than thirty thousand, others more than three hundred thousand pounds. This high price too is not said to have arisen from the dye. In the dress of the people of fashion of both sexes, there seems to have been much less variety, it is observed by Dr. Arbuthnot, in ancient than in modern times; and the very little variety which we find in that of the ancient statues confirms his observation. He infers from this, that their dress must upon the whole have been cheaper than ours: but the conclusion does not seem to follow. When the expence of fashionable dress is very great, the variety must be very small. But when, by the improvements in the productive powers of manufacturing art and industry, the expence of any one dress comes to be very moderate, the variety will naturally be very great. The rich not being able to distinguish themselves by the expence of any one dress, will naturally endeavour to do so by the multitude and variety of their dresses.

<small>Everything which raises the price of manufactures discourages agriculture,</small>

The greatest and most important branch of the commerce of every nation, it has already been observed, is that which is carried on between the inhabitants of the town and those of the country. The inhabitants of the town draw from the country the rude produce which constitutes both the materials of their work and the fund of their subsistence; and they pay for this rude produce by sending back to the country a certain portion of it manufactured and prepared for immediate use. The trade which is carried on between those two different sets of people, consists ultimately in a certain quantity of rude produce exchanged for a certain quantity of manufactured produce. The dearer the latter, therefore, the cheaper the former; and whatever tends in any country to raise the price of manufactured produce, tends to lower that of the rude produce of the land, and thereby to discourage agriculture. The smaller the quantity of manufactured produce which any given quantity of rude produce, or, what comes to the same thing, which the price of any given quantity of rude produce is capable of purchasing, the smaller the exchangeable value of that given quantity of rude produce; the smaller the encouragement which either the landlord has to increase its quantity by improving, or the farmer by cultivating the land. Whatever, besides, tends to

1000迪纳里,即33镑6先令8便士。必须记住,罗马镑仅含今日常衡量12盎司。诚然,这样的高价,似乎主要起因于染料。但若呢绒本身价格不比现在高得多,那么这样昂贵的染料,大概不会用在呢绒上面。这样,附属物与主要物价值间的不均衡,就显得过于巨大了。再据同一作者所说,一种放在靠近桌子的长椅上的毛织枕垫的价格,是难以令人置信的。有些值三万镑以上,有些值30万镑以上。这样高的价格,也没说是起因于染料。阿布诺博士说,古时时髦男女的服装,并不像今天有那么多的花样。我们在古代雕像中,只能看出极少式样的服装,就可证实他的议论。但他从此推论,他们的服装,总的说来,必较今日低廉。这个结论,却似乎不甚妥当。在时装衣服所费很大时,花样必定很少,但在制造技术及制造业的生产力已经改良,以致任何服装所费都不很大时,花样自会多起来。富人们在不能以一件价格昂贵的服装来炫耀自己时,就自然竭力以许许多多各色各样的服装来炫耀他们自己了。

前面已经说过,任何一国的贸易,都以城乡之间的贸易为最大而最重要的部门。城市居民的工作材料及生活资料基金,供给于农村的原生产物,而以一定部分制成了的、适于目前使用的物品送还农村,作为原生产物的代价。这两种人之间的贸易,最终总是以一定数量的原生产物,与一定数量的制造品相交换。前者愈昂贵,后者必愈低廉;在任何一个国家,提高制造品价格,就会减低土地原生产物价格,因而就会妨害农业。一定数量的原生产物或其价格所能购买的制造品量愈小,这一定数量的原生产物的交换价值必愈小,对地主改良土地和农场主耕种土地以增加其产量的鼓励,亦必愈小。此外,在任何一个国家,减少工匠及制造业

每一种提高制造品价格的事情,都会抑制农业。

diminish in any country the number of artificers and manufacturers, tends to diminish the home market, the most important of all markets for the rude produce of the land, and thereby still further to discourage agriculture.

<small>and this is done by systems which restrain manufactures and foreign trade.</small>
Those systems, therefore, which preferring agriculture to all other employments, in order to promote it, impose restraints upon manufactures and foreign trade, act contrary to the very end which they propose, and indirectly discourage that very species of industry which they mean to promote. They are so far, perhaps, more inconsistent than even the mercantile system. That system, by encouraging manufactures and foreign trade more than agriculture, turns a certain portion of the capital of the society from supporting a more advantageous, to support a less advantageous species of industry. But still it really and in the end encourages that species of industry which it means to promote. Those agricultural systems, on the contrary, really and in the end discourage their own favourite species of industry.

<small>So all systems of encouragements and restraints retard the progress of society.</small>
It is thus that every system which endeavours, either, by extraordinary encouragements, to draw towards a particular species of industry a greater share of the capital of the society than what would naturally go to it; or, by extraordinary restraints, to force from a particular species of industry some share of the capital which would otherwise be employed in it; is in reality subversive of the great purpose which it means to promote. It retards, instead of accelerating, the progress of the society towards real wealth and greatness; and diminishes, instead of increasing, the real value of the annual produce of its land and labour.

<small>The system of natural liberty leaves the sovereign only three duties: (1) the defence of the country; (2) the administration of justice; and (3) the maintenance of certain public works.</small>
All systems either of preference or of restraint, therefore, being thus completely taken away, the obvious and simple system of natural liberty establishes itself of its own accord. Every man, as long as he does not violate the laws of justice, is left perfectly free to pursue his own interest his own way, and to bring both his industry and capital into competition with those of any other man, or order of men. The sovereign is completely discharged from a duty, in the attempting to perform which he must always be exposed to innumerable delusions, and for the proper performance of which no human wisdom or knowledge could ever be sufficient; the duty of superintending the industry of private people, and of directing it towards the employments most suitable to the interest of the society. According to the system of natural liberty, the sovereign has only three duties to attend to; three duties of great importance, indeed, but plain and intelligible to common understandings: first, the duty of protecting the society from the violence

工人,就会缩小国内市场,即原生产物的最重要市场,因而就会进一步妨害农业。

所以,为了增进农业而特别重视农业,并主张对制造业及国外贸易加以限制的那些学说,其作用都和其所要达到的目的背道而驰,并且间接妨害他们所要促进的那一种产业。就这一点来说,其矛盾也许比重商主义还要大。重商主义为了鼓励制造业及国外贸易,而不鼓励农业,虽会使一部分社会资本从较有利的产业,转向有较少利益的产业,但实际上,它归根结底仍然算是鼓励了它所要促进的产业。反之,重农学派的学说,却归根到底实际上妨害了它们所爱护的产业。

_{那些制造业和国外贸易的体系就是这样做的。}

这样看来,任何一种学说,如要特别鼓励特定产业,违反自然趋势,把社会上过大一部分的资本投入这种产业,或要特别限制特定产业,违反自然趋势,强迫一部分原来要投在这种产业上的资本离开这个产业,那实际上是和它所要促进的大目的背道而驰。那只能阻碍,而不能促进社会走向富强的发展;只能减少,而不能增加其土地和劳动的年产物的价值。

_{所以,所有特意鼓励或者限制的体系都会阻碍社会的进步。}

一切偏重或限制的制度,一经完全废除,最明白最单纯的自然自由制度就会树立起来。每一个人,在他不违反正义的法律时,都应听其完全自由,让他采用自己的方法,追求自己的利益,以其劳动及资本和任何其他人或其他阶级相竞争。这样,君主们就被完全解除了监督私人产业、指导私人产业、使之最适合于社会利益的义务。要履行这种义务,君主们极易陷于错误;要行之得当,恐不是人间智慧或知识所能做到的。按照自然自由的制度,君主只有三个应尽的义务——这三个义务虽很重要,但都是一般人所能理解的。第一,保护社会,使其不受其他独立社会的侵

_{天由系主三:国;司;维持某种工程。对于自然自由体的君主只需做件事(1)国家防卫(2)司法行政(3)维持某种公共工程。}

and invasion of other independent societies; secondly, the duty of protecting, as far as possible, every member of the society from the injustice or oppression of every other member of it, or the duty of establishing an exact administration of justice; and, thirdly, the duty of erecting and maintaining certain public works and certain public institutions, which it can never be for the interest of any individual, or small number of individuals, to erect and maintain; because the profit could never repay the expence to any individual or small number of individuals, though it may frequently do much more than repay it to a great society.

The next book will treat of the necessary expenses of the sovereign, the methods of contribution towards the expenses of the whole society, and the causes and effects of public debts.

The proper performance of those several duties of the sovereign necessarily supposes a certain expence; and this expence again necessarily requires a certain revenue to support it. In the following book, therefore, I shall endeavour to explain; first, what are the necessary expences of the sovereign or commonwealth; and which of those expences ought to be defrayed by the general contribution of the whole society; and which of them, by that of some particular part only, or of some particular members of the society: secondly, what are the different methods in which the whole society may be made to contribute towards defraying the expences incumbent on the whole society, and what are the principal advantages and inconveniences of each of those methods: and, thirdly, what are the reasons and causes which have induced almost all modern governments to mortgage some part of this revenue, or to contract debts, and what have been the effects of those debts upon the real wealth, the annual produce of the land and labour of the society. The following book, therefore, will naturally be divided into three chapters.

犯。第二,尽可能保护社会上各个人,使其不受社会上任何其他人的侵害或压迫,这就是说,要设立严正的司法机关。第三,建设并维持某些公共事业及某些公共设施(其建设与维持绝不是为着任何个人或任何少数人的利益),这种事业与设施,在由大社会经营时,其利润常能补偿所费而有余,但若由个人或少数人经营,就绝不能补偿所费。

这些义务的适当履行,必须有一定的费用;而这一定的费用,又必须有一定的收入来支付。所以,在下一篇,我将努力说明以下各点。第一,什么是君主或国家的必要费用,其中哪些部分应由对全社会的一般课税来支付,哪些部分应由对社会内特殊部分或特殊成员的课税来支付。第二,应由全社会支付的费用,将用各种什么方法向全社会课税,而这各种方法的主要利弊怎样。第三,近代各国政府几乎都用这种收入的一部分来作抵押以举债,其理由及原因何在,此种债务对社会真实财富即土地和劳动的年产物的影响又怎样。所以,下一篇自然而然地分作三章。

下篇将讨论君主的必要支出,对整个社会支出的贡献方法,以及公债的原因和影响。

BOOK V
Of The Revenue Of The Sovereign Or Commonwealth

CHAPTER I
Of The Expences Of The Sovereign Or Commonwealth

Part I *Of The Expence Of Defence*

<small>The expense of a military force is different at different periods.</small>   The first duty of the sovereign, that of protecting the society from the violence and invasion of other independent societies, can be performed only by means of a military force. But the expence both of preparing this military force in time of peace, and of employing it in time of war, is very different in the different states of society, in the different periods of improvement.

<small>Among hunters it costs nothing.</small>   Among nations of hunters, the lowest and rudest state of society, such as we find it among the native tribes of North America, every man is a warrior as well as a hunter. When he goes to war, either to defend his society, or to revenge the injuries which have been done to it by other societies, he maintains himself by his own labour, in the same manner as when he lives at home. His society, for in this state of things there is properly neither sovereign nor commonwealth, is at no sort of expence, either to prepare him for the field, or to maintain him while he is in it. ①

Among nations of shepherds, a more advanced state of society, such as we find it among the Tartars and Arabs, every man is, in the same manner, a warrior. Such nations have commonly

---

① [*Lectures*, p. 14.]

第五篇　论君主或者国家的收入

第一章　君主或国家的费用

第一节　论防御的费用支出

君主的第一个职责,就是保护国家免受其他独立国家的暴行与侵略,而这只有借助于军事力量才能完成。但由于社会状态不同,进化时期不同,平时准备兵力和战时使用军事力量的费用也不大相同。

在不同的时期,军事力量的费用支出也不相同。

在最低级最粗野的狩猎民族中,像我们在北美土著人中发现的那样,人人都是狩猎者,人人也都是战士。当他走上战场,或去保护社会,或为社会发生的不公正进行复仇时,他用自己的劳动维持自己,像在家中时一样。在他所处的社会状态中,当然既没有君主,也没有国家。他的社会不会为准备他走上战场做出任何开支,也不会为他负担在作战期间的任何费用①。

狩猎者不必开支。

在更高层次的社会状态,即游牧民族时期,像我们在鞑靼及阿拉伯人中发现的那样,人人同时也是战士。这样的民族一般居

---

① 《关于法律、警察、岁入及军备的演讲》,第14页。

国民财富的性质与原理

<blockquote>When shepherds go to war the whole nation moves with its property,</blockquote>

no fixed habitation, but live, either in tents, or in a sort of covered waggons which are easily transported from place to place. The whole tribe or nation changes its situation according to the different seasons of the year, as well as according to other accidents. When its herds and flocks have consumed the forage of one part of the country, it removes to another, and from that to a third. In the dry season, it comes down to the banks of the rivers; in the wet season it retires to the upper country. When such a nation goes to war, the warriors will not trust their herds and flocks to the feeble defence of their old men, their women and children, and their old men, their women and children, will not be left behind without defence and without subsistence. The whole nation, besides, being accustomed to a wandering life, even in time of peace, easily takes the field in time of war. Whether it marches as an army, or moves about as a company of herdsmen, the way of life is nearly the same, though the object proposed by it be very different. They all go to war together, therefore, and every one does as well as he can. Among the Tartars, even the women have been frequently known to engage in battle. If they conquer, whatever belongs to the hostile tribe is the recompence of the victory. But if they are vanquished, all is lost, and not only their herds and flocks, but their women and children, become the booty of the conqueror. Even the greater part of those who survive the action are obliged to submit to him for the sake of immediate subsistence. The rest are commonly dissipated and dispersed in the desert.

<blockquote>and the sovereign is at no expense.</blockquote>

The ordinary life, the ordinary exercises of a Tartar or Arab, prepare him sufficiently for war. Running, wrestling, cudgel-playing, throwing the javelin, drawing the bow, &c. are the common pastimes of those who live in the open air, and are all of them the images of war. When a Tartar or Arab actually goes to war, he is maintained, by his own herds and flocks which he carries with him, in the same manner as in peace. His chief or sovereign, for those nations have all chiefs or sovereigns, is at no sort of expence in preparing him for the field; and when he is in it, the chance of plunder is the only pay which he either expects or requires.

<blockquote>Shepherds are far more formidable than hunters.</blockquote>

An army of hunters can seldom exceed two or three hundred men. The precarious subsistence which the chace affords could seldom allow a greater number to keep together for any considerable time. An army of shepherds, on the contrary, may sometimes amount to two or three hundred thousand. As long as nothing stops their progress, as long as they can go on from one district, of which they have consumed the forage, to another which is yet entire; there seems to be

无定所。他们生活在帐篷里或是有棚的马车上,这样易于迁移。整个部落或民族随着一年四季的变化及其他状况而迁移,牛羊吃光了一个地方的草场,就会向下一个地方迁移,再从那里迁到第三个地方。在枯水季节,他们就迁到河岸边;在潮湿季节则回到高地。这样的民族如若参战,士兵不会把牛羊交给老人、妇女、儿童看管,也不会让老人、妇女、儿童留下来无依无靠,失去供给。整个民族不仅习惯了流浪的生活,即使到了战争时期也容易走上战场。他们无论是战斗行军抑或是牧民迁移,生活方式几乎相差无几,虽然目的不同。因此,人人参战,人人尽其所能。据悉,在鞑靼人中,甚至妇女也频频参战。若他们获胜,则敌对方的一切物品皆属于他们的战利品;如若战败,则失去一切,不仅他们的羊群,还有他们的妻儿也成为征服者的战利品。为了迅速补给,即使在战役中存活下来的人,大部分也必须臣服于胜利者,其余的人则被驱逐到沙漠中去。

牧民战争。当牧场上走时,整个民族及其财产一起迁移。

鞑靼人或阿拉伯人的普通生活,即日常训练使他们对战争有充分的准备。赛跑、摔跤、耍棒、掷标枪、拉弓等是那些在户外运动的人们日常的消遣,而这些又都是战争的形式。鞑靼人或阿拉伯人真的参战时,会像和平时期那样,以自己带的牛羊为生。他们的部落酋长或君主——这些民族都有酋长或君主的——绝不会为他们准备作战的费用的。他参战所期望得到的或要求的唯一报酬就是能有机会掠夺他人。

君主不需要花钱。

狩猎人群很少会超过二三百人。狩猎带来的供给很不确定,故大批的人长期待在一起很难。相反,游牧人群有时数目则达二三十万人。只要他们前进不受阻碍,只要他们消耗掉一个草原后能从一个地方迁移到另一片牧草丰盛的地方,在一起前进的人数

游牧人比狩猎人更可怕。

scarce any limit to the number who can march on together. A nation of hunters can never be formidable to the civilized nations in their neighbourhood. A nation of shepherds may. Nothing can be more contemptible than an Indian war in North America. Nothing, on the contrary, can be more dreadful than a Tartar invasion has frequently been in Asia. The judgment of Thucydides, ① that both Europe and Asia could not resist the Scythians united, has been verified by the experience of all ages. The inhabitants of the extensive, but defenceless plains of Scythia or Tartary, have been frequently united under the dominion of the chief of some conquering horde or clan; and the havoc and devastation of Asia have always signalized their union. The inhabitants of the inhospitable desarts of Arabia, the other great nation of shepherds, have never been united but once; under Mahomet and his immediate successors. ② Their union, which was more the effect of religious enthusiasm than of conquest, was signalized in the same manner. If the hunting nations of America should ever become shepherds, their neighbourhood would be much more dangerous to the European colonies than it is at present.

<small>Husbandmen with little commerce and only household manufactures are easily converted into soldiers, and it seldom costs the sovereign anything to prepare them for the field,</small>   In a yet more advanced state of society, among those nations of husbandmen who have little foreign commerce, and no other manufactures but those coarse and houshold ones which almost every private family prepares for its own use; every man, in the same manner, either is a warrior, or easily becomes such. They who live by agriculture generally pass the whole day in the open air, exposed to all the inclemencies of the seasons. The hardiness of their ordinary life prepares them for the fatigues of war, to some of which their necessary occupations bear a great analogy. The necessary occupation of a ditcher prepares him to work in the trenches, and to fortify a camp as

---

① [What Thucydides says (ii. , 97) is that no European or Asiatic nation could resist the Scythians if they were united. Ed. 1 reads here and on next page 'Thucydides '.]

② [*Lectures*, pp. 20, 21.]

第五篇 第一章

似乎就没有任何限制。狩猎民族对邻近的文明民族不构成任何威胁,但游牧民族则会构成威胁。再没有什么比北美印第安人的战争更令人嗤之以鼻了。相反,鞑靼人频繁在亚洲的侵略则是十分可怕的。修希德狄斯[1]认为,无论欧洲还是亚洲,都无法抵御西斯亚人的联合进攻,一直以来的经验已证明了他的判断无误①。西斯亚人或鞑靼人居住的平原辽阔而无防御,他们常常在某个征服者部落或种族的酋长的统治下联合起来,而亚洲遭受的蹂躏或破坏正是这种联合的象征。居住在不毛沙漠的阿拉伯人是另外一个伟大的游牧民族。他们只有一次是在穆罕默德及其直接继承者②的统治下联合过,之外他们再也没有联合过。而他们的联合是出于对宗教的热忱而不是征服的结果,其象征方式也是相同的。倘若美洲的狩猎民族成为游牧民族的话,对于欧洲殖民地来说,邻近地区的危险性要比现在大得多。

在更高层次的农业社会状态下,那些没有对外贸易的小农经济民族,只有粗糙的家庭手工业,没有其他制造业,几乎每个家庭都自给自足。同样,每个人都是战士,或者是很容易成为战士。靠农业为生的人一般一整天都在野外度过,一年四季栉风沐雨。他们的日常生活艰难竭蹶,这使得他们能承受战争的煎熬。而他们必须从事的职务也和战争的某些方面极为相似。他们必须从

<small>没有商业,只有家庭手工业的农民很容易成为兵士;需要君主去花很少钱准备他们作战。</small>

---

① 修昔底德说的是(《历史》II,97)。如果西斯亚人联合起来,欧洲民族或亚洲民族都不能抵御他们。
② 《关于法律、警察、岁入及军备的演讲》,第20,21页。
[1] 修昔底德(Thucydides),约前460—前404年以后,希腊最伟大的历史学家;希腊历史学家,曾被认为是远古时代最伟大的历史学家,著有一部关于伯罗奔尼撒战争的批评史,其中有佩里克莱斯的葬礼演讲。

国民财富的性质与原理

well as to enclose a field. The ordinary pastimes of such husbandmen are the same as those of shepherds, and are in the same manner the images of war. But as husbandmen have less leisure than shepherds, they are not so frequently employed in those pastimes. They are soldiers, but soldiers not quite so much masters of their exercise. Such as they are, however, it seldom costs the sovereign or commonwealth any expence to prepare them for the field.

<small>or to maintain them when they have taken the field.</small>

Agriculture, even in its rudest and lowest state, supposes a settlement; some sort of fixed habitation which cannot be abandoned without great loss. When a nation of mere husbandmen, therefore, goes to war, the whole people cannot take the field together. The old men, the women and children, at least, must remain at home to take care of the habitation. All the men of the military age, however, may take the field, and, in small nations of this kind, have frequently done so. In every nation the men of the military age are supposed to amount to about a fourth or a fifth part of the whole body of the people. If the campaign too should begin after seed-time, and end before harvest, both the husbandman and his principal labourers can be spared from the farm without much loss. He trusts that the work which must be done in the mean time can be well enough executed by the old men, the women and the children. He is not unwilling, therefore, to serve without pay during a short campaign, and it frequently costs the sovereign or commonwealth as little to maintain him in the field as to prepare him for it. The citizens of all the different states of ancient Greece seem to have served in this manner till after the second Persian war; and the people of Peloponesus till after the Peloponesian war. The Peloponesians, Thucydides observes, generally left the field in the summer, and returned home to reap the harvest. The Roman people under their kings, and during the first ages of the republic, served in the same manner. It was not till the siege of Veii, that they, who staid at home, began to contribute something towards maintaining those who went to war. In the European monarchies, which were founded upon the ruins of the Roman empire, both before and for some time after the establishment of what is properly called the feudal law, the great lords, with all their immediate dependents, used to serve the crown at their own expence. In the field, in the same manner as at home, they maintained themselves by their own revenue, and not by any stipend or pay which they received from the king upon that particular occasion.

<small>Later it becomes necessary to pay those who take the field,</small>

In a more advanced state of society, two different causes contribute

第五篇 第一章

事挖掘之职,以至于可在战场上挖掘沟壕,圈占土地,加固堡垒。农民的日常消遣也和游牧民族相同,俨然是从事战争。但因农民的娱乐比游牧民族少,所以他们不大常从事那些消遣。他们是士兵,但却不大精于军训。尽管如此,备战却不会花费君主或国家任何费用。

农业,即使是在最原始最低级的状态下,也要求有稳定的住所。一旦放弃这样固定的住所,农民就会蒙受巨大的损失。因此,农耕民族一旦参战,不可能全民族都出战。至少老人、妇女和儿童留在家中照看住所。但所有符合兵役年龄的男子则必须走上战场。那些小民族常常如此。每个民族的符合兵役年龄的男子应当占整个民族人口的1/4或1/5。若战役在播种之后开始收获之前结束,那么农民及主要劳力不务农也不会有大损失。因为他们相信老人、妇女和儿童完全可以把该干的活干好。因此能够在短期战役内无偿报效祖国,他们会相当乐意。而他们作战和备战,也花不了君主或国家多少费用。古希腊各国公民在第二次波斯战争以前都是以这种方式服兵役的。伯罗奔尼撒人在伯罗奔尼撒战争以前,也是按这种方式服兵役的。修昔底德观察到伯罗奔尼撒人一般在夏季离开战场,回到家中收割庄稼。罗马人在国王统治之下的共和国初期,也是以这种方式服兵役的。直到围攻维伊之后呆在后方的人才纳贡,维持前线作战的人生活费用。建立在罗马废墟上的欧洲君主国,在所谓的封建法制定之前及之后的相当长的时期内,大封建主及其直接仆从自己出资以效忠国王。在战场和在家庭一样,农民通过自己的收入维持生计,而不是从国王那里拿到的薪俸或报酬。

当他们走上战场时也不必花钱去维持他们。

随后,必须付钱给走上战场的人,

在更高级的社会状态下,有两个原因促使作战的人靠自己的

to render it altogether impossible that they, who take the field, should maintain themselves at their own expence. Those two causes are, the progress of manufactures, and the improvement in the art of war.

<small>since artificers and manufacturers must be maintained by the public when away from their work,</small> Though a husbandman should be employed in an expedition, provided it begins after seed-time and ends before harvest, the interruption of his business will not always occasion any considerable diminution of his revenue. Without the intervention of his labour, nature does herself the greater part of the work which remains to be done. But the moment that an artificer, a smith, a carpenter, or a weaver, for example, quits his workhouse, the sole source of his revenue is completely dried up. Nature does nothing for him, he does all for himself. When he takes the field, therefore, in defence of the public, as he has no revenue to maintain himself, he must necessarily be maintained by the public. But in a country of which a great part of the inhabitants are artificers and manufacturers, a great part of the people who go to war must be drawn from those classes, and must therefore be maintained by the public as long as they are employed in its service.

<small>and the greater length of campaigns makes service without pay too heavy a burden even for husbandmen.</small> When the art of war too has gradually grown up to be a very intricate and complicated science, when the event of war ceases to be determined, as in the first ages of society, by a single irregular skirmish or battle, but when the contest is generally spun out through several different campaigns, each of which lasts during the greater part of the year; it becomes universally necessary that the public should maintain those who serve the public in war, at least while they are employed in that service. Whatever in time of peace might be the ordinary occupation of those who go to war, so very tedious and expensive a service would otherwise be by far too heavy a burden upon them. After the second Persian war, accordingly, the armies of Athens seem to have been generally composed of mercenary troops; consisting, indeed, partly of citizens, but partly too of foreigners; and all of them equally hired and paid at the expence of the state. From the time of the siege of Veii, the armies of Rome received pay for their service during the time which they remained in the field. Under the feudal governments the military service both of the great lords and of their immediate dependents was, after a certain period, universally exchanged for a payment in money, which was employed to maintain those who served in their stead.

<small>The possible proportion of soldiers to the rest of the population is much smaller in civilised times.</small> The number of those who can go to war, in proportion to the whole number of the people, is necessarily much smaller in a civilized, than in a rude state of society. In a civilized society, as the soldiers are maintained altogether by the labour of those who are not soldiers, the number of the former can never exceed what the latter can maintain, over and above maintaining, in a manner

第五篇 第一章

收入维持生计不再可能。这两个原因即是制造业的进步和战争技术的改进。

即便是农民参加远征,若时间是在播种之后收获之前,农耕的中断也不见得会大大影响其收入。即使他们不加入劳动,大自然自会替他们打理剩余的工作。可一旦技工、铁匠、木匠或织工离开了工场,其收入来源会彻底断绝。大自然可不会为他们做任何事情,他们须自食其力。因此,他们保家卫国打仗时,没有收入养活自己,不得不依靠国家。一国的大部分人若是技工和制造业者,征兵作战时大部分人就来自这些阶层。只要他们在服兵役,国家就须养活他们。

_{因为制造者必须离开工作,国家由来维持}

而且,战争技术逐渐成为一门错综复杂的科学。战争也已不像初期那样由一两场小小的冲突或战斗就能决定胜负,战争往往要消磨上几场战役的时间,一场战役都要历时大半年。国家必须养活为国作战的人,至少在服役期间是如此,这一点已成为共识。无论作战的人和平时期从事何种职业,服兵役对他们来说都是一件既乏味又昂贵的差事,是一个沉重的负担。因此,第二次波斯战争后,雅典的军队似乎一般都是由雇佣军组成。雇佣军的一部分由本国公民组成,一部分则是外国人。所有雇佣军皆由国家雇佣,薪俸平等。自维伊之围以来,罗马军队留守前方期间享受服役报酬。在封建政府统治之下,经过一段时期之后,大封建主及其直接仆从一般都用金钱取代所服兵役,这些钱可以用来养活代替他们服兵役的人。

_{持续期间越长,服役对农民也是重要的负担。战役无偿役民沉。}

论作战人口和总人口的比例,文明民族必然要比原始社会状态小得多。在文明社会,士兵的给养全部来自非士兵者的劳动,因此士兵的人数永远超不过劳动者所维持的范围。劳动者按

_{文明民族,在人的要得兵部例在民士全口比小多。}

suitable to their respective stations, both themselves and the other officers of government, and law, whom they are obliged to maintain. In the little agrarian states of ancient Greece, a fourth or a fifth part of the whole body of the people considered themselves as soldiers, and would sometimes, it is said, take the field. Among the civilized nations of modern Europe, it is commonly computed, that not more than one hundredth part of the inhabitants of any country can be employed as soldiers, without ruin to the country which pays the expence of their service.

<small>The expense of preparing for the field was long inconsiderable.</small> The expence of preparing the army for the field seems not to have become considerable in any nation, till long after that of maintaining it in the field had devolved entirely upon the sovereign or commonwealth. In all the different republics of ancient Greece, to learn his military exercises, was a necessary part of education imposed by the state upon every free citizen. In every city there seems to have been a public field, in which, under the protection of the public magistrate, the young people were taught their different exercises by different masters. In this very simple institution, consisted the whole expence which any Grecian state seems ever to have been at, in preparing its citizens for war. In ancient Rome the exercises of the Campus Martius answered the same purpose with those of the Gymnasium in ancient Greece. Under the feudal governments, the many public ordinances that the citizens of every district should practise archery as well as several other military exercises, were intended for promoting the same purpose, but do not seem to have promoted it so well. Either from want of interest in the officers entrusted with the execution of those ordinances, or from some other cause, they appear to have been universally neglected; and in the progress of all those governments, military exercises seem to have gone gradually into disuse among the great body of the people.

<small>Soldiers were not a distinct class in Greece and Rome, nor at first in feudal times.</small> In the republics of ancient Greece and Rome, during the whole period of their existence, and under the feudal governments for a considerable time after their first establishment, the trade of a soldier was not a separate, distinct trade, which constituted the sole or principal occupation of a particular class of citizens. Every subject of the state, whatever might be the ordinary trade or occupation by which he gained his livelihood, considered himself, upon all ordinary occasions, as fit likewise to exercise the trade of a soldier, and upon many extraordinary occasions as bound to exercise it.

The art of war, however, as it is certainly the noblest of all arts, so in the progress of improvement it necessarily becomes one of the most complicated among them. The state of the mechanical, as well as of some other arts, with which it is necessarily connected, determines the degree of perfection to which it is capable of being carried at any particular time. But in order to carry it to this degree of perfection, it is necessary that it should become the sole or principal

第五篇 第一章

照和他们各自身份相符的方式,首先要养活自己,还有必须养活的其他政府工作人员和司法官员。在古希腊小农业国家中,整个民族人口的 1/4 或 1/5 都自认为是士兵,据说有时也作战。一般推算,现在的欧洲文明社会,要想不因军事费用负担而危害国家,士兵的人数必须不足国家人口的 1%。

直到维持军费开支完全依赖于君主或国家之后很久,备战费用似乎才成为国家的一项巨大开支。古希腊的各个共和国均要求每个公民都参加军训,这是教育的必要部分。每个城市似乎都有一个公共军训场地。在国家官员的监护下,年轻人在那里由不同的业师进行不同的军训。这种简单的制度似乎是希腊共和国让其臣民备战的所有费用支出。在古罗马,竞技场的军事训练和古希腊的体育馆的目的是相同的。封建政府颁布了很多法令,规定各区公民都要操练箭术及其他军事训练,也是为了相同的目的。但效果似乎不尽如人意。因为委任执行该法令的官员对此缺乏兴趣,抑或是其他原因,总之这些法令都被忽视了。随着政府的演变更迭,人民大众似乎渐渐不再进行军事训练。

> 为准备作战,国家所做的支出,在长期内数目不大。

在古希腊和古罗马共和国存在的整个期间,及封建政府首次成立后的相当长的时期内,士兵职业并不是一项分开的独立职业,不构成某一阶层唯一主要工作。国家每个臣民无论其靠何种普通职业或行业谋生,在一切通常场合,都自认为自己适合从军;在有些特殊场合,还认为有义务从军。

> 在希腊罗马及封建时代初期,军人不是一个特殊阶级。

但是,战争技术当然是一切技术中最高贵的,在改良过程中,必然会成为最复杂的技术。机械技术以及与战争必然相关的其他技术,决定着战争在特定时间能够达到的完善程度。可是为了完善战争这一技术,有必要使它成为某个阶层唯一主要职业。正

国民财富的性质与原理

<small>But as war becomes more complicated, division of labour becomes necessary to carry the art to perfection.</small> occupation of a particular class of citizens, and the division of labour is as necessary for the improvement of this, as of every other art. Into other arts the division of labour is naturally introduced by the prudence of individuals, who find that they promote their private interest better by confining themselves to a particular trade, than by exercising a great number. But it is the wisdom of the state only which can render the trade of a soldier a particular trade separate and distinct from all others. A private citizen who, in time of profound peace, and without any particular encouragement from the public, should spend the greater part of his time in military exercises, might, no doubt, both improve himself very much in them, and amuse himself very well; but he certainly would not promote his own interest. It is the wisdom of the state only which can render it for his interest to give up the greater part of his time to this peculiar occupation: and states have not always had this wisdom, even when their circumstances had become such, that the preservation of their existence required that they should have it.

<small>As society advances the people become unwarlike.</small> A shepherd has a great deal of leisure; a husbandman, in the rude state of husbandry, has some; an artificer or manufacturer has none at all. The first may, without any loss, employ a great deal of his time in martial exercises; the second may employ some part of it; but the last cannot employ a single hour in them without some loss, and his attention to his own interest naturally leads him to neglect them altogether. Those improvements in husbandry too, which the progress of arts and manufactures necessarily introduces, leave the husbandman as little leisure as the artificer. Military exercises come to be as much neglected by the inhabitants of the country as by those of the town, and the great body of the people becomes altogether unwarlike. That wealth, at the same time, which always follows the improvements of agriculture and manufactures, and which in reality is no more than the accumulated produce of those improvements, provokes the invasion of all their neighbours. An industrious, and upon that account a wealthy nation, is of all nations the most likely to be attacked; and unless the state takes some new measures for the public defence, the natural habits of the people render them altogether incapable of defending themselves.

<small>There are only two methods of providing for defence,</small> In these circumstances, there seem to be but two methods, by which the state can make any tolerable provision for the public defence.

<small>(1) to enforce military exercises and service,</small> It may either, first, by means of a very rigorous police, and in spite of the whole bent of the interest, genius and inclinations of the people, enforce the practice of military exercises, and oblige either all the citizens of the military age, or a certain number of them, to join in some measure the trade of a soldier to whatever other trade or profession they may happen to carry on.

第五篇 第一章

如其他任何一项职业,为了改良战争,就要实行劳动分工。个别人出于审慎,自然的引进了劳动分工。他们发觉,若专门从事某个行业,而不是涉猎各个方面,则更易于增加个人利益。然而只有国家的智慧才使得士兵职业成为区别于其他职业的独立职业。一个公民倘若在和平年代没有公众鼓励情况下能把一生大部分时光用于军事训练,毋庸置疑,他不但可以在这方面提高自身,还可以得到很大乐趣。可是,他当然无法增加个人利益。只有国家的智慧才会促使他为了个人利益把医生大部分时光献身于这个特定的职业。可是,即使条件使然,让他们的生存必须赖于此智慧,国家也并不见得就有这样的智慧。

<small>战争更为复杂,但当实行劳动分工以使技术趋完善,必须</small>

牧民有很多闲暇时间,农民在农业的初级阶段也有一些闲暇时间,而技工或制造业者则无闲暇时间。牧民可以花大部分时间进行军事训练而没有损失,农民可以腾出部分时间。但技工或制造业者即使花费1个小时军训也会有损失,他们自然会关注自己的利益,故而忽视了军事训练。技术以及制造业的进步必然引起农业的改进。农民也就和技工一样没有闲暇时间。不但是农村居民,就是城市市民也都逐渐忽视了军事训练,人民大众都不再尚武。同时,农业和制造业改良总会产生财富,事实上,财富也就是改良积累起来的。邻国垂涎这笔财富,因而会发动侵略。勤劳而富裕的国家也就最易成为各国进攻的对象。国家如不采取新举措防卫,人民的自然习惯会使他们无法自卫。

<small>社会进步了,人们不再尚武了。</small>

<small>只有两种方法来进行防卫。</small>

在这种情况下,国家似乎只有两种方法可以进行公共防卫。

第一,实行严格的管制。不管人民的利益、资质和倾向如何,强制他们进行军事操练。所有符合兵役年龄的人,或者一定数目的人,在某种程度上,加入到军队行列,不管各人以前从事何种

<small>(1)强制实行军事训练和服役,</small>

| 国民财富的性质与原理

or (2) to make the trade of the soldier a separate one,

  Or, secondly, by maintaining and employing a certain number of citizens in the constant practice of military exercises, it may render the trade of a soldier a particular trade, separate and distinct from all others.

  If the state has recourse to the first of those two expedients, its military force is said to consist in a militia; if to the second, it is said to consist in a standing army. The practice of military exercises is the sole or principal occupation of the soldiers of a standing army, and

in other words the establishment of a militia or a standing army.

the maintenance or pay which the state affords them is the principal and ordinary fund of their subsistence. The practice of military exercises is only the occasional occupation of the soldiers of a militia, and they derive the principal and ordinary fund of their subsistence from some other occupation. In a militia, the character of the labourer, artificer, or tradesman, predominates over that of the soldier: in a standing army, that of the soldier predominates over every other character; and in this distinction seems to consist the essential difference between those two different species of military force.

Militias were anciently only exercised and not regimented.

  Militias have been of several different kinds. In some countries the citizens destined for defending the state, seem to have been exercised only, without being, if I may say so, regimented; that is, without being divided into separate and distinct bodies of troops, each of which performed its exercises under its own proper and permanent officers. In the republics of ancient Greece and Rome, each citizen, as long as he remained at home, seems to have practised his exercises either separately and independently, or with such of his equals as he liked best; and not to have been attached to any particular body of troops till he was actually called upon to take the field. In other countries, the militia has not only been exercised, but regimented. In England, in Switzerland, and, I believe, in every other country of modern Europe, where any imperfect military force of this kind has been established, every militia-man is, even in time of peace, attached to a particular body of troops, which performs its exercises under its own proper and permanent officers.

Fire-arms brought about the change by making dexterity less important,

  Before the invention of fire-arms, that army was superior in which the soldiers had, each individually, the greatest skill and dexterity in the use of their arms. Strength and agility of body were of the highest consequence, and commonly determined the fate of battles. But this skill and dexterity in the use of their arms, could be acquired only, in the same manner as fencing is at present, by practising, not in great bodies, but each man separately, in a particular school, under a particular master, or with his own particular equals and companions. Since

行业。

第二，维持或雇佣一定数目的公民成为常备军，这使得士兵这个职业成为独立的特定职业，有别于其他职业。

（2）使士兵职业成为一个单独的职业，

国家若用第一种方案，其军队就称为民兵，若用第二种，其军队就称为常备军。常备军士兵的唯一主要职责就是进行军事训练。他们的主要日常生活来源是国家发的生活费或薪俸。民兵只是偶尔进行军事训练，他们的主要日常生活来源来自其他职业。对于民兵来说，普通工人、技工或商人的性质要远远大于士兵的性质。对于常备军来说，士兵的性质远远大于其他职业的性质，这种区别是军队两个工种的本质区别。

换言之，就是建立民兵和常备军。

民兵又可分几种。在有些国家，捍卫国家的民兵似乎只进行军事训练而没有编成队伍（如果我可以这样说的话）。也就是说，他们没有编成独立可区分的军队，没有在各自专门固定军官的带领下进行军事训练。在古希腊和古罗马共和国，各个公民只要是留在后方，似乎就进行过军事训练。他们或者单独分开练习，或者和最喜欢的同伴一起练习。直到实际作战时，他们才会隶属于某个部队。在别的一些国家，民兵不仅军训，而且编队。在英国，瑞典，乃至近代欧洲各个其他国家，都成立有这种不完善的民兵。即使是在和平时期，每个民兵也都隶属于特定的部队，都在专门固定军官的带领下军训。

古代的民兵只进行操练和编队。

在枪炮发明以前，军队的优越程度取决于各个士兵使用武器时具有的高超技能和灵巧程度。身体的力气和敏捷性最为重要，一般决定着战斗的胜负。使用武器的技能和技巧也像箭术一样，现在不能集体训练习得，而是个人进入专门的学校，师从术有专攻的教师，或者与自己关系较好的同辈或同伴一起练习。枪炮发

枪炮使成次要，因为造成了这变化。

the invention of fire-arms, strength and agility of body, or even extraordinary dexterity and skill in the use of arms, though they are far from being of no consequence, are, however, of less consequence. The nature of the weapon, though it by no means puts the awkward upon a level with the skilful, puts him more nearly so than he ever was before. All the dexterity and skill, it is supposed, which are necessary for using it, can be well enough acquired by practising in great bodies.

<small>and discipline much more so.</small>
Regularity, order, and prompt obedience to command, are qualities which, in modern armies, are of more importance towards determining the fate of battles, than the dexterity and skill of the soldiers in the use of their arms. But the noise of fire-arms, the smoke, and the invisible death to which every man feels himself every moment exposed, as soon as he comes within cannon-shot, and frequently a long time before the battle can be well said to be engaged, must render it very difficult to maintain any considerable degree of this regularity, order, and prompt obedience, even in the beginning of a modern battle. In an ancient battle there was no noise but what arose from the human voice; there was no smoke, there was no invisible cause of wounds or death. Every man, till some mortal weapon actually did approach him, saw clearly that no such weapon was near him. In these circumstances, and among troops who had some confidence in their own skill and dexterity in the use of their arms, it must have been a good deal less difficult to preserve some degree of regularity and order, not only in the beginning, but through the whole progress of an ancient battle, and till one of the two armies was fairly defeated. But the habits of regularity, order, and prompt obedience to command, can be acquired only by troops which are exercised in great bodies.

<small>A militia is always inferior to a standing army, being less expert,</small>
A militia, however, in whatever manner it may be either disciplined or exercised, must always be much inferior to a well-disciplined and well-exercised standing army.

The soldiers, who are exercised only once a week, or once a month, can never be so expert in the use of their arms, as those who are exercised every day, or every other day; and though this circumstance may not be of so much consequence in modern, as it was in ancient times, yet the acknowledged superiority of the Prussian troops, owing, it is said, very much to their superior expertness in their exercise, may satisfy us that it is, even at this day, of very considerable consequence.

<small>and less well disciplined.</small>
The soldiers, who are bound to obey their officer only once a week or once a month, and who are at all other times at liberty to manage their own affairs their own way, without being in any respect accountable to him, can never be under the same awe in his presence, can never have

明以来,力气和敏捷性,甚至使用武器的特别熟练和技巧,虽不是说全无是处,但也不是那么重要了。武器的性质虽然没有把笨拙者提高到和灵巧者同一水准,但他们的水平却比以往任何时候都更为接近。人们认为,使用武器所必需的敏捷性和技能只有集体训练才能恰当掌握。

在近代战争中,纪律、秩序和迅速服从命令比使用武器的敏捷性和技能更能决定战争的命运。但即使是在近代战争的初期,只要士兵进入战场,就会有枪炮声、烟雾,在战争开始前很久每个人还会无时无刻不在感受看不到的死神,因此要想维持纪律、秩序和迅速服从命令是很困难的。在古代战争中,没有枪炮声,只有人们的厮杀声,没有烟雾,没有看不见的杀手使人受伤或死亡。没有致命的武器向他靠近,倘若的确有他会看得一清二楚。在这种情况下,不仅在战争初期,即使在古代战争的整个过程中,直至双方的一方败北,对使用武器的熟练和技能有信心的部队,要想维持纪律和秩序也容易得多。然而,只有集体训练的部队才能养成纪律严明、秩序井然和迅速服从命令的习惯。

<small>纪律更为重要。</small>

但是民兵无论用何种方式约束或训练,总是远远不及纪律严明、训练有素的常备军。

<small>民兵总是不及常备军优越,不是那么娴熟,</small>

在武器的熟练使用上,一周或一月训练一次的士兵不及每日或隔日训练的士兵。虽然这种情况在近代战争不及古代战争那么重要,然而,据说普鲁士军队之所以具有世所公认的优越性很大程度上就在于他们训练时无比的纯熟。这点足以证明,即使在现在,熟练的技能也是至关重要的。

一种士兵,每周或每月听长官命令一次,其余时间则自由处理自己的事务,不必向长官负责;另一种士兵,整个生活及行为都

<small>民兵纪律较差。</small>

the same disposition to ready obedience, with those whose whole life and conduct are every day directed by him, and who every day even rise and go to bed, or at least retire to their quarters, according to his orders. In what is called discipline, or in the habit of ready obedience, a militia must always be still more inferior to a standing army, than it may sometimes be in what is called the manual exercise, or in the management and use of its arms. But in modern war the habit of ready and instant obedience is of much greater consequence than a considerable superiority in the management of arms.

<small>The best militias are those which go to war under the chieftains who rule in time of peace.</small>

Those militias which, like the Tartar or Arab militia, go to war under the same chieftains whom they are accustomed to obey in peace, are by far the best. In respect for their officers, in the habit of ready obedience, they approach nearest to standing armies. The highland militia, when it served under its own chieftains, had some advantage of the same kind. As the highlanders, however, were not wandering, but stationary shepherds, as they had all a fixed habitation, and were not, in peaceable times, accustomed to follow their chieftain from place to place; so in time of war they were less willing to follow him to any considerable distance, or to continue for any long time in the field. When they had acquired any booty they were eager to return home, and his authority was seldom sufficient to detain them. In point of obedience they were always much inferior to what is reported of the Tartars and Arabs. As the highlanders too, from their stationary life, spend less of their time in the open air, they were always less accustomed to military exercises, and were less expert in the use of their arms than the Tartars and Arabs are said to be.

<small>A militia kept long enough in the field becomes a standing army.</small>

A militia of any kind, it must be observed, however, which has served for several successive campaigns in the field, becomes in every respect a standing army. The soldiers are every day exercised in the use of their arms, and, being constantly under the command of their officers, are habituated to the same prompt obedience which takes place in standing armies. What they were before they took the field, is of little importance. They necessarily become in every respect a standing army, after they have passed a few campaigns in it. Should the war in America drag out through another campaign, the American militia may become in every respect a match for that standing army, of which the valour appeared, in the last war, at least not inferior to that of the hardiest veterans of France and Spain.

<small>History shows the superiority of the standing army.</small>

This distinction being well understood, the history of all ages, it will be found, bears testimony to the irresistible superiority which a well-regulated standing army has over a militia.

要听命于长官,每日早上起床晚上睡觉,或至少返回军营时都要听从长官的命令。前者绝对不会像后者那样对长官毕恭毕敬,也绝对不会乐意迅速服从命令。至于所谓的纪律或迅速服从命令的习惯,在有时所谓的徒手训练或对武器的操作和使用上,民兵往往远远不及常备军。但在近代战争,立即服从命令的习惯的重要性要远远高于熟练操作武器。

民兵若跟和平时期惯于遵从的部落酋长一道作战,像鞑靼民兵或阿拉伯民兵那样,那是最好不过了。他们尊重长官,惯于迅速听从命令,最接近于常备军。苏格兰高地的民兵如果是在自己的酋长带领下作战,就有这样的优势。可是,高地人是不习惯流浪而有固定住处的牧民,在和平时期,不习惯跟酋长到处流浪。所以,和鞑靼民兵或阿拉伯民兵相比,他们战时不大愿意跟酋长长期纵横沙场。他们一旦获得战利品,就急于回家,酋长的威严也不能够阻挡他们。和鞑靼人以及阿拉伯人相比,据说高地人在服从命令方面很差;此外,高地人生活固定,野外活动时间少,往往不习惯军事训练,使用武器也不够熟练。

<small>最好的民兵是在和平时期由他们的酋长来带领的民兵。</small>

但是,我们要注意到,无论是哪种民兵,只要是连续在战场打过仗,就会成为面面俱到的常备军。民兵每天操练武器,常常听命于长官,像常备军那样,就习惯了迅速服从命令。他们战前是什么样子已无关紧要。重要的是,他们经过几场战役已经成为地地道道的常备军。美洲的战争倘若再拖延长一点,美洲民兵就会在各方面与常备军旗鼓相当,这些常备军在最后一场战争中骁勇善战,其表现绝不逊色于法国及西班牙最顽强的老兵。

<small>在上战场长期作战的民兵会变成常备军。</small>

知道了这个区别就会发现,历史上的一切时代都证明了训练有素的常备军比民兵有着无可比拟的优越。

<small>历史表明了常备军的优越性。</small>

国民财富的性质与原理

That of Macedon defeated the Greek militias.

One of the first standing armies of which we have any distinct account, in any well authenticated history, is that of Philip of Macedon. His frequent wars with the Thracians, Illyrians, Thessalians, and some of the Greek cities in the neighbourhood of Macedon, gradually formed his troops, which in the beginning were probably militia, to the exact discipline of a standing army. When he was at peace, which he was very seldom, and never for any long time together, he was careful not to disband that army. It vanquished and subdued, after a long and violent struggle, indeed, the gallant and well exercised militias of the principal republics of ancient Greece; and afterwards, with very little struggle, the effeminate and ill-exercised militia of the great Persian empire. The fall of the Greek republics and of the Persian empire, was the effect of the irresistible superiority which a standing army has over every sort of militia. It is the first great revolution in the affairs of mankind, of which history has preserved any distinct or circumstantial account.

In the wars of Carthage and Rome standing armies defeated militias.

The fall of Carthage, and the consequent elevation of Rome, is the second. All the varieties in the fortune of those two famous republics may very well be accounted for from the same cause.

The Carthaginian standing army defeated the Roman militia in Italy,

From the end of the first to the beginning of the second Carthaginian war, the armies of Carthage were continually in the field, and employed under three great generals, who succeeded one another in the command; Amilcar, his son-in-law Asdrubal, and his son Annibal; first in chastising their own rebellious slaves, afterwards in subduing the revolted nations of Africa, and, lastly, in conquering the great kingdom of Spain. The army which Annibal led from Spain into Italy must necessarily, in those different wars, have been gradually formed to the exact discipline of a standing army. The Romans, in the mean time, though they had not been altogether at peace, yet they had not, during this period, been engaged in any war of very great consequence; and their military discipline, it is generally said, was a good deal relaxed. The Roman armies which Annibal encountered at Trebia, Thrasymenus and Cannæ, were militia opposed to a standing army. This circumstance, it is probable, contributed more than any other to determine the fate of those battles.

and Spain.

The standing army which Annibal left behind him in Spain, had the like superiority over the militia which the Romans sent to oppose it, and in a few years, under the command of his brother, the younger Asdrubal, expelled them almost entirely from that country.

第五篇　第一章

　　史料中有明确记载的首支出色的常备军就是马其顿国王菲利普率领的军队。他常常与色雷斯人、伊里利亚人、色萨利亚人以及马其顿邻近的希腊各城市作战,就逐渐带出了有严格纪律的常备军。开始时,这支军队或许也不过是民兵罢了。和平时期——对他来说这样的时期很少,总共也持续不了多久,他努力不遣散军队。的确,经过长期的激战,这支军队一举打败了古希腊各主要共和国骁勇善战、训练有素的民兵。后来,又不费吹灰之力打败了大波斯帝国柔弱而缺乏训练的民兵。希腊各共和国及波斯帝国的衰落,就是常备军比民兵具有无可比拟的优越性的结果。这是历史上有明确详细记载的人类事务的首次伟大革命。 马其顿常备军挫败了希腊民兵。

　　迦太基的衰落,以及取而代之的罗马的崛起,是人类历史上第二次伟大革命。这两个著名共和国的一切兴衰胜败,均可由同一原因解释。 在迦太基和罗马的战争中,常备军击败了民兵。

　　从第一次迦太基战争结束到第二次迦太基战争开始,迦太基的军队连年作战,相继由三名著名将军率领,即哈米尔卡尔、他的女婿哈斯德拉巴及儿子哈尼巴。他们首先惩治了反叛的奴隶,后来镇压了非洲叛乱民族,最后又征服了西班牙大王国。哈尼巴率领的军队,从西班牙进攻意大利,经历种种战争,必然渐渐锻炼成为纪律严明的常备军。当时,罗马人虽然没有完全过着和平的生活,但在此期间也没有经历过大规模的战争。一般认为,罗马的军队纪律大为松弛。罗马的军队在特雷比亚、色斯雷米纳以及坎尼与哈尼巴的军队遭遇,其实是民兵和常备军的对抗。这一情况或许比任何其他情况更能决定这些战争的命运。 迦太基常备军在意大利击败了罗马民兵。

　　哈尼巴留在西班牙的常备军,对于罗马派去对抗它的民兵,具有同样的优越性。短短几年,这支常备军就在他的弟弟小哈斯 在西班牙也是如此。

When the Roman militias became a standing army they defeated the Carthaginian standing army in Italy,

Annibal was ill supplied from home. The Roman militia, being continually in the field, became in the progress of the war a well disciplined and well exercised standing army; and the superiority of Annibal grew every day less and less. Asdrubal judged it necessary to lead the whole, or almost the whole of the standing army which he commanded in Spain, to the assistance of his brother in Italy. In this march he is said to have been misled by his guides; and in a country which he did not know, was surprized and attacked by another standing army, in every respect equal or superior to his own, and was entirely defeated.

and the Carthaginian militia in Spain, and both standing army and militia in Africa.

When Asdrubal had left Spain, the great Scipio found nothing to oppose him but a militia inferior to his own. He conquered and subdued that militia, and, in the course of the war, his own militia necessarily became a well-disciplined and well-exercised standing army. That standing army was afterwards carried to Africa, where it found nothing but a militia to oppose it. In order to defend Carthage it became necessary to recall the standing army of Annibal. The disheartened and frequently defeated African militia joined it, and, at the battle of Zama, composed the greater part of the troops of Annibal. The event of that day determined the fate of the two rival republics.

Thenceforward the Roman republic had standing armies, which found little resistance except from the standing army of Macedon.

From the end of the second Carthaginian war till the fall of the Roman republic, the armies of Rome were in every respect standing armies. The standing army of Macedon made some resistance to their arms. In the height of their grandeur, it cost them two great wars, and three great battles, to subdue that little kingdom; of which the conquest would probably have been still more difficult, had it not been for the cowardice of its last king. The militias of all the civilized nations of the ancient world, of Greece, of Syria, and of Egypt, made but a feeble resistance to the standing armies of Rome. The militias of some barbarous nations defended themselves much better. The Scythian or Tartar militia, which Mithridates drew from the countries north of the Euxine and Caspian seas, were the most formidable enemies whom the Romans had to encounter after the second Carthaginian war. The Parthian and German militias too were always respectable, and, upon several occasions, gained very considerable advantages over the Roman armies. In general, however, and when the Roman armies were well commanded, they appear to have

第五篇 第一章

德鲁巴的指挥下,将罗马的民兵通通逐出了西班牙。

汉尼巴的后方供给不足。而罗马民兵久经沙场,渐渐在战争过程中锻炼成为纪律严明、训练有素的常备军。哈尼巴的优越性却江河日下。小哈斯德鲁巴认为有必要率领他在西班牙的全部或几乎全部的常备军,支援在意大利作战的兄长。在进军中,据说他被向导带错了路,陷入一个陌生的国度,遭到另一支各方面都与他旗鼓相当甚至优于他的常备军的突袭,结果全军覆没。

哈斯德鲁巴离开西班牙时,伟人的西皮阿发觉和他对抗的只不过是劣于他的民兵。他大败了这支民兵,而他自己的民兵在战争中也必然成为了纪律严明、训练有素的常备军。后来,这支正规军被派往非洲,却发现抵抗它的只不过是民兵罢了。为了保卫迦太基,召回哈尼巴的常备军势在必行。伤心欲绝、屡战屡败的非洲民兵加入到常备军中,在查马战斗中,构成哈尼巴军队的大部分。而当日的决战决定了两个敌对共和国的命运。

从第二次迦太基战争结束到罗马共和国的衰落,罗马军队已成为地地道道的常备军。马其顿的常备军,曾对罗马军队进行过抵抗。当时的罗马正处于鼎盛时期,发动了两场大战争、三次大会战,才征服了这个小国家。要不是这个国家的最后一个国王生性懦弱,征服这小国或许也会更加困难。一切古老文明国家的民兵,如希腊的民兵,叙利亚的民兵以及埃及的民兵,对罗马的常备军都只进行了微弱的抵抗。而一些野蛮民族的民兵则誓死捍卫祖国。米斯里德斯率领的西斯亚民兵及鞑靼民兵来自黑海和里海以北各国,是罗马在第二次迦太基战争后遭遇到的最可怕的敌人。帕斯阿民兵及日耳曼的民兵,也令人敬佩,有几次给罗马军队以重创。然而,一般来说,罗马军队倘若指挥得当,还是大有优

been very much superior; and if the Romans did not pursue the final conquest either of Parthia or Germany, it was probably because they judged, that it was not worth while to add those two barbarous countries to an empire which was already too large. The ancient Parthians appear to have been a nation of Scythian or Tartar extraction, and to have always retained a good deal of the manners of their ancestors. The ancient Germans were, like the Scythians or Tartars, a nation of wandering shepherds, who went to war under the same chiefs whom they were accustomed to follow in peace. Their militia was exactly of the same kind with that of the Scythians or Tartars, from whom too they were probably descended.

<small>Under the emperors these armies degenerated into militias.</small>
Many different causes contributed to relax the discipline of the Roman armies. Its extreme severity was, perhaps, one of those causes. In the days of their grandeur, when no enemy appeared capable of opposing them, their heavy armour was laid aside as unnecessarily burdensome, their laborious exercises were neglected as unnecessarily toilsome. Under the Roman emperors besides, the standing armies of Rome, those particularly which guarded the German and Pannonian frontiers, became dangerous to their masters, against whom they used frequently to set up their own generals. In order to render them less formidable, according to some authors, Dioclesian, according to others, Constantine, first withdrew them from the frontier, where they had always before been encamped in great bodies, generally of two or three legions each, and dispersed them in small bodies through the different provincial towns, from whence they were scarce ever removed, but when it became necessary to repel an invasion. Small bodies of soldiers quartered in trading and manufacturing towns, and seldom removed from those quarters, became themselves tradesmen, artificers, and manufacturers. The civil came to predominate over the military character; and the standing armies of Rome gradually degenerated into a corrupt, neglected, and undisciplined militia, incapable of resisting the attack of the German and Scythian militias, which soon afterwards invaded the western empire. It was only by hiring the militia of some of those nations to oppose to that of others, that the emperors were for some time able to defend themselves. The fall of the western empire is the third great revolution in the affairs of mankind, of which ancient history has preserved any distinct or circumstantial account. It was brought about by the irresistible superiority which the militia of a barbarous, has over that of a civilized nation;

第五篇 第一章

势的。罗马人不曾彻底征服帕斯阿及日耳曼,或许在于他们认为帝国已经足够大了,不值得再增加两个野蛮民族。古代帕斯阿人,似乎是西斯亚或鞑靼系属的民族,一直保留着祖先遗留下来的风俗习惯。古日耳曼人和西斯亚人或鞑靼人一样,是流浪的游牧民族。他们和平时期习惯于跟随酋长;战时依然在他的率领下作战。古日耳曼民兵跟西斯亚及鞑靼民兵一样,或许还是他们的后裔呢。

罗马军队之所以纪律松弛,原因很多。而纪律过分严厉或许是原因之一。在罗马处于鼎盛时期时,似乎没有军队能与之匹敌,他们认为沉重的盔甲负担累累,因而漠然置之,并且把辛苦操练当作无谓之劳,等闲视之。而且,罗马皇帝统治下的那些常备军,特别是保卫边疆防御日耳曼人及班诺尼亚人的常备军,成为皇帝的心头大患。为对付朝廷,他们常常拥立自己的将军。在某些作家看来,为削弱常备军的强大兵权,德奥克里希恩大帝,或是根据其他作家的看法,是康斯坦丁大帝,首先把他们从边疆撤走。过去,这些常备军往往是由两三个军团组成的大部队,一直驻守在边疆;现在,把他们分散成小部队,驻扎在各省省会。自此,除非为了驱除外来侵略,他们再也很少移动。小队士兵驻守在商业及制造业城市,很少从这些地方移动,就渐渐成了商人、技工或制造业者。市民的性质渐渐超过了军士的性质,而罗马的常备军也堕落了,成为簠簋不饬,玩忽职守、纪律涣散的民兵,再也无力抵抗日耳曼及西斯亚民兵的入侵。后来日耳曼及西斯亚民兵很快就入侵了西罗马帝国。皇帝一度为了自卫,只好雇佣别国民兵来抵抗外国民兵。西罗马帝国的衰落是人类事务中第三次伟大革命。古代历史对此有明确详细的记载。究其原因,是野蛮民族的

各个罗马皇帝统治下,军队退化成民兵。

which the militia of a nation of shepherds, has over that of a nation of husbandmen, artificers, and manufacturers. The victories which have been gained by militias have generally been, not over standing armies, but over other militias in exercise and discipline inferior to themselves. Such were the victories which the Greek militia gained over that of the Persian empire; and such too were those which in later times the Swiss militia gained over that of the Austrians and Burgundians.

<small>Militias were gradually superseded by standing armies in Western Europe.</small>

The military force of the German and Scythian nations who established themselves upon the ruins of the western empire, continued for some time to be of the same kind in their new settlements, as it had been in their original country. It was a militia of shepherds and husbandmen, which, in time of war, took the field under the command of the same chieftains whom it was accustomed to obey in peace. It was, therefore, tolerably well exercised, and tolerably well disciplined. As arts and industry advanced, however, the authority of the chieftains gradually decayed, and the great body of the people had less time to spare for military exercises. Both the discipline and the exercise of the feudal militia, therefore, went gradually to ruin, and standing armies were gradually introduced to supply the place of it. When the expedient of a standing army, besides, had once been adopted by one civilized nation, it became necessary that all its neighbours should follow the example. They soon found that their safety depended upon their doing so, and that their own militia was altogether incapable of resisting the attack of such an army.

<small>A standing army does not lose its valour in time of peace,</small>

The soldiers of a standing army, though they may never have seen an enemy, yet have frequently appeared to possess all the courage of veteran troops, and the very moment that they took the field to have been fit to face the hardiest and most experienced veterans. In 1756, when the Russian army marched into Poland, the valour of the Russian soldiers did not appear inferior to that of the Prussians, at that time supposed to be the hardiest and most experienced veterans in Europe. The Russian empire, however, had enjoyed a profound peace for near twenty years before, and could at that time have very few soldiers who had ever seen an enemy. When the Spanish war broke out in 1739, England had enjoyed a profound peace for about eight and twenty years. The valour of her soldiers, however, far from being corrupted by that long peace, was never more distinguished than in the attempt upon Carthagena, the first unfortunate exploit of

民兵对于文明国民兵有着无可比拟的优越,也是游牧民族的民兵对于农民、技工及制造业者民族的民兵有着无可比拟的优越。这里,民兵所战胜的大都不是常备军,而是训练及纪律都不如他们的民兵。同样,希腊民兵大败波斯民兵,以及后来的瑞士民兵大败奥地利及勃艮第民兵都是如此。

在西罗马帝国的废墟上建立起来的是日耳曼民族和塞西亚民族的国家。他们军队的性质,和原来在自己国家一样,在新占领的土地上依然维持了一段时间。这支军队是由牧人和农民组成的民兵。和平时期,他们惯于服从酋长的命令,战时则由酋长率领奔赴沙场。因此,这支队伍还算训练有素、纪律严明。然而,随着技术及产业的进步,酋长的权威逐渐丧失,大多数人再无更多闲暇时间接受军事训练。所以封建民兵的纪律日趋松弛,训练逐渐荒废,着手建立起常备军取而代之成为趋势。此外,一旦一个文明国家采用建立常备军的策略,邻近国家势必纷纷仿效。他们很快发现自己的安全维系于此;若非如此,自己的民兵根本无法抵抗常备军的进攻。

<small>在西欧,常备军逐渐代替了民兵。</small>

常备军的士兵,虽然从未上阵杀敌,但也往往显出老兵才有的英勇气概,一旦上阵作战,就能配合最顽强、最有经验的老兵大战一场。1756年,俄罗斯军队开进波兰,士兵们骁勇善战,其势绝不亚于当时最顽强最有经验的普鲁士士兵。然而,俄罗斯帝国在此以前享受了近20年的太平盛世;那时士兵很少有机会上阵杀敌。1739年,西班牙战争爆发。当时,英国也享受了约28年的太平盛世。然而,长期的太平生活并没有消磨英国常备军的锐气。在攻打喀他基那的战争中,他们表现得尤为出色。这一进攻,是他们在这次不幸战争中的第一次不幸冒险。和平日子过久了,将

<small>常备军在平时也不会丧失它的英勇气概。</small>

that unfortunate war. In a long peace the generals, perhaps, may sometimes forget their skill ; but, where a well-regulated standing army has been kept up, the soldiers seem never to forget their valour.

<small>and is the only safeguard of a civilised nation,</small>
When a civilized nation depends for its defence upon a militia, it is at all times exposed to be conquered by any barbarous nation which happens to be in its neighbourhood. The frequent conquests of all the civilized countries in Asia by the Tartars, sufficiently demonstrates the natural superiority, which the militia of a barbarous, has over that of a civilized nation. A well-regulated standing army is superior to every militia. Such an army, as it can best be maintained by an opulent and civilized nation, so it can alone defend such a nation against the invasion of a poor and barbarous neighbour. It is only by means of a standing army, therefore, that the civilization of any country can be perpetuated, or even preserved for any considerable time.

<small>also the only means of civilising a barbarous one.</small>
As it is only by means of a well-regulated standing army that a civilized country can be defended; so it is only by means of it, that a barbarous country can be suddenly and tolerably civilized. A standing army establishes, with an irresistible force, the law of the sovereign through the remotest provinces of the empire, and maintains some degree of regular government in countries which could not otherwise admit of any. Whoever examines, with attention, the improvements which Peter the Great introduced into the Russian empire, will find that they almost all resolve themselves into the establishment of a well-regulated standing army. It is the instrument which executes and maintains all his other regulations. That degree of order and internal peace, which that empire has ever since enjoyed, is altogether owing to the influence of that army.

<small>It is not unfavourable to liberty.</small>
Men of republican principles have been jealous of a standing army as dangerous to liberty. It certainly is so, wherever the interest of the general and that of the principal officers are not necessarily connected with the support of the constitution of the state. The standing army of Cæsar destroyed the Roman republic. The standing army of Cromwel turned the long parliament out of doors. But where the sovereign is himself the general, and the principal nobility and gentry of the country the chief officers of the army; where the military force is placed under the command of those who have the greatest interest in the support of the civil authority, because they have themselves the greatest share of that authority, a standing army can never be dangerous to

领或许有时会忘了自己的技能,但常备军却秩序井然,士兵是不大会忘记自己应该英勇杀敌的。

文明民族若依赖民兵保卫国家,随时都有被四邻野蛮民族征服的危险。鞑靼人横扫亚洲文明国家的事实就足以证明,野蛮民族的民兵对于文明民族的民兵有着天然的优越性。训练有素的常备军优于任何民兵。只有富强的文明国家,才能拥有这样的军队;也只有这样的军队,才能保卫这种国家不受贫穷野蛮邻国的入侵。因此,国家也只有拥有常备军,文明才会不朽或是得到长久保存。_{常备军是文明国家的唯一保障,}

只有拥有训练有素的常备军,文明国家的国防才会无忧;也只有训练有素的常备军,野蛮国家才会迅速相当地文明化。常备军凭借其无可抗衡的军力,可以把君主的法令推广到帝国最偏僻的地方,并且在没有常备军就没有统治可言的国家,实行相当正规的统治。凡用心考察俄罗斯帝国彼得大帝改革的人,都会发现这些举措都是为了建立起训练有素的常备军。彼得大帝也就是通过常备军才能执行和维持其他法规。俄罗斯帝国自此以后之所以能够享有相当的秩序和国内和平,归根结底在于这支常备军的威力。_{常备军也是使野蛮国家文明化的唯一方法。}

信仰共和主义的人担心常备军会危害自由。当将领及主要官吏的利益和国家宪法没有必然联系时,当然会出现这种情况。恺撒的常备军就毁坏了罗马共和国;克伦威尔的常备军将英国长期存在的议会驱逐出门。但是,只要君主自己是统帅,王孙贵胄成为军队的主要军官,军队大权掌握在最关心公民权益的人手中,即他们享有的公民权利最大,那么常备军绝不会危害到自由。_{常备军并非不利于自由。}

liberty. On the contrary, it may in some cases be favourable to liberty. ① The security which it gives to the sovereign renders unnecessary that troublesome jealousy, which, in some modern republics, seems to watch over the minutest actions, and to be at all times ready to disturb the peace of every citizen. Where the security of the magistrate, though supported by the principal people of the country, is endangered by every popular discontent; where a small tumult is capable of bringing about in a few hours a great revolution, the whole authority of government must be employed to suppress and punish every murmur and complaint against it. To a sovereign, on the contrary, who feels himself supported, not only by the natural aristocracy of the country, but by a well-regulated standing army, the rudest, the most groundless, and the most licentious remonstrances can give little disturbance. He can safely pardon or neglect them, and his consciousness of his own superiority naturally disposes him to do so. That degree of liberty which approaches to licentiousness can be tolerated only in countries where the sovereign is secured by a well-regulated standing army. It is in such countries only, that the public safety does not require, that the sovereign should be trusted with any discretionary power, for suppressing even the impertinent wantonness of this licentious liberty.

Defence thus grows more expensive.   The first duty of the sovereign, therefore, that of defending the society from the violence and injustice of other independent societies, grows gradually more and more expensive, as the society advances in civilization. The military force of the society, which originally cost the sovereign no expence either in time of peace or in time of war, must, in the progress of improvement, first be maintained by him in time of war, and afterwards even in time of peace.

Fire-arms enhance the expense,   The great change introduced into the art of war by the invention of fire-arms, has enhanced still further both the expence of exercising and disciplining any particular number of soldiers in time of peace, and that of employing them in time of war. Both their arms and their ammunition are become more expensive. A musket is a more expensive machine than a javelin or a bow and arrows; a cannon or a mortar than a balista or a catapulta. The powder, which is spent in a modern review, is lost irrecoverably, and occasions a very considerable expence.

---

① [*Lectures*, p. 263.]

反之,在某些情况下,或许常备军还有利于自由①。君主拥有了常备军,就高枕无忧,省去了不必要的嫉妒和苦恼,就不会像某些近代共和国那样,监视市民的细微行动,还时时干扰公民的平静生活。如果行政长官虽然得到国家大部分人的支持,但其安全会在群众不满情绪下受到威胁;或者如果小小的骚乱也能引发大革命,这时,政府必须运用权势镇压惩处对其不满的群众。反之,君主如果感到自己不仅得到世袭贵族的支持,也得到了训练有素的常备军的支持,这时,即使他遭到了最粗鲁、最无理由、最放肆的抗议,也不会很在意。他可以宽宏大量地饶恕他们,不再过问。他意识到了自己的优越,自然倾向于这样做。只有国君得到了训练有素的常备军的保障,才会容许自由宽延至放肆的地步。也只有在这样的国家,公共安全才不需要赋予君主任意的权利,去镇压肆意无度的自由。

因此,随着社会文明的进步,君主的第一要务,即保卫社会免遭其他独立社会的强暴及欺侮,需要的费用越来越昂贵了。原来,无论是在和平时期还是战争年代,维持军队不需要花费君主一分钱;在社会进步的过程中,起初,君主需要在战时出钱,后来,即使和平时期也需要君主出钱了。这样,国防就变得更加费钱。

随着枪炮的发明,战争技术发生了巨大的变化。无论是和平年代训练一定数额的士兵,还是战争时期雇佣士兵,费用都需要增加了。他们使用的武器及弹药费用也更为昂贵了。步枪的费用比长矛或弓箭高。大炮及迫击炮的费用也比弩炮或石炮高。近代阅兵所消耗的火药,无可回收,开支巨大。古代阅兵投掷的枪炮增加了支出,

---

① 《关于法律、警察、岁入及军备的演讲》,第263页。

The javelins and arrows which were thrown or shot in an ancient one, could easily be picked up again, and were besides of very little value. The cannon and the mortar are, not only much dearer, but much heavier machines than the balista or catapulta, and require a greater expence, not only to prepare them for the field, but to carry them to it. As the superiority of the modern artillery too, over that of the ancients is very great; it has become much more difficult, and consequently much more expensive, to fortify a town so as to resist even for a few weeks the attack of that superior artillery. In modern times many different causes contribute to render the defence of the society more expensive. The unavoidable effects of the natural progress of improvement have, in this respect, been a good deal enhanced by a great revolution in the art of war, to which a mere accident, the invention of gunpowder, seems to have given occasion.

<small>and so give an advantage to rich nations, which is favourable to civilisation.</small>

In modern war the great expence of fire-arms gives an evident advantage to the nation which can best afford that expence; and consequently, to an opulent and civilized, over a poor and barbarous nation. In ancient times the opulent and civilized found it difficult to defend themselves against the poor and barbarous nations. In modern times the poor and barbarous find it difficult to defend themselves against the opulent and civilized. The invention of fire-arms, an invention which at first sight appears to be so pernicious, is certainly favourable both to the permanency and to the extension of civilization.

Part II *Of The Expence Of Justice*

<small>The expense of justice is different at different periods.</small>

The second duty of the sovereign, that of protecting, as far as possible, every member of the society from the injustice or oppression of every other member of it, or the duty of establishing an exact administration of justice requires too very different degrees of expence in the different periods of society.

Among nations of hunters, as there is scarce any property, or at least none that exceeds the value of two or three days labour; so there is seldom any established magistrate or any regular administration of justice. Men who have no property can injure one another only in their persons or reputations. But when one man kills, wounds, beats, or defames another, though he to whom the injury is done suffers, he who does it receives no benefit. It is otherwise with the injuries to property. The benefit of the person who does the injury is often equal

长矛及放射的箭,都易于回收,并且造价很低。与弩炮及石炮相比,大炮及迫击炮不仅价格昂贵,而且是非常笨重的机械,无论是制造起来,还是运往战场,费用都很高昂。近代大炮的优越性要远远大于古代的武器,城市倘若筑防御工事,抵抗大炮的进攻,哪怕只有几个星期也困难得多,费用也极其昂贵,近代社会的国防费用日趋提高,原因有诸多方面。在这方面,是社会自然进步的必然结果,战争技术的大革命又起到推波助澜的作用。这场大革命似乎只不过是偶发事故引起的,即火药的发明。

近代战争的枪炮费用昂贵,能负担此费用的国家就具有显而易见的优势。故富裕文明的国家就比贫穷野蛮的国家有明显的优势。而在古代,富裕文明的国家却难于抵御贫穷野蛮的国家。枪炮的发明,最初看起来似乎是有害的,实际上却对文明的持久与延伸大为有利。_{这就使富国处于有利地位,而这是有利于文明的。}

第二节 论司法的费用支出

君主的第二个职责就是尽可能保护社会每个成员不受其他社会成员的欺侮及压迫,或者是成立严格的司法机构。社会时期不同,执行职责所需费用也大不相同。_{司法费用在不同时期也有所相同。}

在狩猎民族中,几乎没有任何财产,至少没有大于两三天劳动价值的财产。所以也就没有固定的司法官吏或正规的司法行政机构。没有财产的人,相互伤害的也只是各人的身体或者名誉。然而,当某人屠杀、杀伤、殴打另一个人或者让他名誉扫地时,虽然受害人忍受着折磨,害人者却毫无利益可言。可对财产的侵害却不相同。害人者的所得利益往往也就是受害人的损失。

国民财富的性质与原理

<small>Civil government was first rendered necessary by the introduction of property.</small> to the loss of him who suffers it. Envy, malice, or resentment, are the only passions which can prompt one man to injure another in his person or reputation. But the greater part of men are not very frequently under the influence of those passions; and the very worst men are so only occasionally. As their gratification too, how agreeable soever it may be to certain characters, is not attended with any real or permanent advantage, it is in the greater part of men commonly restrained by prudential considerations. Men may live together in society with some tolerable degree of security, though there is no civil magistrate to protect them from the injustice of those passions. But avarice and ambition in the rich, in the poor the hatred of labour and the love of present ease and enjoyment, are the passions which prompt to invade property, passions much more steady in their operation, and much more universal in their influence. Wherever there is great property, there is great inequality. For one very rich man, there must be at least five hundred poor, and the affluence of the few supposes the indigence of the many. The affluence of the rich excites the indignation of the poor, who are often both driven by want, and prompted by envy, to invade his possessions. It is only under the shelter of the civil magistrate that the owner of that valuable property, which is acquired by the labour of many years, or perhaps of many successive generations, can sleep a single night in security. He is at all times surrounded by unknown enemies, whom, though he never provoked, he can never appease, and from whose injustice he can be protected only by the powerful arm of the civil magistrate continually held up to chastise it. The acquisition of valuable and extensive property, therefore, necessarily requires the establishment of civil government. Where there is no property, or at least none that exceeds the value of two or three days labour, civil government is not so necessary.

<small>Property strengthens the causes of subordination.</small> Civil government supposes a certain subordination. But as the necessity of civil government gradually grows up with the acquisition of valuable property, so the principal causes which naturally introduce subordination gradually grow up with the growth of that valuable property.

<small>There are four causes of subordination:</small> The causes or circumstances which naturally introduce subordination, or which naturally, and antecedent to any civil institution, give some men some superiority over the greater part of their brethren, seem to be four in number.

The first of those causes or circumstances is the superiority of

第五篇 第一章

只有嫉妒、怨恨、愤怒等情绪才会使人去伤害另一个人的身体或名誉。但往往大多数人是不会这么被情绪冲昏头脑的,罪大恶极的人也只是偶尔如此。对有些人来说,不管满足自己的情绪是多么惬意,满足感带来的好处却不会是真实、永久的。大部分人一般还是会审慎考虑而加以克制的。即使没有司法官吏保护人们免受不良情绪的危害,人们还是会在一定程度上安全地居住在一起。但是,富人有贪欲和野心;穷人也会憎恨劳动,贪图现实的安逸。这些情绪都会促使人去攫取他人财产,而这些情绪一旦发作,又极其稳固,其影响也就更为普遍。凡是有巨额财产的地方,就存在着巨大的不公平。有一个大富人,就至少有 500 个穷人;少数人的富足是以多数人的贫穷为前提的。富人的富足会激起穷人的义愤,他们为生活需求和嫉妒所驱,就去强取富人的财产。只有在司法官吏的庇护下,富人才能睡上一个安稳觉,而他的贵重财产也是多年劳动或连续几代人劳动才积攒起来的。富人随时都被未知的敌人包围着,他虽然从未招惹这些人,但也无法满足他们。只有司法官吏一贯强有力的保护才能惩处不法之徒,让他免遭不幸。因此,积攒的万贯财产必然要求成立民法政府。凡是没有财产,至少没有大于两三天劳动价值的财产的地方,就没有成立法制政府的必要。

<small>由于采用财产权,首先使民法政府成为必要。</small>

民法政府是以人民的服从为前提的。随着贵重财产的获得,渐渐就有了成立民法政府的需求。因此,人民自然服从的主要原因也随着贵重财产的增产而增长。

<small>财产加强了服从的原因。</small>

人民自然服从的原因或条件,或者在成立民法机构以前,让有些人对大部分同胞有着天然优越的原因或条件,似乎有四种。

<small>有四个服从的原因:</small>

第一个原因或条件就是以下各个方面的优越:个人资质的优

(1) superiority of personal qualifications,

personal qualifications, of strength, beauty, and agility of body; of wisdom, and virtue, of prudence, justice, fortitude, and moderation of mind. The qualifications of the body, unless supported by those of the mind, can give little authority in any period of society. He is a very strong man, who, by mere strength of body, can force two weak ones to obey him. The qualifications of the mind can alone give very great authority. They are, however, invisible qualities; always disputable, and generally disputed. No society, whether barbarous or civilized, has ever found it convenient to settle the rules of precedency of rank and subordination, according to those invisible qualities; but according to something that is more plain and palpable.

(2) superiority of age,

The second of those causes or circumstances is the superiority of age. An old man, provided his age is not so far advanced as to give suspicion of dotage, is every where more respected than a young man of equal rank, fortune, and abilities. Among nations of hunters, such as the native tribes of North America, age is the sole foundation of rank and precedency. Among them, father is the appellation of a superior; brother, of an equal; and son, of an inferior. In the most opulent and civilized nations, age regulates rank among those who are in every other respect equal, and among whom, therefore, there is nothing else to regulate it. Among brothers and among sisters, the eldest always take place; and in the succession of the paternal estate every thing which cannot be divided, but must go entire to one person, such as a title of honour, is in most cases given to the eldest. Age is a plain and palpable quality which admits of no dispute.

(3) superiority of fortune,

The third of those causes or circumstances is the superiority of fortune. The authority of riches, however, though great in every age of society, is perhaps greatest in the rudest age of society which admits of any considerable inequality of fortune. A Tartar chief, the increase of whose herds and flocks is sufficient to maintain a thousand men, cannot well employ that increase in any other way than in maintaining a thousand men. The rude state of his society does not afford him any manufactured produce, any trinkets or baubles of any kind,

越,身体力量的优越,容貌的优越,动作敏捷的优越;智慧的优越、德行的优越,正义的优越,坚忍的优越,克制的优越等。身体的资质,除非得到精神资质的支持,否则在社会的任何时期,都不会拥有权威的。身体强壮之人,只凭身体的强壮,可以降服两个身体虚弱之人来服从他。而单凭精神的资质却可以赢得巨大的权威。但这些资质是看不见的品质,总会引起人们的争议,而且一般受到众人的质疑。无论是野蛮社会还是文明社会,都不曾依据这些看不见的品质,而是依据那些看得见摸得着的东西,来确定等级和服从的法规。

(1)个人资质的优越,

第二个条件或原因就是年龄的优越。老年人,只要他没有衰老到腐朽的地步,各方面都要比同等等级、同等财富及同等能力的年轻人更受到尊重。在北美狩猎民族中,例如北美土著部落,年龄是等级和先后次序的唯一根据。在他们之中,父亲是上级的称呼,兄弟是平等的称呼,儿子是下级的称呼。在富裕文明的国家,给各方面旗鼓相当的人规定等级时,若无其他可以区分的标准,年龄就规定着等级。在兄弟姐妹中,老大总是排第一。当继承父辈财产时,凡是无法分割、必须完全归于一个人的东西,例如爵位称呼,绝大多数会授予年长者。年龄是一个清楚明了的资格,这一点是毋庸置疑的。

(2)年龄的优越,

第三个条件或原因是财产的优越。然而,财产的优越,虽然在社会的每个年代都有很大的优越,但或许在最原始的社会——也是财产分布最不平等的社会——其优越性最大。鞑靼的酋长,随着喂养牛羊数目的增长,足够养活1000人,他也只会凭借牛羊的增殖来养活1000人,再没有其他用途。他所处的原始社会状态,没有制造品,没有小装饰品,也没有小玩意儿,他不可能把消费不了

(3)财产的优越,

for which he can exchange that part of his rude produce which is over and above his own consumption. The thousand men whom he thus maintains, depending entirely upon him for their subsistence, must both obey his orders in war, and submit to his jurisdiction in peace. He is necessarily both their general and their judge, and his chieftainship is the necessary effect of the superiority of his fortune. In an opulent and civilized society, a man may possess a much greater fortune, and yet not be able to command a dozen of people. Though the produce of his estate may be sufficient to maintain, and may perhaps actually maintain, more than a thousand people, yet as those people pay for every thing which they get from him, as he gives scarce any thing to any body but in exchange for an equivalent, there is scarce any body who considers himself as entirely dependent upon him, and his authority extends only over a few menial servants. The authority of fortune, however, is very great even in an opulent and civilized society. That it is much greater than that, either of age, or of personal qualities, has been the constant complaint of every period of society which admitted of any considerable inequality of fortune. The first period of society, that of hunters, admits of no such inequality. Universal poverty establishes there universal equality, and the superiority, either of age, or of personal qualities, are the feeble, but the sole foundations of authority and subordination. There is therefore little or no authority or subordination in this period of society. The second period of society, that of shepherds, admits of very great inequalities of fortune, and there is no period in which the superiority of fortune gives so great authority to those who possess it. There is no period accordingly in which authority and subordination are more perfectly established. The authority of an Arabian scherif is very great; that of a Tartar khan altogether despotical.

and (4) superiority of birth.
The fourth of those causes or circumstances is the superiority of birth. Superiority of birth supposes an ancient superiority of fortune in the family of the person who claims it. All families are equally ancient; and the ancestors of the prince, though they may be better known, cannot well be more numerous than those of the beggar. Antiquity of family means every where the antiquity either of wealth, or of that greatness which is commonly either founded upon wealth, or

的原始物件用来交换这些东西。而他养活的那1000人,因为要完全靠他维持生计,所以战争时必须听从他的命令,和平时期也要服从他的管辖。他就必然成了他们的统帅及法官。他的酋长地位,是财富优越的必然结果。在富裕文明社会,一个人拥有的财产可以比别人多很多,然而他所能支配的人数却不到十几人。虽然他的财产增值物可以养活1000人,或许也确是如此,但那些人从他那里拿走了东西都付了钱,也就是说他没有给别人任何东西,只是交换了同等价值的东西,没有人自认为完全依赖他,他的权威也只有几个仆人才会遵从。但是,即使在富裕文明的社会里,财产的权威,也是很大的。财产的权威比年龄及品质的权威都要大得多。关于这一点,生活在财产极大不平等社会的人们经常抱怨。社会的第一个时期,即狩猎民族时期,容不得半点不平等。这个时期,普遍的贫穷造就了普遍的平等。无论是年龄的优越还是个人品质的优越都是权威和服从的薄弱基础,然而也是唯一的基础。因此,这个社会时期几乎没有或者就没有权威和顺从。社会第二个时期,即游牧民族时期,社会财产出现极大的不平等。在这个时期,财产的优越给予拥有财产的人极大的权威,这一点其他社会时期都难以比拟。因而这个时期也是权威和服从达到极致的时期。阿拉伯酋长的权威非常大,鞑靼可汗的权威完全是专制的。

第四个原因或条件是出身的权威。出身的优越,是以祖上的家族财产的优越为前提的。所有的家族,都是古老的。皇子的祖先,虽然更为出名,但其数目却不及乞丐的祖先多。家族的古老在任何地方都意味着祖上曾家财万贯,或者以财富为基础的或与之相伴的赫赫声势。无论在何处,暴发户名气虽大,但总不及显

(4)出身的优越。

accompanied with it. Upstart greatness is every where less respected than ancient greatness. ① The hatred of usurpers, the love of the family of an ancient monarch, are, in a great measure, founded upon the contempt which men naturally have for the former, and upon their veneration for the latter. As a military officer submits without reluctance to the authority of a superior by whom he has always been commanded, but cannot bear that his inferior should be set over his head; so men easily submit to a family to whom they and their ancestors have always submitted; but are fired with indignation when another family, in whom they had never acknowledged any such superiority, assumes a dominion over them.

<small>The distinction of birth is not present among hunters,</small>

The distinction of birth, being subsequent to the inequality of fortune, can have no place in nations of hunters, among whom all men, being equal in fortune, must likewise be very nearly equal in birth. The son of a wise and brave man may, indeed, even among them, be somewhat more respected than a man of equal merit who has the misfortune to be the son of a fool or a coward. The difference, however, will not be very great; and there never was, I believe, a great family in the world whose illustration was entirely derived from the inheritance of wisdom and virtue.

<small>but always among shepherds.</small>

The distinction of birth not only may, but always does take place among nations of shepherds. Such nations are always strangers to every sort of luxury, and great wealth can scarce ever be dissipated among them by improvident profusion. There are no nations accordingly who abound more in families revered and honoured on account of their descent from a long race of great and illustrious ancestors; because there are no nations among whom wealth is likely to continue longer in the same families.

<small>Distinctions of birth and fortune are both most powerful among shepherds.</small>

Birth and fortune are evidently the two circumstances which principally set one man above another. They are the two great sources of personal distinction, and are therefore the principal causes which naturally establish authority and subordination among men. Among nations of shepherds both those causes operate with their full force. The great shepherd or herdsman, respected on account of his great wealth, and of the great number of those who depend upon him for subsistence, and revered on account of the nobleness of his birth, and of the immemorial antiquity of his illustrious family, has a natural authority over all the inferior shepherds or herdsmen of his horde or clan. He can command the united force of a greater number of people

---

① [*Lectures*, p. 10.]

赫世家受人尊敬[①]。人们憎恨篡夺者，敬爱王孙贵戚，这在很大程度上基于对人们自然对前者的蔑视，对后者的崇拜。军官愿意服从一贯指挥他的上级，但却无法忍受下级军官爬到他的头上。同此道理，人们能坦然服从自己及自己的先人一贯服从的家族，可是，倘若另外一个从未得到他们认可的家族来支配他们，他们就会怒火中烧。

出身的差别在狩猎民族中是不存在的，

出身的差别，起因于财产的不平等。但在狩猎民族中，这点却不存在，因为那里人人财产平等，因而出身也算是平等的。假若该民族中有两人，一个是智慧勇敢者的儿子，另一个不幸生为愚蠢懦弱者的儿子，两人优点相同，前者稍微比后者更受人尊重。然而，差别不会很大。而且，我认为，世上也没有哪个显赫家族的名声完全得益于智慧德行。

但在游牧民族中则总有出身的差别。

出身的差别，在游牧民族中，不但可能存在，而且的确一直是存在的。这样的民族因为一直没有接触过奢侈品，就不会去挥霍浪费巨额财富了。因此，这个民族的家族最多。这些家族的先人声势显赫，源远流长，惠及子孙受人尊重敬仰，因为没有哪个民族像游牧民族那样，财富会持久地保留在同一家族中。

出身和财产两者的区别在牧人中最有势力。

显而易见，出身和财产是使一个人高于另一个人的两个基本条件。他们是人与人之间差别的两大来源，因而也是在众人中自然树立权威和服从的主要根源。在游牧民族中，这两个原因起着充分的作用。大牧羊者因为财富庞大，有很多人靠他为生，所以受人尊重；又因出身高贵、家族古老显赫而受人敬仰。因而他在同部落或同族的下级牧羊者中自然享有权威。与其他任何人相

① 《关于法律、警察、岁入及军备的演讲》，第10页。

than any of them. His military power is greater than that of any of them. In time of war they are all of them naturally disposed to muster themselves under his banner, rather than under that of any other person, and his birth and fortune thus naturally procure to him some sort of executive power. By commanding too the united force of a greater number of people than any of them, he is best able to compel any one of them who may have injured another to compensate the wrong. He is the person, therefore, to whom all those who are too weak to defend themselves naturally look up for protection. It is to him that they naturally complain of the injuries which they imagine have been done to them, and his interposition in such cases is more easily submitted to, even by the person complained of, than that of any other person would be. His birth and fortune thus naturally procure him some sort of judicial authority.

<small>Among shepherds inequality of fortune arises and introduces civil government,</small> It is in the age of shepherds, in the second period of society, that the inequality of fortune first begins to take place, and introduces among men a degree of authority and subordination which could not possibly exist before. It thereby introduces some degree of that civil government which is indispensably necessary for its own preservation: and it seems to do this naturally, and even independent of the consideration of that necessity. The consideration of that necessity comes no doubt afterwards to contribute very much to maintain and secure that authority and subordination. The rich, in particular, are necessarily interested to support that order of things, which can alone secure them in the possession of their own advantages. Men of inferior wealth combine to defend those of superior wealth in the possession of their property, in order that men of superior wealth may combine to defend them in the possession of theirs. All the inferior shepherds and herdsmen feel that the security of their own herds and flocks depends upon the security of those of the great shepherd or herdsman; that the maintenance of their lesser authority depends upon that of his greater authority, and that upon their subordination to him depends his power of keeping their inferiors in subordination to them. They constitute a sort of little nobility, who feel themselves interested to defend the property and to support the authority of their own little sovereign, in order that he may be able to defend their property and to support their authority. Civil government, so far as it is instituted for the security of property, is in reality instituted for the defence of the rich

比,他都能指挥更多的人联合起来,而他的军事能力也是无人能比。在战时,人们自然愿意集结在他的旗帜下,而不愿受别人指挥。因而他的出身和财富自然使他获得了某种行政权力。因为只有他能够指挥更多人的联合力量,他们中间若有人伤害他人,他就最有能力强迫那人做出赔偿。因此,他就是弱者无法自保时自然仰仗的人。无论何人认为受到了伤害,都会自然地向他申诉,在这种情况下,他的干预最能让人折服,即使对受到控诉的人也是如此。他的出身和财富就这样自然地使他获得了某种司法权力了。

在游牧民族时期即社会的第二个时期,才出现了财产的不平等,继而出现了人类历史上从未存在的某种权威和服从。自此引进了某种程度的民法政府,这是维护权威和服从所必不可少的。似乎很自然就这样做,甚至也没有考虑到这么做的必要性。毋庸置疑,对必要性的考虑后来的确大大有助于维持和保护那种权威和服从。特别是富人,必然赞成维护那种制度。只有这种制度,才能保障他们的既得利益。财富较少者联合起来,保护财富较多者的财产,如此,财富较多者才会联合起来保护财富较少者的财产。所有财富较少的牧人都感到自己牛羊的安全都取决于那个大牧羊者牛羊的安全,自己权力的维护取决于他的大权利的维护,自己管制下属的权力取决于自己对他的服从。这些财富较少的牧人就构成了某种小贵族。他们乐于保障小君主的财产,支持小君主的权力。他们感到,只有这样,小君主才会保障自己的财产,支持自己的权力。民法政府,只要是为保护财产而成立的,实际上是为了保护富人防备穷人,或者说是保护有财产的人防备没

> 游牧民族时期,出现了财产的不平等,继而出现了民法政府,

国民财富的性质与原理

against the poor, or of those who have some property against those who have none at all. ①

but the judicial authority was long a source of revenue rather than expense, The judicial authority of such a sovereign, however, far from being a cause of expence, was for a long time a source of revenue to him. The persons who applied to him for justice were always willing to pay for it, and a present never failed to accompany a petition. After the authority of the sovereign too was thoroughly established, the person found guilty, over and above the satisfaction which he was obliged to make to the party, was likewise forced to pay an amercement to the sovereign. He had given trouble, he had disturbed, he had broke the peace of his lord the king, and for those offences an amercement was thought due. In the Tartar governments of Asia, in the governments of Europe which were founded by the German and Scythian nations who overturned the Roman empire, the administration of justice was a considerable source of revenue, both to the sovereign, and to all the lesser chiefs or lords who exercised under him any particular jurisdiction, either over some particular tribe or clan, or over some particular territory or district. Originally both the sovereign and the inferior chiefs used to exercise this jurisdiction in their own persons. Afterwards they universally found it convenient to delegate it to some substitute, bailiff, or judge. This substitute, however, was still obliged to account to his principal or constituent for the profits of the jurisdicdiction. Whoever reads the instructions ② which were given to the judges of the circuit in the time of Henry Ⅱ. will see clearly that those judges were a sort of itinerant factors, sent round the country for the purpose of levying certain branches of the king's revenue. In those days the administration of justice, not only afforded a certain revenue to the sovereign, but to procure this revenue seems to have been one of the principal advantages which he proposed to obtain by the administration of justice.

which produced great abuses, This scheme of making the administration of justice subservient to the purposes of revenue, could scarce fail to be productive of several very gross abuses. The person, who applied for justice with a large present in his hand, was likely to get something more than justice; while he, who applied for it with a small one, was likely to get something less. Justice too might frequently be delayed, in order that this present might be repeated. The amercement, besides, of the person

---

① [*Lectures*, p. 15: Cp. Locke, *Civil Government*, § 94, 'government has no other end but the preservation of property'.]

② They are to be found in Tyrrel's History of England. [*General History of England, both Ecclesiastical and Civil*, by James Tyrrell, vol. ii. , 1700, pp. 576-579. The king is Richard I. , not Henry Ⅱ.]

第五篇 第一章

有财产的人①。

可是,这样一个君主的司法权力,根本没有花费他的任何费用,反而长期成为他的收入来源。凡向他申诉的人都乐意给他报酬,诉状递上时总免不了有份礼物。在君主的权威完全树立以后,被判有罪之人除向对方赔偿损失以外,还得被迫向君主缴纳罚金。因为他闯了祸,搅乱了秩序,破坏了君主的安宁,施以罚款是罪有应得。在亚洲的鞑靼政府,在颠覆了罗马帝国后日耳曼民族和西斯亚民族所成立的欧洲各政府,无论是对君主来说,还是对在君主统治下的某个部落、宗族或领地、地区行使专门权力的酋长或领主来说,司法行政都是巨大的收入来源。起初,无论是君主还是下面的酋长都是亲自行使司法权力。后来,他们都发觉,把权利委托给代理人、执行官或法官行使,会很方便。不过,代理人仍有义务向君主或委托人汇报司法利润收支。凡是读过亨利二世给巡回法官训令的人都会明白②,法官不过是巡回代理人,派往全国各地征收某些部门的国王税收。当时,司法行政不但向君主提供一定的收入,而且获得这笔收入似乎还是他提议通过司法行政得到的一个主要好处。

当司法权力长期以来是收入来源而不是支出原因

司法行政目的是为了敛财,这种做法,不免会产生种种严重的弊端。申诉者若送上重礼,可能得到的不止是公道;申诉者若送上薄礼,可能所得不算公道。法官也往往会延缓判决,以便有人一再送礼。此外,对被告的罚款常常表明,法官会找出充足的

这产生了巨大的弊端,

---

① 《关于法律、警察、岁入及军备的演讲》,第 15 页。比较洛克《文官政府》,第 94 节,"政府没有其他目的,只是为了保持财产"。
② 这些训令见詹姆斯·蒂勒尔《英国通史,教会史和普通史》,第 2 卷,1700 年,第 576～579 页。国王是查理一世,而不是亨利二世。

complained of, might frequently suggest a very strong reason for finding him in the wrong, even when he had not really been so. That such abuses were far from being uncommon, the ancient history of every country in Europe bears witness.

<small>whether the sovereign exercised the judicial authority in person or by deputy.</small> When the sovereign or chief exercised his judicial authority in his own person, how much soever he might abuse it, it must have been scarce possible to get any redress; because there could seldom be any body powerful enough to call him to account. When he exercised it by a bailiff, indeed, redress might sometimes be had. If it was for his own benefit only, that the bailiff had been guilty of any act of injustice, the sovereign himself might not always be unwilling to punish him, or to oblige him to repair the wrong. But if it was for the benefit of his sovereign, if it was in order to make court to the person who appointed him and who might prefer him, that he had committed any act of oppression, redress would upon most occasions be as impossible as if the sovereign had committed it himself. In all barbarous governments, accordingly, in all those ancient governments of Europe in particular, which were founded upon the ruins of the Roman empire, the administration of justice appears for a long time to have been extremely corrupt; far from being quite equal and impartial even under the best monarchs, and altogether profligate under the worst.

<small>These abuses could not be remedied so long as the sovereign depended only on land revenue and court fees,</small> Among nations of shepherds, where the sovereign or chief is only the greatest shepherd or herdsman of the horde or clan, he is maintained in the same manner as any of his vassals or subjects, by the increase of his own herds or flocks. Among those nations of husbandmen who are but just come out of the shepherd state, and who are not much advanced beyond that state; such as the Greek tribes appear to have been about the time of the Trojan war, and our German and Scythian ancestors when they first settled upon the ruins of the western empire; the sovereign or chief is, in the same manner, only the greatest landlord of the country, and is maintained, in the same manner as any other landlord, by a revenue derived from his own private estate, or from what, in modern Europe, was called the demesne of the crown. His subjects, upon ordinary occasions, contribute nothing to his support, except when, in order to protect them from the oppression of some of their fellow-subjects, they stand in need of his authority. The presents which they make him upon such occasions, constitute the whole ordinary revenue, the whole of the emoluments which, except perhaps upon some very extraordinary emergencies, he derives from his dominion over them. When Agamemnon, in Homer, offers to

理由给实际无罪的人定罪。司法上的这些弊害都实在是司空见惯,不足为奇,欧洲各个国家的古代史都印证了这一事实。

当君主或酋长亲自行使司法权力时,无论他如何滥用职权,都无法矫正。因为没有任何人有权去责备他。当他委托代理人行使职权时,的确有时还可以矫正。代理人如果只是为了自身利益而执法不公,犯下罪行,那么君主也不见得就不乐意惩罚他,或强迫他改正错误。但代理人如果是为了君主的利益,或为了谄媚任命他宠爱他的人而压迫他人,犯下罪行,那么在大多数情况下,就像君主本人犯下罪行一样,不可能得到矫正。所以,在一切野蛮国家的政府,特别是建立在罗马帝国废墟上的古代欧洲政府,司法机构长期陷于极度的腐败状态;即使在最好君主的统治下,也根本没有什么平等、公正可言,而在最坏的君主统治下,简直就是无法无天。不论是君主亲自审判还是由代理人行使司法权,种种弊端都无法消除。

在游牧民族中,君主或酋长只不过是部落或宗族中最大的牧羊者或畜牧者。他像他的隶属和臣民一样靠牛羊的增殖为生。在农业民族中,农民只不过刚刚脱离游牧状态,进步不是很大,更没有超越他们所处的农耕状态,例如特洛伊战争时代出现的希腊各部落,以及初次定居在西罗马帝国废墟上的日耳曼人和塞西亚人的祖先。同样,君主或酋长也不过是国家最大的地主;他像其他地主那样,靠自己私有财产的收入为生,或者说是近代欧洲所谓的御用领地的收入。他的臣民,一般情况下不向他纳贡,除非为了保护自己免受其他同胞的压迫而需要他的权力。他们在这种情况下送给他的礼物,构成他的全部经常收入,除了某些特殊的紧急情况外,这就是他管辖他们所得的全部报酬。荷马史诗中讲到,阿伽门农,为了取得阿喀琉斯的友谊,向他赠送七个希腊城君主全土入司法费用,只要君主完全依赖地租收入就无法。

| 国民财富的性质与原理

Achilles for his friendship the sovereignty of seven Greek cities, the sole advantage which he mentions as likely to be derived from it, was, that the people would honour him with presents. ① As long as such presents, as long as the emoluments of justice, or what may be called the fees of court, constituted in this manner the whole ordinary revenue which the sovereign derived from his sovereignty, it could not well be expected, it could not even decently be proposed, that he should give them up altogether. It might, and it frequently was proposed, that he should regulate and ascertain them. But after they had been so regulated and ascertained, how to hinder a person who was all-powerful from extending them beyond those regulations, was still very difficult, not to say impossible. During the continuance of this state of things, therefore, the corruption of justice, naturally resulting from the arbitrary and uncertain nature of those presents, scarce admitted of any effectual remedy.

<small>but when taxes became necessary, the people stipulated that no presents should be taken by judges.</small>

But when from different causes, chiefly from the continually increasing expence of defending the nation against the invasion of other nations, the private estate of the sovereign had become altogether insufficient for defraying the expence of the sovereignty; and when it had become necessary that the people should, for their own security, contribute towards this expence by taxes of different kinds, it seems to have been very commonly stipulated, that no present for the administration of justice should, under any pretence, be accepted either by the sovereign, or by his bailiffs and substitutes, the judges. Those presents, it seems to have been supposed, could more easily be abolished altogether, than effectually regulated and ascertained. Fixed salaries were appointed to the judges, which were supposed to compensate to them the loss of whatever might have been their share of the ancient emoluments of justice; as the taxes more than compensated to the sovereign the loss of his. Justice was then said to be administered gratis.

<small>Justice is never administered gratis.</small>

Justice, however, never was in reality administered gratis in any country. Lawyers and attornies, at least, must always be paid by the parties; and, if they were not, they would perform their duty still worse than they actually perform it. The fees annually paid to lawyers

---

① [Iliad, ix., 149-156, but the presents are not the 'sole advantage' mentioned.]

市的主权,他提到阿喀琉斯从七个城市可能获得的唯一好处,就是人民奉献的礼物①。只要这种礼物,只要这种司法行政的报酬,或者所谓的司法手续费,是构成君主实施统治权所获得的全部经常收入,那就不能期望,也不能够光明正大地建议,他放弃全部收入。臣民建议他规范一下礼物,使之明确化是可以的,而且,臣民也经常这样提议过。但是,在规定、明确之后,要想防止一个具有无上权力的人超出其规定范围,即使不是说完全不可能,起码也是非常困难的。因此,这种状态继续进行下去的恶果,就是由任意的不确定的礼物自然引起的司法的腐败,是无法弥补了。

但是,出于种种原因,主要是为抵御外来侵略的国防费用在不断增加,君主的私有财产已经不够支付国家费用;而人民为了自身安全,必须通过交纳各种税收来填补这笔费用,这时,似乎才普遍规定,在执行司法行政时,无论是君主还是执行官、代理人及法官都不得以任何借口接受礼物。似乎这样看来,完全废止礼物要比做出有效的规定使之明确更容易一些。法官领取固定的薪俸,用以弥补昔日享有的司法报酬的损失。税收的费用远远超过了君主统治费,同样,弥补法官的损失也是绰绰有余。就这样,司法被说成是免费的了。^{但当纳税时,人民规定法官不得接受礼物。}

可是,实际上,司法的执行在任何国家都不是免费的。至少律师或辩护律师的费用一般必须由被告支付。否则,他们履行起职责要比实际情况糟糕。在每场法庭上,付给律师或辩护律师的年平均费用,要远远高于法官的薪俸。国王每年付给法官薪俸,^{审判从来都不是免费的。司法。}

---

① 《伊利亚特》,第 4 卷,第 149~156 页,但礼物并不是上面所说的"唯一好处"。

and attornies amount, in every court, to a much greater sum than the salaries of the judges. The circumstance of those salaries being paid by the crown, can no-where much diminish the necessary expence of a law-suit. But it was not so much to diminish the expence, as to prevent the corruption of justice, that the judges were prohibited from receiving any present or fee from the parties.

The salaries of judges are a small part of the expense of civilised government, The office of judge is in itself so very honourable, that men are willing to accept of it, though accompanied with very small emoluments. The inferior office of justice of peace, though attended with a good deal of trouble, and in most cases with no emoluments at all, is an object of ambition to the greater part of our country gentlemen. The salaries of all the different judges, high and low, together with the whole expence of the administration and execution of justice, even where it is not managed with very good economy, makes, in any civilized country, but a very inconsiderable part of the whole expence of government.

and might be defrayed by fees of court. The whole expence of justice too might easily be defrayed by the fees of court; and, without exposing the administration of justice to any real hazard of corruption, the public revenue might thus be entirely discharged from a certain, though, perhaps, but a small incumbrance. It is difficult to regulate the fees of court effectually, where a person so powerful as the sovereign is to share in them, and to derive any considerable part of his revenue from them. It is very easy, where the judge is the principal person who can reap any benefit from them. The law can very easily oblige the judge to respect the regulation, though it might not always be able to make the sovereign respect it. Where the fees of court are precisely regulated and ascertained, where they are paid all at once, at a certain period of every process, into the hands of a cashier or receiver, to be by him distributed in certain known proportions among the different judges after the process is decided, and not till it is decided, there seems to be no more danger of corruption than where such fees are prohibited altogether. Those fees, without occasioning any considerable increase in the expence of a law-suit, might be rendered fully sufficient for defraying the whole expence of justice. By not being paid to the judges till the process was determined, they might be some incitement to the diligence of the court in examining and deciding it. In courts which consisted of a considerable number of judges, by proportioning the share of each judge to the number of hours and days which he had employed in examining the process, either in the court or in a committee by order of the court, those fees might give some encouragement to the diligence of each particular judge. Public services are never better performed than when their reward comes only in consequence of their

这也根本没有减少诉讼的必要费用。但是禁止法官收受诉讼双方的礼物或费用,与其说是为了减少司法费用,不如说是为了防止司法腐败。

法官是个光荣的职业,薪俸虽少,人们还是乐意去干。职位低下的治安法官,虽然要处理种种麻烦,而且大都没有薪俸,可还是成为国家大部分乡绅的梦想。所有大小法官的费用,无论高低如何,加起来,连同司法审判及执行费用,即使在经济不宽余的地方,在任何文明国家,都只占整个国民费用的一小部分。

_{法官薪俸只占政府支出的一小部分,}

全部司法经费也可用法院手续费来轻松解决。这样,司法行政就不会陷于任何真正的腐败危险,公共收入就可省去一定的负担、或许不过是很小的一笔费用。倘若像君主那样拥有至高无上权力的人插手进来,捞得一大笔收入,就很难再有效规范司法行政收费制度。但如果司法行政收费的主要受益人是法官时,那就容易得多。法律无法使君主遵守规定,但却可以很容易使法官遵从。司法手续费制度在精确规定和明确之后,规定在每个诉讼过程的某个时期,全部付清费用,交到出纳或收款人手中,待诉讼结束后而不是诉讼结束前,由出纳或收款人按照规定的比例分发到各个法官手中。这种制度,和完全废除司法收费制度相比,似乎没有腐败的危险。这些手续费,没有引起诉讼费用大量增加,但却可以足够支付全部司法费用。法官判决完案件之后才能拿到手续费,那么手续费就会激励法院工作人员用心审理及判决。在有众多法官的法院,可以根据每个法官在法院或审判委员会审理案件所花的时数及天数来分配手续费的份额,这些费用可以起到激励每个专门法官用心办案的作用。公共服务工作办好后才发报酬,而且根据他们办案的辛勤程度分配报酬,这样才可以办好

_{可以用手续费支付司法费用。}

being performed, and is proportioned to the diligence employed in performing them. In the different parliaments of France, the fees of court (called Epicès and vacations) constitute the far greater part of the emoluments of the judges. After all deductions are made, the neat salary paid by the crown to a counsel or or judge in the parliament of Toulouse, in rank and dignity the second parliament of the kingdom, amounts only to a hundred and fifty livres, about six pounds eleven shillings sterling a year. About seven years ago ① that sum was in the same place the ordinary yearly wages of a common footman. The distribution of those Epicès too is according to the diligence of the judges. A diligent judge gains a comfortable, though moderate, revenue by his office: An idle one gets little more than his salary. Those parliaments are perhaps, in many respects, not very convenient courts of justice; but they have never been accused; they seem never even to have been suspected of corruption.

<small>The English courts were originally maintained by fees, and this led to their encroachments.</small>   The fees of court seem originally to have been the principal support of the different courts of justice in England. Each court endeavoured to draw to itself as much business as it could, and was, upon that account, willing to take cognizance of many suits which were not originally intended to fall under its jurisdiction. The court of king's bench, instituted for the trial of criminal causes only, took cognizance of civil suits; the plaintiff pretending that the defendant, in not doing him justice, had been guilty of some trespass or misdemeanor. The court of exchequer, instituted for the levying of the king's revenue, and for enforcing the payment of such debts only as were due to the king, took cognizance of all other contract debts; the plaintiff alleging that he could not pay the king, because the defendant would not pay him. In consequence of such fictions it came, in many cases, to depend altogether upon the parties before what court they would chuse to have their cause tried; and each court endeavoured, by superior dispatch and impartiality, to draw to itself as many causes as it could. The present admirable constitution of the courts of justice in England was, perhaps, originally in a great measure, formed by this emulation,

---

① [Smith was in Toulouse from February or March, 1764, to August, 1765. Rae, *Life of Adam Smith*, pp. 174、175、188.]

案件。在法国各个法院,手续费(称为 epicès① 和 vacation)成为法官绝大部分的报酬。法国图卢兹[1]法院是全国第二大法院。根据等级和权限,在减去一切扣除之后,国王发给那里的法律顾问或法官的净薪俸,只有 150 里弗,约合 6 英镑 11 先令。在当地大约七年前,这个数额等于一个普通仆役的一般年工资。这些手续费,也是按法官的辛勤程度分配的。勤奋的法官,虽然收入充裕,也只能算是中等收入;懒惰的法官仅仅拿到自己的薪俸收入。从各方面来讲,这些法院执法差强人意,但却从没遭到过控诉,似乎没有人怀疑他们会贪污腐败。

英国各法院的主要费用,最初似乎也是来自法院手续费。各个法院都竭力兜揽案子,这样,原本不属于自己审理的案件也愿意办理。最高法院,原本只能审理刑事案件,后来也接手民事案件。例如,原告原认定被告对他不公,犯有过失罪或轻罪,高等法院也就接手过来了。财务法庭,原本是为了征收国王收入和强制人民偿清对于国王的债务的而设立的,后来也接手所有其他合同债务案件。例如,原告声称,自己无法偿还国王收入,是因为被告不还钱,法院就以此受理。由于以上种种托词,在大多数情况下,全凭当事人自己决定案件在哪个法庭审理。而且每个法庭都尽力招揽更多的案件,审理也力求快速、公正。现在,英国的法院体制备受人们推崇,或许很大程度上在于昔日法官之间的相互竞

<small>英国的法庭最初是靠手续费来维持的,这导致了越权行为。</small>

---

① 斯密从 1764 年的 2 月或 3 月到 1765 年的 8 月在图卢兹。参见雷《亚当·斯密的生平》,第 174、175、188 页。

[1] 图卢兹:法国南部一城市,位于加龙河沿岸,波尔多东南。最初为罗马高卢地区的一部分。它是西哥特王国(419~507)及阿基但卡洛林王朝(781~843)的首都,图卢兹是中世纪欧洲的一文化中心。

which anciently took place between their respective judges; each judge endeavouring to give, in his own court, the speediest and most effectual remedy, which the law would admit, for every sort of injustice. Originally the courts of law gave damages only for breach of contract. The court of chancery, as a court of conscience, first took upon it to enforce the specific performance of agreements. When the breach of contract consisted in the non-payment of money, the damage sustained could be compensated in no other way than by ordering payment, which was equivalent to a specific performance of the agreement. In such cases, therefore, the remedy of the courts of law was sufficient. It was not so in others. When the tenant sued his lord for having unjustly outed him of his lease, the damages which he recovered were by no means equivalent to the possession of the land. Such causes, therefore, for some time, went all to the court of chancery, to the no small loss of the courts of law. It was to draw back such causes to themselves that the courts of law are said to have invented the artificial and fictitious writ of ejectment, the most effectual remedy for an unjust outer or dispossession of land. ①

Courts might be maintained by a stamp duty on proceedings before them, but this would tempt them to multiply such proceedings.

A stamp-duty upon the law proceedings of each particular court, to be levied by that court, and applied towards the maintenance of the judges and other officers belonging to it, might, in the same manner, afford a revenue sufficient for defraying the expence of the administration of justice, without bringing any burden upon the general revenue of the society. The judges indeed might, in this case, be under the temptation of multiplying unnecessarily the proceedings upon every cause, in order to increase, as much as possible, the produce of such a stamp-duty. It has been the custom in modern Europe to regulate, upon most occasions, the payment of the attornies and clerks of court, according to the number of pages which they had occasion to write; the court, however, requiring that each page should contain so many lines, and each line so many words. In order to increase their payment, the attornies and clerks have contrived to multiply words beyond all necessity, to the corruption of the law language of, I believe, every court of justice in Europe. A like temptation might perhaps occasion a like corruption in the form of law proceedings.

But whether the administration of justice be so contrived as to defray its own expence, or whether the judges be maintained by fixed salaries paid to them from some other fund, it does not

---

① [*Lectures*, p. 49.]

争。对各种不公正行为,法官都尽力在自己的法庭上在法律许可的范围给予最快速、最有效的补救。起初,只有违反了合约,一般法庭才会判决付赔偿金。大法官法庭,作为良心惩戒法庭,首先接管合约的具体强制履行。当违反合约在于不偿还货币时,对遭受到的损失,唯一的办法就是命令其赔偿。这和专门履行合约无异。因此,在这种情况下,法院的补救已经足够了。但在其他情况下则不够。当承租人控告地主非法取消租约时,他所受的损失绝不等于占有土地。因此,这样的案件曾一度属于大法官法庭审理,使一般法庭损失不小。据说,一般法庭为了拉回这样的案例,就编造了虚假的土地驱逐文书,这对于不正当地剥夺土地及侵占土地的事件,是最有效的补救办法①。

各个专门法庭对诉讼程序征收印花税,用以维持该法院法官及其他人员,同样,这笔收入也足够支付全部司法行政费用,而不会给社会一般收入造成任何负担。当然,在这种情况下,法官会在各个案件上增加不必要的诉讼程序,以尽量增加印花税的。在近代欧洲,在大多数情况下,根据惯例辩护律师和法庭文书的报酬是按照他们书写的页码来计算的。可是,法庭要求每页应当有多少行,每行又有多少字。于是,辩护律师和法院文书为了增加报酬就不遗余力地增加毫无必要的字句。我认为,欧洲每个法院的法律语言都是些陈词滥调。同样,诉讼程序形式也许因为诱惑而渐渐成为陈规陋习。

但是,无论是由司法行政费用自行支付开支,还是由某个其他基金支付法官的定额薪俸,都没有必要让具有行政权力的人来

法庭可靠诉讼程序的印花税来维持,但可能使他们增加诉讼程序。

---

① 《关于法律、警察、岁入及军备的演讲》,第49页。

<small>Another way of securing independence would be to endow the courts with a revenue from property.</small>

seem necessary that the person or persons entrusted with the executive power should be charged with the management of that fund, or with the payment of those salaries. That fund might arise from the rent of landed estates, the management of each estate being entrusted to the particular court which was to be maintained by it. That fund might arise even from the interest of a sum of money, the lending out of which might, in the same manner, be entrusted to the court which was to be maintained by it. A part, though indeed but a small part, of the salary of the judges of the court of session in Scotland, arises from the interest of a sum of money. The necessary instability of such a fund seems, however, to render it an improper one for the maintenance of an institution which ought to last for ever.

<small>The separation of the judicial from the executive power is due to the increase of executive business.</small>

The separation of the judicial from the executive power seems originally to have arisen from the increasing business of the society, in consequence of its increasing improvement. The administration of justice became so laborious and so complicated a duty as to require the undivided attention of the persons to whom it was entrusted. The person entrusted with the executive power, not having leisure to attend to the decision of private causes himself, a deputy was appointed to decide them in his stead. In the progress of the Roman greatness, the consul was too much occupied with the political affairs of the state, to attend to the administration of justice. A prætor, therefore, was appointed to administer it in his stead. In the progress of the European monarchies which were founded upon the ruins of the Roman empire, the sovereigns and the great lords came universally to consider the administration of justice as an office, both too laborious and too ignoble for them to execute in their own persons. They universally, therefore, discharged themselves of it by appointing a deputy, bailiff, or judge.

<small>The judicial should be not only separate but independent of the executive power.</small>

When the judicial is united to the executive power, it is scarce possible that justice should not frequently be sacrificed to, what is vulgarly called, politics. The persons entrusted with the great interests of the state may, even without any corrupt views, sometimes imagine it necessary to sacrifice to those interests the rights of a private man. But upon the impartial administration of justice depends the liberty of every individual, the sense which he has of his own security. In order to make every individual feel himself perfectly secure in the possession of every right which belongs to him, it is not only necessary that the judicial should be separated from the executive power, but that it should be rendered as much as possible independent of that power. The judge should not be liable to be removed from his office according to the caprice of that power. The regular payment of his salary should not depend upon the good-will, or even upon the good œconomy of that power.

管理这个基金或支付法官的薪俸。这笔基金可能是来自地产的地租,每片地产都是由专门的法院管理,法院也以此维持生计。这笔基金甚至也可能是出自一笔金钱的利息,同样,贷款权力赋予法院,法院靠利息维持。苏格兰巡回法院法官的薪俸就有一部分,虽只不过一小部分,是来自一笔金钱的利息。但是,这样的基金必然不稳定,对于应当永久维持的机构来说,这似乎是不合适的。

<small>另外一个保证法庭独立的方法就是给予其财产收入。</small>

司法权力和行政权力的分离,似乎最初是社会的不断进步,继而是社会事务的增多的结果。司法行政工作很辛苦、复杂,于是,需要有人专心负责。专门从事行政工作的人,没有闲暇时间审理私人案件,就派遣代理人审理案件。在罗马帝国兴盛之时,大执政官因忙于政事,无法顾及司法行政,就任命裁判官来代行司法权力。后来,罗马帝国衰亡之后,随着各个君主国的建立发展,君主及大领主普遍把司法行政当作出力不讨好的职务,不愿意亲自处理。因此,他们通常摆脱这个包袱,任命代理人、执行官及法官来执行。

<small>司法权和行政权的分开是由于行政事务的增加。</small>

司法权和行政权捆绑在一起,司法公正要想不牺牲给世俗政治,那是不可能的。承担国家重大利益的人,即使没有腐败想法,有时也会认为,为了国家重大利益,必须牺牲个人权益。但是,每个人的自由及每个人的安全感都取决于司法行政能够不偏不倚。为了使每个人在享有属于自己的权力的同时感到绝对安全,司法权不但应与行政权分离,而且应尽可能独立于行政权力之外。法官不应由行政当局随意罢免,法官的一般薪俸也不应随行政当局的意向或经济政策的好坏而改变。

<small>司法权不仅应与行政权分开,还应该独立于行政权。</small>

Part III Of The Expence Of Public Works And Public Institutions

<small>The third duty of the sovereign is the erection and maintenance of those public works and institutions which are useful but not capable of bringing in a profit to individuals.</small>

  The third and last duty of the sovereign or commonwealth is that of erecting and maintaining those public institutions and those public works, which, though they may be in the highest degree advantageous to a great society, are, however, of such a nature, that the profit could never repay the expence to any individual or small number of individuals, and which it therefore cannot be expected that any individual or small number of individuals should erect or maintain. The performance of this duty requires too very different degrees of expence in the different periods of society.

<small>These are chiefly institutions for facilitating commerce and promoting instruction.</small>

  After the public institutions and public works necessary for the defence of the society, and for the administration of justice, both of which have already been mentioned, the other works and institutions of this kind are chiefly those for facilitating the commerce of the society, and those for promoting the instruction of the people. The institutions for instruction are of two kinds; those for the education of the youth, and those for the instruction of people of all ages. The consideration of the manner in which the expence of those different sorts of public wores and institutions may be most properly defrayed, will divide this third part of the present chapter into three different articles.

Article I Of The Public Works And Institutions For Facilitating The Commerce Of The Society And, First, Of Those Which Are Necessary For Facilitating Commerce In General

<small>The expense of such institutions increases.</small>

  That the erection and maintenance of the public works which facilitate the commerce of any country, such as good roads, bridges, navigable canals, harbours, &c. must require very different degrees of expence in the different periods of society, is evident without any proof. The expence of making and maintaining the public roads of any country must evidently increase with the annual produce of the land and labour of that country, or with the quantity and weight of the

第三节　论公共工程和公共机构的费用

君主或国家的第三个职责，也是最后一个职责，就是建立和维持公共机构和公共工程。这些公共机构和工程，虽然对大社会的益处最多，但就其性质来说，个人或少数人即使为其出资，所得利润也不能补偿他们所花费用，因此，不能期望个人或少数人会建立和维持公共机构或工程。社会时期不同，履行职责所需费用也大不相同。

> 君主的第三个职责，是建立和维持那些不能给个人带来利润的公共工程和机构。

以上提到社会防卫和司法行政，两者都需要公共机构和公共工程。除此以外，其他的主要是那些促进社会商业的运作及人民教育的公共机构和工程。人民教育的公共机构有两类：针对年轻人的教育机构和针对一切年龄的人的教育机构。关于以上不同种类的公共工程和公共机构所需费用该如何合理支付，我们将在本章的第三部分分为三个篇幅来论述。

> 这些机构主要是为了促进商业和教育。

第一项　论推动社会商业的公共工程和公共机构

推动一般商业活动所必需的公共工程和公共机构

为促进商业发展，任何国家都要建立和维持公共工程，例如修建宽阔的公路、建造坚固的桥梁、开凿畅通的运河、建造良好的港湾，等等。在不同的时期，建造和维护这些工程所需费用也大不相同，这点自不待言。显而易见，任何国家修建、保养公路所需费用，都会随着该国土地及劳动的年产物的增加而增加，或者说随

> 这些机构的支出在增加。

国民财富的性质与原理

goods which it becomes necessary to fetch and carry upon those roads. The strength of a bridge must be suited to the number and weight of the carriages, which are likely to pass over it. The depth and the supply of water for a navigable canal must be proportioned to the number and tunnage of the lighters, which are likely to carry goods upon it; the extent of a harbour to the number of the shipping which are likely to take shelter in it.

<small>The expense need not be defrayed from the general public revenue,</small>

It does not seem necessary that the expence of those public works should be defrayed from that public revenue, as it is commonly called, of which the collection and application are in most countries assigned to the executive power. The greater part of such public works may easily be so managed, as to afford a particular revenue sufficient for defraying their own expence, without bringing any burden upon the general revenue of the society.

<small>but may be raised by tolls and other particular charges.</small>

A highway, a bridge, a navigable canal, for example, may in most cases be both made and maintained by a small toll upon the carriages which make use of them: a harbour, by a moderate port-duty upon the tunnage of the shipping which load or unload in it. The coinage, another institution for facilitating commerce, in many countries, not only defrays its own expence, but affords a small revenue or seignorage to the sovereign. The post-office, another institution for the same purpose, over and above defraying its own expence, affords in almost all countries a very considerable revenue to the sovereign.

<small>Tolls according to weight of carriages and capacity of boats are very equitable.</small>

When the carriages which pass over a highway or a bridge, and the lighters which sail upon a navigable canal, pay toll in proportion to their weight or their tunnage, they pay for the maintenance of those public works exactly in proportion to the wear and tear which they occasion of them. It seems scarce possible to invent a more equitable way of maintaining such works. This tax or toll too, though it is advanced by the carrier, is finally paid by the consumer, to whom it must always be charged in the price of the goods. As the expence of carriage, however, is very much reduced by means of such public works, the goods, notwithstanding the toll, come cheaper to the consumer than they could otherwise have done; their price not being so much raised by the toll, as it is lowered by the cheapness of the carriage. The person who final-

第五篇 第一章

着公路上运输的货物的数量和重量的增加而增加。桥梁的坚固程度一定要能够承载可能通过它的车辆的数量和重量。运河的深度及水量,一定要和在河上运载货物的船舶的数目和吨位成比例。港湾的大小要和可能停泊的船只成比例。

这部分公共工程的费用,似乎不必从所谓的公共收入中支出。许多国家都把公共收入的征收和使用指派给行政当局负责。大部分此类工程都这样管理,使之可以提供足够的专门收入来支付自己的费用,而无须对社会一般收入增加任何负担。

> 这种支出并不需要由公共收入一般支出

例如,在大多数情况下,修建和维护公路、桥梁、运河的费用,都可出自对过往车辆、船舶所收的小额通行税;建造和维持港湾的费用,都可出在对装货、卸货船只所收的低额港口税。铸币厂也是便利商业的机构。在大多数国家,它不但能够开支自己的费用,而且能向君主提供一笔小收入或货币铸造税。邮局也是一个具有同样目的的机构。它除了支付自己的费用以外,还向君主提供一笔可观的收入,几乎每个国家都是如此。

> 但可以用通行税和其他特种税来支出。

当车辆通过公路或桥梁,船舶驶过运河或港口时,都要按照重量或吨数来缴纳通行税。他们支付的这些维持费,是严格按照使用该公共工程的损耗比例给出的。要维护这些公共工程,似乎再没有比这更公平的办法了。此外,税收或通行税虽然是由运送人预付的,但最终还是由消费者支付,因为税赋是加在消费者所购买货物的价格里了。然而,通过这样的公共工程,货物的运输费大大减少了;消费者买到手的货物,虽然含有通行税,却比在没有通过公共工程的时候便宜得多。通行税并没有使货物的价格抬高,因为使用公共工程时,运输费比以往降低了。因此,最终支付这笔税赋的人,由通行税所得的利益,大于他支付税赋所受

> 根据车辆重量和船舶吨位征收的赋税是非常公平的。

— 1509 —

ly pays this tax, therefore, gains by the application, more than he loses by the payment of it. His payment is exactly in proportion to his gain. It is in reality no more than a part of that gain which he is obliged to give up in order to get the rest. It seems impossible to imagine a more equitable method of raising a tax.

<small>If the tolls are higher on carriages of luxury, the rich contribute in an easy manner to the relief of the poor.</small>

When the toll upon carriages of luxury, upon coaches, post-chaises, &c. is made somewhat higher in proportion to their weight, than upon carriages of necessary use, such as carts, waggons, &c. the indolence and vanity of the rich is made to contribute in a very easy manner to the relief of the poor, by rendering cheaper the transportation of heavy goods to all the different parts of the country.

<small>Roads and canals, etc., thus paid for cannot be made except where they are wanted.</small>

When high roads, bridges, canals, &c. are in this manner made and supported by the commerce which is carried on by means of them, they can be made only where that commerce requires them, and consequently where it is proper to make them. Their expence too, their grandeur and magnificence, must be suited to what that commerce can afford to pay. They must be made consequently as it. is proper to make them. A magnificent high road cannot be made through a desert country where there is little or no commerce, or merely because it happens to lead to the country villa of the intendant of the province, or to that of some great lord to whom the intendant finds it convenient to make his court. A great bridge cannot be thrown over a river at a place where nobody passes, or merely to embellish the view from the windows of a neighbouring palace: things which sometimes happen, in countries where works of this kind are carried on by any other revenue than that which they themselves are capable of affording.

<small>Canals are better in the hands of private persons than of commissioners.</small>

In several different parts of Europe the toll or lock-duty upon a canal is the property of private persons, whose private interest obliges them to keep up the canal. If it is not kept in tolerable order, the navigation necessarily ceases altogether, and along with it the whole profit which they can make by the tolls. If those tolls were put under the management of commissioners, who had themselves no interest in them, they might be less attentive to the maintenance of the works which produced them. The canal of Languedoc cost the king of France and the province upwards of thirteen millions of livres, which (at twenty-eight livres the mark of silver, the value of French money in the end of the last century) amounted to upwards of nine hundred thousand pounds sterling. When that great work was finished, the most likely method, it was found, of keeping it in constant repair was to make a present of the tolls to Riquet the engineer, who planned and conducted the work. Those tolls constitute at present a very large

的损失。他的支出,恰恰和他所得的利益成比例,事实上,他必须放弃的只是一部分利益,这样才能得到其余的利益。征收税赋,再也没有比这更公平的方法了。

如果按照重量对奢侈车辆、四轮大马车、驿站马车征收的通行税略高于对必要用途车辆如二轮运货马车、四轮运货马车等征收的通行税,那么就会降低运往全国各地的笨重货物的运输费,而懒惰和虚荣的富人就会很容易地为救助穷人做出贡献。

<small>对品输较通对奢侈运输较高的征运税,就可以这种方式救济穷人。如果对奢侈品的运输征收较高的通行税,富人可以这种方式救济穷人。</small>

如果由使用公路、桥梁、运河等等的商业来建造和维持它们,这些工程就只会建在商业需要的地方,因而在此地建造它们也是合适的。建造的费用及建筑物的富丽堂皇程度也要和商业能够提供的费用相称。因此,建造工程必须适度。宽广的马路不能建在很少或没有商业的荒凉村庄,也不能仅仅因为可以通到省长的乡村别墅或省长要巴结的某个大领主的别墅就建造。宏伟的桥梁不能架在无人过往的河上,或仅仅因为能增加邻近宫殿的窗外远眺景观而建。这样的事情的确时有发生,这类工程是由其他收入支付而不是工程自身能负担费用的国家建起的。

<small>是要地不一样的,除非在需要的地方,否则支付公路和运河是不会建设的。</small>

欧洲几个地方的运河通行税或水闸通行税是私人财产,个人利益促使他们维护运河。如若不能维持运河正常通行,航运必然停止,征收通行税所得的一切利润也就荡然无存。如果运河的通行税交给那些利益毫不相干的委员管理,那么他们就会不大关心产生通行税的工程的维持。法国兰格多克运河的开凿,花费了国王及该省 1300 万里弗,这(上世纪末法币 28 里弗等于 1 马克白银)合 90 多万英镑。这个大工程竣工时,人们发现,不断维修运河保持运河畅通的最好方法,就是把通行税赠予工程师里格,是他设计并监督了这项工程。现在,通行税已成为里格的子

<small>运河在私人手中比在管理员手中要好。</small>

estate to the different branches of the family of that gentleman, who have, therefore, a great interest to keep the work in constant repair. But had those tolls been put under the management of commissioners, who had no such interest, they might perhaps have been dissipated in ornamental and unnecessary expences, while the most essential parts of the work were allowed to go to ruin.

<small>But tolls on a high road cannot safely be made private property and must be committed to trustees.</small>

The tolls for the maintenance of a high road, cannot with any safety be made the property of private persons. A high road, though entirely neglected, does not become altogether impassable, though a canal does. The proprietors of the tolls upon a high road, therefore, might neglect altogether the repair of the road, and yet continue to levy very nearly the same tolls. It is proper, therefore, that the tolls for the maintenance of such work should be put under the management of commissioners or trustees.

In Great Britain, the abuses which the trustees have committed in the management of those tolls, have in many cases been very justly complained of. At many turnpikes, it has been said, the money lev-

<small>The prevalence of complaints against British turnpike tolls is not remarkable.</small>

ied is more than double of what is necessary for executing, in the completest manner, the work which is often executed in a very slovenly manner, and sometimes not executed at all. The system of repairing the high roads by tolls of this kind, it must be observed, is not of very long standing. We should not wonder, therefore, if it has not yet been brought to that degree of perfection of which it seems capable. If mean and improper persons are frequently appointed trustees; and if proper courts of inspection and account have not yet been established for controlling their conduct, and for reducing the tolls to what is barely sufficient for executing the work to be done by them; the recency of the institution both accounts and apologizes for those defects, of which, by the wisdom of parliament, the greater part may in due time be gradually remedied.

<small>It has been proposed that the government should manage the turnpikes and make a revenue from them.</small>

The money levied at the different turnpikes in Great Britain is supposed to exceed so much what is necessary for repairing the roads, that the savings, which, with proper economy, might be made from it, have been considered, even by some ministers, as a very great resource which might at some time or another be applied to the exigencies of the state. Government, it has been said, by taking the management of the turnpikes into its own hands, and by employing the soldiers, who would work for a very small addition to their pay, could keep the roads in good order at a much less expence than it can be done by trustees, who have no other workmen to employ, but such as

孙后代的一大笔财产,因此,他们对运河不断维修以及保持运河畅通无阻抱有极大的兴趣。倘若当时把通行税交由利益毫不相干的委员管理,那么税收就会浪费在装饰及毫无必要的花销上,工程的最主要部分也会任其毁掉。

维护公路的通行税却不能随便成为个人财产。运河不加疏通就无法通行,但公路则不然,即使完全不管,也不会完全无法通行。因此,征收公路通行税的人可能会不修理路面,马路仍然可以通行,他们却继续征收相同的税收。所以,维护这类工程的通行税,应当交由委员或托管员管理,这样才算合适。

> 公路税安作为私人财产,必须交给委员管理。但通行税不能不加地为财产,而要托管。

在英国,托管员管理通行税的弊端多多,人们对此时有怨言,而人们的怨言也是很中肯的。据说,许多收税公路征收的通行税往往是修理这些公路必须费用的两倍多,而公路却往往马马虎虎地修理了事,有时根本就不修理。应当注意到,用通行税来修理公路的制度,还不算长久。因此,这种制度似乎尚未达到完善的程度,也就不足为奇了。如果常常任命居心叵测、难担此任的人为托管员,并且尚未建立公正的监督机构来约束其行为,并将通行税减少到恰好足够修理路面的额度,那么这个制度存在的缺陷就只能从建立时间不久上得到解释。相信不久,议会自会采取明知之举,绝大部分缺陷也将会得到矫正。

> 对英国通行税的指责是值得注意的。

英国收税公路所收的通行税应当远远超过了修理马路所需的费用。甚至有些大臣也认为,多余款项倘若适当节约,可成为一项巨额费用,用作急需情况救助金。据说,政府管理收税马路的费用要远远少于用托管员管理的费用,因为政府可以雇佣士兵,士兵有自己的收入,为政府干活只拿小额报酬;而托管员所雇佣的是工人,工资则为他们的全部生活来源。有人主张,可以如

> 有人建议政府应该管理收税公路并从中获得收入。

derive their whole subsistence from their wages. A great revenue, half a million, perhaps, ① it has been pretended, might in this manner be gained without laying any new burden upon the people; and the turnpike roads might be made to contribute to the general expence of the state, in the same manner as the post-office does at present.

<small>This plan is open to the following objections:</small>

That a considerable revenue might be gained in this manner, I have no doubt, though probably not near so much, as the projectors of this plan have supposed. The plan itself, however, seems liable to several very important objections.

First, if the tolls which are levied at the turnpikes should ever be considered as one of the resources for supplying the exigencies of the state, they would certainly be augmented as those exigencies were

<small>(1) the tolls would be raised and become a great encumbrance to commerce,</small>

supposed to require. According to the policy of Great Britain, therefore, they would probably be augmented very fast. The facility with which a great revenue could be drawn from them, would probably encourage administration to recur very frequently to this resource. Though it may, perhaps, be more than doubtful, whether half a million could by any œconomy be saved out of the present tolls, it can scarce be doubted but that a million might be saved out of them, if they were doubled; and perhaps two millions, if they were tripled. ② This great revenue too might be levied without the appointment of a single new officer to collect and receive it. But the turnpike tolls being continually augmented in this manner, instead of facilitating the inland commerce of the country, as at present, would soon become a very great incumbrance upon it. The expence of transporting all heavy goods from one part of the country to another would soon be so much increased, the market for all such goods, consequently, would soon be so much narrowed, that their production would be in a great measure discouraged, and the most important branches of the domestic industry of the country annihilated altogether.

Secondly, a tax upon carriages in proportion to their weight, though a very equal tax when applied to the sole purpose of repairing the roads, is a very unequal one, when applied to any other

---

① Since publishing the two first editions of this book, I have got good reasons to believe that all the turnpike tolls levied in Great Britain do not produce a neat revenue that amounts to half a million; a sum which, under the management of Government, would not be sufficient to keep in repair five of the principal roads in the kingdom. [This and the next note appear first in ed. 3.]

② I have now good reasons to believe that all these conjectural sums are by much too large.

上述那样获得这笔或许有 50 万英镑的大收入①,而无须给人民增加新负担。正如现在的邮局那样,收税马路也可促进国家一般费用。

我毫不怀疑,这样可以得到一笔可观收入,虽不如提出计划的人所预测的那么多。但是,这个计划本身似乎应有几个重大缺陷。对这个有以下反对理由:

第一,在收费公路上征收的通行税当作供应突发事件需求的资金来源,那么紧急情况需要时,通行税当然就得随之增加。因此,根据英国的政策,通行税或许会迅速增加。巨额收入可轻易获得,就势必会鼓励政府频繁向这笔资金伸手。至于能否从现在的通行税中节约出 50 万英镑,这十分令人怀疑;但若是加倍征收通行税,那么从中省出 100 万英镑,倒是毫不令人怀疑,倘若加三倍,没准还能省出 200 万英镑呢②。而且,征收这笔巨额收入无需任命新收税官。但是,通行税如果这样不断增加下去,而不是像现在这样便利国内商业,那么通行税很快就会成为商业的累赘。笨重货物从国内一个地方运往另一个地方所需的运输费很快就会增加,结果,这些货物的市场会急剧萎缩,货物的生产也会大大受挫,那么国内最重要的产业部门就会彻底毁灭。(1)这样征收通行税将会大大阻碍商业,

第二,按照重量对车辆征收的通行税,其唯一目的若是修理道路,那么征收税收是极其公平的;但若是为了其他目的,或者是

---

① 自从本书的前两版出版以来,我已经有充足的理由相信,在大不列颠征收的全部通行税并不能产生 50 万镑的净收入;在政府管理下,这个总额并不足以维修王国的五条主要公路。本脚注和下一个脚注首见于第三版。

② 现在我有充足的理由相信所有这些推测的数额都有点太大了。

| 国民财富的性质与原理

(2) a tax on carriages in proportion to weight falls principally on the poor,

purpose, or to supply the common exigencies of the state. When it is applied to the sole purpose above mentioned, each carriage is supposed to pay exactly for the wear and tear which that carriage occasions of the roads. But when it is applied to any other purpose, each carriage is supposed to pay for more than that wear and tear, and contributes to the supply of some other exigency of the state. But as the turnpike toll raises the price of goods in proportion to their weight, and not to their value, it is chiefly paid by the consumers of coarse and bulky, not by those of precious and light commodities. Whatever exigency of the state therefore this tax might be intended to supply, that exigency would be chiefly supplied at the expence of the poor, not of the rich; at the expence of those who are least able to supply it, not of those who are most able.

and (3) the roads would be neglected.

Thirdly, if government should at any time neglect the reparation of the high roads, it would be still more difficult, than it is at present, to compel the proper application of any part of the turnpike tolls. A large revenue might thus be levied upon the people, without any part of it being applied to the only purpose to which a revenue levied in this manner ought ever to be applied. If the meanness and poverty of the trustees of turnpike roads render it sometimes difficult at present to oblige them to repair their wrong; their wealth and greatness would render it ten times more so in the case which is here supposed.

High roads are under the executive in France,

In France, the funds destined for the reparation of the high roads are under the immediate direction of the executive power. Those funds consist, partly in a certain number of days labour which the country people are in most parts of Europe obliged to give to the reparation of the highways; and partly in such a portion of the general revenue of the state as the king chuses to spare from his other expences.

and great post roads are generally good, but all the rest entirely neglected.

By the ancient law of France, as well as by that of most other parts of Europe, the labour of the country people was under the direction of a local or provincial magistracy, which had no immediate dependency upon the king's council. But by the present practice both the labour of the country people, and whatever other fund the king may chuse to assign for the reparation of the high roads in any particular province or generality, are entirely under the management of the intendant; an officer who is appointed and removed by the king's council, who receives his orders from it, and is in constant correspondence with it. In the progress of despotism the authority of the executive power gradually absorbs that of every other power in the

为了供应国家一般的急需,那么征收税收就是非常不公平的。如上所述,如果通行税的唯一目的是修理路面,每辆车就应是严格按照对路面的损耗付费。但如果赋税用于其他目的,每辆车所付费用会大于损耗费,即用于其他国家急需。但是,按照货物的重量而不是货物价值对车辆征收通行税,那么货物的价格就会提高;货物的主要消费者消费的是粗糙笨重的商品而不是贵重轻便的商品。因此,国家征收税收的意图无论是为了应付什么急需,费用却主要出在穷人身上,而不是富人身上;出在最没有能力供应的人身上,而不是最有能力供应的人身上。

(2) 对车辆按照重量征收的赋税将主要落在穷人身上。

第三,如果路面修理一直得不到政府重视,要想强制其正当使用一部分通行税来修理路面,那么就比现在困难得多。如此一来,政府就会对民众征收一大笔收入,但是,却不会把收入的任何部分用于其唯一应当适用的目的。如今,对于卑下贫穷的道路通行税托管员,有时要强迫其矫正错误,还是很困难的,那么要使有钱又有权势的人去矫正错误,恐怕就要难上十倍。

(3) 公路会得不到重视。

法国用于修理公路的基金是由行政当局直接管理的。基金的一部分,是法国大部分地方的村民为修理公路所必须提供的一定日数的劳动;另一部分则是国王从国家一般收入拨出的不用作其他费用的那一部分。

在法国,公路由行政当局管理,

根据法国以及欧洲大多数地方的古典法,地方行政长官或省级行政长官管理村民的劳动,他们不直接隶属于国王的枢密院。但按照现行做法,无论是村民的劳动还是国王在某特定省份或地方为修理公路所拨出的任何基金,都是由省长管理;而省长则由枢密院任命罢黜,接受枢密院的命令,并经常与枢密院保持联络。在专制政体演进过程中,行政当局逐渐吞并了国家任何其他行

而且大路一般是良好的,但其余的公路就完全被忽视了。

state, and assumes to itself the management of every branch of revenue which is destined for any public purpose. In France, however, the great post-roads, the roads which make the communication between the principal towns of the kingdom, are in general kept in good order; and in some provinces are even a good deal superior to the greater part of the turnpike roads of England. But what we call the cross-roads, that is, the far greater part of the roads in the country, are entirely neglected, and are in many places absolutely impassable for any heavy carriage. In some places it is even dangerous to travel on horseback, and mules are the only conveyance which can safely be trusted. The proud minister of an ostentatious court may frequently take pleasure in executing a work of splendour and magnificence, such as a great highway, which is frequently seen by the principal nobility, whose applauses not only flatter his vanity, but even contribute to support his interest at court. But to execute a great number of little works, in which nothing that can be done can make any great appearance, or excite the smallest degree of admiration in any traveller, and which, in short, have nothing to recommend them but their extreme utility, is a business which appears in every respect too mean and paultry to merit the attention of so great a magistrate. Under such an administration, therefore, such works are almost always entirely neglected.

The executive in China and other parts of Asia maintains both high roads and canals, it is said, in good condition, but this would not be the case in Europe.   In China, and in several other governments of Asia, the executive power charges itself both with the reparation of the high roads, and with the maintenance of the navigable canals. In the instructions which are given to the governor of each province, those objects, it is said, are constantly recommended to him, and the judgment which the court forms of his conduct is very much regulated by the attention which he appears to have paid to this part of his instructions. This branch of public police accordingly is said to be very much attended to in all those countries, but particularly in China, where the high roads, and still more the navigable canals, it is pretended, exceed very much every thing of the same kind which is known in Europe. The accounts of those works, however, which have been transmitted to Europe, have generally been drawn up by weak and wondering travellers; frequently by stupid and lying missionaries. If they had been examined by more intelligent eyes, and if the accounts of them had been reported by more faithful witnesses, they would not, perhaps, appear to be so wonderful. The account which Bernier gives of some works of this kind in Indostan, falls very much short of what had

政权力,包揽了对一切用作公共目的的收入的管理。但是,法国联系各个地方城市的大驿路,一般还保护得很完好。甚至有些省份的大驿路比英国大部分收税公路都要好得多。然而,所谓的十字路,即乡村绝大部分的公路却被人们完全弃之不管,在很多地方,重型车辆根本无法通行。在有些地方,甚至骑在马背上旅行也很危险,而骡子是唯一安全可靠的运输工具。崇尚浮华的朝廷,其大吏必然骄奢,常常以建造盛大雄伟、富丽堂皇的工程为荣。例如,那些王公贵族可以经常看到的大道。这些王宫贵族的赞许奉承,不仅会使大吏的虚荣心得到满足,甚至对于他在朝廷的地位还会有所进益。但是,对于众多的小工程,是做不出什么惊天动地的外观的,也无法吸引任何旅行者驻足观望,总之,除了极其有用之外,这些小工程没有什么可圈可点的。从各方面来讲,这些工程都太卑微琐碎,怎么会吸引一位大吏的注意呢。因此,在这样的管理之下,这些小工程几乎完全被置之不理了。

  中国及亚洲其他几个国家的行政当局,既负责修建公路,又负责通航运河的维持。据说,在朝廷颁给各省大员的训示中,总是提到这些目标;朝廷对他政绩的评定,很大程度上也取决于对训示中这部分的执行程度。所以,据说所有这些国家都对这些工程非常关注,尤其是中国,更是如此。人们认为,中国的公路,特别是通航运河,比欧洲著名的公路及运河都要好得多。不过,传到了欧洲的关于那些工程的报告,一般仅仅是些少见多怪的旅行者以及糊涂说谎的传教士所写的传闻异辞罢了。如果用明智眼光来考察这些工程,如果关于工程的报告有更多忠实的见证人,那么工程似乎就不会看起来如此奇妙了。柏尼尔所写的关于印度斯坦的这类工程的报道,比其他好奇尚异的旅行者所写的报道

据说中国和其他一些亚洲国家的行政部门保持了良好的公路和运河,但欧洲情况有所不同。

been reported of them by other travellers, more disposed to the marvellous than he was. ① It may too, perhaps, be in those countries, as it is in France, where the great roads, the great communications which are likely to be the subjects of conversation at the court and in the capital, are attended to, and all the rest neglected. In China, besides, in Indostan, and in several other governments of Asia, the revenue of the sovereign arises almost altogether from a land-tax or land-rent, which rises or falls with the rise and fall of the annual produce of the land. The great interest of the sovereign, therefore, his revenue, is in such countries necessarily and immediately connected with the cultivation of the land, with the greatness of its produce, and with the value of its produce. But in order to render that produce both as great and as valuable as possible, it is necessary to procure to it as extensive a market as possible, and consequently to establish the freest, the easiest, and the least expensive communication between all the different parts of the country; which can be done only by means of the best roads and the best navigable canals. But the revenue of the sovereign does not, in any part of Europe, arise chiefly from a land-tax or land-rent. In all the great kingdoms of Europe, perhaps, the greater part of it may ultimately depend upon the produce of the land: But that dependency is neither so immediate, nor so evident. In Europe, therefore, the sovereign does not feel himself so directly called upon to promote the increase, both in quantity and value, of the produce of the land, or, by maintaining good roads and canals, to provide the most extensive market for that produce. Though it should be true, therefore, what I apprehend is not a little doubtful, that in some parts of Asia this department of the public police is very properly managed by the executive power, there is not the least probability that, during the present state of things, it could be tolerably managed by that power in any part of Europe.

Public works of a local nature should be maintained by local revenue.

Even those public works which are of such a nature that they cannot afford any revenue for maintaining themselves, but of which the conveniency is nearly confined to some particular place or district, are always better maintained by a local or provincial revenue, under the management of a local and provincial administration, than by the

---

① [*Voyages de Francois Bernier*, Amsterdam, 1710. See tom. ii. , p. 249.]

第五篇 第一章

就少了很多渲染。① 亚洲那些国家的大马路,像法国一样,也是通衢大道,并常常成为朝廷及首都人们谈论的话题,因而所受关注也多,而其余道路则被人们忽视了。此外,在中国、印度及亚洲其他几个国家,君主的收入几乎全部来自土地税或地租。而土地税或地租的多少又随着土地年产量的多少而定。因此,这些国家君主的巨额利益,即收入,必然与土地的耕作、土地产量的大小和土地产物价值大小等密切相连。土地生产物要想最大限度地增多产量、提高价值,必须尽可能地占有广大的市场。结果,就要在全国各地修建交通,以期极其自由、方便、便宜,而这只有通过修建四通八达的马路和畅通无阻的运河才能达到目的。但欧洲各国君主的主要收入并非来自土地税或地租。在欧洲所有的大王国里,或许主要收入的大部分归根结底依赖于土地生产物,但这种依赖既非直接又不明显。因此,欧洲各国君主感觉没有直接义务去增加土地生产物的数量和价值,或者维持四通八达的马路和畅通无阻的运河;为生产物提供广大的市场。因此,在亚洲的某些地方,行政当局把这些修建公路河道的公共工程管理得很好,这种说法可能是真的,但据我所知,还是颇让人怀疑的。最起码,在现有状态下,欧洲各国的行政当局要想管理好,还是有难度的。

如果公共工程自身无法提供收入来维持,而其提供的便利又几乎只限于某地方或某地区,那么在地方或省行政当局管理下并由地方或省收入来维持,要比在国家行政当局管理下,由国家一 地方性公共工程应由地方人维持的公工程该由地方收入来持。

---

① 阿姆斯特丹:《德·佛朗克斯·伯尔尼航行记》,1710 年,第 2 卷,第 249 页。

general revenue of the state, of which the executive power must always have the management. Were the streets of London to be lighted and paved at the expence of the treasury, is there any probability that they would be so well lighted and paved as they are at present, or even at so small an expence ? The expence, besides, instead of being raised by a local tax upon the inhabitants of each particular street, parish, or district in London, would, in this case, be defrayed out of the general revenue of the state, and would consequently be raised by a tax upon all the inhabitants of the kingdom, of whom the greater part derive no sort of benefit from the lighting and paving of the streets of London.

<small>The abuses of local administration are small compared with those of the administration of the general revenue.</small>
The abuses which sometimes creep into the local and provincial administration of a local and provincial revenue, how enormous soever they may appear, are in reality, however, almost always very trifling, in comparison of those which commonly take place in the administration and expenditure of the revenue of a great empire. They are, besides, much more easily corrected. Under the local or provincial administration of the justices of the peace in Great Britain, the six days labour which the country people are obliged to give to the reparation of the highways, is not always perhaps very judiciously applied, but it is scarce ever exacted with any circumstance of cruelty or oppression. In France, under the administration of the intendants, the application is not always more judicious, and the exaction is frequently the most cruel and oppressive. Such Corvèes, as they are called, make one of the principal instruments of tyranny by which those officers chastise any parish or communeautè which has had the misfortune to fall under their displeasure.

Of The Public Works And Institutions Which Are Necessary For Facilitating Particular Branches Of Commerce

<small>Some particular institutions are required to facilitate particular branches of commerce.</small>
The object of the public works and institutions above mentioned is to facilitate commerce in general. But in order to facilitate some particular branches of it, particular institutions are necessary, which again require a particular and extraordinary expence.

<small>as trade with barbarous nations requires forts, and trade with other nations requires ambassadors,</small>
Some particular branches of commerce, which are carried on with barbarous and uncivilized nations, require extraordinary protection. An ordinary store or counting-house could give little security to the goods of the merchants who trade to the western coast of Africa. To defend them from the barbarous natives, it is necessary that the place where they are deposited, should be, in some measure, fortified. The disorders in the government of Indostan have been supposed to render a like precaution necessary even among that mild and gentle people; and it was under pretence of securing their persons and property from violence, that both the English and French

般收入来维持更好。如果英国伦敦的街道照明与道路铺砌由财政部出资,会像现在这样街灯明亮、道路平坦吗?所花费用能这么少吗?此外,费用若不是出自伦敦各街道、教区、市区的居民所提供的地方税,那就要从国家一般收入中支出,结果就要对王国的所有居民征税,而他们中大多数人根本没有从伦敦街道的照明和修砌中得到好处。

地方政府和省政府管理地方收入和省收入,有时会产生弊端,然而这与大帝国收入的管理及支出存在的弊端相比,不管看起来是多么严重,事实上,实在是微乎其微;此外,前者的弊端与后者相比也更加容易矫正。在英国,在地方或郡治安推事管理之下,村民为修理公路必须提供六天的劳动。或许对六天劳动的利用并不总是非常得当,但绝没有发生过残忍压迫之举。在法国州长的管理下,劳动的利用,与英国相比,并不是很得当,常常发生极其残忍的强制勒索事件。法国人所谓的强迫劳役制,成为暴政的主要工具。倘若某个教区或社团不幸惹恼了酷吏,必会遭到惩罚。

<small>相比于一般收入管理的弊端,地方政府进行的弊端很小。</small>

为便利特殊商业部门所必需的公共工程和机构

上述公共工程和机构的目的,就是便利一般商业。但为了便利一些特殊部门,就必须建立特殊的机构,也就必然需要特别的额外费用。

<small>为了方便某些特殊商业部门,就要建立特殊机构。</small>

一些特殊商业部门,若与野蛮、不开化民族通商,需要额外保护。对于在非洲西海岸进行交易的商人的货物,普通商店或账房无法提供保障。要让货物不为野蛮土著人抢去,就必须在放置货物的地方建筑防御工事。印度政府管理混乱,即使在最温文儒雅的印度人中,也应当设置相似的防御。英法两国的东印度公司,

<small>野蛮家需要坚固的要塞,而与他们做贸易则需要做贸易时要安全,其国家贸易时需要。</small>

国民财富的性质与原理

East India Companies were allowed to erect the first forts which they possessed in that country. Among other nations, whose vigorous government will suffer no strangers to possess any fortified place within their territory, it may be necessary to maintain some ambassador, minister, or consul, who may both decide, according to their own customs, the differences arising among his own countrymen; and, in their disputes with the natives, may, by means of his public character, interfere with more authority, and afford them a more powerful protection, than they could expect from any private man. The interests of commerce have frequently made it necessary to maintain ministers in foreign countries, where the purposes, either of war or alliance, would not have required any. The commerce of the Turkey Company first occasioned the establishment of an ordinary ambassador at Constantinople. ① The first English embassies to Russia arose altogether from commercial interests. ② The constant interference which those interests necessarily occasioned between the subjects of the different states of Europe, has probably introduced the custom of keeping, in all neighbouring countries, ambassadors or ministers constantly resident even in the time of peace. This custom, unknown to ancient times, seems not to be older than the end of the fifteenth or beginning of the sixteenth century; that is, than the time when commerce first began to extend itself to the greater part of the nations of Europe, and when they first began to attend to its interests.

Branches of commerce which require extraordinary expense for their protection may reasonably bear a particular tax,

It seems not unreasonable, that the extraordinary expence, which the protection of any particular branch of commerce may occasion, should be defrayed by a moderate tax upon that particular branch; by a moderate fine, for example, to be paid by the traders when they first enter into it, or, what is more equal, by a particular duty of so much per cent. upon the goods which they either import into, or export out of, the particular countries with which it is carried on. The protection of trade in general, from pirates and free-booters, is said to have given occasion to the first institution of the duties of customs. But, if it was thought reasonable to lay a general tax upon trade, in order to defray the expence of protecting trade in general, it should seem equally reasonable to lay a particular tax upon a particular branch of trade, in order to defray the extraordinary expence of protecting that branch.

---

① [Anderson, *Commerce*, A. D. 1606.]
② [*Anderson, Commerce*, A. D. 1620, and cp A. D. 1623.]

第五篇　第一章

以保障个人及财产安全不受侵犯为借口,获准建筑了在印度的最早的堡垒。在其他国家,强大的政府是不会容许外人在其领土拥有堡垒的。这时,就必须派遣大使、公使或领事。当本国人之间产生分歧时,可以根据本国习惯做出裁决。当本国人与当地人发生争执时,他可以利用外交官身份,进行有权威的干涉,对本国公民提供有力的保护,这是任何私人都无法做到的。为了商业利益,国家常常有必要在外国派驻公使,本来无论是战争还是结盟,都不需要这样。土耳其公司的商业,是首次在君士坦丁堡设立普通大使的原因①。英国在俄罗斯首次设立大使馆,也完全是出于商业上的利益②。欧洲各国人民因为商业利益不断发生冲突,或许就是这个原因,促使欧洲各国,即使在和平时期,也在所有邻国永久派驻大使或公使。这个闻所未闻的习惯,似乎也不过起始于15世纪末或16世纪初,也就是说,是在商业开始扩展到欧洲大部分国家,欧洲各国开始注意到商业利益的时候。

　　为保护某特殊商业部门而支出特别费用,应通过向该部门征收适当的税收来弥补,这似乎不是不合理。例如,让刚开始做生意的商人,支付适当的加入费,或更公平一些,对商人从特定国家进口、出口的货物,征收一定百分比的特殊税。据说,为了保护一般贸易免受海盗的抢劫,首创了海关税收制度。但是,如果认为为保护一般贸易支出费用,就理应征收一般贸易税,那么,为保护特殊部门的贸易支出特别费用,同样也理应向该贸易征收特殊税收。

---

　　①　安德森:《商业》,1606年。
　　②　安德林:《商业》,1602年,比较1623年。

| 国民财富的性质与原理

The proceeds of such taxes should be at the disposal of the executive, but have often been given to companies of merchants.
　　The protection of trade in general has always been considered as essential to the defence of the commonwealth, and, upon that account, a necessary part of the duty of the executive power. The collection and application of the general duties of customs, therefore, have always been left to that power. But the protection of any particular branch of trade is a part of the general protection of trade; a part, therefore, of the duty of that power; and if nations always acted consistently, the particular duties levied for the purposes of such particular protection, should always have been left equally to its disposal. But in this respect, as well as in many others, nations have not always acted consistently; and in the greater part of the commercial states of Europe, particular companies of merchants have had the address to persuade the legislature to entrust to them the performance of this part of the duty of the sovereign, together with all the powers which are necessarily connected with it.

which have always proved in the long run burdensome or useless.
　　These companies, though they may, perhaps, have been useful for the first introduction of some branches of commerce, by making, at their own expence, an experiment which the state might not think it prudent to make, have in the long-run proved, universally, either burdensome or useless, and have either mismanaged or confined the trade.

They are either regulated or joint-stock companies.
　　When those companies do not trade upon a joint stock, but are obliged to admit any person, properly qualified, upon paying a certain fine, and agreeing to submit to the regulations of the company, each member trading upon his own stock, and at his own risk, they are called regulated companies. When they trade upon a joint stock, each member sharing in the common profit or loss in proportion to his share in this stock, they are called joint stock companies. ① Such companies, whether regulated or joint stock, sometimes have, and sometimes have not, exclusive privileges.

　　Regulated companies resemble, in every respect, the corporations of trades, so common in the cities and towns of all the different countries of Europe; and are a sort of enlarged monopolies of the same kind. As no inhabitant of a town can exercise an incorporated trade, without first obtaining his freedom in the corporation, so in most cases

---

　　① [Sir Josiah Child, *New Discourse of Trade*, etc. , chap. iii. , divides companies into those in joint stock and those 'who trade not by a joint stock, but only are under a government and regulation '.]

第五篇 第一章

保护一般贸易常被看作是国防所必需的,因而也就成了行政当局职责的必要的一部分。因此,一般关税的征收和使用,一直由行政当局负责。但特殊贸易保护是一般贸易保护的一部分,因而也是行政当局职责的一部分。如果国家的行为总是前后一致的,那么为保护特殊贸易而征收的特殊税收,同样也应当一直由行政当局处置。然而,在这方面以及其他很多方面,国家的行为并不总是一致的。在欧洲大部分的商业国家里,特殊商业公司,说服了立法机关,把君主的这部分职责,以及与之必然相关的一切权力,都交给他们去履行。

> 这种税收应当由行政部门支配,但情况经常是将其交给了商业公司来支配。

这些公司自己出资,创建了一些商业部门。这对于部门的创立是非常有用的。对于这种尝试,政府一直很谨慎,不敢自己去实行。虽然如此,长期来说,这些公司都还是变得累赘而无用,不是管理不善就是束缚了贸易。

> 很长的一段时间里,这些公司已经证明它们总是累赘的无用的。

这些公司分两类:一类是所谓的章程公司:经营这类公司,没有共同的股份;只要具备适当的资格,任何人只要支付一定数额的加入费,同意遵守公司章程,即可加入;每个成员靠自己的股份经营,风险自担。另一类是股份公司:这类公司靠共同的股份经营,每个成员根据持有的股份分享一般利润或损失①。无论是章程公司还是股份公司,专营特权的有无都是暂时的。

> 它们是章程公司或者股份公司。

从各方面来讲,章程公司都类似于欧洲各国城市或小城镇普遍存在的行业组织,只不过是某种类似行业组织的扩大化了的垄断团体。城市的居民如果没有先从章程公司取得自由经营权,就

---

① 参见弃赛亚·蔡尔德《商业新论》,第3章,他将公司划分为那些股份公司和那些"非股份公司,只是在政府和规章下运作的公司"。

| 国民财富的性质与原理

Regulated companies are like corporations of trades and act like them. no subject of the state can lawfully carry on any branch of foreign trade, for which a regulated company is established, without first becoming a member of that company. The monopoly is more or less strict according as the terms of admission are more or less difficult; and according as the directors of the company have more or less authority, or have it more or less in their power to manage in such a manner as to confine the greater part of the trade to themselves and their particular friends. In the most ancient regulated companies the privileges of apprenticeship were the same as in other corporations; and entitled the person who had served his time to a member of the company, to become himself a member, either without paying any fine, or upon paying a much smaller one than what was exacted of other people. The usual corporation spirit, wherever the law does not restrain it, prevails in all regulated companies. When they have been allowed to act according to their natural genius, they have always, in order to confine the competition to as small a number of persons as possible, endeavoured to subject the trade to many burdensome regulations. When the law has restrained them from doing this, they have become altogether useless and insignificant.

There are five existing regulated companies, The regulated companies for foreign commerce, which at present subsist in Great Britain, are, the ancient merchant adventurers company, ① now commonly called the Hamburgh Company, the Russia Company, the Eastland Company, the Turkey Company, and the African Company.

of which the Hamburg, Russian and Eastland Companies are merely useless. The terms of admission into the Hamburgh Company, are now said to be quite easy; and the directors either have it not in their power to subject the trade to any burdensome restraint or regulations, or, at least, have not of late exercised that power. It has not always been so. About the middle of the last century, the fine for admission was fifty, and at one time one hundred pounds, ② and the conduct of the company was said to be extremely oppressive. In 1643, in 1645, and in 1661, the clothiers and free traders of the West of England complained

---

① [The company or society of the Merchant Adventurers of England.]

② [Anderson, *Commerce*, A. D. 1643: the fine was doubled in that year, being raised to £ 100 for Londoners and £ 50 for others.]

不能参加联合商业活动。所以,在大多数情况下,国家任何公民,如果不先成为业已成立的章程公司的会员,就不能合法地与外国贸易部门进行交易。垄断权的严格与否与入会条件的难易、与公司董事权力的大小,即把大部分贸易控制在自己及亲朋手中经营的权力的大小相关。在最古老的章程公司里,学徒的特权也和其他公司一样,只要学徒在公司服务过,他就不用交什么加入费用,或所交加入费比别人少得多,就可以成为会员。只要法律不加限制,通常的行业组织精神在所有章程公司中占主导地位。只要允许它们按自然倾向行事,它们为了将竞争限制于尽可能少的人数中,总是力图约束贸易经营,设立种种繁复的规章制度。当法律限制它们这样做的时候,它们就变成完全毫无用处、无关紧要的东西了。

<small>章程公司类似于行业组织,而且也像它一样行事。</small>

现在,英国存在的对外贸易章程公司是以前的商人冒险家公司①,现在通常称为汉堡公司、俄罗斯公司、东方公司、土耳其公司以及非洲公司。

<small>有五家现存的章程公司。</small>

据说现在汉堡公司的入伙条件非常容易。公司董事或许是没有权利设立种种繁复的规章限制来约束贸易经营,至少他们近来没有行使过这种权力。过去它却不是这样的。在上个世纪中叶,该公司的加入费是 50 镑,后又一度改为 100 镑②。据说,公司的行为极其专横。1643 年、1645 年、1661 年,英格兰西部的毛织业者及自由贸易者,先后几次向议会提出控诉,称他们是限制

<small>汉堡公司、俄罗斯公司和东方公司完全是无用的。</small>

---

① "商人冒险团"公司或社会。
② 安德森:《商业》,1643 年:该年的会费增长了一倍,伦敦人提到了 100 镑,其他人则为 50 镑。

of them to parliament, as of monopolists who confined the trade and oppressed the manufactures of the country. ①Though those complaints produced no act of parliament, they had probably intimidated the company so far, as to oblige them to reform their conduct. Since that time, at least, there have been no complaints against them. By the 10th and 11th of William Ⅲ. c. 6. the fine for admission into the Russian Company was reduced to five pounds; and by the 25th of Charles Ⅱ. c. 7. that for admission into the Eastland Company, to forty shillings, while, at the same time, Sweden, Denmark and Norway, all the countries on the north side of the Baltic, were exempted from their exclusive charter. ② The conduct of those companies had probably given occasion to those two acts of parliament. Before that time, Sir Josiah Child had represented both these and the Hamburgh Company as extremely oppressive, and imputed to their bad management the low state of the trade, which we at that time carried on to the countries comprehended within their respective charters. ③ But though such companies may not, in the present times, be very oppressive, they are certainly altogether useless. To be merely useless, indeed, is perhaps the highest eulogy which can ever justly be bestowed upon a regulated company; and all the three companies above mentioned seem, in their present state, to deserve this eulogy.

<small>The Turkey Company is an oppressive monopoly.</small>
The fine for admission into the Turkey Company, was formerly twenty-five pounds for all persons under twenty-six years of age, and fifty pounds for all persons above that age. Nobody but mere merchants could be admitted; a restriction which excluded all shop-keepers and retailers. ④ By a bye-law, no British manufactures could be exported to Turkey but in the general ships of the company; and as those ships sailed always from the port of London, this restriction confined the trade to that expensive port, and the traders, to those who lived in London and in its neighbourhood. By another bye-law, no person living within twenty miles of London, and not free

---

① [Anderson, *Commerce*, A. D. 1661, under which the other two years are also mentioned,]

② [Anderson, *Commerce*, A. D. 1672.]

③ [*New Discourse of Trade*, chap. iii. , quoted by Anderson, *Commerce*, A. D. 1672. This part of the book was not published till long after 1672, but seems to have been written before the closing of the Exchequer in that year.]

④ [Anderson, *Commerce*, A. D. 1605, 1643, 1753.]

国家贸易、压迫国家制造业者的垄断集团①。虽然控诉没有使议会采取什么行动,却也让公司感到了威胁,被迫改正自己的行为。从那时起,至少没有人再控诉它们。根据威廉三世十年、十一年的第 6 号法令,俄罗斯公司的加入费减为 5 镑;根据查理二世二十五年的第 7 号法令,东方公司的加入费减为 40 先令。同时,瑞典、丹麦、挪威以及波罗的海北岸所有国家也都免除了公司的专营特权②。或许这些公司的行为引起议会颁布了这两条法令。在此以前,乔赛亚·蔡尔德曾称这两家公司及汉堡公司极其专横,并把当时本国与这些公司特许状所涵盖的国家间贸易状态不佳,都归咎于公司管理不善③。现在,这些公司也许没有那么专横了,但也完全没用了。诚然,没有用处或许是能够给予章程公司的莫大赞辞。现有阶段的所有上述三家公司似乎也配得上这种赞美。

　　土耳其公司的加入费,对于年龄 26 岁以下者,是 25 镑,对于 26 岁以上者,是 50 镑。只有商人才能加入。这种限制把所有小店主和零售商都排斥在外了④。根据公司一项条例,英国制造品出口到土耳其的,只有用该公司的普通船舶才能运出;而且因为该公司船舶总是从伦敦港驶出,英国对土耳其的贸易就只能局限于这个昂贵的港口了,而商人也只能是伦敦及其附近的居民。根

土耳其公司是专横的垄断组织。

---

　　① 安德森:《商业》,1661 年,其中也提到了其他两年。在序言中详述了公司的历史。
　　② 安德森:《商业》,1672 年。
　　③ 《贸易新论》,第 3 章,被 1672 年安德森的《商业》所援引。该书的这一部分直到 1672 年才出版,但它似乎是在那年财务署关闭之前写的。
　　④ 安德森:《商业》,1605 年,1643 年,1753 年。

of the city, could be admitted a member; another restriction, which, joined to the foregoing, necessarily excluded all but the freemen of London. ① As the time for the loading and sailing of those general ships depended altogether upon the directors, they could easily fill them with their own goods and those of their particular friends, to the exclusion of others, who, they might pretend, had made their proposals too late. In this state of things, therefore, this company was in every respect a strict and oppressive monopoly. Those abuses gave occasion to the act of the 26th of George II. c. 18. reducing the fine for admission to twenty pounds for all persons, without any distinction of ages, or any restriction, either to mere merchants, or to the freemen of London; and granting to all such persons the liberty of exporting, from all the ports of Great Britain to any port in Turkey, all British goods of which the exportation was not prohibited; and of importing from thence all Turkish goods, of which the importation was not prohibited, upon paying both the general duties of customs, and the particular duties assessed for defraying the necessary expences of the company; and submitting, at the same time, to the lawful authority of the British ambassador and consuls resident in Turkey, and to the bye-laws of the company duly enacted. To prevent any oppression by those bye-laws, it was by the same act ordained, that if any seven members of the company conceived themselves aggrieved by any bye-law which should be enacted after the passing of this act, they might appeal to the Board of Trade and Plantations (to the authority of which, a committee of the privy council has now succeeded), provided such appeal was brought within twelve months after the bye-law was enacted; and that if any seven members conceived themselves aggrieved by any bye-law which had been enacted before the passing of this act, they might bring a like appeal, provided it was within twelve months after the day on which this act was to take place. The experience of one year, however, may not always be sufficient to discover to all the members of a great company the pernicious tendency of a

---

① [See the preamble to 26 Geo. II., c. 18. —Anderson, *Commerce*, A. D. 1753.]

据公司的另一条例,居住在伦敦市 20 英里内,拥有伦敦市民权的人,才能成为公司会员。这种限制,和前面的限制一起,必然把没有取得伦敦市民资格的人都排斥在外①。因为公司普通船舶装载及起航的时间完全由公司董事决定,所以董事当然就先装载自己及有与自己有特殊关系的友人的货物,而对于他人的货物,就以他们投保装船日期太迟为借口,将其排除在外。因此,在这种情况下,公司从各方面来讲都是严厉苛刻、专横跋扈的垄断组织。这些弊害,导致乔治二世二十六年第 18 号法令的颁布。法令将入会费减少到 20 镑,并规定任何人,不论年龄大小、纯粹商人与否及是否是伦敦市民,都可以成为公司会员;还准许所有这些入会的人,都有权将货物,除禁止运输的外,从英国任何港口运往土耳其任何港口,或除了禁止进口的货物外,进口土耳其所有的货物;但他们必须缴纳一般海关税,以及为支付该公司必须费用而征收的特定税;同时,他们还必须服从英国驻土耳其大使和领事的合法权力以及公司正式颁布的条例。为防止这些法令过于苛刻,上述法令还规定,在该法令通过之后,公司颁布的任何条例,只要使公司的任何七个成员受到压制,他们即可向贸易殖民部(该部的权力现由枢密院的委员会继承)上诉,矫正条例,但上诉应在该公司条例颁布后的一年内提出。此外,公司的任何七个成员,如果在该法令通过之前公司颁布的任何条例中受到压制,那么他们可在法案实施之日起十二个月内,提起相似的上诉。但是,大公司中所有的成员,凭借为期一年的经验,并不见得就能发现某条例中的有害倾向。如果到后来他们中才有人发现,那么无

---

① 参见乔治二世二十六年第 18 号法令。安德森:《商业》,1753 年。

particular bye-law; and if several of them should afterwards discover it, neither the Board of Trade, nor the committee of council, can afford them any redress. The object, besides, of the greater part of the bye-laws of all regulated companies, as well as of all other corporations, is not so much to oppress those who are already members, as to discourage others from becoming so; which may be done, not only by a high fine, but by many other contrivances. The constant view of such companies is always to raise the rate of their own profit as high as they can; to keep the market, both for the goods which they export, and for those which they import, as much understocked as they can; which can be done only by restraining the competition, or by discouraging new adventurers from entering into the trade. A fine even of twenty pounds, besides, though it may not, perhaps, be sufficient to discourage any man from entering into the Turkey trade, with an intention to continue in it, may be enough to discourage a speculative merchant from hazarding a single adventure in it. In all trades, the regular established traders, even though not incorporated, naturally combine to raise profits, which are no-way so likely to be kept, at all times, down to their proper level, as by the occasional competition of speculative adventurers. The Turkey trade, though in some measure laid open by this act of parliament, is still considered by many people as very far from being altogether free. The Turkey Company contribute to maintain an ambassador and two or three consuls, who, like other public ministers, ought to be maintained altogether by the state, and the trade laid open to all his majesty's subjects. The different taxes levied by the company, for this and other corporation purposes, might afford a revenue much more than sufficient to enable the state to maintain such ministers.

Regulated companies, it was observed by Sir Josiah Child, though they had frequently supported public ministers, had never maintained any forts or garrisons in the countries to which they traded; whereas joint stock companies frequently had. ① And in reality the former seem to be much more unfit for this sort of service than the latter. First, the directors of a regulated company

---

① [*New Discourse of Trade*, chap. iii.]

论是贸易部还是枢密院委员会都无法再矫正条例中的弊病。此外,所有章程公司以及所有其他行业组织制定的大部分条例,是为了阻碍外人的加入,而不是压迫已经加入的成员。要达到这一目的,不仅可以通过设立很高的加入费,而且还有很多其他的计谋。这些公司一贯认为,要不断提高利润率,越高越好;要尽量让市场上的货物保持供应不足,出口货物市场如此,进口货物市场也是如此:要做到这些,就只有限制竞争,或者阻碍新的冒险者进入行业。况且,即使20镑的加入费,或许并不足以阻碍打算继续从事土耳其贸易的人,但足够阻碍只想冒险一次的投机商人。在一切行业中,打拼多年有所成就的商人,即使没有加入任何行业组织,也自然会联合起来提高利润。他们会尽力使商业利润一直不低于应有的水平,这种做法与偶尔竞争的投机商不同。通过议会的这项法令,英国在土耳其的贸易一定程度地开放了,但许多人仍然认为距离完全自由还有很长的路要走。英国一名大使以及两三名领事是由土耳其公司出资维持的,实际上,他们应当像其他国家大臣那样,全部由国家收入维持;而贸易也应当对国王陛下的一切臣民开放。公司为此目的以及其他行业社团的目的征收了各种税收,这些税收所提供的收入不仅足够国家维持这几个外交官的费用,而且还大有节余。

乔赛亚·蔡尔德注意到,章程公司虽然常常维持驻外官员的费用,但从未在与之进行贸易的国家维持任何堡垒或守备队,而股份公司则常常维持堡垒和守备队①。实际上,对于提供这类服务,前者似乎远不如后者合适。首先,章程公司的董事,对于该公

---

① 《贸易新论》,第三章。

> 国民财富的性质与原理

<small>Regulated companies are more unfit to maintain forts than joint-stock companies,</small> have no particular interest in the prosperity of the general trade of the company, for the sake of which, such forts and garrisons are maintained. The decay of that general trade may even frequently contribute to the advantage of their own private trade; as by diminishing the number of their competitors, it may enable them both to buy cheaper, and to sell dearer. The directors of a joint stock company, on the contrary, having only their share in the profits which are made upon the common stock committed to their management, have no private trade of their own, of which the interest can be separated from that of the general trade of the company. Their private interest is connected with the prosperity of the general trade of the company; and with the maintenance of the forts and garrisons which are necessary for its defence. They are more likely, therefore, to have that continual and careful attention which that maintenance necessarily requires. Secondly, The directors of a joint stock company have always the management of a large capital, the joint stock of the company, a part of which they may frequently employ, with propriety, in building, repairing, and maintaining such necessary forts and garrisons. But the directors of a regulated company, having the management of no common capital, have no other fund to employ in this way, but the casual revenue arising from the admission fines, and from the corporation duties, imposed upon the trade of the company. Though they had the same interest, therefore, to attend to the maintenance of such forts and garrisons, they can seldom have the same ability to render that attention effectual. The maintenance of a public minister requiring scarce any attention, and but a moderate and limited expence, is a business much more suitable both to the temper and abilities of a regulated company.

<small>but the African company was charged with this duty.</small> Long after the time of Sir Josiah Child, however, in 1750, a regulated company was established, the present company of merchants trading to Africa, which was expressly charged at first with the maintenance of all the British forts and garrisons that lie between Cape Blanc and the Cape of Good Hope, and afterwards with that of those only which lie between Cape Rouge and the Cape of Good Hope. The act which establishes this company (the 23d of George Ⅱ. c. 31.) seems to have had two distinct objects in view; first, to restrain effectually the oppressive and monopolizing spirit which is natural to the directors of a regulated company; and secondly, to force them, as much as possible, to give an attention, which is not natural to them, towards the maintenance of forts and garrisons.

第五篇 第一章

司一般贸易的繁荣,并没有特殊的兴趣;而为了这种繁荣,才会维持堡垒及守备队。公司一般贸易的衰退甚至常常给他们私人的贸易增添好处。因为如果公司一般贸易衰退,竞争人数就会减少,他们就可以贱买贵卖。反之,股份公司的董事唯一可以分享的利益,是他们负责管理的共同股份所产生的利润。他们没有私人利益可言。即使有,他们的私人利益也和公司的一般贸易所产生的利益是密不可分的。他们的私人利益,与公司一般贸易的繁荣以及保障这繁荣的堡垒或守备队的维持是相联系的。因此,就维持堡垒或守备队所必需的持久认真的注意力来说,他们比章程公司的董事更可能有这份关注。第二,股份公司的董事总是掌管着一大笔资本,即公司的股份。他们常常合理使用其中一部分,用来建设、修理及维持必要的堡垒和守备队。但是,章程公司的董事,并没有掌管什么共同资本,除了加入费、向公司贸易所征收的合伙税等临时收入以外,没有其他资金可以动用。因此,即使两者的利益相同,都会关注堡垒和守备队的维持,但就关注的有效性来讲,两者的能力却不相同。至于驻外官员的维持,根本不需要什么关注,所需费用也少而有限。那么就公司性质和能力来说,股份公司都更为合适。

相比股份公司,章程公司更不适于维持堡垒。

但是,在乔赛亚·蔡尔德爵士的时代以后许久,即1750年,又成立了一个章程公司,就是现在的非洲商业贸易公司。最初,该公司负责非洲沿岸由布朗角至好望角之间所有的英国堡垒和守备队的维持;后来,只负担鲁杰角与好望角之间的堡垒和守备队的维持。设立这个公司的法令(乔治二世二十二年第31号法令),似乎有两个明显目的。第一,有效限制章程公司董事自然拥有的压迫精神和垄断精神;第二,尽力迫使他们去关注堡垒与守

但非洲商业贸易公司有这种责任。

— 1537 —

<small>The statute establishing the company endeavoured ineffectually to restrain the spirit of monopoly,</small> For the first of these purposes, the fine for admission is limited to forty shillings. The company is prohibited from trading in their corporate capacity, or upon a joint stock; from borrowing money upon common seal, or from laying any restraints upon the trade which may be carried on freely from all places, and by all persons being British subjects, and paying the fine. The government is in a committee of nine persons who meet at London, but who are chosen annually by the freemen of the company at London, Bristol and Liverpool; three from each place. No committee-man can be continued in office for more than three years together. Any committee-man might be removed by the Board of Trade and Plantations; now by a committee of council, after being heard in his own defence. The committee are forbid to export negroes from Africa, or to import any African goods into Great Britain. But as they are charged with the maintenance of forts and garrisons, they may, for that purpose, export from Great Britain to Africa, goods and stores of different kinds. Out of the monies which they shall receive from the company, they are allowed a sum not exceeding eight hundred pounds for the salaries of their clerks and agents at London, Bristol and Liverpool, the house-rent of their office at London, and all other expences of management, commission and agency in England. What remains of this sum, after defraying these different expences, they may divide among themselves, as compensation for their trouble, in what manner they think proper. By this constitution, it might have been expected, that the spirit of monopoly would have been effectually restrained, and the first of these purposes sufficiently answered. It would seem, however, that it had not. Though by the 4th of George Ⅲ. c. 20. the fort of Senegal, with all its dependencies, had been vested in the company of merchants trading to Africa, yet in the year following (by the 5th of George Ⅲ. c. 44.), not only Senegal and its dependencies, but the whole coast from the port of Sallee, in south Barbary, to Cape Rouge, was exempted from the jurisdiction of that company, was vested in the crown, and the trade to it declared free to all his majesty's subjects. The company had been suspected of restraining the trade, and of establishing some sort of improper monopoly. It is not, however, very easy to conceive how, under the regulations of the 23d George Ⅱ. they could do so. In the printed debates of the House of Commons, not always the most authentic records of truth, I observe,

备队的维持。这种关注力是他们原本所没有的。

对于第一个目的,法令限定加入费40先令。该法令还禁止公司以组合资格或以共同股份进行贸易;不得以共同印章借入资本进行贸易;对于所有缴纳加入费的英国公民,不能限制其在各地进行的自由贸易。公司的管理层是由九人组成的委员会。会议是在伦敦召开,但委员的选举是从伦敦、布里斯托尔和利物浦三市的公司员工中各选三名。委员的任期不得超过三年。委员有不当行为,贸易殖民局(现由枢密院委员会接管)在听了他本人的辩护后可罢免其职。禁止委员会从非洲贩运黑人,或将非洲货物运入英国。但因为他们负责维持堡垒和守备队,所以,为此目的,可以把不同种类的货物或军需品从英国运往非洲。他们从公司领取的钱,不准超过800镑,这些费用可以用来支付伦敦、布里斯托尔、利物浦三市的公司职员和代理人的薪俸、驻伦敦办事处的房租以及在英国的其他一切管理、委任、代理费用。支付过种种费用以后剩余的金钱,可以让他们自己合理分配,作为他们辛劳的报酬。按照这种严格规定,垄断精神应已得到有效的控制,两个目的中的第一个似乎已充分达到了。然而,实际上似乎并非如此。按照乔治三世四年第20号法令,塞内加尔堡垒及其属地,应归非洲贸易商业公司管理。但在次年(根据乔治三世五年第44号法令),该公司不仅在塞内加尔及其属地,而且从南巴巴利的萨利港至鲁杰角的整个海岸的管理权都被免除了,改由国王支配;而且法令宣称,国王陛下的一切臣民都可以自由进行非洲贸易。人们怀疑,公司限制了贸易,建立了某种不正当垄断。然而,很难想象,在乔治二世二十三年法令如此严密的规定之下,他们竟能这样做。但是,我在下议院的辩论记录里——记录并不总是完全正

<small>这公司有限垄断,建立公家的法律未能有效地制止</small>

however, that they have been accused of this. The members of the committee of nine being all merchants, and the governors and factors in their different forts and settlements being all dependent upon them, it is not unlikely that the latter might have given peculiar attention to the consignments and commissions of the former, which would establish a real monopoly.

<small>and Parliament allots £13,000 a year to the company for forts, which sum they misapply.</small>

For the second of these purposes, the maintenance of the forts and garrisons, an annual sum has been allotted to them by parliament, generally about 13, 000 *l*. For the proper application of this sum, the committee is obliged to account annually to the Cursitor Baron of Exchequer; which account is afterwards to be laid before parliament. But parliament, which gives so little attention to the application of millions, is not likely to give much to that of 13, 000 *l*. a-year; and the Cursitor Baron of Exchequer, from his profession and education, is not likely to be profoundly skilled in the proper expence of forts and garrisons. The captains of his majesty's navy, indeed, or any other commissioned officers, appointed by the Board of Admiralty, may enquire into the condition of the forts and garrisons, and report their observations to that board. But that board seems to have no direct jurisdiction over the committee, nor any authority to correct those whose conduct it may thus enquire into; and the captains of his majesty's navy, besides, are not supposed to be always deeply learned in the science of fortification. Removal from an office, which can be enjoyed only for the term of three years, and of which the lawful emoluments, even during that term, are so very small, seems to be the utmost punishment to which any committee-man is liable, for any fault, except direct malversation, or embezzlement, either of the public money, or of that of the company; and the fear of that punishment can never be a motive of sufficient weight to force a continual and careful attention to a business, to which he has no other interest to attend. The committee are accused of having sent out bricks and stones from England for the reparation of Cape Coast Castle on the coast of Guinea, a business for which parliament had several times granted an extraordinary sum of money. These bricks and stones too, which had thus been sent upon so long a voyage, were said to have been of so bad a quality, that it was necessary to rebuild from the foundation the walls which had been repaired with them. The forts and garrisons which lie north of Cape Rouge, are not only maintained at the expence of the state, but are under the immediate government of the executive power; and why those which lie south of that Cape, and which too are, in part at least, maintained at the expence of the state, should be under a different government, it seems not very easy even to imagine a good reason. The protection of the Mediterranean trade was the original purpose or pretence of the garrisons of Gibraltar and

确——注意到,他们受到这种控告。委员会的九位委员都是商人,在他们的堡垒及殖民地的大大小小的官员都依赖他们,很可能这些官员特别关注委员的交代及委托,这样,就形成了真正的垄断。

对于第二个目的,该法令规定:议会每年一般拨出 13000 镑给该公司,用于维持堡垒和守备队。对于这笔金额的合理使用,公司委员会每年必须向财政部主计官提出报告,之后,财政部主计再将报告递交议会。但是,议会对于数百万镑的使用,都不太在意,更不用提这 13000 镑的小数额的使用,当然不可能去注意了。而从财政部主计官的职务和教育来看,他的技能不是那么精湛,不见得能判断出堡垒和守备队费用的利用是否合理。诚然,王国海军舰长或任何海军部委派遣的其他官员,都可以调查堡垒和守备队的状况,并向海军部报告。但海军部对委员会似乎没有直接管辖权,也没有权力去纠正被调查者的行为;此外,舰长对于建筑防御工事这门科学的学识并不见得总是那么渊博。委员的任期只有三年,任期期间的合法报酬也很少,除非他们贪污受贿或侵吞公款和公司钱财,对于他们所犯错误,最多也不过是罢黜其职务。对这样惩罚的恐惧,绝不可能成为强迫他们一直认真关注对他们没有利益可言的事情的砝码。委员会被指控从英格兰贩运砖石,去修缮几内亚海岸的海岸角堡垒。议会也曾几次下拨特别款项修缮堡垒。据说,这些砖石长途跋涉地运往那里,质量很差,所以,必须在用它们修建的墙垣的基础上重新修建。鲁杰角以北的堡垒和守备队,不但由国家出资维持,而且处于行政当局的直接管辖之下。但鲁杰角以南的堡垒和守备队,至少有一部分是由国家出资维持的,可为什么管辖权却不同,似乎很难让人找出合适的理由去解释。在直布罗陀海峡及米诺卡岛建立守备

而且议会每年给这个公司拨款 13000 镑作为维持堡垒的费用,但他们没有运用得当。

Minorca, and the maintenance and government of those garrisons has always been, very properly, committed, not to the Turkey Company, but to the executive power. In the extent of its dominion consists, in a great measure, the pride and dignity of that power; and it is not very likely to fail in attention to what is necessary for the defence of that dominion. The garrisons at Gibraltar and Minorca, accordingly, have never been neglected; though Minorca has been twice taken, and is now probably lost for ever, that disaster was never even imputed to any neglect in the executive power. I would not, however, be understood to insinuate, that either of those expensive garrisons was ever, even in the smallest degree, necessary for the purpose for which they were originally dismembered from the Spanish monarchy. That dismemberment, perhaps, never served any other real purpose than to alienate from England her natural ally the King of Spain, and to unite the two principal branches of the house of Bourbon in a much stricter and more permanent alliance than the ties of blood could ever have united them.

<small>Joint-stock companies differ from private partnerships:</small>

Joint stock companies, established either by royal charter or by act of parliament, differ in several respects, not only from regulated companies, but from private copartneries.

<small>(1) withdrawals are by sale of shares;</small>

First, In a private copartnery, no partner, without the consent of the company, can transfer his share to another person, or introduce a new member into the company. Each member, however, may, upon proper warning, withdraw from the copartnery, and demand payment from them of his share of the common stock. In a joint stock company, on the contrary, no member can demand payment of his share from the company; but each member can, without their consent, transfer his share to another person, and thereby introduce a new member. The value of a share in a joint stock is always the price which it will bring in the market; and this may be either greater or less, in any proportion, than the sum which its owner stands credited for in the stock of the company.

<small>(2) liability is limited to the share held.</small>

Secondly, In a private copartnery, each partner is bound for the debts contracted by the company to the whole extent of his fortune. In a joint stock company, on the contrary, each partner is bound

队的最初目的或借口是保护地中海贸易,而守备队的维持费和管辖权一直由政府负责,和土耳其公司无关。统治领域的广大,在很大程度上牵涉到行政当局的声誉和尊严,所以,他们不可能对该领域防卫必须的事情不给予关注。因此,对驻扎在直布罗陀海峡及米诺卡岛的守备队,从未受到疏忽。虽然米诺卡曾两次被夺,现在或许也永远丧失了,但从没有人把这灾难归咎于行政当局的疏忽。不过,我不愿被人认为,我是在暗示这些堡垒花费昂贵,最初把它们从西班牙王国手中夺过来的目的是毫无必要的。夺取这些要塞,达不到任何真实的目的,只会使英国与她的自然的同盟者西班牙国王疏远,并使波旁王室的两大分支团结起来,结成超过血缘关系的更紧密更永久的同盟。

根据皇家特诉状或议会法令成立的股份公司,在很多方面,不仅和章程公司不同,而且与私人合伙公司也不相同。〔股份公司和私人公司不一样:〕

第一,在私人合伙公司中,合伙人不经公司同意,不得将股份转让他人,或介绍新成员入伙。但是,每个成员如若退伙,须事先声明,并要求他们支付共同股份中属于自己的股份。股份公司则相反。股东不得要求公司支付属于自己的股份。而且,股东不经公司同意,也可将股份转让他人,因此,也可介绍新成员入股。股票价值,总是通过市场上的价格体现出来。这价格有涨有落,因此,股票所有者的实际股金,就与股票上注明的金额,可能多些或少些。〔(1)通过售出股票退出公司,〕

第二,在私人合伙公司中,每个合伙人对公司的全部债务,都负责任。反之,在股份公司中,股东只对自己的那部分股份负〔(2)责任仅限于持有的股份。〕

国民财富的性质与原理

Such companies are managed by directors, who are negligent and profuse.

only to the extent of his share. ①

The trade of a joint stock company is always managed by a court of directors. This court, indeed, is frequently subject, in many respects, to the controul of a general court of proprietors. But the greater part of those proprietors seldom pretend to understand any thing of the business of the company; and when the spirit of faction happens not to prevail among them, give themselves no trouble about it, but receive contentedly such half yearly or yearly dividend, as the directors think proper to make to them. This total exemption from trouble and from risk, beyond a limited sum, encourages many people to become adventurers in joint stock companies, who would, upon no account, hazard their fortunes in any private copartnery. Such companies, therefore, commonly draw to themselves much greater stocks than any private copartnery can boast of. The trading stock of the South Sea Company, at one time, amounted to upwards of thirty-three millions eight hundred thousand pounds. ② The divided capital of the Bank of England amounts, at present, to ten millions seven hundred and eighty thousand pounds. ③ The directors of such companies, however, being the managers rather of other people's money than of their own, it cannot well be expected, that they should watch over it with the same anxious vigilance with which the partners in a private copartnery frequently watch over their own. Like the stewards of a rich man, they are apt to consider attention to small matters as not for their master's honour, and very easily give themselves a dispensation from having it. Negligence and profusion, therefore, must always prevail, more or less, in the management of the affairs of such a company. It is upon this account that joint stock companies for foreign trade have seldom been able to maintain the competition against private adventurers. They have, accordingly, very seldom succeeded without an exclusive privilege; and frequently have not succeeded with one. Without an exclusive privilege they have commonly mismanaged the trade. With an exclusive privilege they have both mismanaged and confined it.

The Royal African Company, the predecessors of the present African Company, had an exclusive privilege by charter; but as that charter had not been confirmed by act of parliament, the trade, in consequence of the declaration of rights, was, soon after the revolution,

---

① [A joint-stock company here is an incorporated or chartered company. The common application of the term to other companies is later.]

② [Anderson, *Commerce*, A. D. 1723.]

③ [It stood at this amount from 1746 to the end of 1781, but was then increased by a call of 8 per cent. —Anderson, *Commerce*, A. D. 1746, and (Continuation) A. D. 1781.]

责①。

　　股份公司的交易,常常由董事会管理。诚然,董事会在很多方面要受股东大会的支配。但大部分股东不懂公司业务;如果他们没有派别之争,也就不大操心过问,只是心安理得地接受每年或每半年董事会认为应该分配给他们的红利。这样不需要操劳,所冒风险又只限于一定金额的事情,使得很多不愿把财产投资于合伙公司的人都入股冒险。因此,股份公司吸收的资本通常要远远超过合伙公司所鼓吹的资本。南海公司的营业资本一度曾达到3380多万镑②。现在,英格兰银行的分红股本达到了1078万镑③。但是,因为股份公司的董事经营别人的钱财而不是自己的钱财,所以我们不能期望他们会像私人合伙公司的合伙人那样一直焦虑万分地关注自己的资本。股份公司的董事,像富人家的管事那样,为了主人的荣誉,往往不会注意小事。因此,股份公司的业务经营上常常或多或少出现疏忽和浪费。也就是因为这个原因,国外贸易股份公司,是很少能竞争过私人的冒险者的。所以,股份公司就没有专营特权,不大能够成功;即使取得了专营特权,他们常常还是不能成功。没有专营特权,他们会经营不善;有了特权,他们不但经营不善,而且限制了贸易。

这种由董事会来管理的公司,他们是懈怠和浪费的。

　　皇家非洲公司,即现在非洲公司的前身,根据特许状取得了专营特权,但特许状并未经议会通过。因此,作为民权宣布的结

---

　　① 这里所说的股份公司是指法人公司或特许经营公司。这个术语对其他公司的普遍应用是以后的事情了。
　　② 安德森:《商业》,1723年。
　　③ 从1746年到1781年底,这个数额始终没变,但接着增加了8%的股份。参见安德森:《商业》,1746年,1781年《续编》。

国民财富的性质与原理

Some have and some have not exclusive privileges.

laid open to all his majesty's subjects. ① The Hudson's Bay Company are, as to their legal rights, in the same situation as the Royal African Company. ② Their exclusive charter has not been confirmed by act of parliament. The South Sea Company, as long as they continued to be a trading company, had an exclusive privilege confirmed by act of parliament; as have likewise the present United Company of Merchants trading to the East Indies.

The Royal African Company, having lost exclusive privileges, failed.

The Royal African Company soon found that they could not maintain the competition against private adventurers, whom, notwithstanding the declaration of rights, they continued for some time to call interlopers, and to persecute as such. In 1698, however, the private adventurers were subjected to a duty of ten per cent. upon almost all the different branches of their trade, to be employed by the company in the maintenance of their forts and garrisons. But, notwithstanding this heavy tax, the company were still unable to maintain the competition. ③ Their stock and credit gradually declined. In 1712, their debts had become so great, that a particular act of parliament was thought necessary, both for their security and for that of their creditors. It was enacted, that the resolution of two-thirds of these creditors in number and value, should bind the rest, both with regard to the time which should be allowed to the company for the payment of their debts; and with regard to any other agreement which it might be thought proper to make with them concerning those debts. ④ In 1730, their affairs were in so great disorder, that they were altogether incapable of maintaining their forts and garrisons, the sole purpose and pretext of their institution. From that year, till their final dissolution, the parliament judged it necessary to allow the annual sum of ten thousand pounds for that purpose. ⑤ In 1732, after having been for many years losers by the trade of carrying negroes to the West Indies, they at last resolved to give it up altogether; to

---

① [Anderson, *Commerce*, A. D. 1672 and A. D. 1698.]
② [*Anderson, Commerce*, A. D. 1670.]
③ [*Anderson, Commerce*, A. D. 1698.]
④ [10 Ann., c. 27. Anderson, *Commerce*, A. D. 1712.]
⑤ [*Anderson, Commerce*, A. D. 1730. The annual grant continued till 1746.]

果,在革命后不久,非洲贸易就向国王陛下的所有臣民开放了①。哈德逊湾公司的合法权利和皇家非洲公司相同,他们的特许状未经议会通过②。南海公司只要一直还是贸易公司,就始终具有经议会法令确认过的专营特权。现在和东印度进行贸易的联合商业公司也是如此。

有些股份公司有排他特权,而有的则没有。

皇家非洲公司很快就发现,自己无法和私人冒险者竞争,于是不顾民权宣言的发布,一度竟把这些私人冒险者称为无照营业者而加以迫害。但是,1698 年,他们的几乎一切贸易部门都对私人冒险者征收 10% 的税收,公司用这笔税款来维持堡垒和守备队。但尽管向私人竞争者征收了这么高的税收,公司仍无法和私人竞争者竞争。公司的股本及信用逐渐下降③。1712 年,公司负债累累,为公司及债权人的安全,议会有必要制定特别的法令。法令规定,关于公司债务的偿付日期以及关于债务的其他必要协定,就人数和价值来说,只要债权人 2/3 以上的决议赞成,就对其他债权人也有约束力④。1730 年,公司的业务处于极度混乱的状态,完全无法维持堡垒和守备队,而这却是设立公司的唯一目的或借口。从那年起至公司最后解散,议会决定,每年拨款 1 万镑用作这个目的⑤。1732 年,公司因为贩运到印度西岸的黑奴贸易多年都是亏损,最后决定完全放弃,而把在非洲海岸买

丧失专营权的皇家非洲公司破产了。

---

① 安德森:《商业》,1672 年和 1698 年。
② 安德林:《商业》,1670 年。
③ 安德林:《商业》,1698 年。
④ 安妮女士十年第 27 号法令。安德森:《商业》,1712 年。
⑤ 安德森:《商业》,1730 年。每年都拨款,直到 1746 年。安德森:《商业》,1733 年。

国民财富的性质与原理

sell to the private traders to America the negroes which they purchased upon the coast; and to employ their servants in a trade to the inland parts of Africa for gold dust, elephants teeth, dying drugs, &c. But their success in this more confined trade was not greater than in their former extensive one. ① Their affairs continued to go gradually to decline, till at last, being in every respect a bankrupt company, they were dissolved by act of parliament, and their forts and garrisons vested in the present regulated company of merchants trading to Africa. ② Before the erection of the Royal African Company, there had been three other joint stock companies successively established, one after another, for the African trade. ③ They were all equally unsuccessful. They all, however, had exclusive charters, which, though not confirmed by act of parliament, were in those days supposed to convey a real exclusive privilege.

The Hudson's Bay Company have been moderately successful, having in fact an exclusive trade and a very small number of proprietors.

The Hudson's Bay Company, before their misfortunes in the late war, had been much more fortunate than the Royal African Company. Their necessary expence is much smaller. The whole number of people whom they maintain in their different settlements and habitations, which they have honoured with the name of forts, is said not to exceed a hundred and twenty persons. ④ This number, however, is sufficient to prepare beforehand the cargo of furs and other goods necessary for loading their ships, which, on account of the ice, can seldom remain above six or eight weeks in those seas. This advantage of having a cargo ready prepared, could not for several years be acquired by private adventurers, and without it there seems to be no possibility of trading to Hudson's Bay. The moderate capital of the company, which, it is said, does not exceed one hundred and ten thousand pounds, ⑤ may besides be sufficient to enable them to engross the whole, or almost the whole, trade and surplus produce of the miserable, though extensive country, comprehended within their charter. No private adventurers, accordingly, have ever attempted to trade to that country in competition with them. This company, therefore, have always enjoyed an

---

① [Anderson, *Commerce*, A. D. 1733.]

② [23 Geo. Ⅱ. , c. 31; 25 Geo. Ⅱ. , c. 40; Anderson, *Commerce*, A. D. 1750, 1752; above, p. 229.]

③ [Anderson, *Commerce*, A. D. 1618, 1631 and 1662.]

④ [*Anderson, Commere* , A. D. 1743, quoting Captain Christopher Middleton.]

⑤ [Anderson, *Commerce*, A. D. 1670.]

得的黑奴转卖于美洲私人贸易者;并利用公司贸易上的雇员从事非洲内地的金沙、象牙、染料等贸易。但他们从事的贸易范围上受到限制,成功的机会并不比先前范围广泛的贸易多。公司的业务,继续逐渐衰败,直到最后,从各方面来讲公司都破产了。议会的一项法令决定解散公司。而堡垒及防备队则由现在非洲贸易商人所组织的章程公司管理①。在皇家非洲公司建立之前,先后有三家股份公司从事非洲贸易②,但都没有成功。它们都有专营特许状,特许状虽未经议会确认,但在当时被认为赋有真正的专营特权。

在上次战争中遭到不幸打击以前,哈德逊湾公司要比皇家非洲公司幸运得多。它的必要开支很少。据说,在各个殖民地和居留地(这些地方被赞誉为堡垒),公司所维持的总人数不过120名③。可是人数虽少,却足够预先准备装载船舶所必需的羊毛及其他货物。由于结冰期长,船舶很少能在那些海域停泊七八周以上;因此,提前准备货物,大有好处。这是私人冒险者几年内都做不到的。而且,没有这个好处,似乎也就不可能和哈德逊湾进行贸易。哈德逊湾公司资本虽少,据说不到11万镑④,但仍足以使它把特许状所许可的那些虽然广阔但却贫乏的地带的全部或将近全部的贸易和剩余生产物全部垄断。结果,私人贸易者从不敢到那种地方与该公司竞争。所以,该公司虽然在法律上可能没有

哈德逊湾公司比较成功,它事实上从事专营贸易,而且股东人数很少。

---

① 乔治二世二十三年第31号法令;乔治二世二十五年第40号法令。见安德森《商业》,1750年。
② 安德森:《商业》,1618年,1631年,1662年。
③ 安德林:《商业》,1743年。引用科利斯托福·米德尔顿船长的话。
④ 安德森:《商业》,1670年。

exclusive trade in fact, though they may have no right to it in law. Over and above all this, the moderate capital of this company is said to be divided among a very small number of proprietors. ① But a joint stock company, consisting of a small number of proprietors, with a moderate capital, approaches very nearly to the nature of a private copartnery, and may be capable of nearly the same degree of vigilance and attention. It is not to be wondered at, therefore, if in consequence of these different advantages, the Hudson's Bay Company had, before the late war, been able to carry on their trade with a considerable degree of success. It does not seem probable, however, that their profits ever approached to what the late Mr. Dobbs imagined them. ② A much more sober and judicious writer, Mr. Anderson, author of The Historical and Chronological Deduction of Commerce, very justly observes, that upon examining the accounts which Mr. Dobbs himself has given for several years together, of their exports and imports, and upon making proper allowances for their extraordinary risk and expence, it does not appear that their profits deserve to be envied, or that they can much, if at all, exceed the ordinary profits of trade. ③

The South Sea Company failed to make any profit by their annual ship to the Spanish West Indies,

The South Sea Company never had any forts or garrisons to maintain, and therefore were entirely exempted from one great expence, to which other joint stock companies for foreign trade are subject. But they had an immense capital divided among an immense number of proprietors. It was naturally to be expected, therefore, that folly, negligence, and profusion should prevail in the whole management of their affairs. The knavery and extravagance of their stock-jobbing projects are sufficiently known, and the explication of them would be foreign to

---

① ['Eight or nine private merchants do engross nine-tenth parts of the company's stock.' Anderson, *Commerce*, A, D. 1743, quoting from *An Account of the Countries Adjoining to Hudson's Bay . . . with an Abstract of Captain Middleton's Journal and Observations upon his Behaviour*, by Arthur Dobbs, Esq. , 1744, p. 58.]

② [In his *Account*, pp. 3 and 58, he talks of 2,000 per cent, but this, of course, only relers to the difference between buying and selling prices.]

③ [*Commerce*, A. D. 1743, but the examination is not nearly so comprehensive, nor the expression of opinion so ample as is suggested by the text.]

专营特权,但实际上,却一直在享受着专营贸易。除此之外,据说,该公司资本虽少,分享利润的股东却也是少之又少①。一个只有少数股东小额资本构成的股份公司,和私人合伙公司的性质相差无几,所以在经营上,也几乎同样谨慎和小心。因此,有以上种种好处,哈德逊湾公司在上次战争前所进行的贸易仍然取得很大的成功,是不足为奇的。不过,该公司获得的利润,似乎还没有达到已故的多布斯先生所想象的那个程度②。《商业历史和编年推断》的作者安德森先生,是一个比多布斯更为严肃、公正的人,他查看了多布斯关于该公司数年中进出口的全部报告,对公司的特别冒险和特别开支加以扣除后,似乎该公司的利润并不值得羡慕,或者说,并没有大大超过普通的贸易利润,如果真有超过的话。他的观察还是很正确的③。

南海公司从未维持堡垒和守备队,因此,完全不需负担其他国外贸易公司所通常负担的一大笔费用,不过,该公司股本很大,股东人数又多,因而,我们自然可以想到,公司在整个业务经营上,一定会出现荒唐、疏忽和浪费之举。他们代客买卖股票的诈骗无赖之举和铺张浪费行为已是众所周知,和本题无关,毋庸赘述。而南海公司以金钱为目的的商业计划也并不比代客买卖的

南海公司从来没有从他们每年派往西班牙印度的船只中获得利润,

---

① "八九个私人商人垄断了 90% 的公司资本。"见安德森《商业》,1743年,引用了亚瑟·多布斯《哈德逊附近各国概况……附米德尔顿船长日记摘要及对其行为的观察》,1744 年,第 58 页。

② 《哈德逊附近各国概况……附米德尔顿船长日记摘要及对其行为的观察》,第 3 页和第 58 页,他谈到了 2000% 的利润,但这只是指买卖价格之差。

③ 《商业》,1743 年,但是审查并没有这么广泛,里面表达的意思也不像文中那么肯定。

the present subject. Their mercantile projects were not much better conducted. The first trade which they engaged in was that of supplying the Spanish West Indies with negroes, of which (in consequence of what was called the Assiento contract granted them by the treaty of Utrecht) they had the exclusive privilege. But as it was not expected that much profit could be made by this trade, both the Portugueze and French companies, who had enjoyed it upon the same terms before them, having been ruined by it, they were allowed, as compensation, to send annually a ship of a certain burden to trade directly to the Spanish West Indies. ① Of the ten voyages which this annual ship was allowed to make, they are said to have gained considerably by one, that of the Royal Caroline in 1731, and to have been losers, more or less, by almost all the rest. Their ill success was imputed, by their factors and agents, to the extortion and oppression of the Spanish government; but was, perhaps, principally owing to the profusion and depredations of those very factors and agents; some of whom are said to have acquired great fortunes even in one year. In 1734, the company petitioned the king, that they might be allowed to dispose of the trade and tunnage of their annual ship, on account of the little profit which they made by it, and to accept of such equivalent as they could obtain from the king of Spain. ②

lost £ 237,000 in their whale fishery,

In 1724, this company had undertaken the whale-fishery. Of this, indeed, they had no monopoly; but as long as they carried it on, no other British subjects appear to have engaged in it. Of the eight voyages which their ships made to Greenland, they were gainers by one, and losers by all the rest. After their eighth and last voyage, when they had sold their ships, stores, and utensils, they found that their whole loss, upon this branch, capital and interest included, amounted to upwards of two hundred and thirty-seven thousand pounds. ③

In 1722, this company petitioned the parliament to be allowed to divide their immense capital of more than thirty-three millions eight hundred thousand pounds, the whole of which had been lent to government, into two equal parts: The one half, or upwards of sixteen

---

① [Anderson, *Commerce*, A. D. 1713.]

② [*Anderson, Commerce*, A. D. 1731, 1732 and 1734.]

③ [*Anderson, Commerce* , A. D. 1724 and 1732. But there was no successful voyage; the company were 'considerable losers in every one' of the eight years.]

计划好到哪里。该公司首次从事的贸易,就是向西班牙所属的西印度贩运黑人奴隶。对于这项贸易(根据尤特雷特条约认可的所谓阿西思托约定),它有专营特权。但是,他们预料到该贸易不会取得多大利润,因为在这之前,葡萄牙和法国的两家同样享有特权的公司都经营过这一贸易,但已经倒闭了。因此,作为补偿,准许他们每年派遣一定吨数的船舶直接与西班牙属地西印度进行贸易①。公司每年都派遣船舶,共航行十次。据说,其中一次,即1731 年,加洛林皇后号的航行获得了巨额利润,其余九次,或多或少都有损失。公司的代理店及代理人都把不成功归罪于西班牙政府的勒索和压迫。但或许主要还是由于代理店及代理人的浪费和掠夺吧。据说,这些代理人中有些人在一年之内就发了大财。1734 年,该公司以利润微薄为借口,上书请求英王准许变卖贸易权与吨位,许其等价卖给西班牙国王②。

1724 年,该公司开始从事捕鲸业。诚然,对于这项业务,它没有独占权,但只要该公司从事这项贸易,似乎就没有其他英国公民掺和进来。公司的船舶,曾航行到格陵兰岛八次。只有一次赢利,其余几次都遭受了损失。在第八次即最后一次航行结束后,该公司卖掉了船只、储藏商品、渔具,这时才发现这个部门包括资本及利息的全部损失达到 237000 多镑③。在他们的捕鲸业中损失了237000镑,

1722 年,该公司请求议会,准许它把借给政府的全部巨额资本,即 3380 万镑,划分作两个相等的部分;一半即 1690 多万镑,处

---

① 安德森:《商业》,1713 年。
② 安德森:《商业》,1731 年,1732 年,1734 年。
③ 安德森:《商业》,1724 和 1732 年。但是航行都没有成功;该公司八年间"每年都遭受了巨人的损失"。

and finally ceased to be a trading company.

millions nine hundred thousand pounds, to be put upon the same footing with other government annuities, and not to be subject to the debts contracted, or losses incurred, by the directors of the company, in the prosecution of their mercantile projects; the other half to remain, as before, a trading stock, and to be subject to those debts and losses. The petition was too reasonable not to be granted. ① In 1733, they again petitioned the parliament, that three-fourths of their trading stock might be turned into annuity stock, and only one-fourth remain as trading stock, or exposed to the hazards arising from the bad management of their directors. ② Both their annuity and trading stocks had, by this time, been reduced more than two millions each, by several different payments from government; so that this fourth amounted only to 3, 662, 7841. 8s. 6d. ③ In 1748, all the demands of the company upon the king of Spain, in consequence of the Assiento contract, were, by the treaty of Aix-la-Chapelle, given up for what was supposed an equivalent. An end was put to their trade with the Spanish West Indies, the remainder of their trading stock was turned into an annuity stock, and the company ceased in every respect to be a trading company. ④

They had competitor in the trade of the annual ship.

It ought to be observed, that in the trade which the South Sea Company carried on by means of their annual ship, the only trade by which it ever was expected that they could make any considerable profit, they were not without competitors, either in the foreign or in the home market. At Carthagena, Porto Bello, and La Vera Cruz, they had to encounter the competition of the Spanish merchants, who brought from Cadiz, to those markets, European goods, of the same kind with the outward cargo of their ship; and in England they had to encounter that of the English merchants, who imported from Cadiz goods of the Spanish West Indies, of the same kind with the inward cargo. The goods both of the Spanish and English merchants, indeed,

---

① [By 9 Geo. I., c. 6. Anderson, *Commerce*, A. D. 1723.]
② [This was done by 6 Geo. II., c. 28. *Ibid.*, A. D. 1733.]
③ [Anderson, *Commerce*, A. D. 1732 and A. D. 1733.]
④ [Anderson, *Commerce*, A. D. 1748 and A. D. 1750.]

于与其他公债相同的地位。在执行商业计划中,公司董事不得动用这笔资本来偿付和弥补公司商业经营上的债务或损失;其他一半,像以前那样,仍然作为贸易资本,用以偿付和弥补债务或损失。请愿非常合理,议会也就满足该公司的要求①。1733年,该公司再次向议会请求,把贸易资本的3/4作为公债,只有1/4作为贸易资本,或公司董事管理不善引起的风险补偿金。到这时为止,该公司的公债资本和贸易资本两者,因政府的几次偿还,已分别减少了200多万镑,因而,这1/4也只是3662784镑8先令6便士②。1748年,该公司根据艾克斯拉沙佩勒条约,放弃了以前阿西恩托约定中从西班牙国王取得的一切权利,所得的只是所谓的相当等价物。这样,公司就终结了与西班牙属地西印度之间的贸易。剩余的贸易资本就转成了公债,于是公司从各方面讲都不再是一个贸易公司了③。

_{最终停止作为一个贸易公司。}

应当注意到,南海公司每年都派遣船舶到西班牙属地西印度进行贸易,它所期望的唯一贸易就是获得巨额利润。但是无论在国外市场还是在国内市场,它都不乏竞争者。在国外的卡塔赫纳、贝洛港、拉维拉克鲁斯等地,他们遇上了西班牙商人的竞争。这些商人把该公司船舶装载的同种欧洲货物,从加的斯运到那些地方的市场上。在英格兰,他们要面对英格兰商人的竞争。这些商人从加的斯运进的货物,和该公司运进的货物相同,都是来自西班牙属地西印度。诚然,无论西班牙商人还是英国商人的货

_{他们在贸易竞争中,每年的船舶只有一艘。}

---

① 经乔治一世九年第6号法令允许。见安德森《商业》,1723年。
② 安德森:《商业》,1732年,1733年。
③ 安德森:《商业》,1748年,1750年。

were, perhaps, subject to higher duties. But the loss occasioned by the negligence, profusion, and malversation of the servants of the company, had probably been a tax much heavier than all those duties. That a joint stock company should be able to carry on successfully any branch of foreign trade, when private adventurers can come into any sort of open and fair competition with them; seems contrary to all experience.

<small>The old East India Company, unable to support competition, was superseded by the present company, which with exclusive privileges has traded successfully, but has conquered large territories, and mismanaged them so that Parliament has been obliged to make alterations, which are not likely to be of service.</small> The old English East India Company was established in 1600, by a charter from Queen Elizabeth. In the first twelve voyages which they fitted out for India, they appear to have traded as a regulated company, with separate stocks, though only in the general ships of the company. In 1612, they united into a joint stock. ① Their charter was exclusive, and though not confirmed by act of parliament, was in those days supposed to convey a real exclusive privilege. For many years, therefore, they were not much disturbed by interlopers. Their capital which never exceeded seven hundred and forty-four thousand pounds, ② and of which fifty pounds was a share, ③ was not so exorbitant, nor their dealings so extensive, as to afford either a pretext for gross negligence and profusion, or a cover to gross malversation. Notwithstanding some extraordinary losses, occasioned partly by the malice of the Dutch East India Company, and partly by other accidents, they carried on for many years a successful trade. But in process of time, when the principles of liberty were better understood, it became every day more and more doubtful how far a royal charter, not confirmed by act of parliament, could convey an exclusive privilege. Upon this question the decisions of the courts of justice were not uniform, but varied with the authority of government and the humours of the times. Interlopers multiplied upon them; and towards the end of the reign of Charles Ⅱ. through the whole of that of James Ⅱ. and during a part of that of William Ⅲ. reduced them to great distress. ④ In 1698, a proposal was made to parliament of advancing two millions to government at eight per cent. provided the subscribers were erected into

---

① [Anderson, *Commerce*, A. D. 1612.]
② [Anderson, *Commerce*, A. D. 1693.]
③ [Anderson, *Commerce*, A. D. 1676.]
④ [Anderson, *Commerce*, A. D. 1681 and A. D. 1685.]

第五篇　第一章

物,都要缴纳较重的税收,但该公司人员的疏忽、浪费和贪污造成的损失,或许是一种比一切税收都要高的重税吧。如果私人贸易者能够公开地、公平地与股份公司竞争,股份公司还能成功经营国外贸易,这似乎和过去的经验相违背的。

旧的英国东印度公司于 1600 年根据女王伊丽莎白的特许状设立。在前 12 次向印度的航行中,虽然船舶是公司共有的,但资本还是各人的,他们交易的性质显示这似乎还是章程公司。1612 年,他们联合起来成立共同资本①。该公司持有专营特许状。特许状虽然未经议会确认,但当时被认为具有真正的专营特权。因此,多年来他们从未受无证经营者的骚扰。它的股本总额只有 74.4 万镑②。50 镑为一股③,这并不昂贵。公司的营业规模也不大,经营上也没有什么借口去疏忽大意、奢华铺张,更没有资本去贪污腐化。所以,虽然由于荷兰东印度公司的蓄意谋害以及其他的意外事故,它遭受了很大损失,但多年来它所进行的贸易却很成功。但是,随着时间的流逝,一般人逐渐理解了自由的原则,而未经议会确认的皇家特许状,能够多么长久地拥有专营特权,就越来越让人怀疑。关于这个问题,法院的决定并不一致,随政府权力和各时代民意的变化而变化。周围的无证经营者迅速增多。查理二世统治晚年,在詹姆士二世地整个统治时期和在威廉三世初年,公司陷入困境④1698 年,有人向议会建议,愿以 8% 的利息贷给政府 200 万镑,其条件为购买公债者设立一个有专营

旧印度公司无受法竞争,被所有的公司取得了成功,征服了印度,管理所征服的国土,但他们会迫使他们改革,但改革不会产生作用。现在所有贸易做得很成功,他们经营的领域扩大,已使他们改善。

---

① 安德森:《商业》,1612 年。
② 安德森:《商业》,1693 年。
③ 安德森:《商业》,1676 年。
④ 安德森:《商业》,1681 年,1685 年。

— 1557 —

国民财富的性质与原理

a new East India Company with exclusive privileges. The old East India Company offered seven hundred thousand pounds, nearly the amount of their capital, at four per cent. upon the same conditions. But such was at that time the state of public credit, that it was more convenient for government to borrow two millions at eight per cent. than seven hundred thousand pounds at four. The proposal of the new subscribers was accepted, and a new East India Company established in consequence. The old East India Company, however, had a right to continue their trade till 1701. They had, at the same time, in the name of their treasurer, subscribed, very artfully, three hundred and fifteen thousand pounds into the stock of the new. By a negligence in the expression of the act of parliament, which vested the East India trade in the subscribers to this loan of two millions, it did not appear evident that they were all obliged to unite into a joint stock. ① A few private traders, whose subscriptions amounted only to seven thousand two hundred pounds, insisted upon the privilege of trading separately upon their own stocks and at their own risk. ② The old East India Company had a right to a separate trade upon their old stock till 1701; and they had likewise, both before and after that period, a right, like that of other private traders, to a separate trade upon the three hundred and fifteen thousand pounds, which they had subscribed into the stock of the new company. The competition of the two companies with the private traders, and with one another, is said to have well nigh ruined both. Upon a subsequent occasion, in 1730, when a proposal was made to parliament for putting the trade under the management of a regulated company, and thereby laying it in some measure open, the East India Company, in opposition to this proposal, represented in very strong terms, what had been, at this time, the miserable effects, as they thought them, of this competition. In India, they said, it raised the price of goods so high, that they were not worth the buying; and in England, by overstocking the market, it sunk their price so low, that no profit could be made by them. ③ That by a more plentiful supply, to the great advantage and conveniency of the public, it must have reduced, very much, the

---

① [The whole of this history is in Anderson, *Commerce*, A. D. 1698.]
② [Anderson, *Commerce*, A. D. 1701.]
③ [Anderson, *Commerce*, A. D. 1730.]

特权的新东印度公司;旧东印度公司也向议会提出,按照相同条件,愿以4%的利息贷给政府70万镑,这几乎和公司的资本额相等。当时国家公债的状态是这样的:政府以8%的利息贷款200万镑比以4%的利息贷款70万镑更方便。新公债者的建议被采纳了,结果,新东印度公司出现了。不过,旧东印度公司的贸易权利可持续到1701年。同时,该公司以自己会计的名义,极巧妙地认购了新公司的股本31.5万镑。议会法案规定,给认购200万镑公债者授予东印度贸易特权,但由于用词含糊,就应募者的资本是否合为共同资本这一点不很明白①。于是,少数私人贸易者只认购了7200镑的公债,坚持用自己的资本、自担风险进行贸易②。旧东印度公司有权使用其旧资本独立进行贸易直至1701年;而且,他们和其他私人贸易者一样,在这个时期前后,也有权使用其投入新公司的31.5万镑的资本单独进行贸易。据说,新旧东印度公司与私人贸易者之间的竞争,以及两个公司之间彼此的竞争,几乎毁灭了这两个公司。后来在1730年,有人向议会提议,建议把此项贸易交给一个章程公司管辖,使之在某种程度上开放。对于这个建议,东印度公司极力反对;他们措辞非常激烈,描绘了那时这种竞争所带来的悲惨结果。他们说,竞争使印度货物价格提高,根本不值得去购买,而在英国,因为市场存货过多,货物价格跌得很低,以致无利可图③。可是,供给丰足,英国市场上印度货物的价格一定会大跌,给公众带来巨大的利益和好处,

---

① 整个这段历史参见安德森:《商业》,1698年。
② 安德森:《商业》,1701年。
③ 安德森:《商业》,1730年。

price of India goods in the English market, cannot well be doubted; but that it should have raised very much their price in the Indian market, seems not very probable, as all the extraordinary demand which that competition could occasion, must have been but as a drop of water in the immense ocean of Indian commerce. The increase of demand, besides, though in the beginning it may sometimes raise the price of goods, never fails to lower it in the long run. It encourages production, and thereby increases the competition of the producers, who, in order to undersell one another, have recourse to new divisions of labour and new improvements of art, which might never otherwise have been thought of. The miserable effects of which the company complained, were the cheapness of consumption and the encouragement given to production, precisely the two effects which it is the great business of political œconomy to promote. The competition, however, of which they gave this doleful account, had not been allowed to be of long continuance. In 1702, the two companies, were, in some measure, united by an indenture tripartite, to which the queen was the third party; ① and in 1708, they were, by act of parliament, perfectly consolidated into one company by their present name of the United Company of Merchants trading to the East Indies. Into this act it was thought worth while to insert a clause, allowing the separate traders to continue their trade till Michaelmas 1711, but at the same time empowering the directors, upon three years notice, to redeem their little capital of seven thousand two hundred pounds, and thereby to convert the whole stock of the company into a joint stock. By the same act, the capital of the company, in consequence of a new loan to government, was augmented from two millions to three millions two hundred thousand pounds. ② In 1743, the company advanced another million to government. But this million being raised, not by a call upon the proprietors, but by selling annuities and contracting bond-debts, it did not augment the stock upon which the proprietors could claim a dividend. It augmented, however, their trading stock, it being equally liable with the other three millions two hundred thousand pounds to the losses sustained, and debts contracted, by the company in prosecution of their mercantile projects. From 1708, or at least from

---

① ['This coalition was made on the 22nd of July, 1702, by an indenture tripartite between the Queen and the said two companies.'—Anderson, *Commerce*, A. D. 1702.]

② [6 Ann., c. 17. Anderson, Commerce, A. D. 1708.]

这一点是毋庸置疑的。但是，说竞争会使印度市上货物的价格暴涨，似乎也不大可能。因为竞争引起的特别需求，在印度的贸易大洋中，不过是一滴而已。此外，需求的增加，起初或许会提高价格，但长期来说会降低货物的价格。它刺激了生产，从而会增大生产者之间的竞争。生产者为使自己产品的价格比他人的更低，会进行新的分工和新的技术改良，这在其他情况下是连想都不会想到的。该公司所抱怨的悲惨结果，即消费的便宜和对生产的奖励，这两者正是政治经济学努力要促进的结果。但是，他们满怀悲哀提到的竞争，并没有持续很久。1702 年，这两个公司通过三方契约在某种程度上联合起来，其中一方是女王[①]。1708 年，按照议会法案，两者完全合为一个公司，即现在所谓的东印度贸易商人联合公司。在这个法案中，大家认为值得再加上一项条款。条款规定，准许独立商人贸易者继续交易，直至 1711 年米迦勒节为止。同时，授权该公司董事对那些独立商人贸易者发出通知，以三年为期，赎回其 7200 镑的小资本，从而把公司的全部资本变为共同资本。该法案还规定：由于给予政府新的贷款，该公司的资本从 200 万镑增加到 300 万镑[②]。1743 年，该公司又贷给政府 100 万镑。但是，这 100 万镑的筹集，不是通过要求股东增加股本得来的，而是发行公司债得来的，没有增加股东要求分红的资本。但这 100 万镑，增加了他们的贸易资本，和其他 300 万镑一起，对公司在执行商业计划时所受的亏损和债务，负担责任。自 1708

---

① "这个联合是 1702 年 7 月 22 日，由女王与两家公司订立的三方契约。"参见安德森：《商业》，1702 年。

② 安妮女王六年第 17 号法令。参见安德森：《商业》，1708 年。

1711, this company, being delivered from all competitors, and fully established in the monopoly of the English commerce to the East Indies, carried on a successful trade, and from their profits made annually a moderate dividend to their proprietors. During the French war which began in 1741, the ambition of Mr. Dupleix, the French governor of Pondicherry, involved them in the wars of the Carnatic, and in the politics of the Indian princes. After many signal successes, and equally signal losses, they at last lost Madras, at that time their principal settlement in India. It was restored to them by the treaty of Aix-la-Chapelle; and about this time the spirit of war and conquest seems to have taken possession of their servants in India, and never since to have left them. During the French war which began in 1755, their arms partook of the general good fortune of those of Great Britain. They defended Madras, took Pondicherry, recovered Calcutta, and acquired the revenues of a rich and extensive territory, amounting, it was then said, to upwards of three millions a-year. They remained for several years in quiet possession of this revenue: But in 1767, administration laid claim to their territorial acquisitions, and the revenue arising from them, as of right belonging to the crown; and the company, in compensation for this claim, agreed to pay to government four hundred thousand pounds a-year. They had before this gradually augmented their dividend from about six to ten per cent. ; that is, upon their capital of three millions two hundred thousand pounds, they had increased it by a hundred and twenty-eight thousand pounds, or had raised it from one hundred and ninety-two thousand, to three hundred and twenty thousand pounds a-year. They were attempting about this time to raise it still further, to twelve and a half per cent. which would have made their annual payments to their proprietors equal to what they had agreed to pay annually to government, or to four hundred thousand pounds a-year. But during the two years in which their agreement with government was to take place, they were restrained from any further increase of dividend by two successive acts of parliament, ① of which the object was to enable them to make a speedier progress in the payment of their debts, which were at this time estimated at upwards of six or seven millions sterling. In 1769, they renewed their a-

---

① [7 Geo. Ⅲ. , c. 49, and 8 Geo. Ⅲ. , c. 11.]

年,或者至少自 1711 年以来,由于摆脱了一切竞争者,并且完全建立了英国商业在东印度的垄断,该公司的贸易进行得很成功,每年都从利润中向股东支付适度的红利。在 1741 年爆发的对法战争中,法国庞迪彻里的总督杜不勒先生野心勃勃,使东印度公司卷入了卡哪迪克战争和印度亲王间的政治斗争中。有无数次,他们大获全胜;有无数次,他们遭到重创。最后,竟把那时公司在印度的主要殖民地马德拉斯丢掉了。后来根据艾克斯拉沙佩勒条约,马德拉斯重新回到该公司手中。大约这个时候,该公司在印度的人员心中就充满了战斗及征服精神;后来,也没有放弃这种精神。1755 年,爆发了法兰西战争。英国的军队不断打胜仗。该公司的军队在印度也分享了这好运,他们捍卫马德拉斯,占领了庞迪彻里,收复了加尔各答,并获得一个富裕而广大的领土的收入。据说,当时这收入每年达到 300 多万镑。该公司有好几年都安然享有这收入。但 1767 年,政府以该公司占领的领土及其收入属于国王为理由提出要求。作为补偿,公司同意每年付给政府 40 万镑。在此以前,公司逐渐增加股息,利息率从大约 6% 增至 10%。也就是说,在 320 万镑资本上,又增加了 12.8 万镑股息,或者说,每年红利额从 19.2 万镑增加至 32 万镑。但这时候,公司又企图把股息进一步提高至 12.5%。这会使公司每年分派给股东的金额等于每年提供给政府的金额,即 40 万镑。可是,当公司与政府订立的协约就要实施的那两年中,议会相继制定的两个法令限制他们再增加利息①。这些法案的目的,在于使公司加速偿还债务。当时公司的债务估计已达六七百万镑了。1769 年,

---

① 乔治三世七年第 49 号法令和乔治三世八年第 11 号法令。

greement with government for five years more, and stipulated, that during the course of that period they should be allowed gradually to increase their dividend to twelve and a half per cent. ; never increasing it, however, more than one per cent. in one year. This increase of dividend, therefore, when it had risen to its utmost height, could augment their annual payments, to their proprietors and government together, but by six hundred and eight thousand pounds, beyond what they had been before their late territorial acquisitions. What the gross revenue of those territorial acquisitions was supposed to amount to, has already been mentioned; and by an account brought by the Cruttenden East Indiaman in 1768, the nett revenue, clear of all deductions and military charges, was stated at two millions forty-eight thousand seven hundred and forty-seven pounds. They were said at the same time to possess another revenue, arising partly from lands, but chiefly from the customs established at their different settlements, amounting to four hundred and thirty-nine thousand pounds. The profits of their trade too, according to the evidence of their chairman before the House of Commons, amounted at this time to at least four hundred thousand pounds a-year; according to that of their accomptant, to at least five hundred thousand; according to the lowest account, at least equal to the highest dividend that was to be paid to their proprietors. So great a revenue might certainly have afforded an augmentation of six hundred and eight thousand pounds in their annual payments; and at the same time have left a large sinking fund sufficient for the speedy reduction of their debts. In 1773, however, their debts, instead of being reduced, were augmented by an arrear to the treasury in the payment of the four hundred thousand pounds, by another to the custom-house for duties unpaid, by a large debt to the bank for money borrowed, and by a fourth for bills drawn upon them from India, and wantonly accepted, to the amount of upwards of twelve hundred thousand pounds. The distress which these accumulated claims brought upon them, obliged them not only to reduce all at once their dividend to six per cent. but to throw themselves upon the mercy of government, and to supplicate, first, a release from the further payment of the stipulated four hundred thousand pounds a-year; and, secondly, a loan of fourteen hundred thousand, to save them from immediate bankruptcy. The great increase of their fortune had, it seems, only served to furnish their servants with a pretext for greater profusion, and a cover for greater malversation, than in proportion even to that increase of fortune. The conduct of their servants in India, and the general state of their affairs both in India and in Europe, became the subject of a parliamentary inquiry; in consequence of which several very important alterations were made in the constitution of their government, both at home and abroad. In India their principal settlements of Madras, Bombay, and Calcutta, which had before been altogether independent of one another, were subjected to a governor-general, assisted by a council of four assessors, parliament as-

公司把与政府订立的协约延期五年,并约定,在这五年中,准许公司逐渐把股息提高到 12.5%,但在一年之中股息增加不得超过 1%。因此,股息增加到极限时,会使公司每年付给股东以及政府的金额,两者合计比他们在最近占领领土以前的金额增加 60.8 万镑。前面说过,公司最近占领领土的总收入,每年共有 300 余万镑。根据 1768 年东印度贸易船克鲁登敦号提出的报告,除去一切扣除和军事开支,纯收入为 2048747 镑。公司方面据说同时还有其他收入,收入一部分来自土地,但主要则来自殖民地所设的海关,达到 43.9 万镑。当时公司的贸易利润,据公司董事长在下院提出的证言,至少有 40 万镑;据公司会计提出的证言,至少 50 万镑;根据最低计算,至少也会等于每年分给股东的最高股份。这么大的收入,公司当然有能力每年支付增加 60.8 万镑,同时留下一项减债基金,以迅速偿还债务。但是,在 1773 年,公司债务不但没有减少,反而增大了。拖欠财政部的欠款有 40 万镑;拖欠的关税,拖欠英格兰银行的借款,鲁莽地承兑由印度方面向其开出的汇票,三者共达 120 多万镑。这些累计债务所带来的困难,使公司不得不将股息立即减低到 6%,而且不得不乞求政府,哀求答应条件:第一,豁免公司不再交纳 40 万镑的约定;第二,贷款 140 万镑,拯救公司不会立即破产。似乎公司的财富增加只会为职员提供比财富增加更大的借口和进行贪污的掩护。公司人员在印度的行为,以及公司在欧印两方面的一般业务状况成为议会调查的对象。调查的结果使公司对国内外管理机构的组织都实行几种至关重要的变革。在印度的主要殖民地,如马德拉斯、孟买、加尔各答,过去相互独立,现在由一个总督管辖,并有由四名顾问组成的评议会相助。议会提名任命了第一任总督及顾问,

suming to itself the first nomination of this governor and council who were to reside at Calcutta; that city having now become, what Madras was before, the most important of the English settlements in India. The court of the mayor of Calcutta, originally instituted for the trial of mercantile causes, which arose in the city and neighbourhood, had gradually extended its jurisdiction with the extension of the empire. It was now reduced and confined to the original purpose of its institution. Instead of it a new supreme court of judicature was established, consisting of a chief justice and three judges to be appointed by the crown. In Europe, the qualification necessary to entitle a proprietor to vote at their general courts was raised, from five hundred pounds, the original price of a share in the stock of the company, to a thousand pounds. In order to vote upon this qualification too, it was declared necessary that he should have possessed it, if acquired by his own purchase, and not by inheritance, for at least one year, instead of six months, the term requisite before. The court of twenty-four directors had before been chosen annually; but it was now enacted that each director should, for the future, be chosen for four years; six of them, however, to go out of office by rotation every year, and not to be capable of being re-chosen at the election of the six new directors for the ensuing year. In consequence of these alterations, the courts, both of the proprietors and directors, it was expected, would be likely to act with more dignity and steadiness than they had usually done before. But it seems impossible, by any alterations, to render those courts, in any respect, fit to govern, or even to share in the government of a great empire; because the greater part of their members must always have too little interest in the prosperity of that empire, to give any serious attention to what may promote it. Frequently a man of great, sometimes even a man of small fortune, is willing to purchase a thousand pounds share in India stock, merely for the influence which he expects to acquire by a vote in the court of proprietors. It gives him a share, though not in the plunder, yet in the appointment of the plunderers of India; the court of directors, though they make that appointment, being necessarily more or less under the influence of the proprietors, who not only elect those directors, but sometimes overrule the appointments of their servants in India. Provided he can enjoy this influence for a few years, and thereby provide for a certain number of his friends, he frequently cares little about the dividend; or even about the value of the stock upon which his vote is founded. About the prosperity of the great empire, in the government of which that vote gives him a share, he seldom cares at all. No other sovereigns ever

他们常驻加尔各答。加尔各答现已成为英国在印度的最重要殖民地,像过去的马德拉斯一样。加尔各答的市长法庭原为审理该市及其附近的商业案件而设立,后来随着帝国的扩大,其司法管辖权也随之扩大。现在缩小限制其权限,使其回到最初的权限。取代它的是新设立的最高法院。最高法院由审判长一人和审判官三人组成,他们都由国王任命。在欧洲,股东在股东大会的投票权资格,从原来的500镑(原来公司每股股票的价格),增加到1000镑。此外,凭此资格取得的投票权,如果股票不是承继得来而是由自己购买得来,以前在购买后六个月就能行使,现在期限已延长到一年。还有,过去公司的24名董事每年改选一次,现在规定每个董事任期四年,但在24名董事中,每年有六个旧董事出去,六个新董事补充进来,出去的董事,不能重新当选。有了这些改革,预料股东会及董事会的行为会较以前更持重、稳妥,但是,无论怎样变革,要使这些人在各方面都配合管制,甚至分享大帝国的统治,似乎是不可能的,因为大部分成员对这个帝国的繁荣根本不感兴趣,他们是不会对促进帝国繁荣的事情给予认真关注的。有大财产的人,有时甚至是小有产的人,往往只因为要取得股东大会上的投票权,才愿意购买1000镑的东印度公司股票。有了这投票权,纵然自己不能参加对印度的掠夺,也可参加对掠夺者的任命。虽然董事会决定任命权力,但董事会本身必然或多或少受到股东的影响:股东不但选举董事,而且有时还会否决董事会关于派驻印度人员的任命。假若一个股东能享有这权力几年,因而可在公司安插几个亲信,他就会不太在意股息,甚至连他投票权所根据的股份的价值也不太在意,至于投票权使得他有权参与治理的大帝国的繁荣,他根本就不会在意。从来没有哪个君

were, or, from the nature of things, ever could be, so perfectly indifferent about the happiness or misery of their subjects, the improvement or waste of their dominions, the glory or disgrace of their administration; as, from irresistible moral causes, the greater part of the proprietors of such a mercantile company are, and necessarily must be. This indifference too was more likely to be increased than diminished by some of the new regulations which were made in consequence of the parliamentary inquiry. By a resolution of the House of Commons, for example, it was declared, that when the fourteen hundred thousand pounds lent to the company by government should be paid, and their bond-debts be reduced to fifteen hundred thousand pounds, they might then, and not till then, divide eight per cent. upon their capital; and that whatever remained of their revenues and neat profits at home, should be divided into four parts; three of them to be paid into the exchequer for the use of the public, and the fourth to be reserved as a fund, either for the further reduction of their bonddebts, or for the discharge of other contingent exigencies, which the company might labour under. But if the company were bad stewards, and bad sovereigns, when the whole of their nett revenue and profits belonged to themselves, and were at their own disposal, they were surely not likely to be better, when three-fourths of them were to belong to other people, and the other fourth, though to be laid out for the benefit of the company, yet to be so, under the inspection, and with the approbation, of other people.

They tend to encourage waste,   It might be more agreeable to the company that their own servants and dependants should have either the pleasure of wasting, or the profit of embezzling whatever surplus might remain, after paying the proposed dividend of eight per cent. , than that it should come into the hands of a set of people with whom those resolutions could scarce fail to set them, in some measure, at variance. The interest of those servants and dependants might so far predominate in the court of proprietors, as sometimes to dispose it to support the authors of depredations which had been committed in direct violation of its own authority. With the majority of proprietors, the support even of the authority of their own court might sometimes be a matter of less consequence, than the support of those who had set that authority at defiance.

and the company is now in greater distress than ever.   The regulations of 1773, accordingly, did not put an end to the disorders of the company's government in India. Notwithstanding that, during a momentary fit of good conduct, they had at one time collected, into the treasury of Calcutta, more than three millions sterling; notwithstanding that they had afterwards extended, either their dominion, or their depredations over a vast accession of some of the richest and most fertile countries in India; all was wasted and destroyed.

第五篇 第一章

王,按照事物的性质猜度,对于被统治者的幸福或悲惨,对于领土的改良或荒废,对于政府的荣誉或耻辱,会像这个商业公司的大部分股东那样漠不关心。议会根据调查结果,制定出种种新规,但可能只会使漠不关心的程度增加而不会减少。例如,下议院的一个决议宣称:当公司把政府贷给它的债券140万镑还清,所欠私人债务减少到150万镑时,到那时,也只有到那时,公司才能发给8%的股息;该公司留在国内的剩余收入及纯利,应当分为四部分,其中三部分交给财政部,当作国家用途,第四部分,则留作偿还债务或者支付公司可能遇到的急需的基金。但是,如果全部纯收入和利润都归自己所有,由自己自由支配的时候,公司还是管理不好,统治不好,那么当把纯收入和利润的3/4分划给别人,把其余的1/4部分留给公司使用,但在别人监督之下,经别人许可才能使用,这时公司一定不会做得更好。

就公司方面说,在支付了所提出的8%股息后,与其按照下院决议案规定,把一切剩余部分,交给与自己不和的一群人手中,倒不如让公司的雇用人员和隶属人员随便浪费,任意侵吞,来得痛快。此外,公司的这些雇用人员和隶属人员可能在股东会里起支配作用,有时使他们反而去支持贪污舞弊直接违犯自己权益的人。对于大部分股东来说,他们有时甚至把支持自己大会的权威这件事看得较轻,反而把支持公然藐视这种权威的人的事情看得较重。_{他们倾向于鼓励浪费。}

因此,1773年的规定,不能结束东印度公司统治的混乱局面。_{以前公司正在遭受更大的困难相比。}尽管公司因一时的措施得当,在加尔各答金库中,积存了300多万镑,尽管以后占领了印度几个最富裕、最肥沃的地区而使它的支配或掠夺范围,更加扩大,但它所获得的一切,全都被浪费和毁

国民财富的性质与原理

They found themselves altogether unprepared to stop or resist the incursion of Hyder Ali; and, in consequence of those disorders, the company is now (1784) in greater distress than ever; and, in order to prevent immediate bankruptcy, is once more reduced to supplicate the assistance of government. Different plans have been proposed by the different parties in parliament, for the better management of its affairs. And all those plans seem to agree in supposing, what was indeed always abundantly evident, that it is altogether unfit to govern its territorial possessions. Even the company itself seems to be convinced of its own incapacity so far, and seems, upon that account, willing to give them up to government.

<small>Companies misuse the right of making peace and war.</small>

With the right of possessing forts and garrisons in distant and barbarous countries, is necessarily connected the right of making peace and war in those countries. The joint stock companies which have had the one right, have constantly exercised the other, and have frequently had it expressly conferred upon them. How unjustly, how capriciously, how cruelly they have commonly exercised it, is too well known from recent experience.

<small>The grant of a temporary monopoly to a joint-stock company may sometimes be reasonable, but a perpetual monopoly creates an absurd tax.</small>

When a company of merchants undertake, at their own risk and expence, to establish a new trade with some remote and barbarous nation, it may not be unreasonable to incorporate them into a joint stock company, and to grant them, in case of their success, a monopoly of the trade for a certain number of years. It is the easiest and most natural way in which the state can recompense them for hazarding a dangerous and expensive experiment, of which the public is afterwards to reap the benefit. A temporary monopoly of this kind may be vindicated upon the same principles upon which a like monopoly of a new machine is granted to its inventor, and that of a new book to its author. But upon the expiration of the term, the monopoly ought certainly to determine; the forts and garrisons, if it was found necessary to establish any, to be taken into the hands of government, their value to be paid to the company, and the trade to be laid open to all the subjects of the state. By a perpetual monopoly, all the other subjects of the state are taxed very absurdly in two different ways; first, by the high price of goods, which, in the case of a free trade, they could buy much cheaper; and, secondly, by their total exclusion from a branch of business, which it might be both convenient and profitable for many of them to carry on. It is for the most worthless

灭了。到海德·阿利入侵时,公司发觉完全没有准备,无法阻止和抵抗。由于这些混乱,现在(1784年)公司已陷于前所未有的困境。为防止马上破产,公司又再一次向政府请求援助。为了更好地管理公司业务,议会中各个党派提出了种种计划。所有这些计划似乎都同意一点,即该公司完全不适合统治它所占有的领地。诚然,这一点已经是再明白不过了,即使公司自己,也认为自己无统治能力,因此愿意把领地让给政府。

在偏远而野蛮的国家拥有建筑堡垒和守备队的权利,必然会和与这些国家宣战及媾和的权利相联系。拥有一种权利的股份公司,就会不断行使另一权利,且常常要求把这另一权利明白地授予它们。它们行使权利多么不公正、多么反复无常、多么残忍,这点从最近的经验中已经是再熟悉不过了。

<small>公司滥用了与战争讲和的权利。</small>

但一些商人自己出资,甘冒风险,在偏远野蛮的国家进行新的贸易时,许其组成股份公司,并在他们成功时,给他们几年的垄断权,这并没有什么不合理的。他们进行了危险而费钱的尝试,政府给予补偿,这是最容易、最自然的方法。这样一种暂时的垄断权,和给予新机器发明者对机器的专利权以及给予新著述的著作者对该著述的出版权一样,可依同一理由加以辩护。不过,期限到期时,垄断权当然应予取消。如果建立城堡和守备队仍有必要,就应当交由政府管理,由政府给公司补偿价值,并开放当地贸易,让全国人民自由经营。如果垄断是永久的,那么会给全国其他人民增加不合理的负担。负担有两种:第一,垄断会抬高价格。如若人民可以进行自由贸易,那么货物的价格低廉。第二,垄断把很多人排除在外。如果更多的人经营贸易,那么贸易会更方便、更有利可图。他们被这样征收重税,只为了一个最不值得的

<small>给予一股份公司以暂时垄断权有时是合理的,但永久垄断权就会造成不合理负担。</small>

of all purposes too that they are taxed in this manner. It is merely to enable the company to support the negligence, profusion, and malversation of their own servants, whose disorderly conduct seldom allows the dividend of the company to exceed the ordinary rate of profit in trades which are altogether free, and very frequently makes it fall even a good deal short of that rate. Without a monopoly, however, a joint stock company, it would appear from experience, cannot long carry on any branch of foreign trade. To buy in one market, in order to sell, with profit, in another, when there are many competitors in both; to watch over, not only the occasional variations in the demand, but the much greater and more frequent variations in the competition, or in the supply which that demand is likely to get from other people, and to suit with dexterity and judgment both the quantity and quality of each assortment of goods to all these circumstances, is a species of warfare of which the operations are continually changing, and which can scarce ever be conducted successfully, without such an unremitting exertion of vigilance and attention, as cannot long be expected from the directors of a joint stock company. The East India Company, upon the redemption of their funds, and the expiration of their exclusive privilege, have a right, by act of parliament, to continue a corporation with a joint stock, and to trade in their corporate capacity to the East Indies in common with the rest of their fellow-subjects. But in this situation, the superior vigilance and attention of private adventurers would, in all probability, soon make them weary of the trade.

A list of fifty-five companies with exclusive privileges for foreign trade which have failed has been collected by Abbé Morellet.

An eminent French author, of great knowledge in matters of political œconomy, the Abbé Morellet, gives a list of fifty-five joint stock companies for foreign trade, which have been established in different parts of Europe since the year 1600, and which, according to him, have all failed from mismanagement, notwithstanding they had exclusive privileges. He has been misinformed with regard to the history of two or three of them, which were not joint stock companies and have not failed. But, in compensation, there have been several joint stock companies which have failed, and which he has omitted.

Only four trades can be well carried on by a company with no exclusive privilege, namely,

The only trades which it seems possible for a joint stock company to carry on successfully, without an exclusive privilege, are those, of which all the operations are capable of being reduced to what is called a routine, or to such a uniformity of method as admits of little or no variation. Of this kind is, first, the banking trade; secondly, the trade of insurance from fire, and from sea risk and capture in time of war; thirdly, the trade of making and maintaining a navigable cut or canal; and, fourthly, the similar trade of bringing water for the supply of a great city.

理由。这只会使公司支持员工的怠慢、浪费以及侵吞公款的行为。由于这些人员的胡乱行为,公司分派的股息,很少超过其他自由职业者的普通利润率,且往往远远低于普通利润率。但是,根据经验,股份公司如果没有垄断权,似乎无法长久进行任何对外贸易。公司在一个地方购入货物,运往另一地方出售,获得利润,而在这两个地方都有许多竞争者,这需要时时留意需求情况的偶然变动,以及竞争情况或者需求可能从其他人那里得到供给的更大更频繁的变动;运用巧妙的手腕和正确的判断力,使各色货物的数量,都能适应需求、供给和竞争等各方面的变动情况。这俨然像是在进行一场不断变化的战争,如果不加时时注意、警惕,就无胜利希望,而这种举动,股份公司的董事是不可能长期保持的。所以,东印度公司在偿付完贷款,专营特权过期之后,虽然根据议会制定的法令,仍然可以以股份公司的资格,在东印度与其他商人共同竞争。但在这种情形下,私人冒险者的高度警惕与极力关注很快会使公司经营疲惫不堪。

　　法国著名作家、莫雷勒修道院院长阿贝·摩尔莱,对经济学很有研究。他曾列举了1600年以后在欧洲各地设立的国外贸易股份公司共55家;他认为这些公司都取得了专营特权,但都因管理不善,全都失败。他列举的这55家中,其中有两三家不是股份公司,而且没有失败,他把这弄错了。还有几个失败了的股份公司,他没有列出来。^{摩尔莱列举了五家具有专营权的股份公司。}

　　一个股份公司没有取得专营特权而能经营成功的贸易,似乎只有这种的贸易,也就是说,在这个贸易里,所有营业活动都可简化为常规,或者说方法全部一致,很少变化或毫无变化。这类贸易有四种:第一,银行业;第二,水火兵灾保险业;第三,修建并维^{四种行业不具专营权,但可以取得成功,即}

国民财富的性质与原理

<small>tanking,</small>　　Though the principles of the banking trade may appear somewhat abstruse, the practice is capable of being reduced to strict rules. To depart upon any occasion from those rules, in consequence of some flattering speculation of extraordinary gain, is almost always extremely dangerous, and frequently fatal to the banking company which attempts it. But the constitution of joint stock companies renders them in general more tenacious of established rules than any private copartnery. Such companies, therefore, seem extremely well fitted for this trade. The principal banking companies in Europe, accordingly, are joint stock companies, many of which manage their trade very successfully without any exclusive privilege. The Bank of England has no other exclusive privilege, except that no other banking company in England shall consist of more than six persons. The two banks of Edinburgh are joint stock companies without any exclusive privilege.

<small>insurance,</small>　　The value of the risk, either from fire, or from loss by sea, or by capture, though it cannot, perhaps, be calculated very exactly, admits, however, of such a gross estimation as renders it, in some degree, reducible to strict rule and method. The trade of insurance, therefore, may be carried on successfully by a joint stock company, without any exclusive privilege. Neither the London Assurance, nor the Royal Exchange Assurance companies, have any such privilege. ①

<small>canal and aqueduct management and construction.</small>　　When a navigable cut or canal has been once made, the management of it becomes quite simple and easy, and is reducible to strict rule and method. Even the making of it is so, as it may be contracted for with undertakers at so much a mile, and so much a lock. The same thing may be said of a canal, an aqueduct, or a great pipe for bringing water to supply a great city. Such undertakings, therefore, may be, and accordingly frequently are, very successfully managed by joint stock companies without any exclusive privilege,

　　To establish a joint stock company, however, for any undertaking, merely because such a company might be capable of managing it successfully; or to exempt a particular set of dealers from some of the general laws which take place with regard to all their neighbours,

---

　　① [At least as against private persons, Anderson, *Commerce*, A. D. 1720.]

持通航河道或运河;第四,城市饮水供应业。

银行业的原理虽有些深奥,但实际业务做法可规定为严格的规则。如果为了贪图眼前利益去冒险投机而不顾这些规则,那么这总是极其危险的,这对试图这样去做的银行会是致命的打击。但是,股份公司的章程使得公司一般比私人合伙公司更能遵守规章。因此,股份公司就似乎很适于从事银行业。因此,欧洲主要银行都是股份公司。在这些公司当中,有许多并没有专营特权,但经营却非常成功。英格兰银行业没有专营特权,除了议会规定其他银行的组成,股东不得超过六人以上之外。爱丁堡两家银行全为没有取得任何专营权利股份公司。银行业;

由火灾、水灾或者战祸所带来的风险,其价值虽不能很精准地计算出来,但可大概地估算出来,使得在某种程度上能够订出严密规则和一定方法。因此,保险业的生意,有可能比没有特权的股份公司经营得更加成功。例如伦敦保险公司,如皇家贸易保险公司,这些都是没有取得任何特权的①。保险业;

通航河道或运河一旦修造成功,对其的日常管理将变得非常简单且容易,可定出严密的规则与方法。即使修造河道也是如此,修一里的河道,建一闸门,都可以与承包人签订合约。这些规则可以引申到修造引导清水供给城市的运河、水槽或大水管。诸如此类的事业,往往由那些即使未取得特权的股份公司经营,亦可大获其利,而实际情况也往往如此。运河、沟渠的管理和建筑。

然而,建立一个股份公司,仅仅因为其有成功经营管理的能力,或者说,让一群特定的商人在普遍的规则下享受到其他人享

---

① 至少是针对私人的特权。参见安德森:《商业》,1720年。

国民财富的性质与原理

<small>A joint stock company ought not to be established except for some purpose of remarkable utility, requiring a larger capital than can be provided by a private partnership.</small> merely because they might be capable of thriving if they had such an exemption, would certainly not be reasonable. To render such an establishment perfectly reasonable, with the circumstance of being reducible to strict rule and method, two other circumstances ought to concur. First, it ought to appear with the clearest evidence, that the undertaking is of greater and more general utility than the greater part of common trades; and secondly, that it requires a greater capital than can easily be collected into a private copartnery. If a moderate capital were sufficient, the great utility of the undertaking would not be a sufficient reason for establishing a joint stock company; because, in this case, the demand for what it was to produce, would readily and easily be supplied by private adventurers. In the four trades above mentioned, both those circumstances concur.

<small>These conditions are fulfilled by banking,</small> The great and general utility of the banking trade when prudently managed, has been fully explained in the second book of this inquiry. But a public bank which is to support public credit, and upon particular emergencies to advance to government the whole produce of a tax, to the amount, perhaps, of several millions, a year or two before it comes in, requires a greater capital than can easily be collected into any private copartnery.

<small>insurance,</small> The trade of insurance gives great security to the fortunes of private people, and by dividing among a great many that loss which would ruin an individual, makes it fall light and easy upon the whole society. In order to give this security, however, it is necessary that the insurers should have a very large capital. Before the establishment of the two joint stock companies for insurance in London, a list, it is said, was laid before the attorney-general, of one hundred and fifty private insurers who had failed in the course of a few years.

<small>canals and water works,</small> That navigable cuts and canals, and the works which are sometimes necessary for supplying a great city with water, are of great and general utility; while at the same time they frequently require a greater expence than suits the fortunes of private people, is sufficiently obvious.

<small>but not by anything else.</small> Except the four trades above mentioned, I have not been able to recollect any other in which all the three circumstances, requisite for rendering reasonable the establishment of a joint stock company, concur. The English copper company of London, the lead smelting company, the glass grinding company, have not even the pretext of any

受不到的权利,仅仅因为通过这种途径他们能够得到繁荣,这当然是不合理的。通过定出严密规则及方法,使股份公司的建立达到合理化,应当同时附加上其他两个条件:事业的效用,应当能最清晰的显示出比大部分的商业更大、更普及的好处。所需要的资本,一定是私人合伙公司所无法筹集的数额。那些无需很大资本即能兴办的事业,其效用再大也不应当作为设立股份公司的充分理由。因为,在这种情况下,需求可以很容易地由私人企业提供。上述提及的四种事业,这两个条件都同时具备。

建立公司,必须是一些有着显著效用的目的,要可以比合营私人经营提供更多的资本。

本书第一篇已详细说明了银行业管理妥当,会产生巨大的效用。但是,若一家公共银行的设立,其目的是用于维持公共信用,即当国家有特别急需时,对政府垫付某一税收的全部,数额也许达数百万镑,而该税收又需一两年后才能收入,这种银行所需的资本,当然不是私人公司能力所及。

这些条件银行业可以满足。

保险业对个人财产给予了很大的安全保障。巨大的损失原本会轻而易举的使个人趋于没落,但是保险业却会将这种损失分配给许多人,让整个社会毫不费力的共同分担起来。为了给他人提供这种安全保障,保险业者就必须持有很大的资本。伦敦保险股份公司设立以前,检察长处有数据清单显示,150个保险公司全都开业不到几年就失败了。

保险业也可以满足。

通航水道、运河以及必要的城市的供水系统,是最为普遍而重要的。而与此同时,他们所需的巨大费用,亦非个人财力所及。

运河和供水系统也一样。

具备了上述三个条件的股份公司,才有其合理性。除上述提及的四种行业外,我再也不能想出其他的具有这二个条件的事业。位于伦敦的英国铜业公司、熔铅公司以及玻璃公司,他们所追求目标的效用并没有多大,而费用也是许多私人财力所能做到

但任何其他行业都不足以满足这些条件。

great or singular utility in the object which they pursue; nor does the pursuit of that object seem to require any expence unsuitable to the fortunes of many private men. Whether the trade which those companies carry on, is reducible to such strict rule and method as to render it fit for the management of a joint stock company, or whether they have any reason to boast of their extraordinary profits, I do not pretend to know. The mine-adventurers company has been long ago bankrupt. ① A share in the stock of the British Linen Company of Edinburgh sells, at present, very much below par, though less so than it did some years ago. The joint stock companies, which are established for the public-spirited purpose of promoting some particular manufacture, over and above managing their own affairs ill, to the diminution of the general stock of the society, can in other respects scarce ever fail to do more harm than good. Notwithstanding the most upright intentions, the unavoidable partiality of their directors to particular branches of the manufacture, of which the undertakers mislead and impose upon them, is a real discouragement to the rest, and necessarily breaks, more or less, that natural proportion which would otherwise establish itself between judicious industry and profit, and which, to the general industry of the country, is of all encouragements the greatest and the most effectual.

ARTICLE II *Of The Expence Of The Institutions For The Education Of Youth*

_{Institutions for education may also be made to furnish their own expense, or may be endowed.}

The institutions for the education of the youth may, in the same manner, furnish a revenue sufficient for defraying their own expence. The fee or honorary which the scholar pays to the master naturally constitutes a revenue of this kind.

Even where the reward of the master does not arise altogether from this natural revenue, it still is not necessary that it should be derived from that general revenue of the society, of which the collection and application are, in most countries, assigned to the executive power. Through the greater part of Europe, accordingly, the endowment of schools and colleges makes either no charge upon that general revenue, or but a very small one. It every where arises chiefly from some local or provincial revenue, from the rent of some landed estate, or from the interest of some sum of money allotted and put under the management of trustees for this particular purpose, sometimes by the sovereign himself, and sometimes by some private donor.

---

① [Anderson, *Commerce*, A. D. 1690, 1704, 1710, 1711.]

的。至于这些公司所经营的业务,是否能驾驭这些严密法则及方法使其适用于股份公司的管理,是否有理由为他们获得的厚利自豪,在这里我就不能信口开河了。很早以前矿山企业公司就破产了①。目前,爱丁堡英国麻布公司出售的股票,虽没有从前跌落的那么厉害,但较其票面价格,却仍旧跌了许多。那些基于爱国心的为促进国家某一特殊制造业而设立的股份公司往往因为经营不善,以致减少了社会总资本,在其他的各方面,同样是利少害多。董事们的意图即使非常正直,但他们对特殊制造业不可避免的偏爱将会实质性的妨害到其他的制造行业,这或多或少会破坏适当产业与利润间的自然比例。而这一自然比例,对于国家的整个工业来说,是最大且最有效的鼓励。

第二项　论年轻人教育机构的费用

年轻人教育机构,同样也能提供足以应付自己开支的收入。学生付给教师的学费或谢礼,自然构成这类收入。

即使教师的报酬不是完全从自然收入中获得的,那也不必就由社会的一般收入来开支;在许多国家,社会一般收入的征集和使用都交由行政当局负责。因此,在欧洲大部分地方,学校和学院的基金不是来自社会一般收入,或者只有一小部分是来自一般收入。各个地方的教育经费主要来自于地方收入或省收入、地产租金,或指定用作这项用途的专款的利息。专款有时由君主本人拨给,或由私人捐助,交由保管人管理。

边注：教育机构也可以自己负担他们的支出,或者靠募捐来支付。

---

① 安德森:《商业》,1690 年,1704 年,1710 年,1700 年。

| 国民财富的性质与原理

Have endowments really promoted useful education?

Have those public endowments contributed in general to promote the end of their institution ? Have they contributed to encourage the diligence, and to improve the abilities of the teachers ? Have they directed the course of education towards objects more useful, both to the individual and to the public, than those to which it would naturally have gone of its own accord ? It should not seem very difficult to give at least a probable answer to each of those questions.

Exertion is always in proportion to its necessity.

In every profession, the exertion of the greater part of those who exercise it, is always in proportion to the necessity they are under of making that exertion. This necessity is greatest with those to whom the emoluments of their profession are the only source from which they expect their fortune, or even their ordinary revenue and subsistence. In order to acquire this fortune, or even to get this subsistence, they must, in the course of a year, execute a certain quantity of work of a known value; and, where the competition is free, the rivalship of competitors, who are all endeavouring to justle one another out of employment, obliges every man to endeavour to execute his work with a certain degree of exactness. The greatness of the objects which are to be acquired by success in some particular professions may, no doubt, sometimes animate the exertion of a few men of extraordinary spirit and ambition. Great objects, however, are evidently not necessary in order to occasion the greatest exertions. Rivalship and emulation render excellency, even in mean professions, an object of ambition, and frequently occasion the very greatest exertions. Great objects, on the contrary, alone and unsupported by the necessity of application, have seldom been sufficient to occasion any considerable exertion. In England, success in the profession of the law leads to some very great objects of ambition; and yet how few men, born to easy fortunes, have ever in this country been eminent in that profession ?

Endowments diminish the necessity of application,

The endowments of schools and colleges have necessarily diminished more or less the necessity of application in the teachers. Their subsistence, so far as it arises from their salaries, is evidently derived from a fund altogether independent of their success and reputation in their particular professions.

In some universities the salary makes but a part, and frequently but a small part of the emoluments of the teacher, of which the greater part arises from the honoraries or fees of his pupils.

— 1580 —

这些公共捐赠基金一般有助于促进设置该基金的目的吗?基金是否曾激励过教师要勤奋,并增进教师的能力?基金是否曾改变教育的自然过程,使其转向对个人、对社会双方都较有用的目标?针对上述种种问题,只作大概的答复,似乎不会困难的。

> 但这些募捐真正促进了有用的教育吗?

在每个职业中,从事这个职业的大部分人所作努力程度,总与他们不得不作这努力的必要性大小相称。这种必要对一些人来说是最大的,即职业报酬是他们所期望的财产或甚至是他的普通收入及生活资料的唯一源泉。他们为取得这些财产或基本的生活资料,一年中必须完成一定数量有一定价值的工作。如果竞争自由,那么各人相互排挤,相互竞争,于是迫使每个人都努力搞好自己的工作。毋庸置疑,在某些职业,只有成功才会实现伟大的目标,有时这会鼓舞一些意志坚强、志向远大的人去努力。但是,很显然,要做出非凡的努力,也不见得就需要伟大的目标。即使在最卑微的职业中,竞争和比赛也可以使人为了争取优秀而野心勃勃,那么就会做出最大的努力。反之,只有伟大的目标而没有实现目标的必要,那么也不足以激起巨大的努力。在英国,在法律界获得成功,可以让人实现种种宏伟的目标,但国内出身富贵之人又有几个在这个行业声名显赫呢?

> 努力总是和它的必要性成比例。

学校或学院的捐赠基金,必然或多或少减少教师勉励的必要。就教师的生活资料来自工资来说,显而易见,他们靠基金来维持生计,而这和他们在教育行业的成功或名声是没有关系的。

> 捐助会减少教师勤勉的必要性。

有些大学里教师的工资,仅占其报酬的一部分,而且往往是极小的一部分,其余大部分,则来自学生的谢礼或学费。在这种

国民财富的性质与原理

<small>which is not entirely removed where the teacher receives part of his emoluments from fees,</small> The necessity of application, though always more or less diminished, is not in this case entirely taken away. ① Reputation in his profession is still of some importance to him, and he still has some dependency upon the affection, gratitude, and favourable report of those who have attended upon his instructions; and these favourable sentiments he is likely to gain in no way so well as by deserving them, that is, by the abilities and diligence with which he discharges every part of his duty.

<small>but is entirely absent when his whole revenue arises from endowments.</small> In other universities the teacher is prohibited from receiving any honorary or fee from his pupils, and his salary constitutes the whole of the revenue which he derives from his office. His interest is, in this case, set as directly in opposition to his duty as it is possible to set it. It is the interest of every man to live as much at his ease as he can; and if his emoluments are to be precisely the same, whether he does, or does not perform some very laborious duty, it is certainly his interest, at least as interest is vulgarly understood, either to neglect it altogether, or, if he is subject to some authority which will not suffer him to do this, to perform it in as careless and slovenly a manner as that authority will permit. If le is naturally active and a lover of labour, it is his interest to employ that activity in any way, from which he can derive some advantage, rather than in the performance of his duty, from which he can derive none.

<small>Members of a college or university are indulgent to their fellow members.</small> If the authority to which he is subject resides in the body corporate, the college, or university, of which he himself is a member, and in which the greater part of the other members are, like himself, persons who either are, or ought to be teachers; they are likely to make a common cause, to be all very indulgent to one another, and every man to consent that his neighbour may neglect his duty, provided he himself is allowed to neglect his own. In the university of Oxford, the greater part of the public professors have, for these many years, given up altogether even the pretence of teaching.

If the authority to which he is subject resides, not so much in the body corporate of which he is a member, as in some other extraneous persons, in the bishop of the diocese for example; in the governor of the province; or, perhaps, in some minister of state; it is not indeed in this case very likely that he will be suffered to neglect his duty altogether. All that such superiors, however, can

---

① [Rae, *Life of Adam Smith*, p. 48, thinks Smith's salary at Glasgow may have been about £ 70 with a house, and his fees near £ 100.]

情况下,做出努力的必要,虽不免减少一些,但并未完全消失①。教学的名望还是很重要的。此外,他还需要听他授课的学生的爱戴、感激和良好的评价。要抵得上这种种学生对他的好感,他只有竭尽全力、兢兢业业的完成自己的职责,这才问心无愧。

在其他大学里,禁止教师接受学生的谢礼或学费,而他的工资,是他从事教育职业的全部收入。在这种情况下,教师的利益与职责,处于完全对立的地位。每一个人的利益,在于尽力过上安逸的生活。如果无论他履行了还是没有履行辛苦的职责,他的报酬是完全一样的,那么他的利益,至少是通俗所理解的利益,就是要忽视这种职责。或者如果有某种权力,不许他放弃职责,那他就会在权力容许的范围内,尽量敷衍了事。如果他天性积极,热爱劳动,那么他与其把活动用在无利可图的职务上,不如找点有利可图的事去做。

如果他应当服从的权力,掌握在社团即学院或大学手中,而他自己又是学院或大学中的成员,其他成员大部分,也像他一样,是教师或应为教师者,那么这些教师们就有着共同的动机,彼此非常宽容;各人都容许他的同事忽视职责,而他的同事也容许他忽视职责。牛津大学的大部分公职教授,几年来连表面文章也不做了,完全放弃了教育职责。

如果他服从的权力,不由自己所属的社团管理,而由外部的人物如主教、省长或大臣管理,在这种情况下,容许他全然放弃职责就是不大可能的。但是,这些大人物所做的也只是强迫他在一

---

① 雷:《亚当·斯密的生平》,第 48 页认为,斯密在格拉斯格的薪酬可能是 70 镑,外加一所住宅,他的学费接近 100 镑。

<small>External control is ignorant and capricious.</small> force him to do, is to attend upon his pupils a certain number of hours, that is, to give a certain number of lectures in the week or in the year. What those lectures shall be, must still depend upon the diligence of the teacher; and that diligence is likely to be proportioned to the motives which he has for exerting it. An extraneous jurisdiction of this kind, besides, is liable to be exercised both ignorantly and capriciously. In its nature it is arbitrary and discretionary, and the persons who exercise it, neither attending upon the lectures of the teacher themselves, nor perhaps understanding the sciences which it is his business to teach, are seldom capable of exercising it with judgment. From the insolence of office too they are frequently indifferent how they exercise it, and are very apt to censure or deprive him of his office wantonly, and without any just cause. The person subject to such jurisdiction is necessarily degraded by it, and, instead of being one of the most respectable, is rendered one of the meanest and most contemptible persons in the society. It is by powerful protection only that he can effectually guard himself against the bad usage to which he is at all times exposed; and this protection he is most likely to gain, not by ability or diligence in his profession, but by obsequiousness to the will of his superiors, and by being ready, at all times, to sacrifice to that will the rights, the interest, and the honour of the body corporate of which he is a member. Whoever has attended for any considerable time to the administration of a French university, must have had occasion to remark the effects which naturally result from an arbitrary and extraneous jurisdiction of this kind.

<small>To compel young men to attend a university has a bad effect on the teachers.</small> Whatever forces a certain number of students to any college or university, independent of the merit or reputation of the teachers, tends more or less to diminish the necessity of that merit or reputation.

The privileges of graduates in arts, in law, physic and divinity, when they can be obtained only by residing a certain number of years in certain universities, necessarily force a certain number of students to such universities, independent of the merit or reputation of the teachers. The privileges of graduates are a sort of statutes of apprenticeship, which have contributed to the improvement of education, just as the other statutes of apprenticeship have to that of arts and manufactures.

<small>The privileges of graduates are thus like apprenticeship.</small>

The charitable foundations of scholarships, exhibitions, bursaries, &c. necessarily attach a certain number of students to certain colleges, independent altogether of the merit of those particular colleges. Were the students upon such charitable foundations left free to

定的时数内照顾学生,或者一周或一年内上一定时数的课。至于授课内容如何,要看教师的勤勉程度,而教师的勤勉程度,又和努力授课的动机的大小成比例。此外,这种外部的管辖权的行使,可能是无知和反复无常的,其性质往往是任意的、专断的。行使监督权的人,既没有听过教师的课,又不一定理解教师所教的学科,很难公正地行使权力。加之,这种职务自然让他们产生傲慢之心,所以他们往往对怎样行使其职权漠不关心,没有正当理由就任意谴责教师,或开除教师。教师忍受这样的监管,他的品格必然被贬低,他不再是社会上最受尊敬的人,而是最卑贱、最可轻侮的人了。为了避免随时可受到的不良行为,他就要保护自己,那么就只有依赖有权人物了。他最有可能获得的这种保护,不是因为工作上的能力和勤勉,而是趋于奉承监督者的上级的意志。他随时都准备为这种意志而牺牲他所在团体的权利、利益及名誉。凡是在一个相当长的期间关注过法国大学管理的人,都会看到,这种专横的外部的监督权自然会产生什么结果。

<small>外部控制是无知的,而且是反复无常的。</small>

　　凡是强迫一定人数的学生去上学院或大学,而不管教师学识或名声如何的事情,都会或多或少地减少教师学识或名声地必要性。

<small>强迫年轻人上大学对教师不利。</small>

　　如果只要在某些大学住满一定年限就能获得诸如艺术、法律、医学、神学等学科的毕业生的特权,这必然会使一定人数的学生去上这些大学,而不管教师学问或名声如何。毕业生的特权就像学徒制度,有助于教育的改进,正如其他的学徒制度有助于技术及制造的改进一样。

<small>毕业生的特权比就好是学徒制。</small>

　　奖学金、研究费、贫学津贴等等奖励构成的慈善基金,必然会使一定人数的学生去某些大学学习,而不管其优点如何。如果让

Scholarships, regulations against migration,

chuse what college they liked best, such liberty might perhaps contribute to excite some emulation among different colleges. A regulation, on the contrary, which prohibited even the independent members of every particular college from leaving it, and going to any other, without leave first asked and obtained of that which they meant to abandon, would tend very much to extinguish that emulation.

and assignment of students to particular tutors are equally pernicious.

If in each college the tutor or teacher, who was to instruct each student in all arts and sciences, should not be voluntarily chosen by the student, but appointed by the head of the college; and if, in case of neglect, inability, or bad usage, the student should not be allowed to change him for another, without leave first asked and obtained; such a regulation would not only tend very much to extinguish all emulation among the different tutors of the same college, but to diminish very much in all of them the necessity of diligence and of attention to their respective pupils. Such teachers, though very well paid by their students, might be as much disposed to neglect them, as those who are not paid by them at all, or who have no other recompence but their salary.

Where such regulations prevail a teacher may avoid or suppress all visible signs of disapprobation on the part of his pupils.

If the teacher happens to be a man of sense, it must be an unpleasant thing to him to be conscious, while he is lecturing his students, that he is either speaking or reading nonsense, or what is very little better than nonsense. It must too be unpleasant to him to observe that the greater part of his students desert his lectures; or perhaps attend upon them with plain enough marks of neglect, contempt, and derision. If he is obliged, therefore, to give a certain number of lectures, these motives alone, without any other interest, might dispose him to take some pains to give tolerably good ones. Several different expedients, however may be fallen upon, which will effectually blunt the edge of all those incitements to diligence. The teacher, instead of explaining to his pupils himself the science in which he proposes to instruct them, may read some book upon it; and if this book is written in a foreign and dead language, by interpreting it to them into their own; or, what would give him still less trouble, by making them interpret it to him, and by now and then making an occasional remark upon it, he may flatter himself that he is giving a lecture. The slightest degree of knowledge and application will enable him to do this, without exposing himself to contempt or derision, or saying

慈善基金资助的学生能自由选择自己最喜欢的大学,那么这种自由或许会激起各大学之间一定程度的竞争。反之,如果规定禁止某学院的即使是自费的学生,未经准许不得离开该校,转入他校,那么,各学校之间的竞争也就不复存在了。奖学金,规定不准转学。

如果在各个学院,学生不能自由选择教授科学艺术的导师或教师,而由校长指派;如果学生遇到教师怠慢、无能或做法不当,未经申请许可,不得改换教师,那么这种规定,不但会使同一学校内各导师间的竞争,大大减少,而且会使他们勤勉任教以及关注各个学生的必要性,也大大减少。这样的教师虽然收了学生非常优厚的报酬,但也会像那些未收受学生报酬,或除工资以外毫无其他报酬的教师那样,怠误职守,忽视学生。而且给学生指派特定的导师同样也是有害的。

如果教师是一个明达事理的人的话,那么当他意识到他给学生讲的念的都是一些没有意义或者与没有意义相差无几的内容时,他肯定会感到不舒服;如果他看到大部分学生不来听他讲的课,或者明显地以漫不经心、轻蔑、耻笑的态度来听他的课,他也肯定会感到不舒服。所以,如果他必须要讲一定课时的课的话,即便没有其他利益,单是这些动机,也会促使他尽力来讲一些像样的课。不过,几种教师可能采取的不同的对策可能会大大地减少对教师勤勉讲授的激励。教师可能不是自己给学生讲解他计划讲授的知识,而是读那些与这些知识相关的书籍。如果那本书是用外语或者不再使用的语言写的,那么他就把它翻译成本国语言给学生讲述;或者更不费劲的办法,就是让学生解释给他听,他只是中间间或加一些评论,他就可以自吹他给学生讲授了这门课。这样做只需要最些微的知识和努力,就可以避免使他遭到蔑视或者耻笑,或者避免讲出任何真正愚蠢、荒唐或可笑的内容来。在实行这些规定的地方,教师可以避免或压制学生明显的不满。

any thing that is really foolish, absurd, or ridiculous. The discipline of the college, at the same time, may enable him to force all his pupils to the most regular attendance upon this sham-lecture, and to maintain the most decent and respectful behaviour during the whole time of the performance.

<small>University and college discipline is contrived for the ease of the teachers, and quite unnecessary if the teachers are tolerably diligent.</small>

The discipline of colleges and universities is in general contrived, not for the benefit of the students, but for the interest, or more properly speaking, for the ease of the masters. Its object is, in all cases, to maintain the authority of the master, and whether he neglects or performs his duty, to oblige the students in all cases to behave to him as if he performed it with the greatest diligence and ability. It seems to presume perfect wisdom and virtue in the one order, and the greatest weakness and folly in the other. Where the masters, however, really perform their duty, there are no examples, I believe, that the greater part of the students ever neglect theirs. No discipline is ever requisite to force attendance upon lectures which are really worth the attending, as is well known wherever any such lectures are given. Force and restraint may, no doubt, be in some degree requisite in order to oblige children, or very young boys, to attend to those parts of education which it is thought necessary for them to acquire during that early period of life; but after twelve or thirteen years of age, provided the master does his duty, force or restraint can scarce ever be necessary to carry on any part of education. Such is the generosity of the greater part of young men, that, so far from being disposed to neglect or despise the instructions of their master, provided he shows some serious intention of being of use to them, they are generally inclined to pardon a great deal of incorrectness in the performance of his duty, and sometimes even to conceal from the public a good deal of gross negligence.

<small>The parts of education that are not conducted by public institutions are better taught.</small>

Those parts of education, it is to be observed, for the teaching of which there are no public institutions, are generally the best taught. When a young man goes to a fencing or a dancing school, he does not indeed always learn to fence or to dance very well; but he seldom fails of learning to fence or to dance. The good effects of the riding school are not commonly so evident. The expence of a riding school is so great, that in most places it is a public institution. The three most essential parts of literary education, to read, write, and account, it still continues to be more common to acquire in private than in public schools; and it very seldom happens that any body fails of acquiring them to the degree in which it is necessary to acquire them.

同时,学校的规定,还可以使他强迫所有的学生极为规矩地来上他虚伪的授课,而且还要学生们在他整个的上课期间保持一种最礼貌、最恭敬的态度。

总体来说,学院和大学纪律的设计不是为了学生的利益,而是为了教师的利益,或者更恰当地说是为教师的安逸。在所有的情况下,它的目的都在于维护教师的权威。无论教师是否懈怠或者履行了他的责任,学生们在所有的场合都要表现得恭恭敬敬,好像教师已经尽其最大的勤奋和能力来讲课了似的。它看来是假设教师具有尽善尽美的智慧和美德,而学生则是愚蠢白痴之极。然而,如果教师履行了他们的职责,我相信大多数学生是绝不会轻视他们的课程的。如果这些课程真的值得来听,那么不用任何纪律强制,无论任何时候讲课学生们都会来听讲的。当然,对于儿童或者非常年幼的孩子,为了使他们必须接受幼年期的那部分教育,可能需要某种程度的强制和限制。但十二三岁以后,只要教师尽职尽责,无论什么样的教育都很少再需要强制或限制了。大多数年轻人都是非常宽容的,只要教师是真心实意想讲点对学生有用的东西,学生们就远远不会懈怠或者鄙视老师的讲课,甚至如果教师在履行责任时出现了很多失误,他们还对公众掩盖这些重大疏忽。

值得注意的是,通常是没有公共教育机构的那部分教育教授的最好。一个青年进击剑学校或舞蹈学校学习,虽然他未必一定学得很好,但却很少有没有学会击剑或者跳舞的。而马术学校教育的结果就往往没有这么明显了。马术学校的费用非常昂贵,在大多数地方它都是一个公共教育机构。文科教育三项最根本的部分,即读书、写字和计算,迄今为止还普遍主要由私立学校来讲

| 国民财富的性质与原理

English public schools, where the teachers depend more upon fees, are less corrupt than the universities.

In England the public schools are much less corrupted than the universities. In the schools the youth are taught, or at least may be taught, Greek and Latin; that is, every thing which the masters pretend to teach, or which, it is expected, they should teach. In the universities the youth neither are taught, nor always can find any proper means of being taught, the sciences, which it is the business of those incorporated bodies to teach. The reward of the schoolmaster in most cases depends principally, in some cases almost entirely, upon the fees or honoraries of his scholars. Schools have no exclusive privileges. In order to obtain the honours of graduation, it is not necessary that a person should bring a certificate of his having studied a certain number of years at a public school. If upon examination he appears to understand what is taught there, no questions are asked about the place where he learnt it.

What the universities teach badly would not be commonly taught at all but for them.

The parts of education which are commonly taught in universities, it may, perhaps, be said are not very well taught. But had it not been for those institutions they would not have been commonly taught at all, and both the individual and the public would have suffered a good deal from the want of those important parts of education.

They were originally instituted for the education of churchmen in theology;

The present universities of Europe were originally, the greater part of them, ecclesiastical corporations; instituted for the education of churchmen. They were founded by the authority of the pope, and were so entirely under his immediate protection, that their members, whether masters or students, had all of them what was then called the benefit of clergy, that is, were exempted from the civil jurisdiction of the countries in which their respective universities were situated, and were amenable only to the ecclesiastical tribunals. What was taught in

授。但却很少会有学生没有达到他必须学得的教育程度。

在英国,相比于大学,公共学校远远没有那样腐败。在公共学校,年轻人可以学到或者至少可能学到希腊语和拉丁文,也就是说可以学到教师计划讲授的知识,或者期望教师应该讲授的知识。而在大学里面,年轻人既没有学到大学应该讲授的知识,也没有找到学习这些知识的合适的方法。公共学校教师的薪酬大多数情况下主要依靠,有些情况下几乎是全部来自于学生的学费或者酬金。这些学校没有什么排他特权。要想获得毕业证,并不需要学生出示他已经在一个公共学校里学过了一定年限的证明。如果通过考试他展示了他已经理解了那个公共学校所讲授的知识,那么就不会再问他是在哪所学校里学习的这些知识。

> 英国的公共学校更多地依靠学费,他们不像大学那样腐败。

普遍由大学来承担的那部分教育,或许可以说都讲授的不是很好。但是如果没有大学,那么这部分知识就可能根本不会普遍被讲授了,对于个人和公众来说,又会因为缺失这些重要部分的教育而蒙受巨大的损失。

> 尽管这些大学教授的不好,但如果不是大学,那部分知识就不会被普遍地讲授了。

现在欧洲的大学,它们中的大部分最初都是为了教育牧师而设立的宗教团体。它们是教皇授权建立的,学校的教师和学生都完全处于教皇的直接保护之下。他们拥有所有所谓的圣职特权[1],有了这些特权,他们就不再受大学所在国家的民事法庭的管辖,而只服从宗教法庭的管制。在这样的大部分学校里教授的

> 它们最初是为了教育牧师而设立的;

---

〔1〕圣职特权:在 14 世纪的英格兰,"圣职特权(benefit of clergy)"原则最初只适用于教士,它规定犯有重罪的教士只受教会法(ecclesiastical authority)管辖,后来该原则又适用于任何一个能读一节《圣经》的人。然而 1487 年之后,俗人只能使用一次这种特权,使用时要在他的拇指上烙上印记以便将来确认他是否已经使用过这项特权。

the greater part of those universities was suitable to the end of their institution, either theology, or something that was merely preparatory to theology.

<small>for this Latin was necessary,</small>   When christianity was first established by law, a corrupted Latin had become the common language of all the western parts of Europe. The service of the church accordingly, and the translation of the Bible which was read in churches, were both in that corrupted Latin; that is, in the common language of the country. After the irruption of the barbarous nations who overturned the Roman empire, Latin gradually ceased to be the language of any part of Europe. But the reverence of the people naturally preserves the established forms and ceremonies of religion, long after the circumstances which first introduced and rendered them reasonable are no more. Though Latin, therefore, was no longer understood any where by the great body of the people, the whole service of the church still continued to be performed in that language. Two different languages were thus established in Europe, in the same manner as in ancient Egypt; a language of the priests, and a language of the people; a sacred and a profane; a learned and an unlearned language. But it was necessary that the priests should understand something of that sacred and learned language in which they were to officiate; and the study of the Latin language therefore made, from the beginning, an essential part of university education.

It was not so with that either of the Greek, or of the Hebrew language. The infallible decrees of the church had pronounced the Latin

东西,当然是适合于这些机构的教育目的,即要么是神学,要么是神学预备知识。

最初当基督教通过法律被确定为国教时,这种讹误的拉丁文就成了西欧各个地区的普遍语言。所以,教堂举行的礼拜和教堂里诵读的《圣经》译文,都是采用这种讹误的拉丁文,也就是说用教堂所在国家的普通语言。自从野蛮民族入侵推翻了罗马帝国以后,拉丁文在欧洲各地就逐渐停止使用了。但人们的崇敬还是把宗教的既定形式和仪式自然地保存了下来,即便因为年代久远,如今的情形已经与最初引进这些宗教形式和仪式并将其合理化的环境截然不同了。所以尽管拉丁文在各地并没有多少人会,但教堂里的礼拜还是采用拉丁文。于是就像是古埃及一样,在欧洲存在着两种不同的语言,即牧师的语言和人民的语言,神圣的语言和世俗的语言,有学问的语言和没有学问的语言。但是牧师们必须要懂得做司祭时的一些神圣的、有学问的语言,这样拉丁文自开始就成了大学教育的一个重要部分。

为此,拉丁文必不可少。

而希腊语或者希伯来语情况就与此不同。所谓无误的《圣经》,[1] 曾宣称《圣经》的拉丁文译本,即通常所称的拉丁文《圣

---

〔1〕 罗马教的主要教义之一,就是声称教皇为普天下基督教会看得见的元首,并具有至上的权威,可以管理世界各地的主教和教牧人员。此外,更有甚者,就是教皇已僭称了上帝的尊号。他也被称为"主上帝教皇",并被宣布是绝无错误的。教会的宇宙观与神观必须建立在《圣经》基础上,必然和世俗的宇宙观与神观截然不同。历代正统教会相信,神是真理,他是永恒、无限、不变的神;神的启示,必无任何瑕疵、错误、混杂。今天东、西方思想,均有把神相对化的趋势。至少,把神的启示看作是有限、有错的。强调《圣经》的绝对真实、可靠、无谬(infallible)、无误(inerrant),乃强调神的真实(true)性的一部分,或一个必然的结论。

but not Greek or Hebrew, which were introduced by the Reformation. translation of the Bible, commonly called the Latin Vulgate, to have been equally dictated by divine inspiration, and therefore of equal authority with the Greek and Hebrew originals. The knowledge of those two languages, therefore, not being indispensably requisite to a churchman, the study of them did not for a long time make a necessary part of the common course of university education. There are some Spanish universities, I am assured, in which the study of the Greek language has never yet made any part of that course. The first reformers found the Greek text of the new testament, and even the Hebrew text of the old, more favourable to their opinions, than the vulgate translation, which, as might naturally be supposed, had been gradually accommodated to support the doctrines of the catholic church. They set themselves, therefore, to expose the many errors of that translation, which the Roman catholic clergy were thus put under the necessity of defending or explaining. But this could not well be done without some knowledge of the original languages, of which the study was therefore gradually introduced into the greater part of universities; both of those which embraced, and of those which rejected, the doctrines of the reformation. The Greek language was connected with every part of that classical learning, which, though at first principally cultivated by catholics and Italians, happened to come into fashion much about the same time that the doctrines of the reformation were set on foot. In the greater part of universities, therefore, that language was taught previous to the study of philosophy, and as soon as the student had made some progress in the Latin. The Hebrew language having no connection with classical learning, and, except the holy scriptures, being the language of not a single book in any esteem, the study of it did not commonly commence till after that of philosophy, and when the student had entered upon the study of theology.

Greek and Latin continue to be a considerable part of university education. Originally the first rudiments both of the Greek and Latin languages were taught in universities, and in some universities they still continue to be so. In others it is expected that the student should have previously acquired at least the rudiments of one or both of those languages, of which the study continues to make every where a very considerable part of university education.

The ancient Greek philosophy was divided into three great branches; physics, or natural philosophy; ethics, or moral philosophy; and

经》,也是神的灵感所口授,所以与希腊语原本和希伯来语原书有着同样的权威。这样,这两门语言的知识就不是牧师所必须要求学习的内容了,而对这两门语言的研究,很长一段时间也没有成为大学普通课程的必要部分。我可以肯定的是西班牙的一些大学,从来都没有把希腊语的研究作为一门教育课程。最初的宗教改革者们发现《新约全书》的希腊语书,甚至《旧约全书》的希伯来语书,都要比拉丁文《圣经》对他们的观点更为有利。可以非常容易想到,拉丁文译本已经逐渐地适应于支持天主教教义。于是,他们开始揭露拉丁译文中的许多错误,而罗马天主教的牧师们,则不得不站出来辩护或解释。然而,不懂得一些原文的语言肯定是无法进行辩护或者解释的,因此对希腊语和希伯来语的研究,就逐渐被拥护教义改革和反对教育改革的大多数大学引进了学校课程中。希腊语与每一部分古典学问都有联系,尽管最初只有天主教教徒和意大利人主要研究这些古典学问,但当开始教义改革的时候,这方面的研究已经成为了风尚。所以在大部分大学里,一旦学生学习了一些拉丁文,就要学习希腊语,从而进而研究哲学。而由于希伯来语与古典学问没有任何关系,除了《圣经》之外再也没有一本有价值的书是用希伯来语写得了。所以,学习希伯来语要一直等到哲学研究之后,当学生要研究神学时才开始学习。

_{但希腊语与希伯来语情况不同,它是在教改中被引入的。}

最初大学里只讲授希腊语和拉丁文的初步知识,而且直到今天有些大学还是如此。而在其他的一些大学,则希望学生们已经提前修得这两门语言中的至少一门或者两门的初步知识,对他们的进一步学习已经成为了各地大学教育中非常重要的一部分。

_{希腊语和拉丁文仍然是大学教育的重要部分。}

古希腊哲学分有三部分内容,即物理学或者自然哲学;伦理

There are three branches of Greek philosophy, logic. This general division seems perfectly agreeable to the nature of things.

The great phenomena of nature, the revolutions of the heavenly bodies, eclipses, comets; thunder, lightning, and other extraordinary meteors; the generation, the life, growth, and dissolution of plants and animals; are objects which, as they necessarily excite the wonder, so they naturally call forth the curiosity, of mankind to enquire into their causes. Superstition first attempted to satisfy this curiosity, by referring all those wonderful appearances to the immediate agency of the gods. Philosophy afterwards endeavoured to account for them, from more familiar causes, or from such as mankind were better acquainted with, than the agency of the gods. As those great phenomena are the first objects of human curiosity, so the science which pretends to explain them must naturally have been the first branch of philosophy that was cultivated. The first philosophers, accordingly, of whom history has preserved any account, appear to have been natural philosophers.

(1) physics or natural philosophy,

(2) ethics or moral philosophy,

In every age and country of the world men must have attended to the characters, designs, and actions of one another, and many reputable rules and maxims for the conduct of human life, must have been laid down and approved of by common consent. As soon as writing came into fashion, wise men, or those who fancied themselves such, would naturally endeavour to increase the number of those established and respected maxims, and to express their own sense of what was either proper or improper conduct, sometimes in the more artificial form of apologues, like what are called the fables of Æsop; and sometimes in the more simple one of apophthegms, or wise sayings, like the Proverbs of Solomon, the verses of Theognis and Phocyllides, and some

学或道德哲学;逻辑学。这种总体的划分,看来完全符合事物的 _{希腊哲学有三部分内容,}本质。

自然界的伟大现象,天体的运行、日食月食、彗星,雷电和其他异常的大气现象,动植物的生殖、生活、生长和死亡,都必然会使人类感到奇妙无比,所以自然地就会引起人类的好奇心,促使他们去探究其原因。最初迷信是为了满足这种好奇心,把一切奇妙的现象都归结为神的直接力量。后来,哲学试图用比神的力量更为常见的原因,或者说更能为人所理解的原因去解释它们。由于这些伟大的现象是人类好奇心的最初对象,所以试图来解释它们的科学也自然成为哲学研究的第一个分支。因此,历史上有记录的最早的哲学家,似乎都是自然哲学家。_{(1)物理学或者自然哲学,}

无论任何年代、任何国家,人们都必定会相互关注彼此的性格、意图和行为,也必定会产生许多大家共识的规范性的生活行为规则和准则。一旦写作变得流行起来,那些聪明的人或者自认为聪明的人,就会自然地致力于扩大这些确立起来的受人敬重的准则,并表达他们自己对于一些行为的好恶。有时他们采用非常虚假的寓言形式,如我们所说的《伊索寓言》,有时采用非常简单的格言或智谚,如《所罗门的箴言》[1]、提泰奥格尼斯[2]和弗西里_{(2)伦理学或者道德哲学,}

---

[1] 《所罗门的箴言》,是三千年前的所罗门王为青年人撰写的一本流芳千古的道德经,是犹太人智慧的总集,也是整部《圣经》中内容最针对现实生活、最实用的一部书。

[2] 提泰奥格尼斯是梅加拉的贵族,生活在公元前6世纪中期。当时梅加拉的贵族和平民经常为获得这个城市的控制权而斗争。诗人自然站在贵族一边。但在梅加拉的一次政治变革中,他败下阵来,财产被没收,自己被放逐,不得不流亡国外,旧日的朋友也对他冷淡、疏远了。独特的人生遭际使他对世态炎凉有了深刻的理解和感慨。他以格言诗的形式将自己多方面的人生经验记录下来。风格流畅、严肃。他的格言诗在古希腊常被选为修身教材,所以流传较广,数量也有上千行之多。另有《去国行》等若干抒情诗篇。

part of the works of Hesiod. They might continue in this manner for a long time merely to multiply the number of those maxims of prudence and morality, without even attempting to arrange them in any very distinct or methodical order, much less to connect them together by one or more general principles, from which they were all deducible, like effects from their natural causes. The beauty of a systematical arrangement of different observations connected by a few common principles, was first seen in the rude essays of those ancient times towards a system of natural philosophy. Something of the same kind was afterwards attempted in morals. The maxims of common life were arranged in some methodical order, and connected together by a few common principles, in the same manner as they had attempted to arrange and connect the phenomena of nature. The science which pretends to investigate and explain those connecting principles, is what is properly called moral philosophy.

and
(3)
logic.
  Different authors gave different systems both of natural and moral philosophy. But the arguments by which they supported those different systems, far from being always demonstrations, were frequently at best but very slender probabilities, and sometimes mere sophisms, which had no other foundation but the inaccuracy and ambiguity of common language. Speculative systems have in all ages of the world been adopted for reasons too frivolous to have determined the judgment of any man of common sense, in a matter of the smallest pecuniary interest. Gross sophistry has scarce ever had any influence upon the opinions of mankind, except in matters of philosophy and speculation; and in these it has frequently had the greatest. The patrons of each system of natural and moral philosophy naturally endeavoured to expose the weakness of the arguments adduced to support the systems which were opposite to their own. In examining those

第五篇 第一章

迪斯的诗,以及赫西奥德[1]一部分作品。很长一段时间里,他们只是不断的依这样的方式扩充关于审慎与道德的准则,而没有试图去按照非常清楚的、有条理的次序去组织这些准则,更不要说通过一个或者几个一般的规则来把它们联结起来,从而就像那些自然的因果关系一样,根据这些一般的规则就可以推导出其他的规则。通过系统地整理来自不同的观察,并用一些共同的原则联结起来,这种做法范例最早出现在古代自然哲学体系的一些粗浅的论文中。随后在道德方面也产生了类似的做法。就像是对自然现象的研究方式那样,日常生活准则也按照一些有条理的次序整理起来了,并用一些共同的原则将它们联结起来。这种试图研究和解释这些起联结作用的原则的科学,严格地说就称为道德哲学。

针对自然哲学和道德哲学,不同的作者提出了不同的体系。(3)逻辑学。但他们用来支持这些不同体系的论据,却往往毫无根据,至多也不过是一些小概率论据。有时他们的论证仅仅是诡辩,除了不确切的和模棱两可的语言外,毫无根据可言。有史以来,采用推理体系都只是为了一些琐碎的理由,为了极少一点点的金钱利益,不能对任何有常识的人的判断起决定性的作用。纯粹的诡辩除了对哲学和思辨方面影响非常重大以外,对人类的观点几乎没有任何影响。每个自然哲学体系和道德哲学体系的拥护者都自然地致力于揭露与自己观点相对立者的论据的弱点。他们在考察

---

[1] 赫西奥德:希腊诗人。归于他写的主要史诗有《关于古代农耕生活的有价值的叙述工作与时日》和关于众神及世界的起源的描述《神谱》。

arguments, they were necessarily led to consider the difference between a probable and a demonstrative argument, between a fallacious and a conclusive one; and Logic, or the science of the general principles of good and bad reasoning, necessarily arose out of the observations which a scrutiny of this kind gave occasion to. Though in its origin, posterior both to physics and to ethics, it was commonly taught, not indeed in all, but in the greater part of the ancient schools of philosophy, previously to either of those sciences. The student, it seems to have been thought, ought to understand well the difference between good and bad reasoning, before he was led to reason upon subjects of so great importance.

<small>Philosophy was afterwards divided into five branches,</small>
This ancient division of philosophy into three parts was in the greater part of the universities of Europe, changed for another into five.

<small>Metaphysics or pneumatics were added to physics,</small>
In the ancient philosophy, whatever was taught concerning the nature either of the human mind or of the Deity, made a part of the system of physics. Those beings, in whatever their essence might be supposed to consist, were parts of the great system of the universe, and parts too productive of the most important effects. Whatever human reason could either conclude, or conjecture, concerning them, made, as it were, two chapters, though no doubt two very important ones, of the science which pretended to give an account of the origin and revolutions of the great system of the universe. But in the universities of Europe, where philosophy was taught only as subservient to theology, it was natural to dwell longer upon these two chapters than upon any other of the science. They were gradually more and more extended, and were divided into many inferior chapters, till at last the doctrine of spirits, of which so little can be known, came to take up as much room in the system of philosophy as the doctrine of bodies, of which so much can be known. The doctrines concerning those two subjects were considered as making two distinct sciences. What are called Metaphysics or Pneumatics were set in opposition to Physics, and were cultivated not only as the more sublime, but, for the purposes of a particular profession, as the more useful science of the two. The proper subject of experiment and observation, a subject in which a careful attention is capable of making so many useful discoveries, was almost entirely neglected. The subject in which, after a few very simple and almost obvious truths, the most

这些论据时，必然会考虑到这种概率性的论据和实证论据之间的差别、靠不住的论据和确凿性论据之间的差别。这种周密仔细地审查，必然会导致逻辑学的诞生，或者说关于推理好坏的一般原则的科学的诞生。尽管从起源上讲，逻辑学要晚于物理学和伦理学，但古代大部分（尽管不是所有的）哲学学校，都先于物理学和伦理学开设逻辑学。看来它们可能是认为，在学生对如此重要的问题推理之前，首先要深刻理解好坏推理之间的差别。

古代哲学划分的三部分，在欧洲的大部分大学后来又改成了五部分。后来哲学分成了五部分：

在古代哲学中，无论是关于人类精神本质还是关于上帝本质的教学内容，都是物理学体系的一部分。无论它们的本质是由什么构成，它们都是宇宙大体系的一部分，而且也是可以产生许多最重要结果的一部分。无论人类关于这两部分所能做出的结论或者推论是什么，它们无疑都是试图解释宇宙大体系起源和运行的科学最重要的两章。但在欧洲的大学里，哲学只是作为神学的附属部分来讲授，那么很自然对这两章的讲解就要比科学其他部分的讲解多一些。这两章被逐渐地扩充起来，并划分为许多小的章节，直到最后，这种我们很难认识的精神学说，却占据了与哲学体系中人们可以认识到的很多物体学说同样的位置。这两种学说就被看作了截然不同的两种科学。所谓的形而上学或者精神学就放在了与物理学对等的位置。而在两种科学之间，它不仅被看作比较崇高的科学，而且对于某些特定职业来说还被看作比较有用的科学。于是，这种适合实验和观察而且通过仔细观察就可以得到许多有用发现的学科，就几乎完全被忽视了。而那种除了很少一部分几乎非常明显的真理外，大部分情况是最仔细地观

物理学加上形而上学或者精神学，

careful attention can discover nothing but obscurity and uncertainty, and can consequently produce nothing but subtleties and sophisms, was greatly cultivated.

<small>and gave rise to Ontology</small> When those two sciences had thus been set in opposition to one another, the comparison between them naturally gave birth to a third, to what was called Ontology, or the science which treated of the qualities and attributes which were common to both the subjects of the other two sciences. But if subtleties and sophisms composed the greater part of the Metaphysics or Pneumatics of the schools, they composed the whole of this cobweb science of Ontology, which was likewise sometimes called Metaphysics.

<small>Moral philosophy degenerated into casuistry and an ascetic morality,</small> Wherein consisted the happiness and perfection of a man, considered not only as an individual, but as the member of a family, of a state, and of the great society of mankind, was the object which the ancient moral philosophy proposed to investigate. In that philosophy the duties of human life were treated of as subservient to the happiness and perfection of human life. But when moral, as well as natural philosophy, came to be taught only as subservient to theology, the duties of human life were treated of as chiefly subservient to the happiness of a life to come. In the ancient philosophy the perfection of virtue was represented as necessarily productive, to the person who possessed it, of the most perfect happiness in this life. In the modern philosophy it was frequently represented as generally, or rather as almost always inconsistent with any degree of happiness in this life; and heaven was to be earned only by penance and mortification, by the austerities and abasement of a monk; not by the liberal, generous, and spirited conduct of a man. Casuistry and an ascetic morality made up, in most cases, the greater part of the moral philosophy of the schools. By far the most important of all the different branches of philosophy, became in this manner by far the most corrupted.

<small>the order being (1) logic, (2) ontology, (3) pneumatology, (4) a debased moral philosophy, (5) physics,</small> Such, therefore, was the common course of philosophical education in the greater part of the universities in Europe. Logic was taught first: Ontology came in the second place: Pneumatology, comprehending the doctrine concerning the nature of the human soul and of the Deity, in the third: In the fourth followed a debased system of moral philosophy, which was considered as immediately connected with the doctrines of Pneumatology, with the immortality of the human soul, and with the rewards and punishments which, from the justice of the

察也只能发现模糊的、不确定的东西,这样的结果是只能产生难以捉摸的诡辩的学科,却被很多人所研究。

当这两种科学被放在对立的位置时,关于它们之间的比较或者研究这两门科学主题的共同性质或属性的活动,就会自然地产生第三种科学,即所谓的本体论。但如果各个学派大部分的形而上学或精神学都是难以捉摸的诡辩的话,那么这种有时被同样称之为形而上学的混乱无序的本体论,也将全部都是难以捉摸的诡辩。产生了本体论。

古代道德探究的目的在于研究人的幸福和完善到底在何方,这个人不仅仅看作是一个个体,还被看作一个家族、国家和人类社会的一个成员。在古代道德哲学中,人生的各种职责都是为了人生的幸福与完善。但是当道德哲学和自然哲学都只是作为神学的一部分来讲授时,人生的各种职责就主要是为了来世的幸福。在古代哲学,如果一个人的道德尽善尽美,那么拥有这些德行的人今生就可以享受到最完美的幸福。而在现代哲学中,尽善尽美的道德却往往或者几乎总是和今生任何程度的幸福都有矛盾。不是靠慷慨、大方、精神饱满就可以进入天国,而只有靠忏悔、禁欲、修道者的苦修和谦卑才能进入天国。在大多数场合里,是非判断论和苦行道德观都构成了学校道德哲学教育的大部分内容。这样,哲学所有分支中最重要的一部分,就以这种方式变成了最被歪曲的一部分了。哲学退化是非判断论和苦行道德观,道德学变为。

所以,欧洲大部分大学的普通哲学教育课程就是这样:第一,讲授逻辑学;第二,讲授本体论;第三,讲授关于人类灵魂和上帝本质的精神学;第四,讲授一种变质的道德哲学,即那些被认为与精神学说、人类灵魂不灭学说和通过神的裁判可以在来世得到奖次序是(1)逻辑学;(2)本体论;(3)精神学;(4)一种贬值的道德哲学;(5)物理学。

Deity, were to be expected in a life to come: A short and superficial system of Physics usually concluded the course.

University, education was thus made less likely to produce men of the world.   The alterations which the universities of Europe thus introduced into the ancient course of philosophy, were all meant for the education of ecclesiastics, and to render it a more proper introduction to the study of theology. But the additional quantity of subtlety and sophistry; the casuistry and the ascetic morality which those alterations introduced into it, certainly did not render it more proper for the education of gentlemen or men of the world, or more likely either to improve the understanding, or to mend the heart.

This course is still taught in most universities with more or less diligence   This course of philosophy is what still continues to be taught in the greater part of the universities of Europe; with more or less diligence, according as the constitution of each particular university happens to render diligence more or less necessary to the teachers. In some of the richest and best endowed universities, the tutors content themselves with teaching a few unconnected shreds and parcels of this corrupted course; and even these they commonly teach very negligently and superficially.

Few improvements in philosophy have been made by universities, and fewest by the richest universities.   The improvements which, in modern times, have been made in several different branches of philosophy, have not, the greater part of them, been made in universities; though some no doubt have. The greater part of universities have not even been very forward to adopt those improvements, after they were made; and several of those learned societies have chosen to remain, for a long time, the sanctuaries in which exploded systems and obsolete prejudices found shelter and protection, after they had been hunted out of every other corner of the world. In general, the richest and best endowed universities have been the slowest in adopting those improvements, and the most averse to permit any considerable change in the established plan of education. Those improvements were more easily introduced into some of the poorer universities, in which the teachers, depending upon their reputation for the greater part of their subsistence, were obliged to pay more attention to the current opinions of the world.

In spite of all this the universities drew to themselves the education of gentlemen and men of fortune,   But though the public schools and universities of Europe were originally intended only for the education of a particular profession, that of churchmen; and though they were not always very diligent in instructing their pupils even in the sciences which were supposed necessary for that profession, yet they gradually drew to themselves the

惩的学说直接存在联系的学说；然后经常是用简单肤浅的物理学来结束全部的课程。

欧洲大学对古代哲学课程所作的修改，都是为了教育牧师，使哲学成为研究神学的比较合适的入门课程。但这种改变所增加的难以捉摸的诡辩、是非判断论和苦行道德观，当然使它不能适合于绅士或者一般世人的教育，更不可能提高他们的智力或者改善他们的心灵。

<small>这样，大学教育变得不适合于世俗的人了。</small>

欧洲大部分大学仍然在继续讲授这种哲学课程。教师们的勤勉程度，取决于每个大学的教学大纲所要求的必须的勤勉程度。在那些最富裕、受到捐赠最多的大学里，导师们常常满足于讲授这些变质课程的一些断章残篇，而且甚至于对这些内容他们都讲授得非常马虎肤浅。

<small>无论教师们是否勤勉，大多数大学仍讲授着这些课程。</small>

如今，哲学一些不同领域里的进步，尽管毫无疑问有一部分是在大学里取得的，但大部分都不是在大学里取得的。甚至于当取得进步时，大部分大学都不积极地去采用它。当那些被推翻了的体系和陈旧的偏见在世界各地被赶得无路可寻时，有几个这样的学术团体还愿意长期地充当收容、保护它们的庇护所。一般来说，越是这些最富裕、接受捐助捐赠最多的大学，他们越是迟缓地采用这些改进，越是不愿意对已建立起来的教育体系作任何重大的改动。相反，这些改进却很容易的被一些比较贫困的大学所采纳。那里的教师们大部分的生活来源都来自于他们的声望，这就使得他们不得不更加关注当代的各种思想。

<small>大学里取得的哲学改进很少，越是富裕的大学取得的改进就越少。</small>

尽管欧洲公立学校和大学设立之初只是为了特定职业的教育，即牧师职业的教育，而且甚至于对于这种职业所必需的知识他们也并不总是非常勤勉地给学生讲授，然而他们还是逐渐地把

<small>如今，大多绅士家庭教育还是对和把士有的吸引自己这边来了。</small>

education of almost all other people, particularly of almost all gentlemen and men of fortune. No better method, it seems, could be fallen upon of spending, with any advantage, the long interval between infancy and that period of life at which men begin to apply in good earnest to the real business of the world, the business which is to employ them during the remainder of their days. The greater part of what is taught in schools and universities, however, does not seem to be the most proper preparation for that business.

<small>but in England it is becoming more usual to send young men to travel abroad, a plan so absurd that nothing but the discredit of the universities could have brought it into repute.</small>
In England, it becomes every day more and more the custom to send young people to travel in foreign countries immediately upon their leaving school, and without sending them to any university. Our young people, it is said, generally return home much improved by their travels. A young man who goes abroad at seventeen or eighteen, and returns home at one and twenty, returns three or four years older than he was when he went abroad; and at that age it is very difficult not to improve a good deal in three or four years. In the course of his travels, he generally acquires some knowledge of one or two foreign languages; a knowledge, however, which is seldom sufficient to enable him either to speak or write them with propriety. In other respects, he commonly returns home more conceited, more unprincipled, more dissipated, and more incapable of any serious application either to study or to business, than he could well have become in so short a time, had he lived at home. By travelling so very young, by spending in the most frivolous dissipation the most precious years of his life, at a distance from the inspection and controul of his parents and relations, every useful habit, which the earlier parts of his education might have had some tendency to form in him, instead of being rivetted and confirmed, is almost necessarily either weakened or effaced. Nothing but the discredit into which the universities are allowing themselves to fall, could ever have brought into repute so very absurd a practice as that of travelling at this early period of life. By sending his son abroad, a father delivers himself, at least for some time, from so disagreeable an object as that of a son unemployed, neglected, and going to ruin before his eyes.

Such have been the effects of some of the modern institutions for education.

几乎所有其他人的教育,尤其是几乎所有的绅士和富有家庭子女的教育吸引到他们这里来了。如何度过从幼年到开始认真地处理社会实际事务之间这段时光,似乎没有比在学校里受教育这个方式更好的了,而在此之后学生们就要在其人生中投身于社会的实际事务。这期间的有利的消费,在当时似乎没有比进大学还好的方法。不过,这些学校和大学里讲授的大部分知识,似乎都没有为学生们将来要从事的事情做出很好的准备。

在英国,一天一天流行起来的风尚是,一旦年轻人从学校里毕业,接下来不是把他送往大学,而是立即把他送往外国游历。据说我们的年轻人游历归来后,一般来说都提高了很多。一个年轻人出国时十七八岁,回国时21岁,比他出国时大了三四岁,在他这个年龄,要想在三四年间不取得很大的进步都很难。他游历的过程中,一般来说会获得一两门外语的一些知识。不过,这些知识很少能够使他说得流利或写得通顺。另外,通常情况下他回国后,会变得更加骄傲、更加随便、更加放荡、更加不能认真地学习或工作。如果他待在家里,在如此短的时间内,他绝不会变成这样。这样早的去游历,在人生最宝贵的时期过着最放荡不羁的生活,远离了父母和亲戚的监督控制,这样他早前教育可能形成的一些有用的习惯,一般来说不但不会得到巩固和加强,反而还几乎必然会削弱或消失。之所以家长做出送孩子在很年轻时候就出国游历的荒唐行为,没有其他原因,只因为无法相信大学会教育好自己的子女。通过将子女送到国外,为人父者就可以暂时不用亲眼看到自己的儿女无所事事地、漫不经意地走向毁灭这样令人不愉快的事情。

这就是一些现代教育机构的效果。

<small>在英国,年轻人游得普遍,这种荒谬的做法是无任教育造成的。但在英格兰将人送往国外变得非常普遍,完全因为大学法大育的。</small>

Different plans and different institutions for education seem to have taken place in other ages and nations.

<small>In Greece the state directed education in gymnastics and music.</small> In the republics of ancient Greece, every free citizen was instructed, under the direction of the public magistrate, in gymnastic exercises and in music. By gymnastic exercises it was intended to harden his body, to sharpen his courage, and to prepare him for the fatigues and dangers of war; and as the Greek militia was, by all accounts, one of the best that ever was in the world, this part of their public education must have answered completely the purpose for which it was intended. By the other part, music, it was proposed, at least by the philosophers and historians who have given us an account of those institutions, to humanize the mind, to soften the temper, and to dispose it for performing all the social and moral duties both of public and private life.

<small>The Romans had the Campus Martius, resembling the gymnasium, but no music. They were none the worse for its absence.</small> In ancient Rome the exercises of the Campus Martius answered the same purpose as those of the Gymnazium in ancient Greece, and they seem to have answered it equally well. But among the Romans there was nothing which corresponded to the musical education of the Greeks. The morals of the Romans, however, both in private and public life, seem to have been, not only equal, but, upon the whole, a good deal superior to those of the Greeks. That they were superior in private life, we have the express testimony of Polybius ① and of Dionysius of Halicarnassus, ② two authors well acquainted with both nations; and the whole tenor of the Greek and Roman history

---

① [*Hist.* , vi. , 56; xviii. , 34.]
② [*Ant.* Rom. , ii. , xxiv. to xxvii. , esp. xxvi.]

不同的时期和不同的国家,似乎有不同的教育计划和教育机构。

在古希腊的各个共和国,所有的自由公民在国家官员的指导下,接受体育训练和音乐教育。体育锻炼的目的在于强身健体、磨炼意志,为应对战争的疲劳和危险做准备。根据所有的记载,希腊的民兵都是世界上最好的民兵之一。所以,至少根据记载这些教育机构的哲学家和历史学家的意见,这部分公共教育完全达到了教育的目的。而另一部分教育即音乐教育的目的在于使人通情达理、性情温和,可以履行公共生活和私人生活的所有的社会责任和道德义务。

在古罗马,战神广场[1]的训练就起着与古希腊体育场的训练一样的用途,而且看来古罗马的体育训练也同样很好地完成了训练目的。但在罗马,没有与希腊的音乐教育相对应的教育计划。然而,无论从私人生活上来讲还是从公共生活上来讲,罗马人的道德似乎不仅仅不比希腊人差,而且整体上来说,还要远胜于希腊人。罗马人在私人生活上优于希腊人,这点可由通晓两国的波里比乌斯①和哈利卡纳素斯[2]的狄奥尼西奥斯两人来证明②。而希腊和罗马的整个历史进程则可以证明罗马人在公共道德方

---

① 《历史》,第6章,第56页;第18章,第34页。
② 《古罗马生活及习俗》,第2卷,第14~27章,尤其是第26章。
〔1〕战神广场,战神原义(Campus Martius)与"三月校场"名称相同。Martius在拉丁文中意为"三月"或"马尔斯的"(马尔斯为战神,此地在《罗马史》下册第47页前的地图上可以找到,位于罗马塞维阿·图利阿城墙和台伯河之间,有城门和罗马相通。
〔2〕哈利卡纳素斯(Halicarnassus),小亚细亚西南部卡里西亚地区的一座希腊古城。希腊历史学家希罗多德的诞生地。

bears witness to the superiority of the public morals of the Romans. The good temper and moderation of contending factions seems to be the most essential circumstance in the public morals of a free people. But the factions of the Greeks were almost always violent and sanguinary; whereas, till the time of the Gracchi, no blood had ever been shed in any Roman faction; and from the time of the Gracchi the Roman republic may be considered as in reality dissolved. Notwithstanding, therefore, the very respectable authority of Plato, ① Aristotle, ② and Polybius, ③ and notwithstanding the very ingenious reasons by which Mr. Montesquieu endeavours to support that authority, ④ it seems probable that the musical education of the Greeks had no great effect in mending their morals, since, without any such education, those of the Romans were upon the whole superior. The respect of those ancient sages for the institutions of their ancestors, had probably disposed them to find much political wisdom in what was, perhaps, merely an ancient custom, continued, without interruption, from the earliest period of those societies, to the times in which they had arrived at a considerable degree of refinement. Music and dancing are the great amusements of almost all barbarous nations, and the great accomplishments which are supposed to fit any man for entertaining his society. It is so at this day among the negroes on the coast of Africa. It was so among the ancient Celtes, among the ancient Scandinavians, and, as we may learn from Homer, among the ancient Greeks in the times preceding the Trojan war. ⑤ When the Greek tribes had formed themselves into little republics, it was natural that the study of those accomplishments should, for a long time, make a part of the public and common education of the people.

---

① [*Repub.* , iii. , 400~401.]

② [*Politics*, 1340 *a*.]

③ [*Hist.* , iv. , 20.]

④ [*Esprit des lois*, liv. iv. chap. viii. , where Plato, Aristotle and Polybius are quoted.]

⑤ [*Iliad*, xiii. , 137; xviii. , 494, 594; *Odyssey*, i. , 152; viii. , 265; xviii. , 304; xxiii. , 134.]

面的优越性。党派间争执时保持良好的脾气和节制,是一个自由的民族对公共道德最基本的要求。希腊人的党派斗争基本上都是充满暴力和血腥的。反观,在格拉茨时代之前,罗马人从来没有因为党派争执发生流血事件。格拉茨时代以后,罗马共和国实际上已经认为是解体了。所以,尽管有柏拉图①、亚里士多德②和波里比乌斯③这样非常令人尊敬的权威,尽管孟德斯鸠为了支持这些权威试图提出了相当睿智的理由④,但看来希腊人的音乐教育对改善道德方面并没有什么显著的成效。因为没有这样的音乐教育,罗马人的整体道德却要胜于希腊人。这些古代先圣对他们祖先制度的尊敬,或许也使得他们倾向于仅仅从古代习俗中寻求政治智慧,这些习俗从远古时期开始就一直不间断地延续到了社会有了一定程度的文明发展。音乐和舞蹈是几乎所有野蛮民族的主要娱乐,同时也是适合任何人来款待友伴的主要社交礼仪。今天非洲海岸的黑人之间是这样,古凯尔特人之间[1]、斯堪的纳维亚人间是如此,而且我们从荷马史诗中也可以看到,古希腊人在特洛伊战争之前也是如此⑤。当希腊各部落组成许多小共和国时,很长一段时间内,这些社交礼仪的研究将会构成国民

---

① 《共和国》,第 3 章,第 400~401 页。
② 《政治学》,公元 1340 年。
③ 《历史》,第 4 章,第 20 页。
④ 《法的精神》,liv. iv. 第 8 章,这里引用了柏拉图、亚里士多德和波里比乌斯的话。
⑤ 《伊利亚特》,第 8 章,第 137 页;第 18 章,第 494、594 页。《奥德赛》,第 1 章,第 152 页;第 8 章,第 265 页;第 18 章,第 364 页。
[1] 凯尔特人(Celt),印欧民族的一支,最初分布在中欧,在前罗马帝国时期遍及欧洲西部、不列颠群岛和加拉提亚东南部。尤指不列颠人或高卢人。

国民财富的性质与原理

<small>The teachers of military exercises and music were not paid or appointed by the state.</small>

The masters who instructed the young people either in music or in military exercises, do not seem to have been paid, or even appointed by the state, either in Rome or even in Athens, the Greek republic of whose laws and customs we are the best informed. The state required that every free citizen should fit himself for defending it in war, and should, upon that account, learn his military exercises. But it left him to learn them of such masters as he could find, and it seems to have advanced nothing for this purpose, but a public field or place of exercise, in which he should practise and perform them.

<small>Reading, writing and arithmetic were taught privately.</small>

In the early ages both of the Greek and Roman republics, the other parts of education seem to have consisted in learning to read, write, and account according to the arithmetic of the times. These accomplishments the richer citizens seem frequently to have acquired at home, by the assistance of some domestic pedagogue, who was generally, either a slave, or a freed-man; and the poorer citizens, in the schools of such masters as made a trade of teaching for hire. Such parts of education, however, were abandoned altogether to the care of the parents or guardians of each individual. It does not appear that the state ever assumed any inspection or direction of them. By a law of Solon, indeed, the children were acquitted from maintaining those parents in their old age, who had neglected to instruct them in some profitable trade or business. ①

In the progress of refinement, when philosophy and rhetoric

---

① [Plutarch, *Life of Solon*, quoted by Montesquieu, *Esprit des Lois*, liv., xxvi., ch. v.]

公共教育和普通教育的一部分,这是很自然的事情。

无论是在罗马,还甚至是在法律和习俗为我们所熟知的希腊共和国的雅典,[1] 给年轻人讲授音乐或者军事训练的教师们似乎都不是由国家支付报酬的,甚至也不是由国家任命的。国家要求每个自由公民能够在战时保卫国家,故此要求每个自由公民必须接受军事训练。但是国家只是让公民自己去寻找讲授军训的教师,国家除了提供公共的训练场地或地点以供操练演习外,似乎没有提供其他什么了。

军事训练和音乐教师,不是由国家支付报酬或者任命的。

在希腊共和国和罗马共和国早期,教育的其他部分似乎包括学习读、写和根据当时的算术学会计算。富裕的公民往往是在家中通过家庭教师的帮助获得这些技能,这些家庭教师一般来说是奴隶或者自由人。而贫穷的公民,则是到学校里面去学习这些技能,这些教师以讲授为职业。不过,这部分教育完全由每个人的父母或监护人负责,国家似乎不承担任何监督或指导的责任。的确,根据棱伦的法律,[2] 如果父母忽视了让子女接受一些有益的职业或事物教育,子女们就可以免除父母晚年时赡养的义务。①

读、写和算术是通过私人讲授的。

随着文明的发展,当哲学和修辞学成为时尚时,家境比较好

---

① 孟德斯鸠在《论法的精神》第 26 章第 6 节中引用了普鲁塔克(Plutarch)《棱伦生平》。

〔1〕 雅典(Athens),希腊的首都及最大城市,位于该国东部,萨罗尼克湾附近。公元前 5 世纪培利克里斯时代,文化成就和国势达到巅峰状态。雅典在 1834 年成为现代希腊的首都,两年后希腊摆脱土耳其独立。

〔2〕 棱伦(Solon),公元前(638? ~559?)古雅典的立法者及诗人。他的改革保留了建立在财富基础之上的阶级系统,但却以出生特权而告终。

| 国民财富的性质与原理 |

<small>Philosophical education was independent of the state.</small> came into fashion, the better sort of people used to send their children to the schools of philosophers and rhetoricians, in order to be instructed in these fashionable sciences. But those schools were not supported by the public. They were for a long time barely tolerated by it. The demand for philosophy and rhetoric was for a long time so small, that the first professed teachers of either could not find constant employment in any one city, but were obliged to travel about from place to place. In this manner lived Zeno of Elea, Protagoras, Gorgias, Hippias, and many others. As the demand increased, the schools both of philosophy and rhetoric became stationary; first in Athens, and afterwards in several other cities. The state, however, seems never to have encouraged them further than by assigning to some of them a particular place to teach in, which was sometimes done too by private donors. The state seems to have assigned the Academy to Plato, the Lyceum to Aristotle, and the Portico to Zeno of Citta, the founder of the Stoics. But Epicurus bequeathed his gardens to his own school.

的人们为了让子女接受这些最流行的知识,一般都把他们的子女送到哲学家和修辞学家们设立的学校那里去学习。但是这些学校并不受国家的支持。在很长的一段时期内,国家对它们只是容许而已。一个长的时期内,对哲学和修辞学的需求很小,最初这些专业的教师们在任何一个城市都无法找到持久的工作,而不得不游历于各地之间。埃利亚的齐诺、普罗塔哥拉、高尔吉亚、希帕斯和其他许多学者[1]都过着这样漂泊的生活。后来对哲学和修辞学需求的增加,这些方面的学校也固定了下来。首先在雅典开办了这方面的学校,接着在其他几个城市也有了类似的学校。不过,国家除了给有些人拨了一个特定的场所作为讲学之处外,再也没有其他进一步的鼓励了。有些学校讲学的场所还是私人捐助的。国家似乎拨建了柏拉图的学园、亚里士多德的吕克昂学府和斯多噶学派创建者齐诺的学府。[2] 但伊壁鸠鲁[3]则是将他的花园捐给了自己的学校。不过,在马库斯·安东尼时代以

哲学教育独立于国家。

---

[1] 埃利亚的齐诺(Zeno of Elea),公元前5世纪前后古希腊埃利亚学派哲学家。普罗塔哥拉(Protagoras),希腊的哲学家,被认为是第一个诡辩家。他根据他自己的格言"人类是衡量所有事物的标准"来教授哲学。高尔吉亚(Gorgias),古希腊智者派,他有段著名的话:无物存在;即使有物存在,也不可知;即使可知,也不可说。著有《论非在或论自然》。

[2] 西希昂的齐诺(Zeno of Citium 前340? ~前265?),希腊哲学家,斯多噶派的创始人。斯多噶派学者(Stoics),希腊哲学学校的成员,为芝诺约于公元前380年创立。他们认为人不应为情感所动,应把各种事情当作神意或自然法则的不可避免的结果来坦然地接受

[3] 伊壁鸠鲁(Epicurus),古希腊哲学家,于公元前306年在雅典创立了其颇具影响力的伊壁鸠鲁学派。

Till about the time of Marcus Antoninus, however, no teacher appears to have had any salary from the public, or to have had any other emoluments, but what arose from the honoraries or fees of his scholars. The bounty which that philosophical emperor, as we learn from Lucian, bestowed upon one of the teachers of philosophy, probably lasted no longer than his own life. There was nothing equivalent to the privileges of graduation, and to have attended any of those schools was not necessary, in order to be permitted to practise any particular trade or profession. If the opinion of their own utility could not draw scholars to them, the law neither forced any body to go to them, nor rewarded any body for having gone to them. The teachers had no jurisdiction over their pupils, nor any other authority besides that natural authority, which superior virtue and abilities never fail to procure from young people towards those who are entrusted with any part of their education.

<small>No public institutions for teaching law existed at Rome, where law was first developed into an orderly system.</small>
At Rome, the study of the civil law made a part of the education, not of the greater part of the citizens, but of some particular families. The young people, however, who wished to acquire knowledge in the law, had no public school to go to, and had no other method of studying it, than by frequenting the company of such of their relations and friends, as were supposed to understand it. It is perhaps worth while to remark, that though the laws of the twelve tables were, many of them, copied from those of some ancient Greek republics, yet law never seems to have grown up to be a science in any republic of ancient Greece. In Rome it became a science very early, and gave a considerable degree of illustration to those citizens who had the reputation of understanding it. In the republics of ancient Greece, particularly in Athens, the ordinary courts of

前,[1]似乎没有一个教师曾经从国家领得薪俸,除了学生的谢礼或学费外,教师再也没有其他的报酬了。我们从卢西恩[2]那里可以知道,安东尼这个喜爱哲学的皇帝曾经给一位哲学教师发放了津贴,不过在他死后这个津贴可能也就停发了。从这些学校毕业的毕业生并没有什么特权,上这些学校也不是从事某种特定职业或事业必备的条件。如果这些学校效用的舆论不能吸引学生们来此读书,那么法律既不会强迫任何人去那里学习,也不会奖励任何在那里学习过的学生。教师们对他们的学生没有管辖权,除了凭借出众的品行能力来赢得学生对他们的教育信任从而获得自然权威外,再也没有其他的权威了。

在罗马,民法的学习不是大部分公民教育的一部分,而只是一些特殊家庭教育的一部分。不过,一个想学习法律方面知识的年轻人,并没有公立学校可以去学习法律。他们只有和亲戚朋友中懂得法律的人时常在一起才能学得这些知识。值得注意的是,尽管十二铜表法中的许多部分都是从一些古希腊共和国的法律中抄来的,但法律似乎在古希腊的任何一个共和国都没有发展成为一种科学。而在罗马,法律很早就成为了一种科学,凡是具有通晓法律名声的公民,都会被给予相当的荣耀。在古希腊共和国,尤其是在雅典,一般的法庭都是由人数众多因而也是无序的

罗马没有讲授法律的公共机构,那里的法律最先发展为一种有序的体系。

---

[1] 安东尼(Marcus Aurelius Antoninus),罗马皇帝是罗马帝国后期五贤王之一,他写了一本《沉思录》是自省之意,一共有12卷,是用陈述和问答的方式记录了他的各种思想,可以代表当时的哲学思想,后世也把它作为一部论述修养的哲学名著而广为流传。

[2] 卢西恩(Lucian),希腊讽刺家。他的两部主要作品《众神的对话》和《死者的对话》讽刺了希腊的哲学和神学。

justice consisted of numerous, and therefore disorderly, bodies of people, who frequently decided almost at random, or as clamour, faction and party spirit happened to determine. The ignominy of an unjust decision, when it was to be divided among five hundred, a thousand, or fifteen hundred people (for some of their courts were so very numerous), could not fall very heavy upon any individual. At Rome, on the contrary, the principal courts of justice consisted either of a single judge, or of a small number of judges, whose characters, especially as they deliberated always in public, could not fail to be very much affected by any rash or unjust decision. In doubtful cases, such courts, from their anxiety to avoid blame, would naturally endeavour to shelter themselves under the example, or precedent, of the judges who had sat before them, either in the same, or in some other court. This attention to practice and precedent, necessarily formed the Roman law into that regular and orderly system in which it has been delivered down to us; and the like attention has had the like effects upon the laws of every other country where such attention has taken place. The superiority of character in the Romans over that of the Greeks, so much remarked by Polybius and Dionysius of Halicarnassus, was probably more owing to the better constitution of their courts of justice, than to any of the circumstances to which those authors ascribe it. The Romans are said to have been particularly distinguished for their superior respect to an oath. But the people who were accustomed to make oath only before some diligent and well-informed court of justice, would naturally be much more attentive to what they swore, than they who were accustomed to do the same thing before mobbish and disorderly assemblies.

  The abilities, both civil and military, of the Greeks and Romans, will readily be allowed to have been, at least, equal to those of any modern nation. Our prejudice is perhaps rather to overrate them. But except in what related to military exercises, the state seems to have been at no pains to form those great abilities: for I cannot be induced to believe, that the musical education of the Greeks could be of much consequence in forming them. Masters, however, had been found, it seems, for instructing the better sort of people among those nations in every art and science in which the circumstances of their society rendered it necessary or convenient for them to be instructed. The demand for such instruction produced, what it always produces,

人民团体组成。他们常常几乎是随意地做出判决，或者通过争吵或宗派、党派意志做出判决。一个不公正的判决带来的骂名，会由500人、1000人或1500人（希腊的一些法庭人数就有如此之众）来共同承担，这样每个人所承担的骂名也就很轻了。而与之相反，在罗马，主要的法院要不是就一个法官，要不就是很少数量的法官，尤其是在公审场合，如果裁决草率或不公，那么法官的人格就难免受到很大的损害。所以，当遇到不能确定的案子时，这些法官为了避免受到谴责以保护自己，他们自然就会试图按照本法庭或者其他法院以前的法官所做的先例或判例进行判决。这种对惯例和先例的关注，必然会使罗马法成为能传至今日的这样规则的、有条理的体系。在其他国家如果有类似的对先例和惯例关注的话，也同样会形成这样有条理的、规则的法律。波里比乌斯和哈利卡纳素斯的狄奥尼西奥斯所极力评说的罗马人在性格上要优于希腊人，与其说是因为这两位作者分析的种种情况，不如说是由于罗马拥有较好的法庭组织。据说罗马人尤其以他们特别尊重誓言而闻名。习惯于在做事勤勉而且消息灵通的法庭面前发誓的人，自然要比习惯于在暴乱而又无序的集会前发誓的人更加尊重他们自己的誓言。

　　希腊和罗马人的文明和军事能力可以说与现代任何一个民族不相上下。我们的偏见可能是对他们的这些能力估价过高了。不过，除了军事训练外，国家似乎没有为这些能力的形成尽什么力，因为我不会相信希腊的音乐教育会对这些能力的形成有什么大的影响。但如果这个国家比较富裕的人民想要学习他们社会认为是必须的或有用的技术和科学的话，就总是可以找到传授这些知识的教师。由于对于这种传授知识的需求，就总是会产生传

国民财富的性质与原理

<small>The ancient system was more successful than the modern, which corrupts public teaching and stifles private.</small> the talent for giving it; and the emulation which an unrestrained competition never fails to excite, appears to have brought that talent to a very high degree of perfection. In the attention which the ancient philosophers excited, in the empire which they acquired over the opinions and principles of their auditors, in the faculty which they possessed of giving a certain tone and character to the conduct and conversation of those auditors; they appear to have been much superior to any modern teachers. In modern times, the diligence of public teachers is more or less corrupted by the circumstances, which render them more or less independent of their success and reputation in their particular professions. Their salaries too put the private teacher, who would pretend to come into competition with them, in the same state with a merchant who attempts to trade without a bounty, in competition with those who trade with a considerable one. If he sells his goods at nearly the same price, he cannot have the same profit, and poverty and beggary at least, if not bankruptcy and ruin will infallibly be his lot. If he attempts to sell them much dearer, he is likely to have so few customers that his circumstances will not be much mended. The privileges of graduation, besides, are in many countries necessary, or at least extremely convenient to most men of learned professions; that is, to the far greater part of those who have occasion for a learned education. But those privileges can be obtained only by attending the lectures of the public teachers. The most careful attendance upon the ablest instructions of any private teacher, cannot always give any title to demand them. It is from these different causes that the private teacher of any of the sciences which are commonly taught in universities, is in modern times generally considered as in the very lowest order of men of letters. A man of real abilities can scarce find out a more humiliating or a more unprofitable employment to turn them to. The endowments of schools and colleges have, in this manner, not only corrupted the diligence of public teachers, but have rendered it almost impossible to have any good private ones.

Were there no public institutions for education, no system, no science would be taught for which there was not some demand; or which the circumstances of the times did not render it either

授这些知识的人才,就是说,需求促成了满足此种需要的人才的产生。而且,看来没有限制的竞争所激发的竞赛,也使得这些人才达到了非常完美的程度。古代的哲学家们在唤起听讲者的注意力、影响听讲者的信念和情操、培养听讲者的言谈举止等方面,似乎都要远胜于现代的教师。现代公立教师的勤勉或多或少地受到他们所处环境的腐蚀,因为这些环境使他们或多或少地不依赖于自己在特定职业上的成功或名望。这些公立老师的薪俸,也使得想与这些公立教师竞争的私人教师,就处在类似一个没有津贴的商人想与拥有大量津贴的商人竞争那样的境地。如果这个没有津贴的商人以几乎相同的价格出售商品,他就无法得到相同的利润,这样即便不会破产没落,至少也难逃赤贫困苦的命运。如果他试图以很高的价格出售,那么他的顾客就会很少,他的处境也不会改善多少。而且在许多国家,毕业的特权对于大多数从事有学问职业的人来说,也是必需的或者至少是非常有利的。也就是说对于有机会受到教育的绝大部分人来说,这种毕业的特权是必不可少的。然而,只有听公立教师的课才能获得这些特权。即便是再仔细地听最有讲授能力的私人教师的课,也总是无法取得获得这些特权的资格。由于以上种种原因,当代那些讲授大学普通课程的私人教师,通常被看作文人中最低等的一类人。一个具有真才实学的人再也找不到比这种更加耻辱、更加无利可图得足以令他们掉头就走的职业了。这样,给学校和大学的捐赠金,不但腐蚀了公立教师的勤勉精神,并且也使得几乎不可能再找到优秀的私人教师了。

如果没有公共教育机构,那么对于那些没有一定需求的知识或知识体系就不会被讲授;或者说如果当时的情形没有使这些知

If there were no public institutions for education nothing except what was useful would be taught.

necessary, or convenient, or at least fashionable, to learn. A private teacher could never find his account in teaching, either an exploded and antiquated system of a science acknowledged to be useful, or a science universally believed to be a mere useless and pedantic heap of sophistry and nonsense. Such systems, such sciences, can subsist no where, but in those incorporated societies for education whose prosperity and revenue are in a great measure independent of their reputation, and altogether independent of their industry. Were there no public institutions for education, a gentleman, after going through, with application and abilities, the most complete course of education which the circumstances of the times were supposed to afford, could not come into the world completely ignorant of every thing which is the common subject of conversation among gentlemen and men of the world.

Women's education is excellent in consequence of the absence of public institutions.

There are no public institutions for the education of women, and there is accordingly nothing useless, absurd, or fantastical in the common course of their education. They are taught what their parents or guardians judge it necessary or useful for them to learn; and they are taught nothing else. Every part of their education tends evidently to some useful purpose; either to improve the natural attractions of their person, or to form their mind to reserve, to modesty, to chastity, and to œconomy; to render them both likely to become the mistresses of a family, and to behave properly when they have become such. In every part of her life a woman feels some conveniency or advantage from every part of her education. It seldom happens that a man, in any part of his life, derives any conveniency or advantage from some of the most laborious and troublesome parts of his education.

Ought the state to give no attention to education?

Ought the public, therefore, to give no attention, it may be asked, to the education of the people ? Or if it ought to give any, what are the different parts of education which it ought to attend to in the different orders of the people ? And in what manner ought it to attend to them?

In some cases the state of the society necessarily places the greater part of individuals in such situations as naturally form in them, without any attention of government, almost all the abilities

第五篇 第一章

识或者知识体系成为必须的、有用的或者说至少是流行的,那么也就没有人会学习这些知识或知识体系。一个私人教师绝不会讲授那些过去有用但现在已经被推翻了的过时的知识体系,或一种普遍都认为是无用的、迂腐的诡辩或胡言乱语的知识体系,因为从中他得不到什么好处。这样的知识、这样的体系只能存在于教育机构这样的团体中,这里教师的荣耀和收入很大程度上不依赖于他们的名声,也完全不依赖于他们的勤勉程度。如果没有公共教育机构,那么一个绅士尽其可能接受了当时所能提供的最完整的教育之后,就不可能在进入社会后对社会上绅士和一般人谈论的普通话题还会完全地一无所知。

> 如果没有公共教育机构,没用的知识就不会被讲授了。

由于没有对女子教育的公共机构,所以女子教育的普通课程里也就因此没有那些无用的、荒谬的或者空想的知识。她们学习的内容都是她们的父母或者监护人认为是必须学习的知识或者对他们有用的知识,而其他的知识一概不学。她们教育的每一部分都明显地是为了一些有用的目的,要么是提高她们的形体美,要么是从思想上培养她们谨慎、谦逊、贞洁和节俭的品德,使她们成为好的家庭主妇,或者她们成为家庭主妇后举止适当。在一个女人生活的点点滴滴,都会感到这些教育处处都给她带来便利或者好处。而对于一个男人来说,他的生活每一部分都很少会受益于他受的教育中最辛苦、最麻烦的那部分知识。

> 女子教育非常出色,因为没有公共教育机构。

所以,有人可能会问,国家不应该关注人民的教育吗?或者如果应该关注的话,那么对于不同的社会阶层应该关注什么样不同的教育内容呢?而且,应该按照什么样的方式关注呢?

> 国家是否应该关注教育呢?

在某些场合,即便没有政府的关注,社会状态也必然会使大多数人可以自然而然地养成这个社会状态所要求的或者所可能

| 国民财富的性质与原理

In some cases it ought, in others it need not.
and virtues which that state requires, or perhaps can admit of. In other cases the state of the society does not place the greater part of individuals in such situations, and some attention of government is necessary in order to prevent the almost entire corruption and degeneracy of the great body of the people.

Division of labour destroys intellectual, social and martial virtues unless government takes pains to prevent it,
In the progress of the division of labour, the employment of the far greater part of those who live by labour, that is, of the great body of the people, comes to be confined to a few very simple operations; frequently to one or two. But the understandings of the greater part of men are necessarily formed by their ordinary employments. The man whose whole life is spent in performing a few simple operations, of which the effects too are, perhaps, always the same, or very nearly the same, has no occasion to exert his understanding, or to exercise his invention in finding out expedients for removing difficulties which never occur. He naturally loses, therefore, the habit of such exertion, and generally becomes as stupid and ignorant as it is possible for a human creature to become. The torpor of his mind renders him, not only incapable of relishing or bearing a part in any rational conversation, but of conceiving any generous, noble, or tender sentiment, and consequently of forming any just judgment concerning many even of the ordinary duties of private life. Of the great and extensive interests of his country he is altogether incapable of judging; and unless very particular pains have been taken to render him otherwise, he is equally incapable of defending his country in war. The uniformity of his stationary life naturally corrupts the courage of his mind, and makes him regard with abhorrence the irregular, uncertain, and adventurous life of a soldier. It corrupts even the activity of his body, and renders him incapable of exerting his strength with vigour and perseverance, in any other employment than that to which he has been bred. His dexterity at his own particular trade seems, in this manner, to be acquired at the expence of his intellectual, social, and martial virtues. But in every improved and civilized society this is the state into which the labouring poor, that is, the great body of the people, must necessarily fall, unless government takes some pains to prevent it.

It is otherwise in the barbarous societies, as they are commonly called, of hunters, of shepherds, and even of husbandmen in that

容许的几乎所有的能力和美德。而在其他的场合,如果社会状态不能使大多数人自然地养成这些能力或美德,政府就必须给予一定的关注,以防止大多数民众几乎完全腐化和退化。

> 在某些场合应予以关注,而其他场合则不需要关注。

随着劳动分工的发展,绝大多数依靠劳动为生的人的职业,即大多数民众的职业,就局限于一些非常简单的操作,往往只有一两种操作。但是大多数人们的智力必然是通过他们日常的工作来形成。如果一个人的一生都消耗在一些非常简单的操作上,而且这些操作的结果又总是相同的或几乎完全相同的,那么他就没有机会运用他的智力或者发明创造力,来解决以前从来没有碰到过的困难。这样,他就会自然地丧失运用智力的习惯,往往变成了最愚钝、最无知的那种人。这种思想上的迟钝,不但会使他无法领会或者参与任何合理的谈话,而且会使他无法拥有宽容、高尚、慈爱的胸怀,结果也就使他甚至无法对私人生活的日常义务做出正确的判断。至于国家重大的、广泛的利益,他更是完全无法做出正确判断了。除非为他付出非常大的努力,不然他同样也无法在战时捍卫自己的祖国。他静止生活的单调性自然会腐蚀他精神上的勇气,使他厌恶士兵的那种不规则、不确定和冒险的生活。这种单调性甚至腐蚀了他身体的活力,使他除了自己从事的职业外,没有在任何其他职业中劲道十足、坚定不移地去施展自己的力量。所以,他对自己特定行业的熟练,是以牺牲他的智力、社会美德和军事能力的这种方式来获得的。可是,在所有改良的、文明的社会,如果政府不设法阻止的话,穷苦的劳动民众,也就是大多数民众,必然会陷入这样的状态。

> 劳动分工会破坏智力、社会美德、军事能力,非政府设法阻止能除去它。

在通常我们称为狩猎时期、放牧时期的野蛮社会里,情况就与此不同;甚至在制造业改良以前和对外贸易扩张以前的农业原

<small>Whereas in barbarous societies those virtues are kept alive by constant necessity.</small> rude state of husbandry which precedes the improvement of manufactures, and the extension of foreign commerce. In such societies the varied occupations of every man oblige every man to exert his capacity, and to invent expedients for removing difficulties which are continually occurring. Invention is kept alive, and the mind is not suffered to fall into that drowsy stupidity, which, in a civilized society, seems to benumb the understanding of almost all the inferior ranks of people. In those barbarous societies, as they are called, every man, it has already been observed, is a warrior. Every man too is in some measure a statesman, and can form a tolerable judgment concerning the interest of the society, and the conduct of those who govern it. How far their chiefs are good judges in peace, or good leaders in war, is obvious to the observation of almost every single man among them. In such a society indeed, no man can well acquire that improved and refined understanding, which a few men sometimes possess in a more civilized state. Though in a rude society there is a good deal of variety in the occupations of every individual, there is not a great deal in those of the whole society. Every man does, or is capable of doing, almost every thing which any other man does, or is capable of doing. Every man has a considerable degree of knowledge, ingenuity, and invention; but scarce any man has a great degree. The degree, however, which is commonly possessed, is generally sufficient for conducting the whole simple business of the society. In a civilized state, on the contrary, though there is little variety in the occupations of the greater part of individuals, there is an almost infinite variety in those of the whole society. These varied occupations present an almost infinite variety of objects to the contemplation of those few, who, being attached to no particular occupation themselves, have leisure and inclination to examine the occupations of other people. The contemplation of so great a variety of objects necessarily exercises their minds in endless comparisons and combinations, and renders their understandings, in an extraordinary degree, both acute and comprehensive. Unless those few, however, happen to be placed in some very particular situations, their great abilities, though honourable to themselves, may contribute very little to the good government or happiness of their society. Notwithstanding the great abilities of those few, all the nobler

始状态下,情形也与此不同。在这些社会中,各式各样的工作就迫使每个人都倍尽其力,找到不断出现的问题的解决办法。这样各种发明定会层出不穷,人的思想也不会陷入呆滞的昏沉状态。在文明社会里,正是这种呆滞昏沉的状态使得几乎所有下层人民的智力变得迟钝起来。正如我们前面说过的,在这些所谓的野蛮社会里,每个人都是一个战士。而且,所有的人在一定程度上也都是政治家,对于社会的利益、统治者的行动,他们都能做出适当的判断。几乎每一个人都可以清楚地观察到他们的首领在平时是多好的法官,在战时是多好的指挥官。不过,在这样的社会里,的确没有人会获得在文明状态下有些人有时所具有的那种改良的训练有素的智力。尽管在原始状态下每个人的职业有多种多样,但整个社会的职业却只有那么多。每个人在做的或者能够做的几乎所有事情,也正是其他人在做的或者能够做的事情。每个人都具有一定程度的知识、技巧和发明才能,但却很少会有人具有更大程度的知识、技巧和发明才能。不过,普遍拥有的那种程度,一般来说已经足以应付社会的全部简单事物了。与之相反,在文明社会里,尽管大部分人的职业几乎没有变化,但对整个社会而言,却有不计其数的职业。这些千差万别的职业,对于那些自己没有从事任何职业从而有空闲和心思去研究别人的职业的少数人来说,就提供了几乎是不计其数的思考对象。要想思考这么多数量的对象,就必然需要研究者运用他们的心智进行无穷无尽的对比和组合,从而使他们的智力变得非凡的敏锐和广泛。然而,除非这些人刚好处于一些非常特殊的职位,不然他们杰出的才能虽然对他们自己是一种荣耀,但对整个社会的良好治理和幸福却贡献不多。尽管这些少数人拥有杰出的才能,但大多数民众

在野蛮社会里,经常的必要性使得这些美德要得以持续下去。

国民财富的性质与原理

The education of the common people requires attention from the state more than that of people of rank and fortune, whose parents can look after their interests, and who spend their lives in varied occupations chiefly intellectual,

parts of the human character may be, in a great measure, obliterated and extinguished in the great body of the people.

The education of the common people requires, perhaps, in a civilized and commercial society, the attention of the public more than that of people of some rank and fortune. People of some rank and fortune are generally eighteen or nineteen years of age before they enter upon that particular business, profession, or trade, by which they propose to distinguish themselves in the world. They have before that full time to acquire, or at least to fit themselves for afterwards acquiring, every accomplishment which can recommend them to the public esteem, or render them worthy of it. Their parents or guardians are generally sufficiently anxious that they should be so accomplished, and are, in most cases, willing enough to lay out the expence which is necessary for that purpose. If they are not always properly educated, it is seldom from the want of expence laid out upon their education; but from the improper application of that expence. It is seldom from the want of masters; but from the negligence and incapacity of the masters who are to be had, and from the difficulty, or rather from the impossibility which there is, in the present state of things, of finding any better. The employments too in which people of some rank or fortune spend the greater part of their lives, are not, like those of the common people, simple and uniform. They are almost all of them extremely complicated, and such as exercise the head more than the hands. The understandings of those who are engaged in such employments can seldom grow torpid for want of exercise. The employments of people of some rank and fortune, besides, are seldom such as harass them from morning to night. They generally have a good deal of leisure, during which they may perfect themselves in every branch either of useful or ornamental knowledge of which they may have laid the foundation, or for which they may have acquired some taste in the earlier part of life.

unlike the children of the poor.

It is otherwise with the common people. They have little time to spare for education. Their parents can scarce afford to maintain them even in infancy. As soon as they are able to work, they must apply to some trade by which they can earn their subsistence. That trade too is generally so simple and uniform as to give little exercise to the understanding; while, at the same time, their labour is both so constant and so severe, that it leaves them little leisure and less inclination to apply to, or even to think of any thing else.

人性中所有比较高尚的部分，却可能会在很大程度上消亡泯灭了。

在一个文明的商业社会里，或许对普通人民教育要比对一些显贵和富裕的人的教育，更需要国家的关注。一般来说，那些显贵和富裕的人在十八九岁以后，才从事于他们想借以出名的特定业务、职业或艺业。在此以前他们有充足的时间获得或者有充足的时间来准备自己以便在将来获得那些可以让他们博得世人尊敬或者值得世人尊敬的一切才能。一般来说他们的父母或者监护人都十分地渴望他们能拥有这样的才能，因此大多数情况下，也非常愿意为达此目的付出必要的费用。如果他们不是总能受到适当的教育，很少是由于缺乏教育支出，而是由于没有恰当地运用那些教育支出；很少是由于缺乏教师，而是由于讲授教师的懈怠与无能，或者是在目前状态下很难甚至不可能找到更好的教师。而且，显贵们或者富裕的人们一生中大部分时间从事的职业，也不像普通人民的职业那样简单、单调。他们几乎所有人的职业都是非常复杂的，用脑的时候多，用手的时候少。从事这些职业的人的智力，很少会因为大脑缺少使用而变得迟钝起来。而且，他们这些人所从事的职业也很少会从早到晚地烦扰他们。一般来说他们有大量的空闲时间，来完善他们早年已经打下基础或已经养成的一些嗜好的各种有用的或装饰性的知识。

普通人民的情况则与此不同。他们很少有空闲时间接受教育。甚至在幼年时期，他们的父母也几乎不能养活他们。所以一旦他们可以工作了，就必须马上从事一些可以赚取生活费的职业。他们从事的这些职业，一般来说都很简单、单调，不需要运用多少智力。同时，他们的劳动又是持续的、繁重的，使得他们很少

| 国民财富的性质与原理

The state can encourage or insist on the general acquirement of reading, writing, and arithmetic,

But though the common people cannot, in any civilized society, be so well instructed as people of some rank and fortune, the most essential parts of education, however, to read, write, and account, can be acquired at so early a period of life, that the greater part even of those who are to be bred to the lowest occupations, have time to acquire them before they can be employed in those occupations. For a very small expence the public can facilitate, can encourage, and can even impose upon almost the whole body of the people, the necessity of acquiring those most essential parts of education.

by establishing parish schools,

The public can facilitate this acquisition by establishing in every parish or district a little school, where children may be taught for a reward so moderate, that even a common labourer may afford it; the master being partly, but not wholly paid by the public; because, if he was wholly, or even principally paid by it, he would soon learn to neglect his business. In Scotland the establishment of such parish schools has taught almost the whole common people to read, and a very great proportion of them to write and account. In England the establishment of charity schools has had an effect of the same kind, though not so universally, because the establishment is not so universal. If in those little schools the books, by which the children are taught to read, were a little more instructive than they commonly are; and if, instead of a little smattering of Latin, which the children of the common people are sometimes taught there, and which can scarce ever be of any use to them; they were instructed in the elementary parts of geometry and mechanics, the literary education of this rank of people would perhaps be as complete as it can be. There is scarce a common trade which does not afford some opportunities of applying to it the principles of geometry and mechanics, and which would not therefore gradually exercise and improve the common people in those principles, the necessary introduction to the most sublime as well as to the most useful sciences.

giving prizes,

The public can encourage the acquisition of those most essential parts of education by giving small premiums, and little badges of distinction, to the children of the common people who excel in them.

有空闲和意向去从事、甚至去思考任何其他的事情。

不过,在任何一个文明社会里,尽管普通民众无法像那些显贵或者富有的人们那样受到良好的教育,不过教育中最基本的部分即读、书和计算,却可以在他们幼年时期就能学习到。他们中的绝大部分,甚至是那些从事最低级职业的人,在工作以前都有时间学习这些基本的知识。国家只需要花很少的费用,就可以促进、鼓励,甚至是强制几乎所有的人务必获得这些最基本的教育。_{国家可以鼓励或者要求坚决一般获得读、写和计算知识的}

国家可以通过在各个教区或地方建立小学校来促进这些基本教育的获得,孩子们在这里只需要支付很少的酬金就可以获得教育,即便是一个普通的劳动者也能负担得起。这些学校里教师的薪酬可以部分地但不能全部地由国家负担,因为如果全部或者甚至大部分由国家负担,教师很快就会变得懈怠了。在苏格兰,这些教区学校的建立已经几乎教会了所有的普通民众读书,他们中的一大部分还学会了书写、计算。在英格兰,慈善学校的建立也产生了同样的效果。不过,这种效果并没有那么普遍,因为这样的学校建立的没有那样普遍。如果这些小学校里用来教孩子们识字的课本,比现在经常用的课本更加有用;如果不是给那些在此学习的普通人家的孩子们讲授对他们毫无用处的一知半解的拉丁语,而是给他们讲授最基本的几何、机械知识,那么这个阶层民众的文化教育,也许就能达到所可能达到的最完善程度。那些普通的行业很少会有不给懂得几何学和机械学原理的人提供机会的,这样就能使普通民众可以逐渐地应用和改进这方面的原理,而这些原理也正是最高尚最有用的科学的入门知识。_{通过建立教区学校,}

国家可以用小小的奖金和荣誉奖章,来奖励那些普通家庭的_{发给奖金,}

| 国民财富的性质与原理

<small>and requiring men to pass an examination before setting up in trade.</small>　　The public can impose upon almost the whole body of the people the necessity of acquiring those most essential parts of education, by obliging every man to undergo an examination or probation in them before he can obtain the freedom in any corporation, or be allowed to set up any trade either in a village or town corporate.

<small>In this way the Greeks and Romans maintained a martial spirit.</small>　　It was in this manner, by facilitating the acquisition of their military and gymnastic exercises, by encouraging it, and even by imposing upon the whole body of the people the necessity of learning those exercises, that the Greek and Roman republics maintained the martial spirit of their respective citizens. They facilitated the acquisition of those exercises by appointing a certain place for learning and practising them, and by granting to certain masters the privilege of teaching in that place. Those masters do not appear to have had either salaries or exclusive privileges of any kind. Their reward consisted altogether in what they got from their scholars; and a citizen who had learnt his exercises in the public Gymnasia, had no sort of legal advantage over one who had learnt them privately, provided the latter had learnt them equally well. Those republics encouraged the acquisition of those exercises, by bestowing little premiums and badges of distinction upon those who excelled in them. To have gained a prize in the Olympic,

孩子中成绩优异者,以鼓励获得这种最基本的教育。

　　国家可以通过要求所有的人在获得加入任何行业组织的权利以前,或者在被允许可以在农村或城镇从事某种行业以前,必须得通过国家的考试或检定,这样就可以强制几乎所有的民众不得不获得最基本的教育了。

> 要求人们从事行业以前并在任何业都必须通过考试。

　　希腊共和国和罗马共和国就是通过这种方式,促进、鼓励全体民众接受军事训练和体育训练,甚至是强迫他们必须得进行这样的训练,从而才能保持他们的尚武精神。为了方便人民接受这种训练,国家指定了一个特定的地区作为学习和训练之用,并给予一定的教师在此教授的特权。不过,似乎这些教师没有就此领有任何薪俸或者享有任何独有的特权。他们的报酬完全来自于学生。在公共体育场进行训练的人并不比那些私下学习训练的人在法律上有什么优势,如果后者也学得一样好的话。希腊共和国和罗马共和国是通过用少量的奖金和荣誉奖章来奖励学习优胜者,以此来鼓励接受这些训练。如果能在奥林匹克运动会、科林斯地峡运动会或尼米亚运动会上获奖,〔1〕就不仅仅能给获赏者

> 希腊和罗马人通过这种方式保持了尚武精神。

---

〔1〕 古希腊有四大著名的运动会,除了祭祀宙斯的奥林匹克运动会外,还有三大运动会。庇底亚运动会(Pythian Games)创始于公元前582年,四年一次,目的是祭奠阿波罗。科林斯地峡运动会(Isthmian Gmnes)创始于公元前581年,两年一次,目的是为了祭祀波塞冬。尼米亚运动会(Nemean Games)创始于公元前573年,两年一次,目的是祭祀宙斯。由于每个运动会都与某一个泛希腊的神祇崇拜中心联系在一起,因此它们的影响遍及全希腊。希腊人认为宙斯是众神之主,拥有至高无上的权力和力量,因此祭祠天神宙斯的奥林匹克竞技会,也就特别受到重视。上列四大集会活动,形成每年在不同地点举行的传统,刚好四年轮到一次,轮到奥林匹克竞技会时,规模尤其盛大,这也就是后来形成奥林匹克运动会四年举办一次的由来。

Isthmian or Nemæan games gave illustration, not only to the person who gained it, but to his whole family and kindred. The obligation which every citizen was under to serve a certain number of years, if called upon, in the armies of the republic, sufficiently imposed the necessity of learning those exercises without which he could not be fit for that service.

<small>Martial spirit in the people would diminish both the necessary size and the danger of a standing army.</small>
That in the progress of improvement the practice of military exercises, anless government takes proper pains to support it, goes gradually to decay, and, together with it, the martial spirit of the great body of the people, the example of modern Europe sufficiently demonstrates. But the security of every society must always depend, more or less, upon the martial spirit of the great body of the people. In the present times, indeed, that martial spirit alone, and unsupported by a welldisciplined standing army, would not, perhaps, be sufficient for the defence and security of any society. But where every citizen had the spirit of a soldier, a smaller standing army would surely be requisite. That spirit, besides, would necessarily diminish very much the dangers to liberty, whether real or imaginary, which are commonly

<small>The Greek and Roman institutions were more effectual than modern militias, which only include a small portion of the people. It is the duty of government to prevent the growth of cowardice,</small>
apprehended from a standing army. As it would very much facilitate the operations of that army against a foreign invader, so it would obstruct them as much if unfortunately they should ever be directed against the constitution of the state.

The ancient institutions of Greece and Rome seem to have been much more effectual, for maintaining the martial spirit of the great body of the people, than the establishment of what are called the militias of modern times. They were much more simple. When they were once established, they executed themselves, and it required little or no attention from government to maintain them in the most perfect vigour. Whereas to maintain, even in tolerable execution, the complex regulations of any modern militia, requires the continual and painful attention of government, without which they are constantly falling into total neglect and disuse. The influence, besides, of the ancient institutions was much more universal. By means of them the whole body of the people was completely instructed in the use of arms. Whereas it is but a very small part of them who can ever be so instructed by the regulations of any modern militia; except, perhaps, that

第五篇 第一章

本人带来荣耀,也能给他的整个家族和亲戚都带来荣耀。每个公民市民在被召唤时,都有在共和国军队中服役一定年限的义务,这就足以使他们必须学习接受这些训练,否则他们就无法胜任兵役。

欧洲现代的例子已经足以说明,军事训练改进的过程中,如果政府不采取适当的方法予以支持,则这种军事训练就会日渐衰退,大多数人民的尚武精神也随之减弱。然而,每个社会的安全,都或多或少地依赖于大多数人民的尚武精神。当然,在现代社会,如果没有训练有素的常备军,单靠尚武精神也许并不足以保障任何社会的安全。但是如果所有的公民都具有战斗精神,那么肯定就会只需要较少的常备军。而且,无论是真实的还是想象的,大家对于常备军会严重危害自由都普遍存在忧虑,那么这种民众的战斗精神,就必然会减少这种危害自由的危险。就像这种战斗精神可以大大帮助常备军反抗外敌入侵一样,当常备军不幸发生违反国家宪法时,这种精神也可以极大地阻止常备军的违法行为。

减少常备军的规模和危险。人民的战斗精神

就保持大部分人民的战斗精神而言,古希腊和古罗马的制度似乎要远比我们现代建立的所谓民兵制度有效得多。古希腊和古罗马时期的制度相当的简单。但当它们一旦确立,就可以自行运作,不需要政府的关注就可以维持他们最佳的状态。而要想维持,甚至是勉强实行现代复杂的民兵制度,都需要政府不断的、费力的关注,不然这些制度就会陷入完全被忽视或者废弃不用的境地。而且,古代制度的影响也相当的普遍。通过这种制度,全体人民都完全学会了如何使用武器。而现代恐怕除了瑞士外,只有极少一部分人可以通过民兵制度学习到如何使用武器。一个

希腊和罗马的制度比现代民兵更有效,现代民兵含一部分人,防止怯懦的发展是政府的职责。

— 1635 —

of Switzerland. But a coward, a man incapable either of defending or of revenging himself, evidently wants one of the most essential parts of the character of a man. He is as much mutilated and deformed in his mind as another is in his body, who is either deprived of some of its most essential members, or has lost the use of them. He is evidently the more wretched and miserable of the two; because happiness and misery, which reside altogether in the mind, must necessarily depend more upon the healthful or unhealthful, the mutilated or entire state of the mind, than upon that of the body. Even though the martial spirit of the people were of no use towards the defence of the society, yet to prevent that sort of mental mutilation, deformity, and wretchedness, which cowardice necessarily involves in it, from spreading themselves through the great body of the people, would still deserve the most serious attention of government; in the same manner as it would deserve its most serious attention to prevent a leprosy or any other loathsome and offensive disease, though neither mortal nor dangerous, from spreading itself among them; though, perhaps, no other public good might result from such attention besides the prevention of so great a public evil.

gross ignorance and stupidity.
The same thing may be said of the gross ignorance and stupidity which, in a civilized society, seem so frequently to benumb the understandings of all the inferior ranks of people. A man without the proper use of the intellectual faculties of a man, is, if possible, more contemptible than even a coward, and seems to be mutilated and deformed in a still more essential part of the character of human nature. Though the state was to derive no advantage from the instruction of the inferior ranks of people, it would still deserve its attention that they should not be altogether uninstructed. The state, however, derives no inconsiderable advantage from their instruction. The more they are instructed, the less liable they are to the delusions of enthusiasm and superstition, which, among ignorant nations, frequently occasion the most dreadful disorders. An instructed and intelligent people besides, are always more decent and orderly than an ignorant and stupid one. They feel themselves, each individually more respectable, and more likely to obtain the respect of their lawful superiors, and they are therefore more disposed to respect those superiors. They are

不能保卫自己或者不能为自己复仇的懦夫,显然是缺少人性中最根本的一部分。一个在精神上残废和畸形的人,与另一个身体丧失了某些最重要的部位或这些部位丧失功能的人没有两样。而且两者当中,这种精神上残废和畸形的人还要更可怜、更可悲。因为快乐悲伤都完全在于心间,必定更多的依靠于健康的或不健康的精神状态,一个损伤的或完整的精神状态并不依靠身体的这些方面。尽管人类的武术精神对于社会的防御没有什么用处,然而为防止怯懦必定引发的那种精神的残缺、畸形和可怜在广大民众中传播,将会受到政府最严肃的关注;同样的,它也将会受到最严肃的关注来防止麻风病和其他令人讨厌的、令人不愉快的既不会致死也不会有危险的疾病在他们自己中间传播。或许尽管除了阻止如此大的公共灾害之外,公共的好处并不能从这些关注中产生。

在文明社会中,下层阶级的无知和愚昧似乎使所有下层阶级的人民理解力变得迟钝麻木,同样也可以这样说。如果一个人的智力没有得到合适的使用,甚至比一个懦夫更可耻,并且似乎也是人类天性特点的更本质方面的残废和变形。尽管国家不能从下层阶级民众的教育中获得好处,它仍然值得关注,防止下层阶级民众完全处于不受教育的状态。然而,国家还是能从他们的教育中获得好处。他们受到的教育越多,他们会越少受到迷信和狂热的迷惑,在无知的国家中会经常发生这样最可怕的混乱。并且,受到良好教育和聪明的民众比无知愚蠢的人民更加得体大方,更加守秩序。他们自己觉得每一个单独的个体更加值得尊重,并且更可能获得他们上司的尊重,因而他们就更加尊敬那些上级。他们更倾向于检查,更能看透派别性的和煽动性的抱怨;

_{完全的无知和愚昧。}

more disposed to examine, and more capable of seeing through, the interested complaints of faction and sedition, and they are, upon that account, less apt to be misled into any wanton or unnecessary opposition to the measures of government. In free countries, where the safety of government depends very much upon the favourable judgment which the people may form of its conduct, it must surely be of the highest importance that they should not be disposed to judge rashly or capriciously concerning it.

ARTICLE III Of The Expence Of The Institutions For The Instruction Of People Of All Ages

These institutions are chiefly for religious instruction. Religious like other teachers are more vigorous if unestablished and unendowed.

The institutions for the instruction of people of all ages are chiefly those for religious instruction. This is a species of instruction of which the object is not so much to render the people good citizens in this world, as to prepare them for another and a better world in a life to come. The teachers of the doctrine which contains this instruction, in the same manner as other teachers, may either depend altogether for their subsistence upon the voluntary contributions of their hearers; or they may derive it from some other fund to which the law of their country may entitle them; such as a landed estate, a tythe or land tax, an established salary or stipend. Their exertion, their zeal and industry, are likely to be much greater in the former situation than in the latter. In this respect the teachers of new religions have always had a considerable advantage in attacking those ancient and established systems of which the clergy, reposing themselves upon their benefices, had neglected to keep up the fervour of faith and devotion in the great body of the people; and having given themselves up to indolence, were become altogether incapable of making any vigorous exertion in defence even of their own establishment. The clergy of an established and well-endowed religion frequently become men of learning and elegance, who possess all the virtues of gentlemen, or which can recommend them to the esteem of gentlemen; but they are apt gradually to lose the qualities, both good and bad, which gave them authority and influence with the inferior ranks of people, and which had perhaps been the original causes of the success and establishment of their religion. Such a clergy, when attacked by a set of popular and bold, though perhaps stupid and ignorant enthusiasts, feel themselves as perfectly defenceless as the indolent, effeminate, and full-fed nations of the southern parts of Asia, when they were invaded by the

因此，他们更加不会被误导去对政府的措施作任何不必要的恣意的反对。在自由的国家中，那里政府的安全对人民对政府的行为做出的有利判断有很大的依赖性，非常重要的是他们不能草率地轻易地对政府的行为作出判断。

第三项 论各种年龄人们的教育的机构经费

对各种年龄人民的教育机构主要是进行宗教教育的教育机构。这是一种教育的类型，其目的与其说使人们成为这个世界上的良好公民，倒不如说是让民众为了另一个更好的生活世界做准备。抱有这种教育信条的老师跟其他老师一样，可能为了他们的生存完全依靠他们听众的资源贡献；或者他们可能从他们国家赋予他们的某种其他基金中获得；例如地产、什一税、土地税，固定的工资或薪水等。他们的努力，他们的热心和勤奋，处在前一种情况下的很可能比在后一种情况下的要多。就这一方面，新教的老师在攻击那些古代的和已经建立的体系时，总是具有更大的优势。这种体系中，牧师依靠自己的圣俸，已经忽略了在大部分民众中保持信仰和献身的热情；并且是他们自己放纵懒散，不能在保护自己教会方面完全奋发。一个国教并且是受到大量捐赠的教会的牧师，经常变成有知识并且很优雅，他拥有所有绅士的优点，或者使得他们受到绅士的尊敬；但是他们容易逐渐丧失那些在下层阶级中给他们带来威信和影响的好的或坏的品质，而这些品质也可能正是他们成功和成为国教的根本原因。当这些牧师受到一群受欢迎的勇敢的尽管有点愚笨和无知狂热的人的攻击时，就感觉到他们自己完全无助得像亚洲南部懒惰的、柔弱的、饱

这些机构主要是宗教机构，也像其他教师一样，如果工资固定并不是捐赠不定且受到的，加就更有精力充沛。

active, hardy, and hungry Tartars of the North. Such a clergy, upon such an emergency, have commonly no other resource than to call upon the civil magistrate to persecute, destroy, or drive out their adversaries, as disturbers of the public peace. It was thus that the Roman catholic clergy called upon the civil magistrate to persecute the protestants; and the church of England, to persecute the dissenters; and that in general every religious sect, when it has once enjoyed for a century or two the security of a legal establishment, has found itself incapable of making any vigorous defence against any new sect which chose to attack its doctrine or discipline. Upon such occasions the advantage in point of learning and good writing may sometimes be on the side of the established church. But the arts of popularity, all the arts of gaining proselytes, are constantly on the side of its adversaries. In England those arts have been long neglected by the well-endowed clergy of the established church, and are at present chiefly cultivated by the dissenters and by the methodists. The independent provisions, however, which in many places have been made for dissenting teachers, by means of voluntary subscriptions, of trust rights, and other evasions of the law, seem very much to have abated the zeal and activity of those teachers. They have many of them become very learned, ingenious, and respectable men; but they have in general ceased to be very popular preachers. The methodists, without half the learning of the dissenters, are much more in vogue.

In the church of Rome, the industry and zeal of the inferior clergy are kept more alive by the powerful motive of self-interest, than perhaps in any established protestant church. The parochial clergy derive, many of them, a very considerable part of their subsistence from the voluntary oblations of the people; a source of revenue which confession gives them many opportunities of improving. The mendicant orders derive their whole subsistence from such

食的民族,受到了北方充满活力、勇敢和饥饿的鞑靼人的攻击一样。这样一个民族在这样紧急的情况下,通常除了号召国内官员来将他们的竞争者作为公共和平的扰乱者来迫害、毁灭和驱逐之外,没有其他办法。就是这样,罗马天主教牧师号召国内官员来残害新教徒;英格兰教会残害非国教派。在每一个宗教派别享受了一两个世纪的法律保障的安全后,发现自己不能对任何攻击其信条和戒律的新教做出任何有力的对抗。在这种情况下,学习和良好的写作有时候对国教有利。但是受欢迎的艺术,改变宗教信仰的所有艺术,往往对它的竞争者有利。在英格兰这些艺术长期被国教中享受大量圣俸的牧师所忽略,而目前却主要由反抗者和循道宗信徒[1]加以培养。不过,通过自愿捐赠、信托权利以及其他法律的逃避,在许多地方为这些反抗教会的老师提供的独立的生活资料,似乎大大减少了这些老师的热情和积极性。他们中的很多人变得非常有学问、非常机灵并且受人尊敬;但是他们一般都已经不再是非常受群众欢迎的老师了。这些循道宗信徒教徒没有反对者一半的学问,却更加受到欢迎。

在罗马教会中,由于自身利益强有力的驱使,下层阶级牧师的热情和勤奋比任何清教徒教会的牧师更有活力。教区中很多牧师从民众的自愿的慈善捐赠中获得了他们生活资料中的相当大的部分;秘密的忏悔又给他们增加了这种收入的源泉。托钵[2]

---

[1] 循道宗信徒(Methodist),基督教新教路德教会的成员,此教会建立在英格兰的约翰和查尔斯·卫斯理在18世纪初期提出的原则之上,以积极关心社会福利和公众道德为特点。

[2] 托钵僧(mendicant),一种不允许拥有私人财产的僧人,以工作或化缘维持生活。

The inferior clergy of the Church of Rome are more stimulated by self-interest than those of any established Protestant Church.

oblations. It is with them, as with the hussars and light infantry of some armies; no plunder, no pay. The parochial clergy are like those teachers whose reward depends partly upon their salary, and partly upon the fees or honoraries which they get from their pupils; and these must always depend more or less upon their industry and reputation. The mendicant orders are like those teachers whose subsistence depends altogether upon their industry. They are obliged, therefore, to use every art which can animate the devotion of the common people. The establishment of the two great mendicant orders of St. Dominic and St. Francis, it is observed by Machiavel,① revived, in the thirteenth and fourteenth centuries, the languishing faith and devotion of the catholic church. In Roman catholic countries the spirit of devotion is supported altogether by the monks and by the poorer parochial clergy. The great dignitaries of the church, with all the accomplishments of gentlemen and men of the world, and sometimes with those of men of learning, are careful enough to maintain the necessary discipline over their inferiors, but seldom give themselves any trouble about the instruction of the people.

Hume says the state may leave the promotion of some arts to individuals who benefit by them,

"Most of the arts and professions in a state," says by far the most illustrious philosopher and historian of the present age, "are of such a nature, that, while they promote the interests of the society, they are also useful or agreeable to some individuals; and in that case, the constant rule of the magistrate, except, perhaps, on the first introduction of any art, is, to leave the profession to itself, and trust its encouragement to the individuals who reap the benefit of it. The artizans, finding their profits to rise by the favour of their customers, increase, as much as possible, their skill and industry; and as matters are not disturbed by any injudicious tampering, the commodity is always sure to be at all times nearly proportioned to the demand."

"But there are also some callings, which, though useful and even necessary in a state, bring no advantage or pleasure to any individual, and the supreme power is obliged to alter its conduct

---

① [In 'Discourses on the First Decade of Titus Livius,' book iii., chap. i.]

教团从这些捐献中获得了他们全部的生活资料。对他们而言,就像对敌人的轻骑兵和轻步兵一样,没有掠夺、没有供养。他们很像那些轻骑快步的军队,不行掠夺,就没有给养。教区牧师很像那些收入依靠他们的工资的教师,部分依靠他们从学生那里获得的费用和报酬;或多或少总是依靠他们的勤奋和名誉。托钵教团很像那些生活资料完全依靠他们的勤奋的教师。因此他们必须使用种种技术来激发普通人的皈依。两大托钵教团——圣多米尼克及圣佛兰西斯教团的建立,据马基弗利尔观察,①在13世纪及14世纪,复活了天主教会日趋衰弱的信仰和皈依。在罗马天主教的国家,皈依的精神完全受到修道僧及贫苦的教区牧师的支持。教会大人物,以及所有绅士和世俗人士的才能,有时还有有学问的人的才能,对于维持下层阶级必要的纪律是足够小心的,但是很少给他们自己带来关于教育人民的麻烦。

罗马教会下层阶级的牧师,出于自身的利益,比耶稣会牧师更易受到激励。

现代最著名的哲学家和历史学家说:"一个国家的大部分工艺和技术具有这样的性质:当他们促进社会利益的同时,他们对于某些个人也是有用的,令人愉悦的;在那种情况下,政府的通常规定是让这种职业自由发展,可能除了任何技术首次引进来,并且将它的鼓励交给从它那里收获好处的个人。这些工匠发现他们的利润可以由他们消费者的青睐而上升,他们就会尽可能多的改进他们的技术更加勤奋;如果事情不被不明智的干扰所打扰,商品总是肯定在任何时候都和需求成比例。"

谟国家可以受个人去促进某种技术的发展,凭益人理的休说,任理以进术发展。

"但是也存在一些职业,尽管有用,甚至在一个国家是必须的,却不会给个人带来任何的好处或愉悦。对于这些行业的从业

---

① 《有关提图斯利维阿斯头十年的讲道》,第三编第一章。

others must be promoted by the state;
with regard to the retainers of those professions. It must give them public encouragement in order to their subsistence; and it must provide against that negligence to which they will naturally be subject, either by annexing particular honours to the profession, by establishing a long subordination of ranks and a strict dependance, or by some other expedient. The persons employed in the finances, fleets, and magistracy, are instances of this order of men. "

it might be thought that the teaching of religion belonged to the first class,
"It may naturally be thought, at first sight, that the ecclesiastics belong to the first class, and that their encouragement, as well as that of lawyers and physicians, may safely be entrusted to the liberality of individuals, who are attached to their doctrines, and who find benefit or consolation from their spiritual ministry and assistance, Their industry and vigilance will, no doubt, be whetted by such an additional motive; and their skill in the profession, as well as their address in governing the minds of the people, must receive daily increase, from their increasing practice, study, and attention. "

but it does not, because the interested zeal of the clergy should be discouraged.
"But if we consider the matter more closely, we shall find, that this interested diligence of the clergy is what every wise legislator will study to prevent; because, in every religion except the true, it is highly pernicious, and it has even a natural tendency to pervert the true, by infusing into it a strong mixture of superstition, folly, and delusion. Each ghostly practitioner, in order to render himself more precious and sacred in the eyes of his retainers, will inspire them with the most violent abhorrence of all other sects, and continually endeavour, by some novelty, to excite the languid devotion of his audience. No regard will be paid to truth, morals, or decency in the doctrines inculcated. Every tenet will be adopted that best suits the disorderly affections of the human frame. Customers will be drawn to each conventicle by new industry and address in practising on the passions and credulity of the populace. And in the end, the civil magistrate will find, that he has dearly paid for his pretended frugality, in saving a fixed establishment for the priests; and that in reality the most decent and advantageous composition, which he can make with the spiritual guides, is to bribe their indolence, by assigning stated salaries to their profession, and rendering it superfluous for them to be farther

者,最高当权者必须要改变自己的做法。为了使他们生存下去, <small>必须由国家来促进;其他</small>
必须要给予他们公共的鼓励;并且为防止他们自然会受到的疏
忽,必须给这种职业增加特殊的荣耀,为其建立一系列长期的等
级附属和严格的依存关系,或者采用其他的对策来予以防止。从
事财政、海军及政治的人,都是这一类人的实例。"

"乍一看可能很自然地被认为:教士属于第一类,对他们以及 <small>有人认为教授宗教可能属于第一类,</small>
律师和医师的鼓励,可以很安全的依赖于个人,这些个人信仰他
们的教义,从他们的精神服务和帮助中得到了好处或者安慰。这
样这些教士、律师或者医师的勤奋和警惕意识毫无疑问会被这样
的额外动机加强,他们的专业技能以及他们统治人们心灵的技
巧,也必然会通过他们的不断练习、学习和注意日益增加。"

"但是,如果我们更加仔细地考虑一下这件事情,我们会发 <small>但是并非这样,因为牧师的利己热心应该被挫抑。</small>
现:牧师出于自己利益的勤奋,正是每一个明智的立法者所要研
究防止的。因为除了真正宗教之外每一个宗教,这种利己的勤奋
都是极端有害的,而且它有一种歪曲真理将迷信、愚昧和幻想混
在一起灌入真正的宗教的自然倾向。每一个宗教的从业者,为了
使他自己在他信徒眼中更加尊贵、更加神圣,都要激起对其他所
有教派强烈的厌恶,并且不断用一些新奇的方法来激发听众们日
渐懈怠的宗教热情。在传授教义时,他们丝毫不注意真理、道德
或礼节。最适合于人体结构中最混乱的感情的教义都被采用了。
他们利用普通民众的热情和轻信,吸引了大量的普通民众。最
后,政府将会发现,由于不给牧师提供固定的圣俸,国家为这表面
虚假的节约付出昂贵的代价。实际上,政府和精神领袖们最体
面、最有利的组合,就是给这些职业的人员分配固定的工资以抑
制他们的懒惰,使他们感到除了防止羊群误寻新的牧场而外,其

active, than merely to prevent their flock from straying in quest of new pastures. And in this manner ecclesiastical establishments, though commonly they arose at first from religious views, prove in the end advantageous to the political interests of society."①

Establishments and public endowments have not been due to reasoning like this, but to the needs of political faction.

But whatever may have been the good or bad effects of the independent provision of the clergy; it has, perhaps, been very seldom bestowed upon them from any view to those effects. Times of violent religious controversy have generally been times of equally violent political faction. Upon such occasions, each political party has either found it, or imagined it, for its interest, to league itself with some one or other of the contending religious sects. But this could be done only by adopting, or at least by favouring, the tenets of that particular sect. The sect which had the good fortune to be leagued with the conquering party, necessarily shared in the victory of its ally, by whose favour and protection it was soon enabled in some degree to silence and subdue all its adversaries. Those adversaries had generally leagued themselves with the enemies of the conquering party, and were therefore the enemies of that party. The clergy of this particular sect having thus become complete masters of the field, and their influence and authority with the great body of the people being in its highest vigour, they were powerful enough to over-awe the chiefs and leaders of their own party, and to oblige the civil magistrate to respect their opinions and inclinations. Their first demand was generally, that he should silence and subdue all their adversaries; and their second, that he should bestow an independent provision on themselves. As they had generally contributed a good deal to the victory, it seemed not unreasonable that they should have some share in the spoil. They were weary, besides, of humouring the people, and of depending upon their caprice for a subsistence. In making this demand therefore they consulted their own ease and comfort, without troubling themselves about the effect which it might have in

---

① [Hume, *History*, chap. xxix., vol. iv, pp. 30, 31, in ed. of 1773, which differs verbally both from earlier and from later editions.]

第五篇　第一章

他任何进一步的活动都是多余的。按照这种方式来说,宗教上的定俸制度,尽管最初是起源于宗教观点,却通常也是有利于社会政治利益的。"①

但是,不论给予牧师独立的给养的效果是好是坏,这样规定或许很少是由于对效果好坏的看法而产生的。充满激烈宗教争论的时代,一般也是政治派系斗争同样激烈的时代。在这种情况下,每一个政党发现或者认为为了自身的利益,应该和某一个或其他竞争的宗教派别联合起来。但是要想达到这样的目的,只有采纳或者至少赞成那个教派的教理才行。这个教派如果有幸能和胜利的政党联合,就必定会分享他们联盟的胜利果实。通过同盟的支持和保护,在某种程度上这个教派很快就压制和征服了所有的竞争教派。这些竞争教派一般是和胜利政党的敌对党派联合的,所以也就是胜利政党的敌人。于是这个教派的牧师就成为了这个领域完全的领导者,他们对最广大人民的影响和权威达到了最高的巅峰,他们有足够的力量威慑己方政党的领袖们,也迫使政府尊重他们的观点和倾向。他们的第一个要求一般是,政府首脑必须制服和压制他们所有的反对者;第二个要求是,政府必须给他们提供独立的供奉。因为一般来说他们对于胜利都做出了很大的贡献,似乎他们分享战利品并不是不合理。另外,他们非常厌倦于迎合人民、依靠他们的反复无常来获得生活资料。因此在这样的要求中,他们考虑了自己的舒适和自在,而至于这样做在将来对于他们教派的影响和权威会产生什么后果,他们并没

_{但是国捐助不是这样出于这原因,而是由于政治派系的斗争。}

---

① 休谟:《英格兰史》,1773 年,第 4 卷第 29 章,第 30、31 页,这一版同早先的和以后的版本在文字上略有不同。

future times upon the influence and authority of their order. The civil magistrate, who could comply with this demand only by giving them something which he would have chosen much rather to take, or to keep to himself, was seldom very forward to grant it. Necessity, however, always forced him to submit at last, though frequently not till after many delays, evasions, and affected excuses.

<small>If politics had never called in the aid of religion, sects would have been so numerous that they would have learnt to tolerate each other,</small> But if politics had never called in the aid of religion, had the conquering party never adopted the tenets of one sect more than those of another, when it had gained the victory, it would probably have dealt equally and impartially with all the different sects, and have allowed every man to chuse his own priest and his own religion as he thought proper. There would in this case, no doubt, have been a great multitude of religious sects. Almost every different congregation might probably have made a little sect by itself, or have entertained some peculiar tenets of its own. Each teacher would no doubt have felt himself under the necessity of making the utmost exertion, and of using every art both to preserve and to increase the number of his disciples. But as every other teacher would have felt himself under the same necessity, the success of no one teacher, or sect of teachers, could have been very great. The interested and active zeal of religious teachers can be dangerous and troublesome only where there is, either but one sect tolerated in the society, or where the whole of a large society is divided into two or three great sects; the teachers of each acting by concert, and under a regular discipline and subordination. But that zeal must be altogether innocent where the society is divided into two or three hundred, or perhaps into as many thousand small sects, of which no one could be considerable enough to disturb the public tranquillity. The teachers of each sect, seeing themselves surrounded on all sides with more adversaries than friends, would be obliged to learn that candour and moderation which is so seldom to be found among the teachers of those great sects, whose tenets, being supported by the civil magistrate, are held in veneration by almost all the inhabitants of extensive kingdoms and empires, and who therefore see nothing round them but followers, disciples, and humble admirers. The teachers of each little sect, finding themselves almost alone, would be obliged to respect those of almost every other sect, and the concessions which they would mutually find it both convenient and agreeable

有费心去考虑。政府要想满足他们这些要求，只有选择把自己想要的或想留下来的一部分东西分给他们，所以政府很少愿意答应给予他们。然而，这种需求最终还是迫使他屈服，尽管往往要在找一些回避和造作的借口推脱拖延数次之后。

但是如果政治斗争从来没有请求宗教的援助，胜利的党派在胜利后不是只采用任何一个教派的教理，它就可能公平地、毫无偏见地对待所有的党派，允许每一个人选择他自己认为合适的牧师和宗教。在这种情况下，毫无疑问会存在大量的宗教党派，而几乎每一个不同的宗教集会都很可能形成自己的一个小派系，保持它自己的特殊教理。这样所有的牧师都肯定会觉得有必要尽自己最大的努力，利用每一种技巧来保持和增加信徒的数量。但是每一个其他的教派的牧师同样也会感到这种必要性，因此没有一个牧师或教派可以取得非常大的成功。利己的和极端热情的宗教牧师，只有在社会中仅允许存在一个教派或者整个社会被划分为两三个教派的时候，教派的牧师在统一的纪律和服从之下行动一致，那时他们或许才是危险麻烦的。如果一个社会被划分为两三百或者上千的小党派，其中没有一个足够大到危害社会安宁，在这种情况下，热情必定毫无危险可言。每个党派的老师，发现自己四周被敌人而不是被朋友包围，他们将不得不学习那些大教派的牧师们很少拥有的真诚和温和。大教派的牧师们之所以缺乏这种真诚和温和，原因在于大教派的教理受到政府的支持、受到最广阔国家和王国的几乎所有居民的尊敬，因此大教派的牧师们周围看到的只有追随者、信徒和谦卑的崇拜者。而小教派的老师发现自己是孤立的，就不得不尊敬每一个其他教派的宗教牧师，他们人人都感到相互让步的便利和必要。这样就可能会使大

| 国民财富的性质与原理

to make to one another, might in time probably reduce the doctrine of the greater part of them to that pure and rational religion, free from every mixture of absurdity, imposture, or fanaticism, such as wise men have in all ages of the world wished to see established; but such as positive law has perhaps never yet established, and probably never will establish in any country: because, with regard to religion, positive law always has been, and probably always will be, more or less influenced by popular superstition and enthusiasm. This plan of ecclesiastical government, or more properly of no ecclesiastical government, was what the sect called Independents, a sect no doubt of very wild enthusiasts, proposed to establish in England towards the end of the civil war. If it had been established, though of a very unphilosophical origin, it would probably by this time have been productive of the most philosophical good temper and moderation with regard to every sort of religious principle. It has been established in Pensylvania, where, though the Quakers happen to be the most numerous, the law in reality favours no one sect more than another, and it is there said to have been productive of this philosophical good temper and moderation.

<small>and if they did not, their zeal could do no harm.</small> But though this equality of treatment should not be productive of this good temper and moderation in all, or even in the greater part of the religious sects of a particular country; yet provided those sects were sufficiently numerous, and each of them consequently too small to disturb the public tranquillity, the excessive zeal of each for its particular tenets could not well be productive of any very hurtful effects, but, on the contrary, of several good ones: and if the government was perfectly decided both to let them all alone, and to oblige <small>Of the two systems of morality,</small> them all to let alone one another, there is little danger that they would not of their own accord subdivide themselves fast enough, so as soon to become sufficiently numerous.

<small>the strict or austere and the liberal or loose, the first is favoured by the common people, the second by people of fashion.</small> In every civilized society, in every society where the distinction of ranks has once been completely established, there have been always two different schemes or systems of morality current at the same time; of which the one may be called the strict or austere; the other the liberal, or, if you will, the loose system. The former is generally admired and revered by the common people: the latter is commonly more esteemed and adopted by what are called people of fashion. The degree of disapprobation with which we ought to mark the vices of levity, the vices which are apt to arise from great prosperity, and from the excess of gaiety and good humour, seems to constitute the principal distinction between those two opposite schemes or systems. In the

部分教派成为纯粹的理性的宗教,而避免了荒谬、欺骗或盲信,这正是世界上所有时代明智的人所希望建立的宗教。但是这样的成文法或许从来没有建立,或许将来也不会建立这样的宗教:因为,关于宗教的成文法,总是、或许永远会或多或少地受到流行的迷信和狂热的影响。这种教会的管理方案,或者更适当地说没有管理的教会方案,就是极端狂热的所谓独立教派在英国内战结束时提议建立。如果它被建立起来的话,尽管它的起源是非常非哲学的,但到今日也许会产生最富哲理的和平气质和温和精神。宾夕法尼亚建立了这个方案,虽然那里教友派占最多数,但实际上法律并没有任何偏爱任何教派,据说在那里存在这种哲理的和平气质和温和精神。

尽管这些平等的待遇,不可能使一个国家的所有甚至大部分教派中产生这种良好气质和温和精神,但是只要这些派系足够多,并且他们中的每一个都太小而不足以扰乱社会的安宁。每个派系对它自己的特别教理的过分热情就不会产生非常有害的结果,而且相反,可能还会产生一些好的结果:如果政府决定完全任由这些教派自由发展,并且迫使他们互不干涉,那么他们肯定就会自愿迅速分裂从而变得数目众多,这样也就不存在危险了。[如果他们不这样,他们的热情也没有什么害处。]

在每一个文明社会,社会中的阶级区别已经完全建立,往往同时存在两种不同的道德体系和道义。其中一个被称为严肃的或严格的体系,另一个被称为自由的或者不妨说松散的体系。前者一般被普通人赞赏和尊敬;后者一般更受到所谓社会名流的更大的尊重和采用。对于轻率这种恶习我们应该持有的非难程度,这种恶习容易产生于巨大的繁荣,产生于过度的欢情乐意,似乎是这两种相反体系或系统之间的主要区别。在自由或松散的体[在两种道德体系中,严格的或严肃的体系,由松散的体系,前者受普通人欢迎,后者受社会上流会的欢迎。]

liberal or loose system, luxury, wanton and even disorderly mirth, the pursuit of pleasure to some degree of intemperance, the breach of chastity, at least in one of the two sexes, &c. provided they are not accompanied with gross indecency, and do not lead to falshood or injustice, are generally treated with a good deal of indulgence, and are easily either excused or pardoned altogether. In the austere system, on the contrary, those excesses are regarded with the utmost abhorrence and detestation. The vices of levity are always ruinous to the common people, and a single week's thoughtlessness and dissipation is often sufficient to undo a poor workman for ever, and to drive him through despair upon committing the most enormous crimes. The wiser and better sort of the common people, therefore, have always the utmost abhorrence and detestation of such excesses, which their experience tells them are so immediately fatal to people of their condition. The disorder and ex travagance of several years, on the contrary, will not always ruin a man of fashion, and people of that rank are very apt to consider the power of indulging in some degree of excess as one of the advantages of their fortune, and the liberty of doing so without censure or reproach, as one of the privileges which belong to their station. In people of their own station, therefore, they regard such excesses with but a small degree of disapprobation, and censure them either very slightly or not at all.

<small>Religious sects usually begin with the austere system,</small>　　Almost all religious sects have begun among the common people, from whom they have generally drawn their earliest, as well as their most numerous proselytes. The austere system of morality has, accordingly, been adopted by those sects almost constantly, or with very few exceptions; for there have been some. It was the system by which they could best recommend themselves to that order of people to whom they first proposed their plan of reformation upon what had been before established. Many of them, perhaps the greater part of them, have even endeavoured to gain credit by refining upon this austere system, and by carrying it to some degree of folly and extravagance; and this excessive rigour has frequently recommended them more than any thing else to the respect and veneration of the common people.

　　A man of rank and fortune is by his station the distinguished member of a great society, who attend to every part of his conduct, and who thereby oblige him to attend to every part of it himself. His authority and consideration depend very much upon the respect which

系中，放肆，甚至扰乱秩序的欢乐，无节制的寻欢作乐，贞节的破坏，至少是两性中的一方面破坏贞操等等，只要不伴随着下流，不导致虚妄或不公正，一般都受到很大的宽容，很容易得到完全的原谅或谅解。相反，在严格的体系中，那些过度的放纵都被视为极其憎恶和讨厌。轻率这种恶习总是有害于人民，仅仅一周的粗心大意和挥霍浪费往往足以永远毁了一个贫穷的工人，驱使他由于绝望而犯更大的罪。因此，比较明智、比较善良的普通人总是极度厌恶鄙视这些放荡行为。经验告诉他们，这些行为对于处于他们这种境地的人来说是立即致命的。相反，多年的不羁和浪费不会毁掉一个上流人士，这种阶层的人非常容易将某种程度的过度放纵视为他们拥有财富的好处之一，这样恣意而为没有受到责难和责备也是处于这种境地的人所拥有的特权之一。因此，这个阶层处于同一地位的人，对于这种放纵只作小小的不满非难、很轻微地责备，或者干脆根本不予责备。

几乎所有的宗教派系都始于普通的民众，宗教派系一般从这些普通民众那里吸取最早的、人数最多的新信徒。因此，严肃的道德体系不断被那些派系所采用（或者存在少数几个例外）。这个体系使这些教派能接近这些阶级的民众，向他们提出改革以前建立的宗教的计划方案。他们中的许多人，甚至是绝大多数人，都试图努力通过改革这些严肃的体系来博取信任，使之达到某种愚蠢过分的程度；这种过分的严格，往往比任何其他事情更能获得普通人民的尊敬和崇拜。

_{宗教派系通常始于严格的体系，}

有身份有财产的人，就其地位来说，是社会中引人注目的人物，社会关注他的所有言行举动，因此迫使他自己注意自己的所有言行举止。他的权威和重要性非常依靠社会对他的尊敬。他

国民财富的性质与原理

_{and in small religious sects morals are regular and orderly and even disagreeably rigorous and unsocial.} this society bears to him. He dare not do any thing which would disgrace or discredit him in it, and he is obliged to a very strict observation of that species of morals, whether liberal or austere, which the general consent of this society prescribes to persons of his rank and fortune. A man of low condition, on the contrary, is far from being a distinguished member of any great society. While he remains in a country village his conduct may be attended to, and he may be obliged to attend to it himself. In this situation, and in this situation only, he may have what is called a character to lose. But as soon as he comes into a great city, he is sunk in obscurity and darkness. His conduct is observed and attended to by nobody, and he is therefore very likely to neglect it himself, and to abandon himself to every sort of low profligacy and vice. He never emerges so effectually from this obscurity, his conduct never excites so much the attention of any respectable society, as by his becoming the member of a small religious sect. He from that moment acquires a degree of consideration which he never had before. All his brother sectaries are, for the credit of the sect, interested to observe his conduct, and if he gives occasion to any scandal, if he deviates very much from those austere morals which they almost always require of one another, to punish him by what is always a very severe punishment, even where no civil effects attend it, expulsion or excommunication from the sect. In little religious sects, accordingly, the morals of the common people have been almost always remarkably regular and orderly; generally much more so than in the established church. The morals of those little sects, indeed, have frequently been rather disagreeably rigorous and unsocial.

There are two possible remedies, There are two very easy and effectual remedies, however, by whose joint operation the state might, without violence, correct whatever was unsocial or disagreeably rigorous in the morals of all the little sects into which the country was divided.

(1) the requirement of a knowledge of science and philosophy from candidates for professions and offices; The first of those remedies is the study of science and philosophy, which the state might render almost universal among all people of middling or more than middling rank and fortune; not by giving salaries to teachers in order to make them negligent and idle, but by instituting some sort of probation, even in the higher and more difficult sciences, to be undergone by every person before he was permitted to exercise any liberal profession, or before he could be received as a

不敢做任何有损他体面和名声的事情,被迫严格遵守社会一般认同的他那种地位和财产的人所应该的道德准则,无论这是自由的还是严肃的。相反,下层阶级的人远远不是社会的显赫人物。当他留在乡村,他的行为可能受到自己的关注,并且可能不得不自己小心。在这种情况下,也仅仅在这种情况下,他很可能才有所谓的人格丧失。但是当他来到大城市的时候,他就没入卑贱和低微之中。他的行为不受任何人的关注,因此很可能他自己都忽略这些行为,并且委身于一切卑劣的游荡和罪恶。要从这种卑微中抽身,要使自己的行动引起体面社会的关注,就只有加入一个小的宗教派系中。从加入教派的那时起,他获得了前所未有的尊重。为了教派的名誉,他的教派教友都要关注他的行为;如果他引发了丑闻,或者他的所作所为大大违反了同门教友所彼此要求的严肃的道德规定,他就要受到被认为是极其严峻的一种惩罚,即将他驱逐出教会,即便这种惩罚不带任何民法的效力。因此,在小教派中,普通人民的道德几乎总是非常有规则有秩序的,比在国教要严肃得多。的确,这些小教派的道德,往往过于严格,不合人情。

<small>在小教派中,道德律是有秩序的,其至是过于严格和不合人情的。</small>

不过,对于一国划分的所有小教派道德上的任何不合人情和过于严肃之处,国家不需要武力,只需两种非常容易和有效的方法就可以予以弥补。

<small>存在两种补救的办法:</small>

第一种办法就是学习科学和哲学,国家可以使几乎所有的中等阶级或中等阶级以上的地位和财产的人来学习;不是给老师工资来使他们变得疏忽和懒惰,而是制定某一种鉴定和考验期,在每个人从事自由职业之前,或者在他成为受信托的或有俸给的光荣职位的候选人之前,必须经过甚至更高级更困难的学科检

<small>(1)要求各种职业的人和公职的选举候选人掌握科学和哲学知识;</small>

——1655——

candidate for any honourable office of trust or profit. If the state imposed upon this order of men the necessity of learning, it would have no occasion to give itself any trouble about providing them with proper teachers. They would soon find better teachers for themselves than any whom the state could provide for them. Science is the great antidote to the poison of enthusiasm and superstition; and where all the superior ranks of people were secured from it, the inferior ranks could not be much exposed to it.

<small>and (2) the encouragement of public diversions.</small>

The second of those remedies is the frequency and gaiety of public diversions. The state, by encouraging, that is by giving entire liberty to all those who for their own interest would attempt, without scandal or indecency, to amuse and divert the people by painting, poetry, music, dancing; by all sorts of dramatic representations and exhibitions, would easily dissipate, in the greater part of them, that melancholy and gloomy humour which is almost always the nurse of popular superstition and enthusiasm. Public diversions have always been the objects of dread and hatred, to all the fanatical promoters of those popular frenzies. The gaiety and good humour which those diversions inspire were altogether inconsistent with that temper of mind, which was fittest for their purpose, or which they could best work upon. Dramatic representations besides, frequently exposing their artifices to public ridicule, and sometimes even to public execration, were upon that account, more than all other diversions, the objects of their peculiar abhorrence.

<small>Where no one religion was favoured the sovereign would not require to influence the teachers of religion,</small>

In a country where the law favoured the teachers of no one religion more than those of another, it would not be necessary that any of them should have any particular or immediate dependency upon the sovereign or executive power; or that he should have any thing to do, either in appointing, or in dismissing them from their offices. In such a situation he would have no occasion to give himself any concern about them, further than to keep the peace among them, in the same manner as among the rest of his subjects; that is, to hinder them from persecuting, abusing, or oppressing one another. But it is quite otherwise in countries where there is an established or governing religion. The sovereign can in this case never be secure, unless he has the means of influencing in a considerable degree the greater part of the teachers of that religion.

The clergy of every established church constitute a great incorpo-

定。如果一个国家对这个阶层的人们强迫他们学习,那么就不需要费神给他们提供合适的老师。他们将会很快发现对于他们自己而言,好老师比国家所能提供给他们的任何人都要好。科学是对狂热和迷信这类毒药最好的治疗方法;如果所有的上层阶级的人们都不受这种毒害,下层阶级的人们也就不大可能受到它的影响。

第二种办法是经常和欢乐的公共娱乐。一个国家为了自己的利益,鼓励那些试图通过绘画、诗歌、音乐、舞蹈来娱乐大众而又不伤风败俗的人,给予完全的自由。通过各种戏剧化的展示和表演,很容易驱散大部分人的忧郁和悲观情绪,这些心情正是流行的迷信和狂热的哺育者。对于这些所有流行狂热的疯狂煽动者,公共娱乐一直都是其害怕和仇恨的目标。由公共娱乐所引起的欢乐与快适与符合他们目的的那种情绪是完全不一致的。另外,戏剧的表演经常会揭露他们的伎俩,使他们受到公众的嘲笑,甚至是公众的谴责。由于这个原因,比起所有其他娱乐,公共娱乐更容易成为他们憎恨的目标。

（2）公众娱乐的鼓励。

相比其他宗教的牧师,当一个国家的法律不会偏爱某种宗教的牧师时,他们中间的任何人都不必和君主或者行政部门保持特殊的或直接的从属关系;君主对他们的任免无需过问。在这种情况下,君主除了保持他们之间的和平,以同样的方式对待其余的臣民之外,就不必再去关心他们了;也就是阻止他们之间相互伤害、毁谤或压迫。但是在一个存在国教或者统治宗教的国家中,情况就并非如此了。在这种情况下,君主绝不是安全的,除非他有办法在很大程度上影响那个宗教大部分的牧师。

爱宗教的国家中,没有必要影响牧师,君主不必去影响宗教牧师,

每个国家的牧师组成一个巨大的团体。他们行动一致,在同

<small>as he must where there is an established church,</small> ration. They can act in concert, and pursue their interest upon one plan and with one spirit, as much as if they were under the direction of one man; and they are frequently too under such direction. Their interest as an incorporated body is never the same with that of the sovereign, and is sometimes directly opposite to it. Their great interest is to maintain their authority with the people; and this authority depends upon the supposed certainty and importance of the whole doctrine which they inculcate, and upon the supposed necessity of adopting every part of it with the most implicit faith, in order to avoid eternal misery. Should the sovereign have the imprudence to appear either to deride or doubt himself of the most trifling part of their doctrine, or from humanity attempt to protect those who did either the one or the other, the punctilious honour of a clergy who have no sort of dependency upon him, is immediately provoked to proscribe him as a profane person, and to employ all the terrors of religion in order to oblige the people to transfer their allegiance to some more orthodox and obedient prince. Should he oppose any of their pretensions or usurpations, the danger is equally great. The princes who have dared in this manner to rebel against the church, over and above this crime of rebellion, have generally been charged too with the additional crime of heresy, notwithstanding their solemn protestations of their faith and humble submission to every tenet which she thought proper to prescribe to them. But the authority of religion is superior to every other authority. The fears which it suggests conquer all other fears. When the authorised teachers of religion propagate through the great body of the people doctrines subversive of the authority of the sovereign, it is by violence only, or by the force of a standing army, that he can maintain his authority. Even a standing army cannot in this case give him any lasting security; because if the soldiers are not foreigners, which can seldom be the case, but drawn from the great body of the people, which must almost always be the case, they are likely to be soon corrupted by those very doctrines. The revolutions which the turbulence of the Greek clergy was continually occasioning at Constantinople, as long as the eastern empire subsisted; the convulsions which, during the course of several centuries, the turbulence of the Roman clergy was continually occasioning in every part of Europe, sufficiently demonstrate how precarious and insecure must always be the situation of the sovereign who has no proper means of influencing the clergy of the established and governing religion of his country.

一个计划之下按照同一种精神追求他们的利益,就像他们受到一个人的指挥一样,事实上他们也常常是受到一个人的指挥。作为一个社团,他们的利益和君主的利益绝不相同,有时候还会直接对立。他们最大的利益就是维持他们在群众中的威信;并且这种威信依靠假想的宗教教义所谆谆教诲的确定性和重要性,依靠为了避免永久的痛苦假定的必须以毫无保留的忠诚去接受这种教义的每一部分的必要性。如果君主的轻率行为显示出嘲笑或怀疑他们教义中即便最无关紧要的部分,或者出于人道主义试图保护那些有这种或那种表现之一的人们,那么一个和对他没有任何依赖的牧师由于体面受到伤害,就会被激怒并立即宣布他是一个渎神的人,并且利用宗教中所有的恐怖手段来迫使人们改变他们的忠贞,服从另一个更加正统、更加顺从的君主。如果他反对他们的任何借口或者篡夺行为,同样存在很大的危险。敢于以这种方式反抗教会的君主,除了这种反抗的罪行之外,一般也被指控犯有另外的异教罪,尽管他庄严的宣称他对教会所认为适于他的教义都是忠诚和温顺服从的。但是宗教的权威高于其他任何权威。它所暗示的担心超过了其他所有一切担心。当宗教的授权牧师向大部分民众宣传颠覆君主权威的教义时,君主只有通过武力或者常备军的力量才能维持他的权威。在这种情况下,即使是常备军也不可能给予他长久的安全。因为士兵都是外国人的情况很少,大部分情况是士兵的大部分都来自人民,士兵们很快就被这些教义所腐化。在东罗马帝国存在的时候,希腊的牧师在君士坦丁堡不断地制造动乱;在这几个世纪里,罗马牧师动乱引发的骚乱经常发生在欧洲的每一个地方,足以展示如果君主没有适当的办法来影响他自己国家的国教和统治阶级,情况将是多么不

_{在有国教的国家,君主必须那样去做,}

since he cannot directly oppose the doctrines of the clergy.

Articles of faith, as well as all other spiritual matters, it is evident enough, are not within the proper department of a temporal sovereign, who, though he may be very well qualified for protecting, is seldom supposed to be so for instructing the people. With regard to such matters, therefore, his authority can seldom be sufficient to counter-balance the united authority of the clergy of the established church. The public tranquillity, however, and his own security, may frequently depend upon the doctrines which they may think proper to propagate concerning such matters. As he can seldom directly oppose their decision, therefore, with proper weight and authority, it is necessary that he should be able to influence it; and he can influence it only by the fears and expectations which he may excite in the greater part of the individuals of the order. Those fears and expectations may consist in the fear of deprivation or other punishment, and in the expectation of further preferment.

The clergy hold their benefices for life, and violence used against them would be ineffectual; so management must be resorted to.

In all Christian churches the benefices of the clergy are a sort of freeholds which they enjoy, not during pleasure, but during life, or good behaviour. If they held them by a more precarious tenure, and were liable to be turned out upon every slight disobligation either of the sovereign or of his ministers, it would perhaps be impossible for them to maintain their authority with the people, who would then consider them as mercenary dependents upon the court, in the sincerity of whose instructions they could no longer have any confidence. But should the sovereign attempt irregularly, and by violence, to deprive any number of clergymen of their freeholds, on account, perhaps, of their having propagated, with more than ordinary zeal, some factious or seditious doctrine, he would only render, by such persecution, both them and their doctrine ten times more popular, and therefore ten times more troublesome and dangerous than they had been before. Fear is in almost all cases a wretched instrument of government, and ought in particular never to be employed against any order of men who have the smallest pretensions to independency. To attempt to terrify them, serves only to irritate their bad humour, and to confirm them in an opposition which more gentle usage perhaps might easily induce

稳定和不安全。

　　各种信条,以及所有其他精神方面的事情,非常明显不在世俗君主的部门管辖之内。尽管他可能非常有资格来保护好人民,但是很少被认为可以有资格来教导人民。因此,就这样的事情,他的权威很少足以与国家教会牧师们的联合权力相抗衡。不过,公众的安宁和他自己的安全往往依赖于牧师们认为有关这样事情适于宣传的教义。因此,由于君主不能用适当的力量和权威来直接反对教会的决定,他就必须可以影响这种决定。要想做到影响教会决定,君主只能通过激起这个阶级大部分个人的害怕和期望来达到目的。这种害怕和期望可能是害怕被剥夺职务或其他的惩罚以及能得到进一步升迁的期望。

　　在所有的基督教会中,牧师的圣俸是他们享受的一种不动产,他们可以终生享用,只要行为端正就可以享受,不随君主的好恶变化。如果他们拥有圣俸的时期不是那么确定,对君主或大臣们稍有不从就可能被裁撤,那么对他们来说就不可能维持他们在人民中的威信。人民将把他们看成是依靠宫廷的唯利是图的附庸,对于牧师布道的真诚,他们也没有任何的信心。但是如果君主试图不规则地并且使用武力来剥夺牧师的不动产,即便可能是因为这些牧师带着超出平常的热情宣传了某些党派或煽动性的教义,那么由于这种迫害,将会使得牧师们和牧师们的教义比以前受欢迎十倍以上,并且因此比以前麻烦十倍、危险十倍以上。在几乎所有的情况下,让别人害怕是政府一种最糟糕的工具,尤其不应该用来反对任何拥有稍微自主独立性的人们。企图恐吓这种人,只能激起他们的厌恶感,使他们更坚定地反对。而如果采用比较温和的办法,或许能使其缓和,甚至完全放弃。为

旁注:由于它不能直接反对牧师的教义。

旁注:牧师终享受圣俸,他们的暴没有因此必须诉诸控制和操纵。

them, either to soften, or to lay aside altogether. The violence which the French government usually employed in order to oblige all their parliaments, or sovereign courts of justice, to enregister any unpopular edict, very seldom succeeded. The means commonly employed, however, the imprisonment of all the refractory members, one would think were forcible enough. The princes of the house of Stewart sometimes employed the like means in order to influence some of the members of the parliament of England; and they generally found them equally intractable. The parliament of England is now managed in another manner; and a very small experiment, which the duke of Choiseul made about twelve years ago upon the parliament of Paris, demonstrated sufficiently that all the parliaments of France might have been managed still more easily in the same manner. That experiment was not pursued. For though management and persuasion are always the easiest and the safest instruments of government, as force and violence are the worst and the most dangerous, yet such, it seems, is the natural insolence of man, that he almost always disdains to use the good instrument, except when he cannot or dare not use the bad one. The French government could and durst use force, and therefore disdained to use management and persuasion. But there is no order of men, it appears, I believe, from the experience of all ages, upon whom it is so dangerous, or rather so perfectly ruinous, to employ force and violence, as upon the respected clergy of any established church. The rights, the privileges, the personal liberty of every individual ecclesiastic, who is upon good terms with his own order, are, even in the most despotic governments, more respected than those of any other person of nearly equal rank and fortune. It is so in every gradation of despotism, from that of the gentle and mild government of Paris, to that of the violent and furious government of Constantinople. But though this order of men can scarce ever be forced, they may be managed as easily as any other; and the security of the sovereign, as well as the public tranquillity, seems to depend very much upon the means which he has of managing them; and those means seem to consist altogether in the preferment which he has to bestow upon them.

In the ancient constitution of the Christian church, the bishop of each diocese was elected by the joint votes of the clergy and of the people of the episcopal city. The people did not long retain their right of election; and while they did retain it, they almost always acted under

了迫使所有的国会和最高法院不登记不受欢迎的命令,法国政府经常诉诸武力,但很少成功。不过,经常使用的手段是囚禁所有难以控制的人员,人们会认为这是非常厉害的了。斯图亚特王室的君主有时也用与此相类似的手段来达到影响英国议会某些成员的目的。他们往往发现这些议员同样难以对付。英格兰国会现在采用另一种方式去操纵;舒瓦瑟尔公爵大约在十二年前曾对巴黎国会进行一个极小的实验,那个实验充分表明法国所有的国会很可能更容易地以这样的方式去操纵。这个实验没有再继续下去。尽管控制和劝说是政府最容易、最安全的工具,正如暴力和强制是最坏、最危险的手段一样,但似乎人傲慢的自然天性总是放弃使用好的工具,除非他不能或不敢运用坏的工具的时候。法国政府可以并且敢于使用武力,因此不屑于使用控制和劝说。但是我相信从所有年代的经验来看,似乎没有对哪一阶级的人运用武力和暴力,像对国家备受尊敬的牧师运用武力和暴力那样危险,或者不如说那样做是具有毁灭性的。每一个与他们自己阶级相处很好的神职人员,他们的特权和自由,即使是在最专制的政府中,也比同等阶级和财富的其他任何人更受尊敬。在每一个专制主义之下也是这样的,从巴黎宽大温和的专制政府到君士坦丁堡猛烈狂暴的专制政府都是如此。虽然这样的人很难加以控制,但是也像很多阶级的人那样容易被控制;君主的安全以及公共的安宁,似乎很多都是依靠君主的管理方法和手段,这些手段似乎就是他能给予他们的高位。

基督教教会古代的组织法中,主教通过每个主教教区的牧师和教区城市的人民共同投票来选举。人们不会长期保留这种选举权;当他们保留时,他们几乎总是在牧师的影响下行动,牧师在

Bishops were originally elected by the clergy and people, afterwards by the clergy alone,

the influence of the clergy, who in such spiritual matters appeared to be their natural guides. The clergy, however, soon grew weary of the trouble of managing them, and found it easier to elect their own bishops themselves. The abbot, in the same manner, was elected by the monks of the monastery, at least in the greater part of abbacies. All the inferior ecclesiastical benefices comprehended within the diocese were collated by the bishop, who bestowed them upon such ecclesiastics as he thought proper. All church preferments were in this manner in the disposal of the church. The sovereign, though he might have some indirect influence in those elections, and though it was sometimes usual to ask both his consent to elect, and his approbation of the election, yet had no direct or sufficient means of managing the clergy. The ambition of every clergyman naturally led him to pay court, not so much to his sovereign, as to his own order, from which only he could expect preferment.

still later to a large extent by the Pope.

Through the greater part of Europe the Pope gradually drew to himself first the collation of almost all bishoprics and abbacies, or of what were called Consistorial benefices, and afterwards, by various machinations and pretences, of the greater part of inferior benefices comprehended within each diocese; little more being left to the bishop than what was barely necessary to give him a decent authority with his own clergy. By this arrangement the condition of the sovereign was still worse than it had been before. The clergy of all the different countries of Europe were thus formed into a sort of spiritual army, dispersed in different quarters, indeed, but of which all the movements and operations could now be directed by one head, and conducted upon one uniform plan. The clergy of each particular country might be considered as a particular detachment of that army, of which the operations could easily be supported and seconded by all the other detachments quartered in the different countries round about. Each detachment was not only independent of the sovereign of the country in which it was quartered, and by which it was maintained, but dependent upon a foreign sovereign, who could at any time turn its arms against the sovereign of that particular country, and support them by the arms of all the other detachments.

Those arms were the most formidable that can well be imagined. In the ancient state of Europe, before the establishment of arts and manufactures, the wealth of the clergy gave them the same

第五篇 第一章

精神事情方面似乎是他们天生的领导。不过,牧师很快就厌烦了这种对他们的操纵,并且发现他们自己选举自己的主教更容易一些。同样的,修道院院长由院中修道士选举,至少大部分修道院是这样的。在主教教区内,所有下层阶级神职人员的圣俸被主教授予,主教在他认为合适的时候给予他们这样的任命。所有教会的升迁都是以这种方式由教会来支配。君主尽管对这些选举有一些间接的影响,尽管有时候申请君主的同意和批准选举结果的事情也很常见,但是君主仍然没有控制操纵的直接或充分的手段。每个牧师的勃勃野心自然使他去奉承他自己阶级的人而不是奉承君主,他仅仅希望能从中得到升迁。

<small>主教开始是由牧师和人们来选举,后来由牧师单独来选举。</small>

在欧洲的大部分地区,罗马教皇首先逐渐将几乎所有的主教职、修道院院长职的任命权收归自己手中,这也是所谓的枢机主教全体会议的圣职。后来是用种种计谋和借口,在每个主教区都任命大部分拥有圣俸的下层阶级圣职,留给君主任命的只有他自己的牧师,这仅仅是为了给予他适当的权威所必要的。通过这种安排,君主的状况比以前更糟糕了。欧洲所有国家的牧师,也因此形成了一个精神方面的军队。他们分散在各个不同的方向,但是所有的行动和操作都要听从一个人的指挥,并且按统一的计划来实施。每个特定国家的牧师被看作是那个军队特定的分队,他们的行动很容易受到周围不同国家驻扎的其他分队的支持。每一个分队不仅仅独立于所驻扎国家受其维持的君主,而且隶属于国外的君主,他们可以在任何时候调动军队反对军队所在的那个国家的君主,并且受到其他所有分队所有驻军的支持。

<small>到后来,在很大范围内由教皇任命。</small>

这些军队是我们所能想象的最可怕的军队。在古代欧洲,制造业和手工业建立之前,牧师的财产对于普通民众的影响,跟大

sort of influence over the common people, which that of the great barons gave them over their respective vassals, tenants, and retainers. In the great landed estates, which the mistaken piety both of princes and private persons had bestowed upon the church, jurisdictions were established of the same kind with those of the great barons; and for the same reason. In those great landed estates, the clergy, or their bailiffs, could easily keep the peace without the support or assistance either of the king or of any other person; and neither the king nor any other person could keep the peace there without the support and assistance of the clergy. The jurisdictions of the clergy, therefore, in their particular baronies or manors, were equally independent, and equally exclusive of the authority of the king's courts, as those of the great temporal lords. The tenants of the clergy were, like those of the great barons, almost all tenants at will, entirely dependent upon their immediate lords, and therefore liable to be called out at pleasure, in order to fight in any quarrel in which the clergy might think proper to engage them. Over and above the rents of those estates, the clergy possessed, in the tythes, a very large portion of the rents of all the other estates in every kingdom of Europe. The revenues arising from both those species of rents were, the greater part of them, paid in kind, in corn, wine, cattle, poultry, &c. The quantity exceeded greatly what the clergy could themselves consume; and there were neither arts nor manufactures for the produce of which they could exchange the surplus. The clergy could derive advantage from this immense surplus in no other way than by employing it, as the great barons employed the like surplus of their revenues, in the most profuse hospitality, and in the most extensive charity. Both the hospitality and the charity of the ancient clergy, accordingly, are said to have been very great. They not only maintained almost the whole poor of every kingdom, but many knights and gentlemen had frequently no other means of subsistence than by travelling about from monastery to monastery, under pretence of devotion, but in reality to enjoy the hospitality of the clergy. The retainers of some particular prelates were often as numerous as those of the greatest lay-lords; and the retainers of all the clergy taken together were, perhaps, more numerous than those of all the lay-lords. There was always much more union among the clergy than among the lay-lords. The former were under a regular discipline and subordination to the papal authority. The latter were under no regular discipline or subordination, but almost always equally jealous of

地主对于其家臣、佃农和侍从的影响一样。在各国王室和私人由于错误的虔诚捐赠赠给教会的大地产上,建立了类似的审判权和大地主的审判权。同样的原因,在那些大地主的领地上,牧师或他们的管家,没有国王或其他任何人的帮助和支持就能很容易地维持和平;但是没有牧师的支持和帮助,国王和任何其他人却不可能维持和平。因此,牧师的审判权在特定的领地或庄园同样地独立,如同大地主的审判权一样,同样排除了国王法庭的权威。牧师的佃农跟其他大地主的佃农一样,几乎全都是可以随意令其退佃的佃农,他们完全依靠他们的直接领主,因此就有义务被任意召唤,去他们牧师认为适合使用他们的地方作战。除了这些不动产的地租,牧师从什一税中还得到了欧洲所有王国所有其他不动产地租的相当大的部分。来自这两种租金的收入大部分是用实物来支付,用谷物、葡萄酒、牲畜、家禽等等来支付。其数量大大超过了牧师所能自己消费的数量,既不存在手工业品也不存在制造品可供他们来交换自己的剩余。除了如同大地主那样用自己的巨大剩余来款宴客人和实施最大规模的慈善行为,牧师没有其他的办法来从这巨大的剩余中获得好处。因此,古代牧师的款宴和慈善行为据说非常大。他们不仅仅维持了几乎每个国家所有的穷人,而且许多骑士和绅士经常没有其他生存办法,除了从一个修道院到另一个修道院,他们假皈依之名,实则是为了款待。一些高级教士的奴仆和最大世俗领主的奴仆数量差不多;所有牧师的奴仆总共加起来可能比所有世俗领主的奴仆数量还要多。在牧师中存在团结联合要比在大地主中存在的要多。前者处于罗马教皇权威的正规纪律和从属关系之下。后者没有正规纪律和从属关系,而且几乎总是同样的相互猜忌,并且还猜忌国王。

> 国民财富的性质与原理

<small>This, joined with the clergy, great wealth of the clergy, rendered them exceedingly formidable.</small> one another, and of the king. Though the tenants and retainers of the clergy, therefore, had both together been less numerous than those of the great lay-lords, and their tenants were probably much less numerous, yet their union would have rendered them more formidable. The hospitality and charity of the clergy too, not only gave them the command of a great temporal force, but increased very much the weight of their spiritual weapons. Those virtues procured them the highest respect and veneration among all the inferior ranks of people, of whom many were constantly, and almost all occasionally, fed by them. Every thing belonging or related to so popular an order, its possessions, its privileges, its doctrines, necessarily appeared sacred in the eyes of the common people, and every violation of them, whether real or pretended, the highest act of sacrilegious wickedness and profaneness. In this state of things, if the sovereign frequently found it difficult to resist the confederacy of a few of the great nobility, we cannot wonder that he should find it still more so to resist the united force of the clergy of his own dominions, supported by that of the clergy of all the neighbouring dominions. In such circumstances the wonder is, not that he was sometimes obliged to yield, but that he ever was able to resist.

<small>Benefit of clergy and other privileges were the natural result.</small> The privileges of the clergy in those ancient times (which to us who live in the present times appear the most absurd), their total exemption from the secular jurisdiction, for example, or what in England was called the benefit of clergy; were the natural or rather the necessary consequences of this state of things. How dangerous must it have been for the sovereign to attempt to punish a clergyman for any crime whatever, if his own order were disposed to protect him, and to represent either the proof as insufficient for convicting so holy a man, or the punishment as too severe to be inflicted upon one whose person had been rendered sacred by religion? The sovereign could, in such circumstances, do no better than leave him to be tried by the ecclesiastical courts, who, for the honour of their own order, were interested to restrain, as much as possible, every member of it from committing enormous crimes, or even from giving occasion to such gross scandal as might disgust the minds of the people.

In the state in which things were through the greater part of Europe during the tenth, eleventh, twelfth, and thirteenth centuries, and for some time both before and after that period, the constitution of the church of Rome may be considered as the most formidable combination that ever was formed against the authority and security of civil

第五篇 第一章

因此,尽管牧师的奴仆和佃农总数少于大地主的奴仆和佃农数量,他们的佃农很可能数量更少,但他们的团结却使他们更可怕。牧师的款宴和慈善行为不仅使他们可以支配一种很大的世俗力量,而且可以增加他们精神武器方面的力量。这些优点使他们在所有下层阶级人民中获得了最大的尊重和敬奉,这些下层阶级的人民不断地几乎总是被他们来供养。与如此受欢迎的阶级相关和有联系的每一件事情,它的所有物,它的特权,它的信条,必定在普通人民眼中是神圣的,对于这些神圣事物的侵犯,不论是真的还是伪装的,都是最大的亵渎圣灵的罪恶和不敬。在这种情况下,如果君主发现抵抗许多贵族阶级的联盟非常困难,我们毫不奇怪他会感到更难抵抗自己国内牧师的联盟,这些联盟受到所有周围国家牧师的支持。在这种情况下,奇怪的不是他有时候不得不服从,而是他还能抵抗。

> 这一点和牧师的巨大财富一起,使他们无比可怕。

古代时期牧师的特权(对于我们居住在当代的人而言似乎很可笑),完全不受世俗审判权的约束。例如,英格兰所谓牧师的特典,是这种事态的自然结果或者说是必然的结果。对于一个试图惩罚牧师任何罪行的君主来说,如果牧师自己的阶级要保护他,说证据不足以证明这样一个神圣的人有罪,或者说对一个宗教使他的人身成为神圣不可侵犯的人判刑过于严格,这是多么危险的啊?在这种情况下,君主除了让他去宗教法庭审判,再找不到比这更好的方法。法庭为了他们自己阶级的名誉,会尽可能地约束每一个成员不让他犯重罪,或者不去做引起人民厌恶的事。

> 圣职特权和其他特权都是自然的结果。

在 10 世纪、11 世纪、12 世纪、13 世纪以及这时期前后的一段时间内,欧洲大部分地区都处于这样的情况。罗马教会的组织被认为是前所未有最可怕的联盟,它的存在会反对政府的权威和安

国民财富的性质与原理

<small>The Church of Rome in the Middle Ages was the most formidable combination against liberty, reason and happiness.</small> government, as well as against the liberty, reason, and happiness of mankind, which can flourish only where civil government is able to protect them. In that constitution the grossest delusions of superstition were supported in such a manner by the private interests of so great a number of people as put them out of all danger from any assault of human reason: because though human reason might perhaps have been able to unveil, even to the eyes of the common people, some of the delusions of superstition; it could never have dissolved the ties of private interest. Had this constitution been attacked by no other enemies but the feeble efforts of human reason, it must have endured for ever. But that immense and well-built fabric, which all the wisdom and virtue of man could never have shaken, much less have overturned, was by the natural course of things, first weakened, and afterwards in part destroyed, and is now likely, in the course of a few centuries more, perhaps, to crumble into ruins altogether.

<small>Its power was destroyed by the improvement of arts, manufactures and commerce.</small> The gradual improvements of arts, manufactures, and commerce, the same causes which destroyed the power of the great barons, destroyed in the same manner, through the greater part of Europe, the whole temporal power of the clergy. In the produce of arts, manufactures, and commerce, the clergy, like the great barons, found something for which they could exchange their rude produce, and thereby discovered the means of spending their whole revenues upon their own persons, without giving any considerable share of them to other people. Their charity became gradually less extensive, their hospitality less liberal or less profuse. Their retainers became consequently less numerous, and by degrees dwindled away altogether. The clergy too, like the great barons, wished to get a better rent from their landed estates, in order to spend it, in the same manner, upon the gratification of their own private vanity and folly. But this increase of rent could be got only by granting leases to their tenants, who thereby became in a great measure independent of them. The ties of interest, which bound the inferior ranks of people to the clergy, were in this manner gradually broken and dissolved. They were even broken and dissolved sooner than those which bound the same ranks of people to the great barons: because the benefices of the church being, the greater part of them, much smaller than the estates of the great barons, the

全,反对人类的自由、理性和幸福(自由、理性和幸福只有在政府权力范围内才能发扬)。在这种制度下,最荒谬的迷信幻想受到如此众多数量民众私人利益的支持,使他们不受到任何人类理性的攻击:因为人类理性很可能揭穿某些封建迷信的幻想,甚至普通人民的眼睛也能识破,但却从来不会打断私人利益的纽带。倘若这种制度没有受到其他敌人的攻击而只是受到人类理性微弱的攻击,那么它必定会永远持续下去。然而,这种不会为人类的智慧和德行所动摇,毋宁说被推翻的巨大顽固的组织,会随着事物的自然发展,首先被削弱,然后部分被毁灭,随后经过数个世纪的过程可能会完全瓦解。

> 中世纪罗马教会是反对自由、理性和幸福的最可怕的联盟。

工艺、制造业及商业的逐渐改良,会摧毁掉大地主的力量,而且同样也会在欧洲的大部分地方,摧毁牧师的所有世俗力量。在工艺、制造业及商业的生产物中,如同大地主一样牧师们也发现了可以交换他们剩余原始产物的东西,于是他们就发现了将他们全部收入用在自己的身上的渠道,不用再给其他任何人很大的份额了。他们的慈善行动的范围逐渐变窄,他们的款宴变得不再那么慷慨、不再那么丰富。他们的奴仆也变少了,乃至逐渐完全消失。牧师也像大地主那样,为了以同样的方式将收入用在他们自己身上,希望从他们自己的不动产上获得更好的地租,来满足自己私人的虚荣和荒唐。但是这种地租的增加只能通过和佃农签订租约来获得,因此佃农很大程度上也独立于他们。利益纽带将下层人民与牧师联系在一起的方式,现在逐步被打破和化解了。打破和化解的过程甚至比将同样的阶级和大地主之间的联系化解的过程还要更快:由于圣职特权的存在,他们的大部分人享有的不动产比大地主的不动产要少很多,每一个特定的享有者将很

> 它的力量被手工业、制造业和商业的改良所毁灭。

possessor of each benefice was much sooner able to spend the whole of its revenue upon his own person. During the greater part of the fourteenth and fifteenth centuries the power of the great barons was, through the greater part of Europe, in full vigour. But the temporal power of the clergy, the absolute command which they had once had over the great body of the people, was very much decayed. The power of the church was by that time very nearly reduced through the greater part of Europe to what arose from her spiritual authority; and even that spiritual authority was much weakened when it ceased to be supported by the charity and hospitality of the clergy. The inferior ranks of people no longer looked upon that order, as they had done before, as the comforters of their distress, and the relievers of their indigence. On the contrary, they were provoked and disgusted by the vanity, luxury, and expence of the richer clergy, who appeared to spend upon their own pleasures what had always before been regarded as the patrimony of the poor.

<small>The sovereigns endeavoured to deprive the Pope of the disposal of the great benefices, and succeeded, especially in France and England.</small>

In this situation of things, the sovereigns in the different states of Europe endeavoured to recover the influence which they had once had in the disposal of the great benefices of the church, by procuring to the deans and chapters of each diocese the restoration of their ancient right of electing the bishop, and to the monks of each abbacy that of electing the abbot. The re-establishing of this ancient order was the object of several statutes enacted in England during the course of the fourteenth century, particularly of what is called the statute of provisors; and of the Pragmatic sanction established in France in the fifteenth century. In order to render the election valid, it was necessary that the sovereign should both consent to it before-hand, and afterwards approve of the person elected; and though the election was still supposed to be free, he had, however, all the indirect means which his situation necessarily afforded him, of influencing the clergy in his own dominions. Other regulations of a similar tendency were established in other parts of Europe. But the power of the pope in the collation of the great benefices of the church seems, before the reformation, to have been nowhere so effectually and so universally restrained as in France and England. The Concordat afterwards, in the sixteenth century, gave to the kings of France the absolute right of presenting to all the great, or what are called the consistorial benefices of the Gallican church.

第五篇 第一章

快就能将自己的所有收入用在自己身上。在 14 世纪 15 世纪大部分时期的欧洲大部分地方,大地主的力量处于鼎盛时期。但是牧师的世俗力量,他们曾经对大多数人民所拥有的控制力量,却大大衰落了。到后来,教会的力量在欧洲大部分地区,已经减少到几乎仅仅是它的精神权威所能产生的力量。而且甚至当这种精神力量不再受到牧师慈善行为和款宴的支持时。这种精神力量也大大减弱了。到此时,教会在欧洲大部分的势力,几乎就只剩下了心灵上的权威。下层阶级的人民不再像以前那样,视他们为苦恼的安慰者和贫穷的救济者。相反,他们为富裕牧师的虚荣、奢侈和耗费感到愤怒和反感,这些牧师似乎在把以前被看作是穷人的财产用在自己的享乐上。

在这种情况下,欧洲各国的君主力图恢复他们曾经拥有的支配教会重要圣职的影响力。达到这个目的是通过恢复以前每个教区的主教和教会全体成员所拥有的选举主教的权力,恢复每一个修道院的道士选举院长的权力。这种古代秩序的重新建立,是 14 世纪期间英国制定一些法令的目标,尤其是所谓的圣职候补者法令。这同样也是 15 世纪在法国建立的"国事诏书"目的。为了使选举生效,君主必须事先同意选举,事后同意被选举的人。尽管选举被认为是自由的,不过由于君主的地位,他必然会利用他所能利用的一切间接方法,去影响自己领土上的牧师。就这样同样目的的其他规定在欧洲的其他地方也建立起来。但在改革之前,罗马教皇对于教会大圣职的集权受到如此普遍限制的程度,似乎没有一个地方像在英国和法国那样严重。在 16 世纪时,又建立了一项"罗马教皇和各国政府有关宗教事务之协定"的协定,罗马教皇授予法国国王推荐所有的大圣职(即所谓的枢机主教会

> 君主努力剥夺教皇处理各大圣职的权力,在法国和英格兰尤为成功。

1673

国民财富的性质与原理

<small>Ever since the French clergy have been less devoted to the Pope.</small>   Since the establishment of the Pragmatic sanction and of the Concordat, the clergy of France have in general shown less respect to the decrees of the papal court than the clergy of any other catholic country. In all the disputes which their sovereign has had with the pope, they have almost constantly taken party with the former. This independency of the clergy of France upon the court of Rome, seems to be principally founded upon the Pragmatic sanction and the Concordat. In the earlier periods of the monarchy, the clergy of France appear to have been as much devoted to the pope as those of any other country. When Robert, the second prince of the Capetian race, was most unjustly excommunicated by the court of Rome, his own servants, it is said, threw the victuals which came from his table to the dogs, and refused to taste any thing themselves which had been polluted by the contact of a person in his situation. ① They were taught to do so, it may very safely be presumed, by the clergy of his own dominions.

<small>So even before the Reformation the clergy had less power and inclination to disturb the state.</small>   The claim of collating to the great benefices of the church, a claim in defence of which the court of Rome had frequently shaken, and sometimes overturned the thrones of some of the greatest sovereigns in Christendom, was in this manner either restrained or modified, or given up altogether, in many different parts of Europe, even before the time of the reformation. As the clergy had now less influence over the people, so the state had more influence over the clergy. The clergy therefore had both less power and less inclination to disturb the state.

The authority of the church of Rome was in this state of declension, when the disputes which gave birth to the reformation, began in Germany, and soon spread themselves through every part

---

① [Hénault's account is similar, *Nouvel Abrégé chronologique*, 1768, tom. i., p. 114, A. D. 996.]

— 1674 —

第五篇 第一章

议圣职)的绝对推荐权。[1]

自"国事诏书"和上述协定建立以后,一般来说法国牧师对于罗马教皇命令尊敬的程度已经远不如其他任何天主教国家牧师对罗马教皇命令的尊敬程度。在所有君主和罗马教皇的争执中,他们几乎总是站在君主那边。法国牧师对于罗马教皇的独立,似乎主要建立在"国事诏书"和协定之上。在君主政体的早期,法国牧师和其他任何国家的牧师们一样忠于罗马教皇。当卡佩王室[2]的第二君主罗伯特被罗马教廷非常不公平地逐出去时,据说他的奴仆将桌上的食物扔给狗,拒绝自己品尝任何被他接触玷污过的东西。① 据此可以非常确定地推测,他们是受他们领土上的自己的牧师指使来这样做的。

> 自此以后,法国牧师还很少会像以前那样对罗马教皇忠心了。

甚至在宗教改革以前,就保卫任命教会中大圣职的权力这点,罗马教廷都经常动摇。罗马教廷有时是会推翻基督教国家一些大君主的王位,但在欧洲的很多不同国家,罗马教廷任命大圣职的权力还是被限制、修改或完全放弃了。由于牧师对人民的影响不是很大的时候,因此国家对牧师的影响也就会变大。所以,牧师扰乱国家的力量和倾向就变小了。

> 因此在改革之前,牧师扰乱国家的力量和倾向变小了。

当产生改革的争执出现时,罗马教皇的权威处于衰落状态。

---

① 赫诺的记载相同,《新编年史简编》,1768 年,第 1 卷,第 114、996 页。

[1] 丹尼尔:《法国史》,1775 年,第 7 卷,第 158、159 页。第 9 卷,第 40 页。

[2] 卡佩王朝(Capet),法兰西的一个王朝(987~1328),其中有雨果·卡佩(940?~996),他于 987 年被推选为国王并因此永久地使加洛林王室丧失了权力。他一直统治到逝世时为止。卡佩王朝期间的领土扩张和中央集权开始了统一法兰西的运动。

The Reformation doctrines were recommended to the common people by the zeal of their teachers, of Europe. The new doctrines were every where received with a high degree of popular favour. They were propagated with all that enthusiastic zeal which commonly animates the spirit of party, when it attacks established authority. The teachers of those doctrines, though perhaps in other respects not more learned than many of the divines who defended the established church, seem in general to have been better acquainted with ecclesiastical history, and with the origin and progress of that system of opinions upon which the authority of the church was established, and they had thereby some advantage in almost every dispute. The austerity of their manners gave them authority with the common people, who contrasted the strict regularity of their conduct with the disorderly lives of the greater part of their own clergy. They possessed too in a much higher degree than their adversaries, all the arts of popularity and of gaining proselytes, arts which the lofty and dignified sons of the church had long neglected, as being to them in a great measure useless. The reason of the new doctrines recommended them to some, their novelty to many; the hatred and contempt of the established clergy to a still greater number; but the zealous, passionate, and fanatical, though frequently coarse and rustic, eloquence with which they were almost every where inculcated, recommended them to by far the greatest number.

and enabled sovereigns on bad terms with Rome to overturn the Church with ease,   The success of the new doctrines was almost every where so great, that the princes who at that time happened to be on bad terms with the court of Rome, were by means of them easily enabled, in their own dominions, to overturn the church, which, having lost the respect and veneration of the inferior ranks of people, could make scarce any resistance. The court of Rome had disobliged some of the smaller princes in the northern parts of Germany, whom it had probably considered as too insignificant to be worth the managing. They universally, therefore, established the reformation in their own dominions. The tyranny of Christiern II. and of Troll archbishop of Upsal, enabled Gustavus Vasa to expel them both from Sweden. The pope favoured the tyrant and the archbishop, and Gustavus Vasa found no difficulty in establishing the reformation in Sweden. Christiern II. was afterwards deposed from the throne of Denmark, where his conduct had rendered him as odious as in Sweden. The pope, however, was still disposed to favour him, and Frederic of Holstein, who had

第五篇　第一章

改革始于德国,后来迅速扩展到欧洲的每一个地方。新的教义在每一个地方都大受欢迎。它们受到最大热情地宣传,当它攻击国教的时候通常会激起党派的精神。宣讲这些教义的牧师,尽管可能在其他方面不如保护国教的牧师更有学问,但一般似乎都更熟悉宗教的历史,以及教会权威赖以建立的那种观念体系的起源和发展,因此他们几乎在每一次的争执中都处于优势地位。他们严肃的态度在普通人民面前树立了威信,人民把他们自己严于律己的行为和大部分牧师们无序的生活比较。他们比其对手在博得群众欢心和吸收信徒方面高出许多,这种技艺被教会高傲尊贵的儿子长期忽略,他们认为在很大程度上没有用处。新教义的理论大受欢迎,许多人对它的新奇之处表示欢迎,它对已有牧师的憎恨和鄙视更加受到欢迎。它们是热情的、激情的、狂热的,尽管往往是通过粗犷的雄辩来处处宣讲它们,使它们受到最大多数人的欢迎。

<small>宗教的改革,由于他们热情之广,而受大众的欢迎。</small>

新教义几乎到外都取得了很大的成功。那时候君主恰好与自己领土上的罗马教廷关系不和,凭借这些新教义很容易就颠覆了教会。而教会已经失去了下层阶级对它的尊敬和崇拜,他们根本不可能有任何的抵抗。德意志北部有一些小君主,由于一向受到罗马教皇宫廷的轻视,因此,他们就在自己领土内进行宗教改革。克雷蒂恩二世和阿普索大主教特诺尔的暴虐无道,使卡斯塔瓦斯·瓦萨能够把他们驱逐出瑞典;教皇要袒护这个暴君及主教,所以卡斯塔瓦斯·瓦萨在瑞典进行宗教改革,并未遇到什么困难。后来,克雷蒂恩二世又在丹麦被废,因其行为不改,也像在瑞典时一样招人讨厌。但教皇还是袒护他;于是继承王位的霍斯

<small>使与教会不从容颠覆并且主教关系不和,而很易地颠覆了教会。</small>

mounted the throne in his stead, revenged himself by following the example of Gustavus Vasa. The magistrates of Berne and Zurich, who had no particular quarrel with the pope, established with great ease the reformation in their respective cantons, where just before some of the clergy had, by an imposture somewhat grosser than ordinary, rendered the whole order both odious and contemptible.

<small>while in countries the sovereigns of which were friendly to Rome the Reformation was suppressed or obstructed.</small> In this critical situation of its affairs, the papal court was at sufficient pains to cultivate the friendship of the powerful sovereigns of France and Spain, of whom the latter was at that time emperor of Germany. With their assistance it was enabled, though not without great difficulty and much bloodshed, either to suppress altogether, or to obstruct very much the progress of the reformation in their dominions. It was well enough inclined too to be complaisant to the king of England. But from the circumstances of the times, it could not be so without giving offence to a still greater sovereign, Charles V. king of Spain and emperor of Germany. Henry VIII. accordingly, though he did not embrace himself the greater part of the doctrines of the reformation, was yet enabled, by their general prevalence, to suppress all the monasteries, and to abolish the authority of the church of Rome in his dominions. That he should go so far, though he went no further, gave some satisfaction to the patrons of the reformation, who having got possession of the government in the reign of his son and successor, completed without any difficulty the work which Henry VIII. had begun.

<small>In some countries the Reformation overturned both church and state.</small> In some countries, as in Scotland, where the government was weak, unpopular, and not very firmly established, the reformation was strong enough to overturn, not only the church, but the

坦[1]的弗雷德里克为了报复教皇,仿效卡斯塔瓦斯·瓦萨的前例实行宗教改革。伯尔尼和苏黎世政府原来和教皇并没有很大的争执,但由于少数牧师一时的越轨行为,导致这两个地方人民憎恶轻视全体教会阶级;在这种事故发生不久,宗教改革就很容易在这两个地方完成了。

在事态万分危急的关头,教廷不得不不辞辛劳地讨好法兰西和西班牙的强势君主,后者在当时为德国的皇帝。仰仗他们的援助,教廷在费尽艰难和血流成河的代价下,才把他们领土范围内的宗教改革运动全部镇压下去或者牢牢地控制住。对于英格兰国王,教皇宫廷也分明是持有意拉拢的态度,但从当时所处的时代背景来看,因为害怕冒犯更有实力的西班牙国王兼德国皇帝的查理五世,这种友好只好作罢。英王亨利八世尽管对宗教改革的新教义并不完全赞赏,但由于新教义已经在国内普遍流行开来,所以他就很愿意顺水推舟,镇压领土范围内一切寺院,消除一切罗马教会权威。他虽然只做到这里就停止下来,没有再前进一步;但是,那些宗教改革的拥护者却对此已经有几分满意了。往后在英王儿孙后嗣继承王位执政时,政权却操纵在这帮宗教改革论者的手中,亨利八世未竟的事业,就由他们轻而易举地完成了。

有些国家,如苏格兰,其政府软弱无能,不得民心,政权本身并不十分牢固。那里进行宗教改革运动力量强大,不仅能够推翻

有些国家君主对教廷友好,罗马教廷的改革运动被镇压下去或被控制住

有些国家宗教改革不翻了教会,还翻了国家,在这些国家里,宗教改革运动仅仅推翻了罗马教会

──────────

〔1〕 霍斯坦:德国北部一个曾为公爵领地的地区,位于日德兰半岛的基地,在1474年成为神圣罗马帝国管辖之下的公爵领地,后来经常被丹麦控制。

state likewise for attempting to support the church.

<small>The followers of the Reformation had no common authority like the court of Rome, and divided into Lutherans and Calvinists.</small>

Among the followers of the reformation, dispersed in all the different countries of Europe, there was no general tribunal, which, like that of the court of Rome, or an œcumenical council, could settle all disputes among them, and with irresistible authority prescribe to all of them the precise limits of orthodoxy. When the followers of the reformation in one country, therefore, happened to differ from their brethren in another, as they had no common judge to appeal to, the dispute could never be decided; and many such disputes arose among them. Those concerning the government of the church, and the right of conferring ecclesiastical benefices, were perhaps the most interesting to the peace and welfare of civil society. They gave birth accordingly to the two principal parties or sects among the followers of the reformation, the Lutheran and Calvinistic sects, the only sects among them, of which the doctrine and discipline have ever yet been established by law in any part of Europe.

The followers of Luther, together with what is called the church of England, preserved more or less of the episcopal government, established subordination among the clergy, gave the sovereign the disposal of all the bishoprics, and other consistorial benefices within his dominions, and thereby rendered him the real head of the church; and without depriving the bishop of the right of collating to the smaller benefices within his diocese, they, even to those benefices, not only admitted, but favoured the right of presentation both in the sovereign

罗马教会,并且同样还能有力推翻那些企图支持罗马教会的国家。

宗教改革运动的信奉者遍布欧洲各个国家。但他们之间,迄今为止还没有一个最高法庭,就像罗马教皇宫廷或罗马全体教会会议那样,能够解决一切信奉教义者之间引起的争端,并且以不可抗拒的权威向教义信奉者规定正教的正确范围。所以,如果一个国家宗教改革的信徒碰巧与另一个国家主张宗教改革的信徒的意见相左,由于没有可以共同诉求的仲裁官进行裁决,他们的争论也就得不到解决;而在他们彼此之间发生这类争论又很多。在各种争论中,教会的统治和教会职务的任命也许与平民社会里的和平和福祉关系最大。因此,在所有信徒中间,就产生了两个主要派别或教派,即路德教派[1]和加尔文教派。新的教派有很多分支,但是,在欧洲各地,其教义和教律以法律的形式加以规定下来的却只有这两个教派。

路德教派的信奉者和所谓的英格兰教会,都多多少少保存了主教统治制度,在牧师之间形成一定的隶属关系。一国领土内一切主教职务和其他主教会议牧师职务的任免权,都授予给该国的君主来行使;这样一来,就使各国的君主成为了教会的真正首脑。至于主教辖区内下级牧师职务的任免权,尽管仍然操纵在主教手里,但君主和其他新教拥护者,不但有推荐权,而且还对君主和世俗的拥护者拥有推荐权表示支持和鼓励。这种教会管理制度从

---

[1] 马丁·路德(1483~1546):德国神学家、欧洲宗教改革运动的领袖。他反对教会阶层的富有和腐败,认为只要在信仰的基础上即可获得超度,而不须借助于教会的典籍,这些观点使他于1521年与天主教会脱离。他肯定了1530年的奥格斯堡忏悔会,成功地建立了路德教会。

| 国民财富的性质与原理

The Lutherans and the Church of England preferred episcopacy, and gave the disposal of benefices to the sovereign and other lay patrons.

and in all other lay patrons. This system of church government was from the beginning favourable to peace and good order, and to submission to the civil sovereign. It has never, accordingly, been the occasion of any tumult or civil commotion in any country in which it has once been established. The church of England in particular has always valued herself, with great reason, upon the unexceptionable loyalty of her principles. Under such a government the clergy naturally endeavour to recommend themselves to the sovereign, to the court, and to the nobility and gentry of the country, by whose influence they chiefly expect to obtain preferment. They pay court to those patrons, sometimes, no doubt, by the vilest flattery and assentation, but frequently too by cultivating all those arts which best deserve, and which are therefore most likely to gain them the esteem of people of rank and fortune; by their knowledge in all the different branches of useful and ornamental learning, by the decent liberality of their manners, by the social good humour of their conversation, and by their avowed contempt of those absurd and hypocritical austerities which fanatics inculcate and pretend to practise, in order to draw upon themselves the veneration, and upon the greater part of men of rank and fortune, who avow that they do not practise them, the abhorrence of the common people. Such a clergy, however, while they pay their court in this manner to the higher ranks of life, are very apt to neglect altogether the means of maintaining their influence and authority with the lower. They are listened to, esteemed and respected by their superiors; but

Zwinglian and Calvinists gave the right of election to the people, and established equality among the clergy.

before their inferiors they are frequently incapable of defending, effectually and to the conviction of such hearers, their own sober and moderate doctrines against the most ignorant enthusiast who chuses to attack them.

The followers of Zuinglius, or more properly those of Calvin, on the contrary, bestowed upon the people of each parish, whenever the church became vacant, the right of electing their own pastor; and established at the same time the most perfect equality among the clergy. The former part of this institution, as long as it remained in vigour,

一开始就对和平和良好秩序的形成有利,对君主的服从效忠也有利。所以,不论在任何一个国家,这种教会管理制度一经确立下来,就从来没有成为任何骚扰或内乱的根源。特别是英格兰教会,它自诩对于它所信奉的教义忠心恪守如一,这背后确实理由充分。在这种教会管理制度之下,牧师们自然会努力博取该国君主、宫廷以及达官显贵们的欢心,因为他们所期待的升迁就依赖这些人的意向。为了讨这些人的欢心,他们肯定有时会沦落到卑鄙下贱的阿谀奉承和曲迎拍和,但他们通常都对那最值得尊敬和最易赢得那些达官巨富们敬重的技巧很有研究,如各种有用的和附庸风雅的学识呀,姿态仪表的庄重祥和呀,社交谈吐的温恭风趣呀,对狂信者所教导的和假装的可耻和伪善的朴素苦行表示公然蔑视等等,不一而足。他们之所以公然轻蔑那些狂言者,是因为这些狂言者要博取普通人民的尊敬,同时为了使普通人民对大部分宣称自己不能刻苦的达官巨富们抱有憎恶感,才教诲和假装实行伪善的苦行行为。但是,这种牧师,在以这种方式献媚于上流阶级的同时,很容易全然忽视了维持他们对下层人民的感化力量和权威的手段。他们得到了上层人物的关注、称赞和尊敬,但是,当他们在下层人民面前受到那些最无知的狂热信徒的攻击时,常常不能有效地、使听众信服地去捍卫他们稳重和中庸的教义。

茨温克利斯的信奉者,或者比较恰当地说,加尔文教派的信奉者,和路德教派的信奉者不同。他们把各教会牧师职务的选举权交由各教区人民行使,牧师职位随时出缺,人民随时可以选举。此外,他们在各牧师之间树立最完全的平等关系。就该制度的前一部分来说,在它盛行的期间,似乎也只不过导致了无秩序和混

| 国民财富的性质与原理

seems to have been productive of nothing but disorder and confusion, and to have tended equally to corrupt the morals both of the clergy and of the people. The latter part seems never to have had any effects but what were perfectly agreeable.

Election by the people gave rise to great disorders, and after trial was abolished in Scotland, though the concurrence of the people is still required.

As long as the people of each parish preserved the right of electing their own pastors, they acted almost always under the influence of the clergy, and generally of the most factious and fanatical of the order. The clergy, in order to preserve their influence in those popular elections, became, or affected to become, many of them, fanatics themselves, encouraged fanaticism among the people, and gave the preference almost always to the most fanatical candidate. So small a matter as the appointment of a parish priest occasioned almost always a violent contest, not only in one parish, but in all the neighbouring parishes, who seldom failed to take part in the quarrel. When the parish happened to be situated in a great city, it divided all the inhabitants into two parties; and when that city happened either to constitute itself a little republic, or to be the head and capital of a little republic, as is the case with many of the considerable cities in Switzerland and Holland, every paltry dispute of this kind, over and above exasperating the animosity of all their other factions, threatened to leave behind it both a new schism in the church, and a new faction in the state. In those small republics, therefore, the magistrate very soon found it necessary, for the sake of preserving the public peace, to assume to himself the right of presenting to all vacant benefices. In Scotland, the most extensive country in which this presbyterian form of church government has ever been established, the rights of patronage were in effect abolished by the act which established presbytery in the beginning of the reign of William III①. That act at least put it in the power of certain classes of people in each parish, to purchase, for a very small price, the right of electing their own pastor. The constitution which this act established was allowed to subsist for about two and twenty years, but was abolished by the 10th of queen Anne, ch. 12. on account of the confusions and disorders which this more popular mode of election had almost every where occasioned. In so extensive a country as Scotland, however, a tumult in a remote parish was not so likely to give disturbance to government, as in a smaller state. The 10th of queen Anne restored the rights of patronage. But though in Scotland the law gives the benefice without any exception to the person presented by the patron; yet the church requires sometimes

---

① [The 'Act concerning Patronages,' 53rd of the second session of the first parliament of William and Mary.]

乱的状态,并使牧师们和人民双方道德沦丧。就制度的后一部分来说,除了达到完全平等以外,似乎还没有何影响。

如果各个教区人民拥有自己牧师选举权,他们几乎常常是深受牧师们的影响而行事,而这些牧师又一般是最富有党派精神和最为狂热的。为了保持他们对这些民众选举的影响力,他们多数人自己变成了狂热信徒,或者装成了狂热信徒,他们鼓动民众信奉狂热主义,并经常把优先权给予那些最狂热的候选人。一个教区牧师的任命原本是一件小事,但结果不但在本教区,而且时不时所有邻近的教区都会参与进来,引起猛烈的争斗。教区如果在大城市里,这种争斗便会把全区的居民分成两派。碰巧假若那个城市本身就是一个小的共和国家,或者是小共和国的首都,如瑞士、荷兰许多大城市那样,那么,这种无聊的争斗,除了激起其他派别的憎恶反感以外,有可能在教会内留下新的宗派和在国家内留下新的党派的后果。因此,在那些小共和国里,政府为出于维持社会治安的考虑,不久就发现,必须把牧师职务推荐权掌握在自己手中。苏格兰,也即建立长老管理教会制度的最大国家,在威廉三世执政之初,①颁布一个有关长老会的法令,事实上就取消了这种推荐权。这个法令使各个教区某些阶级的人,至少以少许的代价购买本区牧师的选举权。那项法令所形成的制度大约存续了22年;由于这种比较普遍选举的制度到处惹起无秩序和混乱,才被安妮女王十年第12号法令所废除。不过,苏格兰是一个幅员辽阔的国家,在僻远教区发生纷乱,毕竟不像在一个小国那样容易惊动中央政府。所以安妮女王同年的法令恢复了牧师职推荐权。根据这个法令,对于有推荐权者所推荐的人选,法律尽管都毫无例外地一律授予牧师职位;可是,教会(教会至于这个方

---

① 《推荐法案》,威廉和玛利上议院第二次会议。

(for she has not in this respect been very uniform in her decisions) a certain concurrence of the people, before she will confer upon the presentee what is called the cure of souls, or the ecclesiastical jurisdiction in the parish. She sometimes at least, from an affected concern for the peace of the parish, delays the settlement till this concurrence can be procured. The private tampering of some of the neighbouring clergy, sometimes to procure, but more frequently to prevent this concurrence, and the popular arts which they cultivate in order to enable them upon such occasions to tamper more effectually, are perhaps the causes which principally keep up whatever remains of the old fanatical spirit, either in the clergy or in the people of Scotland.

The equality of the Presbyterian clergy makes them independent and respectable.

The equality which the presbyterian form of church government establishes among the clergy, consists, first, in the equality of authority or ecclesiastical jurisdiction; and, secondly, in the equality of benefice. In all presbyterian churches the equality of authority is perfect: that of benefice is not so. The difference, however, between one benefice and another, is seldom so considerable as commonly to tempt the possessor even of the small one to pay court to his patron, by the vile arts of flattery and assentation, in order to get a better. In all the presbyterian churches, where the rights of patronage are thoroughly established, it is by nobler and better arts that the established clergy in general endeavour to gain the favour of their superiors; by their learning, by the irreproachable regularity of their life, and by the faithful and diligent discharge of their duty. Their patrons even frequently complain of the independency of their spirit, which they are apt to construe into ingratitude for past favours, but which at worst, perhaps, is seldom any more than that indifference which naturally arises from the consciousness that no further favours of the kind are ever to be expected. There is scarce perhaps to be found any where in Europe a more learned, decent, independent, and respectable set of men, than the greater part of the presbyterian clergy of Holland, Geneva, Switzerland, and Scotland.

Where the church benefices are all nearly equal, none of them can be very great, and this mediocrity of benefice, though it may no doubt be carried too far, has, however, some very agreeable effects. Nothing but the most exemplary morals can give dignity to a man of

面的决定,并不一致)在授予被推荐者以灵魂监督权或教区的教会管辖权以前,有时要求必须首先得到人民的赞同。至少,它有时以教区治安为借口,一直拖延到得到这种赞同时才授予被推荐人以牧师职务和权力。邻近有些牧师有时为了得到这赞同,但更多的是经常为了阻止这种赞同而进行的私下干涉,以及为了利用这样的机会更有效地研究出颇为有名的手段和技巧,也许就是苏格兰人民或牧师中间还存有旧时狂热遗风的主要原因。

长老管理教会制度在牧师之间建立的平等关系,有两种组成:第一是权力或教会管辖权的平等,第二是圣俸的平等。在所有长老教会中,完全做到了权力的平等,圣俸的平等却没有做到。不过,圣俸之间的差距还不太大,不至于使一般牧师们为了获取较优厚的圣俸,不惜对推荐者做出下贱的阿谀奉承行为。在完全确立牧师职务推荐权制度的长老教会中,牧师要获其上级的青睐,大概都是凭着学问、生活严整规范、履行职务忠实勤勉这一类比较高尚和比较冠冕的技术。甚至,提拔他们的人往往埋怨他们过于独立自主,并把他们看作是忘恩负义之徒。其实,说得最坏之处,或许也不过是由于没有再进一步的要求,态度归于冷淡而已。因此,欧洲各地最有学问、最有礼节、最有独立精神、最值得敬重的牧师们,恐怕要数荷兰、日内瓦、瑞士及苏格兰长老教会里的那些大部分牧师了。

长老教会里的牧师们之间的平等,使他们更加独立和更令人尊敬。

在教会圣俸几乎相同的地方,在它们中间不可能有一个人圣俸很多;圣俸这样的拉平状况,尽管有时肯定会有点过头,但对教会本身来说却有一些令人满意的影响。一个小有产者想保持尊

> The mediocrity of their benefices gives them influence with the common people.

small fortune. The vices of levity and vanity necessarily render him ridiculous, and are, besides, almost as ruinous to him as they are to the common people. In his own conduct, therefore, he is obliged to follow that system of morals which the common people respect the most. He gains their esteem and affection by that plan of life which his own interest and situation would lead him to follow. The common people look upon him with that kindness with which we naturally regard one who approaches somewhat to our own condition, but who, we think, ought to be in a higher. Their kindness naturally provokes his kindness. He becomes careful to instruct them, and attentive to assist and relieve them. He does not even despise the prejudices of people who are disposed to be so favourable to him, and never treats them with those contemptuous and arrogant airs which we so often meet with in the proud dignitaries of opulent and well-endowed churches. The presbyterian clergy, accordingly, have more influence over the minds of the common people than perhaps the clergy of any other established church. It is accordingly in presbyterian countries only that we ever find the common people converted, without persecution, completely, and almost to a man, to the established church.

> It also enables the universities to draw on them for professors, who are thus the most eminent men of letters.

In countries where church benefices are the greater part of them very moderate, a chair in a university is generally a better establishment than a church benefice. The universities have, in this case, the picking and chusing of their members from all the churchmen of the country, who, in every country, constitute by far the most numerous class of men of letters. Where church benefices, on the contrary, are many of them very considerable, the church naturally draws from the universities the greater part of their eminent men of letters; who generally find some patron who does himself honour by procuring them church preferment. In the former situation we are likely to find the universities filled with the most eminent men of letters that are to be found in the country. In the latter we are likely to find few eminent men among them, and those few among the youngest members of the society, who are likely too to be drained away from it, before they can

严,唯一的方法就是拥有最令人效仿的德行。要是浅薄虚伪和行为乖张,肯定会惹人耻笑,而且与一般浮浪者一样会使他趋于毁灭。因此,他们这种人在自己行为举止上,就不得不遵循普通人最尊敬的道德体系。他博得普通人的尊敬和好感的生活方式,就是他自己的利益和地位指导他所遵循的生活方式。一个人的情况,如多少同我们自己情况接近,而且在我们看来应该优于我们;那么我们对于这个人,就自然而然会产生亲切的感情。所以,普通人对这种牧师就同我们对上述人那样亲切,而牧师也变得很小心教导他们,很关心帮助并救济他们。对于对他这样亲切的人,他甚至不会鄙视他们的私心偏见,他绝不会像富裕和财大气粗教会的那些傲慢牧师那样,动辄以傲慢和蔑视的态度对待他们。因此,长老教会的牧师对普通人民思想的影响,要胜过其他任何国教教会的牧师。由于这个原因,对普通人民不加迫害,他们就全部改信国教教会这种事实,只有在实行长老教会制度的国家才能见到。

一般的圣俸水平也会对普通人民产生影响。

在大部分的教会圣俸很一般的国家里,其大学教职所得的报酬一般要比教会担任教职人员的报酬优厚。在这种情况下,大学从全国所有牧师中挑选教学人员,因为在任何国家里,牧师是人数最多的文人阶级。反之,在一个教会里大部分人的圣俸相当可观的国家里,教会自然会把大学中大部分知名的学者吸引进来;这些学者一般不难找到有权推荐他们的人,因为这些人常以推荐他们为荣。在前一种情况下,全国知名的学者将云集于各个大学;在后一种情况下,留在各大学的知名学者数量有限,而就在这些留下不多的人当中,最年轻的教师早在他们获有充分的教学经验

薪水也使大学能够吸收那些著名的学者到大学任教。

have acquired experience and knowledge enough to be of much use to it. It is observed by Mr. de Voltaire, that father Porrée, a jesuit of no great eminence in the republic of letters, was the only professor they had ever had in France whose works were worth the reading. In a country which has produced so many eminent men of letters, it must appear somewhat singular, that scarce one of them should have been a professor in a university. The famous Gassendi was, in the beginning of his life, a professor in the university of Aix. Upon the first dawning of his genius, it was represented to him, that by going into the church he could easily find a much more quiet and comfortable subsistence, as well as a better situation for pursuing his studies; and he immediately followed the advice. The observation of Mr. de Voltaire may be applied, I believe, not only to France, but to all other Roman catholic countries. We very rarely find, in any of them, an eminent man of letters who is a professor in a university, except, perhaps, in the professions of law and physic; professions from which the church is not so likely to draw them. After the church of Rome, that of England is by far the richest and best endowed church in Christendom. In England, accordingly, the church is continually draining the universities of all their best and ablest members; and an old college tutor, who is known and distinguished in Europe as an eminent man of letters, is as rarely to be found there as in any Roman catholic country. In Geneva, on the contrary, in the protestant cantons of Switzerland, in the protestant countries of Germany, in Holland, in Scotland, in Sweden, and Denmark, the most eminent men of letters whom those countries have produced, have, not all indeed, but the far greater part of them, been professors in universities. In those countries the universities are continually draining the church of all its most eminent men of letters.

It may, perhaps, be worth while to remark, that, if we except

和学识以前,就有可能已经被教会网罗挖走。根据伏尔泰[1]的观察,耶稣教徒波雷在学者中原来并不是著名的人物,但在法国各个大学的教授中,还只有他的著作值得一读。在产生这么多知名学者的国家里,竟然几乎没有一个人是合格的大学教授,看起来似乎有点奇怪。有名的加桑迪,在他青年时代原是艾克斯大学的教授。后来正当他天才展现的初期,有人就劝他进教会去,说在那里容易得到比较安静和比较愉快的生活,并且容易得到比较适合于研究的环境。他很快就接受辞去大学教职的建议,投奔教会而去。我相信,伏尔泰的观察不但可以适用于法国,对一切其他罗马天主教的国家也可以适用。除了从事法律和医学这两方面的人才以外,我们很难从这些国家的大学教授中找出一个知名学者。在罗马教会以后,在一切基督教国家中英格兰教会要算最富裕、受捐赠的财产最多的教会。因此,英格兰各个大学的一切最优秀和最有能力的学者,就不断被教会吸引挖走。其结果,想在那里找到一个学问驰名于欧洲的大学老教师,其难度几乎与在任何罗马天主教国家里不相上下。反之,在日内瓦、瑞士新教各州、德意志新教各个邦、荷兰、瑞士、瑞典和丹麦,它们培养出来的最著名学者,虽然不完全是,但至少相当大的一部分是在大学里担任教授。在这些国家里,教会中一切最有名的学者不断被大学吸引挖走。

在古代希腊和罗马,除了诗人、少数雄辩家和历史学家以外,

---

〔1〕 伏尔泰:法国哲学家和作家,其作品是启蒙时代的代表,常常攻击不公正和不宽容。他著有《老实人》(1759)和《哲学辞典》(1764)。

> Eminent men of letters in Greece and Rome were mostly teachers

the poets, a few orators, and a few historians, the far greater part of the other eminent men of letters, both of Greece and Rome, appear to have been either public or private teachers; generally either of philosophy or of rhetoric. This remark will be found to hold true from the days of Lysias and Isocrates, of Plato and Aristotle, down to those of Plutarch and Epictetus, of Suetonius and Quintilian. ① To impose upon any man the necessity of teaching, year after year, any particular branch of science, seems, in reality, to be the most effectual method for rendering him completely master of it himself. By being obliged to go every year over the same ground, if he is good for any thing, he necessarily becomes, in a few years, well acquainted with every part of it: and if upon any particular point he should form too hasty an opinion one year, when he comes in the course of his lectures to reconsider the same subject the year thereafter, he is very likely to correct it. ② As to be a teacher of science is certainly the natural employment of a mere man of letters; so is it likewise, perhaps, the education which is most likely to render him a man of solid learning and knowledge. The mediocrity of church benefices naturally tends to draw the greater part of men of letters, in the country where it takes place, to the employment in which they can be the most useful to the public, and, at the same time, to give them the best education, perhaps, they are capable of receiving. It tends to render their learning both as solid as possible, and as useful as possible.

The revenue of every established church, such parts of it excepted as may arise from particular lands or manors, is a branch, it ought to be observed, of the general revenue of the state, which is thus diverted to a purpose very different from the defence of the state. The tythe, for example, is a real land-tax, which puts it out of the power

---

① [Ed. I continues here 'Several of those whom we do not know with certainty to have been public teachers appear to have been private tutors. Polybius, we know, was private tutor to Scipio Emilianus]

② [The *Lectures* leave little doubt that this is a fragment of autobiography.]

其余绝大部分知名学者似乎都成为哲学或修辞学的公私教师,这件事也许值得我们思考一下。从里西阿斯、伊索克拉底、柏拉图以及亚里士多德时代,一直到普鲁塔克、埃皮克提图[1]、斯韦托尼阿和昆蒂里恩①时代,这个说法都可以适用。把某一特定部门的学科,年年专门责成某一个人来教授,那实际上就是让他自己精通掌握那门学科的最有效方法。因为他年年重复教这一门,如果他还不是一个一事无成的人,在数年之内,他一定能够通晓该门学问的各个部分;并且,如果他在今年对某点的见解还欠斟酌,到明年讲到同一个主题时,他多半会加以改正。② 成为一名科学的教师是真正想成为学者的人的自然职业,而同时这个职业又是使他受到扎实学问和见解的最适当教育。一个国家教会的圣俸水平一般,大部分学者自然会从事这个对国家和社会最有用的教学职业,同时还可以由此获得他所能接受的最良好的教育。这样一来,他们的学问就尽可能地扎实和有用起来。

在希腊和罗马,最著名的学者都是教师。

应该指出的是,各国国教教会的收入,除了特定土地或庄园收入以外,虽然也是国家一般收入的一部分,但这一部分收入并没用在国防上,而转用到与国防非常不同的目的上。例如,向教会缴纳的什一税是一种真正的土地税;教会如果不把它收上去,

---

① 第一版这里接下来是:"我们不能确切地知道有几个已经成为公办教师的人似乎又已经成为私人教师。"我们知道,波里比斯是西皮罗·阿米里鲁斯的私人教师。

② 《关于法律、警察、岁入及军备的演讲》几乎肯定这是自传的一部分。

[1] 埃皮克提图(Epictetus),公元前1世纪时的希腊斯多噶派哲学家、教师。他以为人生如宴会,人只应在所有提供的东西中有礼貌地拿取一份。

The revenue of the church except that part which arises from endowments is a branch of that of the state. In some cantons of Switzerland the old revenue of the church now maintains both church and state. The whole revenue of the Church of Scotland is a trifling amount, but that church produces all possible good effects. This is also true in a still higher degree of the Swiss Protestant churches.

of the proprietors of land to contribute so largely towards the defence of the state as they otherwise might be able to do. The rent of land, however, is, according to some, the sole fund, and according to others, the principal fund, from which, in all great monarchies, the exigencies of the state must be ultimately supplied. The more of this fund that is given to the church, the less, it is evident, can be spared to the state. It may be laid down as a certain maxim, that, all other things being supposed equal, the richer the church, the poorer must necessarily be, either the sovereign on the one hand, or the people on the other; and, in all cases, the less able must the state be to defend itself. In several protestant countries, particularly in all the protestant cantons of Switzerland, the revenue which anciently belonged to the Roman catholic church, the tythes and church lands, has been found a fund sufficient, not only to afford competent salaries to the established clergy, but to defray, with little or no addition, all the other expences of the state. The magistrates of the powerful canton of Berne, in particular, have accumulated out of the savings from this fund a very large sum, supposed to amount to several millions, part of which is deposited in a public treasure, and part is placed at interest in what are called the public funds of the different indebted nations of Europe; chiefly in those of France and Great Britain. What may be the amount of the whole expence which the church, either of Berne, or of any other protestant canton, costs the state, I do not pretend to know. By a very exact account it appears, that, in 1755, the whole revenue of the clergy of the church of Scotland, including their glebe or church lands, and the rent of their manses or dwelling-houses, estimated according to a reasonable valuation, amounted only to 68,514 *l.* 1 *s.* 5 *d.* 1/12. This very moderate revenue affords a decent subsistence to nine hundred and forty-four ministers. The whole expence of the church, including what is occasionally laid out for the building and reparation of churches, and of the manses of ministers, cannot well be supposed to exceed eighty or eighty-five thousand pounds a-year. The most opulent church in Christendom does not maintain better the uniformity of faith, the fervour of devotion, the spirit of order, regularity, and austere morals in the great body of the people, than this very poorly endowed church of Scotland. All the good effects, both civil and religious, which an established church can be supposed to produce, are produced by it as

土地所有者对国防所能提供的贡献要大得多。国家紧急支出的资源,有些人说是单靠土地地租,有些人说是主要依靠土地地租。很显然,教会从这种资金拿去的部分越多,国家能够从这部分资金中分得的部分就越少。如果一切其他情况都一样,教会就越富有,君主和人民就必然越贫穷,而国家防御外来侵犯的能力也就愈加薄弱。在一些新教国家,特别是在所有瑞士的新教州中,过去属于罗马天主教教会的收入,也就是什一税和教会所有土地的收入这两项,就已经被发现为资金充裕,不但足够向国教牧师们提供体面的薪水,而且只要略加补充或者不需要补充,就足够国家其他一切费用的开支。尤其是强大的伯尔尼州政府,它把以前供给宗教的一大笔资金储蓄起来,大约有几百万镑,其中一部分存贮在国库里,另一部分则投资于欧洲各个债务国的公债用来生息,主要是法兰西和大不列颠国家公债。伯尔尼或瑞士其他新教州的各个教会花费国家多少费用,我不敢冒称知晓。根据非常准确的计算,1755 年苏格兰教会牧师们的全部收入,包括教会所有土地和他们住宅的房租收入在内,合理估算也不会超过 68514 镑 1 先令 5$\frac{1}{12}$便士。这样极其平常的收入,每年要供应 944 名牧师适量的生活资料,再加上教堂和牧师住宅不时维修或新建的支出,汇总计算每年也不会超过 80000 镑或 85000 镑。苏格兰教会资金过于匮乏自不待言;可是,就维持大多数人民信仰的统一、皈依的热忱以及秩序、端正和严肃的道德精神上来说,没有一个基督教国家的最富裕教会能够超过苏格兰的教会。凡是被认为国教教会所能产生的一切良好效果,在社会方面和宗教方面,其他教会能产生的效果,苏格兰教会也能够有同样的效果。而与

completely as by any other. The greater part of the protestant churches of Switzerland, which in general are not better endowed than the church of Scotland, produce those effects in a still higher degree. In the greater part of the protestant cantons, there is not a single person to be found who does not profess himself to be of the established church. If he professes himself to be of any other, indeed, the law obliges him to leave the canton. But so severe, or rather indeed so oppressive a law, could never have been executed in such free countries, had not the diligence of the clergy before-hand converted to the established church the whole body of the people, with the exception of, perhaps, a few individuals only. In some parts of Switzerland, accordingly, where, from the accidental union of a protestant and Roman catholic country, the conversion has not been so complete, both religions are not only tolerated but established by law.

<small>Large revenue is unsuitable to the office of clergymen.</small>
The proper performance of every service seems to require that its pay or recompence should be, as exactly as possible, proportioned to the nature of the service. If any service is very much under-paid, it is very apt to suffer by the meanness and incapacity of the greater part of those who are employed in it. If it is very much over-paid, it is apt to suffer, perhaps, still more by their negligence and idleness. A man of a large revenue, whatever may be his profession, thinks he ought to live like other men of large revenues; and to spend a great part of his time in festivity, in vanity, and in dissipation. But in a clergyman this train of life not only consumes the time which ought to be employed in the duties of his function, but in the eyes of the common people destroys almost entirely that sanctity of character which can alone enable <small>The expense of supporting the dignity of the sovereign increases as the expenditure of the people increases,</small> him to perform those duties with proper weight and authority.

PART IV   *Of The Expence Of Supporting The Dignity Of The Sovereign*

Over and above the expence necessary for enabling the sovereign to perform his several duties, a certain expence is requisite for the support of his dignity. This expence varies both with the different periods of improvement, and with the different forms of government.

苏格兰教会相比,并不一定更加富裕的瑞士新教教会,却能够产生更大的效果。在瑞士大部分信奉新教的州中,差不多找不到一个人,公然宣称他不是新教教会的信徒。的确,如果有人宣称他是其他教会的信徒,法律就会强迫他离开州境。但是,要不是勤勉的牧师们事先劝导全体人民——或许有少数例外——改信国教,像这样苛刻或者更确切地说是压迫性的法律,是很难在这种自由国家里实行的。因此,在瑞士某些地方,由于新教国家和罗马天主教国家偶然的联合,宗教信仰改变并不像其他地方那么普遍,这两种宗教不但一起为法律所默认,而且同被依法确认为国教。

良好地履行任何一种职务似乎都要求其报酬或薪水应该尽可能地与该职务的性质相称。如果报酬过低,那就会很容易地受损于从事这一职务的大多数人的平庸和无能;如果报酬过多,那就很容易由他们的疏忽怠惰而受到更大的损害。一个收入不菲的人,无论他从事何种职业,他总会认为他应该与其他收入不菲者过一样的生活,并且在娱乐、虚荣以及放荡上面浪费其大部分时间。但是,对于一个牧师来说,这样的生活方式不仅会把他应该用在履行职务上的时间消费掉,而且还会使他人格上的庄严在人民心目中完全被破坏掉,而他只能凭其人格的尊严,才使得他能够以适当的势力和权威去履行其职责。

收入不宜过高 牧师的职责履行

第四节 论维护君主尊严的费用

一个国家的君主,除了执行种种职责所必要花费的费用以外,还要花费一笔费用用来维护他的尊严。费用的大小随社会发展的不同时期而有所变化,随政体形态的不同而不同。

君主用人出增加 维护主尊严的费用随着支出的增加而加

In an opulent and improved society, where all the different orders of people are growing every day more expensive in their houses, in their furniture, in their tables, in their dress, and in their equipage; it cannot well be expected that the sovereign should alone hold out against the fashion. He naturally, therefore, or rather necessarily becomes more expensive in all those different articles too. His dignity even seems to require that he should become so.

<small>and is greater in a monarchy than in a republic</small>   As in point of dignity, a monarch is more raised above his subjects than the chief magistrate of any republic is ever supposed to be above his fellow-citizens; so a greater expence is necessary for supporting that higher dignity. We naturally expect more splendor in the court of a king, than in the mansion-house of a doge or burgo-master.

在富裕而发达的社会里，所有不同阶层人民的房屋、家具、食品、服装和各种家庭工具都日益奢华贵重起来，在这种情况下想要君主独自逆时尚潮流而动，恐怕难以做到。因此，在君主一切所用的不同物品上的花费自然或肯定也会日益增多。要维护他的尊严似乎要求就应该如此。

就尊严一点来说，与共和国的行政长官对其同胞市民相比，一国君主对于他的臣民的尊严要更加高不可攀，望尘莫及；为了维护这个较高的尊严，必须要花费较大的费用。我们很自然地想到，总督或市长的官邸不如国王的宫廷华丽壮观。

在制费在共和制下，君主所用的花费比共和国更要多，并且君主所用的费用比共和国要多。